The Saturday Afternoon War

British wrestling in the 1980's

By

Tony Earnshaw

Copyright © 2020 Tony Earnshaw

ISBN: 9798578914850

All rights reserved, including the right to reproduce this book, or portions thereof in any form. No part of this text may be reproduced, transmitted, downloaded, decompiled, reverse engineered, or stored, in any form or introduced into any information storage and retrieval system, in any form or by any means, whether electronic or mechanical without the express written permission of the author.

Introduction

Before the infamous American Monday night wrestling wars in the 1990's between WWF and WCW, which ended with the WCW promotion no longer existing, a similar war took place in the UK during the 1980's.

On one side of the fence there was the Joint Promotions organisation headed by Max Crabtree, with the crucial ITV contract and exclusive promoting rights to most of the major venues in Britain. On the other side were the independent promoters, the most notable being Brian Dixon who ran the Wrestling Enterprises promotion from Birkenhead, and Jackie Pallo who had promoted his own shows since leaving Joint Promotions in 1974.

Joint Promotions' number one draw was Big Daddy, with a supporting cast of veteran talents such as Mick McManus, as well as a host of excellent wrestlers at all weights such as Wayne Bridges, Tony St Clair, Pat Roach, Mark Rocco, Marty Jones, Johnny Saint, Jim Breaks and Steve Grey.

Brian Dixon's main attraction was his wife, Mitzi Mueller; ladies' contests featured heavily on his bills. His main male wrestlers were those such as Les Kellett, Ricki Starr and Adrian Street, who had fallen out with Max Crabtree and left Joint Promotions.

Jackie Pallo was the feature on his own shows. Although at the veteran stage of his career, his name was still remembered by enough of the general public to be a draw. Pallo also relied on his son JJ, as well as using the likes of Kellett, Starr and the lady wrestlers.

The one thing that gave Joint Promotions the competitive edge was the ITV contract. However, over a tumultuous decade not only would they have to share coverage with Brian Dixon's promotion but in the end lose it completely.

This is the story of the decade, of how traditional British wrestling went from the heights of a ten-thousand strong crowd at Wembley Arena to losing the ITV contract less than ten years later.

CHAPTER ONE – 1980

The new decade started with Joint Promotions on a high, thanks to the Wembley Arena show back in June that had led to an upturn in crowds at the box office as well as cementing Big Daddy as a national treasure.

Wayne Bridges was fresh from winning the World Heavyweight Title from the 'Iron Greek' Spiros Arion at the Royal Albert Hall a week before Christmas, although this title did not have any linear heritage in an historical sense. Arion's tour and the build-up to the title match, as well as 'The Sheik' Adnan Al Kaissy's return to the UK (he had visited here in the 1960's as Billy White Wolf) was somewhat spoilt by the ITV technicians' strike. This had halted coverage from August to the middle of November with no wrestling seen on TV during that time.

The end of 1979 saw the retirement of several familiar faces through injury or old age taking its toll. Amongst the names to leave the scene were 'Big' Bruno Elrington, Johnny Czeslaw, Johnny Yearsley and Steve Logan. Czeslaw had been left blind as a result of a tumour, and Yearsley died within a few weeks of the new year. Several new faces, both newcomers and returnees, took their place including the former amateur star Keith Haward, and Jon Cortez who made a welcome return to Joint Promotions.

The new year was only a few days old when a notable event happened. Following his exile as a condition of losing to Big Daddy, 'Mighty' John Quinn returned to British rings. Although his emphatic loss to Daddy made a return pointless, there was another route for Quinn to follow: challenging Wayne Bridges for his newly won World Heavyweight Title and belt.

At the same time as Quinn arrived, two new faces arrived from South Africa. They were billed as African Kruger and African Rand, Thys Kruger and Don Charles to give them their proper names. Their visit turned out to be very brief as Kruger was forced to return home due to illness. Nothing else was heard from them.

The first *World of Sport* wrestling of the year, shown on January 5th, was a notable event. The TV authorities declared that the match between Mark Rocco and Tony St Clair was too violent an affair to be shown at 4pm on a Saturday afternoon. It wouldn't be the only match that year to be deemed unsuitable to be broadcast on *World of Sport*. So the show had to feature only two matches without the planned Rocco v St Clair top of the bill. The return of Steve Veidor after an absence of a couple of years from the TV thus became the main match shown, and his contest with Colin Joynson ended in the sixth round with neither of them able to continue because of injury. The other match that week saw Mal Sanders take on Zoltan Boscik, who was making an infrequent TV appearance. Sanders got the winning fall in the final round of six.

The other half of the Leeds show was seen on *World of Sport* on January 12th, with the new World Heavyweight Champion Wayne Bridges making his first TV appearance with the belt. His opponent on the show, John Cox, was no match for him and Bridges coasted to an easy two-straight-falls win in the fourth round. Marty Jones beat Ringo Rigby by knockout in the fourth round, and Tally Ho Kaye beat Pat Patton, who was unable to continue for the sixth round after submitting in the fifth.

John Quinn and Giant Haystacks took on Honey Boy Zimba and Butcher Bond when Quinn reappeared on *World of Sport* on January 19th. The match was part of a show recorded at Leamington Spa. Referee Dave Reese had the job of keeping control, which he failed to do as Haystacks and Quinn did a number on their opponents. The end came when a big splash from Haystacks landed on Zimba, who had no chance of beating the count in the ninth minute. Quinn grabbed Brian Crabtree's microphone to berate the crowd, showing he still had the ability to wind everyone up. Referee Reese refused to allow Bond to carry on alone, so the match was stopped in favour of Quinn and Haystacks. That was the cue for more of Quinn shouting into the microphone. Lucky Gordon was called into replace the billed Johnny Yearsley against Chris Adams, who beat the Irishman by two falls to one in the fifth round. In something of a veterans' match, Ken Joyce beat Tony Costas, with the winner coming in the sixth round.

Strangely, the opening show at the Royal Albert Hall on January 24th 1980 was held on a Thursday rather than the usual Wednesday night. The main event was advertised as Giant Haystacks and John Quinn versus The African Krugers, but Haystacks had left Britain for overseas engagements and his place was taken by Rex Strong. Even without Haystacks in the match, the South Africans offered little and were easily beaten inside fifteen minutes. Former Albert Hall favourite Jon Cortez made a welcome return when he took on Zoltan Boscik and beat him in the sixth round. Old rivals Jim Breaks and Steve Grey once again clashed in a major show, this time with Grey coming out as the winner with his surfboard submission seeing off Breaks in the fifth round. Mick McManus beat Mick McMichael who was unable to continue after submitting in the fourth round. Finally, fans of heavyweight wrestling were catered for in the other two matches that night. Firstly, Caswell Martin defeated Honey Boy Zimba by the one fall required to win in twelve minutes. The other superb heavyweight contest saw British Heavyweight Champion Tony St Clair beat Pete Roberts by two falls to one in the sixth round.

A battle royale was the centrepiece of the second half of the Leamington Spa show on January 26th's *World of Sport*. A surprising entrant was Mick McManus; as it had been a long time (perhaps never) that he gone flying over the top rope, it was interesting to see what would happen. The three singles matches saw Catweazle beat TV newcomer Steve Peacock by two falls to one in round five. Jackie Turpin beat Mick McManus, who got himself disqualified in the fourth round. That was very convenient as the rules stated that those disqualified were barred from the over-the-top-rope finale. The final match saw Jon Cortez beat Tommy Lorne in the fifth round. Cortez was the last man standing in the battle royale after just over two minutes.

The month ended with the departure of one of the weirder characters seen in British rings who was billed as Kendo Nagasaki Mk II. His real name was Nick Heywood and he first appeared around November 1979. Apart from wearing a similar striped mask, he bore no resemblance to the great masked man in features, weight (he was a lightweight) or wrestling skill. This was a Max Crabtree promotional gimmick that didn't work.

February was an interesting month for viewers of *World of Sport*. The action started on the 2nd during a show recorded at Reading. Topping the bill was Big Daddy who teamed up with 'Farmer's Boy' Pete Ross against the African Krugers. Daddy and Ross came out on top when a body slam and big splash finished off 'African Rand' Don Charles for the winning fall. After a long wait for a TV appearance by Jon Cortez, he was back on again a week later when he took on the other half of 'The Rockers', Pete LaPaque. Despite Lapaque's flagrant rule breaking, he was no match for Cortez with the winner coming in the fifth round from a cross press. The other match shown saw Steve Grey repeat a previous victory against Johnny Saint with a folding press bringing Grey the winning fall in the seventh round. Commentator Kent Walton sounded most excited when Grey got the winner, but it was a tremendous match between the two.

February 9th on *World of Sport* saw the other half of the show recorded at Reading. The main match was billed to be former World Heavyweight Champion Spiros Arion against John Elijah. Arion had left Britain as soon as he had lost his title to Wayne Bridges in December rather than stay for a return match. He didn't return, so Elijah's opponent was the second of the famous Canadian Hart wrestling family to visit these shores: 'Cowboy' Smith Hart. Hart was not a patch on other members of the family who had visited this country and he lost to Elijah with a reverse back-breaker submission in the fifth round. Smith Hart had the dubious record of losing every match on his UK tour. Banger Walsh was booked in a rare singles match against Jeff Kaye. Walsh got the win in the fourth round when his version of the 'Kamakazi Crash' left Kaye unable to beat referee Peter Szakacs' count of ten. Completing that week's show, Brian Maxine took on Mick McMichael. The match ended in the sixth round when McMichael suffered a dislocated shoulder. The now sporting Maxine refused the win and so the verdict was a No Contest.

John Quinn was featured in a singles match on *World of Sport* on February 16th in a show recorded at Southend where he took on West Indian Caswell Martin. After grabbing MC Fred Downes' microphone, Quinn made his usual speech. First he stated he would pulverise Big Daddy if they ever met, and secondly he would beat Wayne Bridges and take the World Heavyweight title back to North America. To Quinn's surprise, Wayne Bridges was there and entered the ring with his belt to confront him. After a few verbals, Bridges took off his jacket and shirt. Quinn the grabbed the shirt and ripped it apart. In retaliation, Bridges got hold of Quinn's gown and tore that apart. Whilst all this happened, Caswell Martin waited patiently for the match. Martin was no match for Quinn; a forearm smash sent him flying over the top rope in the third round and there was no hope of him beating referee Joe D'Orazio's count of ten. A lively opener that week saw Bobby Barnes and Mal Sanders share a one fall each draw over six rounds. The final bout shown that week was between Pat Roach and Pete Roberts. Roberts got the first fall in the second round with a reversal from an attempted 'Brumagen Bump' by Roach. Roach, who by this time was mainly wrestling within the rules, got the equaliser in the fourth round with a hip toss followed by a cross press. He got the winner in the fifth round when another attempt at the 'Brumagen Bump' was more successful and left Roberts in no fit state to continue.

Once again the Royal Albert Hall show for February took place on a Wednesday night, the 20th. The main event was a non-title match between World Heavyweight Champion Wayne Bridges and the man who stated he was on a mission to return the title to the USA, John Quinn. To the surprise of most fans at the ringside, Quinn won when his over-the-top forearm smash landed cleanly on Bridges' chin in the fourth round and knocked him out. Immediately Quinn demanded a shot at Bridges' title and it seemed Bridges' reign as a champion would be a short one. Another American heavyweight was booked to appear, but the former American football star Butts Giraud was delayed on his arrival and didn't appear till later in the year. His place against Steve Veidor was taken by Ed Wensor. Veidor had an easy night, winning in the fourth round.

This was the second time that season that Veidor's opponent in a featured international match didn't appear after Adnan Al-Kaissy was replaced by John Elijah back in October. A third heavyweight match saw Pat Roach face Colin Joynson. Roach's weight advantage was too much for Joynson to overcome and the match ended in the fifth round when, yet again, Roach's 'Brumagen Bump' left Joynson with no chance of beating the count of ten. The fourth heavyweight match of the night was a lively show opener in which both Terry Rudge and opponent Butcher Bond were disqualified in the sixth round. The evening's tag match saw the duo of Chris Adams and Ringo Rigby gain their second Albert Hall win when they overcame the challenge of 'The Odd Couple', Bobby Barnes and Steve Peacock, with a two falls to one win in twenty minutes. Finally Catweazle sent the punters home happy when he beat his old rival Sid Cooper by two falls to one in the sixth round.

As one feud started, another one came to an end when the Jim Breaks vs Young David series ended after a one fall each title match draw seen on World of Sport on February 23rd. This was the second half of the show recorded at Southend. Going forward, Alan Dennison picked up the matches against Breaks as David was relegated out of the picture. It was a case of Max Crabtree being burnt once by the departure of Dynamite Kid to Canada and saw the same thing happening with his cousin David. Also shown that week was Len Hurst, whose scheduled opponent Mark Rocco didn't apppear as he was still overseas. Rocco was replaced by Romany Riley. The match saw both of them unable to continue through injury. whilst the preliminary contest that week saw Alan Dennison get the one submission needed to beat Bob Anthony.

At the end of February another foreign visitor arrived, the Japanese heavyweight Mr Yasu Fuji. He made an immediate impact when he destroyed Bert Royal in a match from Lincoln shown on *World of Sport* on March 1st. The contest was part of a team match between a squad headed by Big Daddy, of which Royal was a member, and a team captained by Mick McManus. Big Daddy won his match when he knocked out Mike Dean, whilst Marty Jones beat John Naylor by two falls to one to leave the first half of the match two to one in McManus's team's favour.

On March 8th of the following week, the team match continued. Bobby Ryan beat Mick McManus by disqualification. Chris Adams beat Blackjack Mulligan by count out when the Tynesider was thrown outside the ring. TV newcomer Keith Haward beat Sid Cooper by two falls to one to give a four wins to two victory to Big Daddy's team.

John Quinn was back on *World of Sport* the next week on March 15th when he faced Johnny Wilson in another singles match on a bill recorded at Digbeth. Digbeth was one of those venues where the crowd was close to the ring and they were always very excitable in cheering their favourites but vociferous in letting the villains know what they thought. Despite the crowd's hostility, Quinn easily dispatched Wilson with the over-the-top forearm smash, leaving the Hampshire man unable to beat the count. Wayne Bridges was on the same show when he faced Balham's Lee Bronson in a match seen numerous times in the past. As with Quinn's match, Bridges didn't have to break sweat for a two–nil victory and continued on the build-up to the championship match everyone wanted to see. Ringo Rigby won the opening match, beating Steve Peacock by two falls to one.

The March 22nd show on *World of Sport* saw a curious ending to the Vic Faulkner v Mick McMichael contest. The score was one each in the fifth round when Faulkner pinned McMichael with a bridge but, in doing so, had his shoulders on the mat too. Referee Dave Reese counted both wrestlers shoulders down for three. Kent Walton hadn't noticed it and thought Faulkner was the winner but MC Brian Crabtree explained all, so the result was a rare two falls each draw. Colin Joynson beat the Japanese visitor Yasu Fuji by disqualification in a heated encounter, with the crowd enraged at Fuji's underhand tactics and trying to get their own retaliation in at times. Tally Ho Kaye won the other match that was shown when his opponent Jackie Turpin was unable to continue.

In something of a turn up, it was announced wrestling would return to the BBC, where it would be featured as part of the *Big Time* series. A young Lancashire school teacher called Keith

Rawlinson would be filmed as he attempted to become a professional wrestler; the aim would be for him to wrestle John Naylor in front of the cameras at the Royal Albert Hall show on March 26th.

The completed show was broadcast on June 11th, which was a poor piece of scheduling as it was also the date of the second Wembley Arena show. Before the days of affordable video recorders, a lot of fans missed the show when it was originally broadcast. The programme was an enjoyable watch as Rawlinson was trained before the date at the Albert Hall by Tally Ho Kaye at his gym, with input from Max Crabtree, Sid Cooper, Big Daddy and others. Crabtree renamed him Rip Rawlinson for the show in something of a joke. During the match, Naylor pulled him one way and then the other before the contest was mercifully halted and Rawlinson was taken to hospital to get checked over. After the beating from Naylor, we never saw Rawlinson wrestle again – but a lot more was seen of Sheena Easton who featured on another episode.

During the programme there was also brief footage of the evening's top-of-the-bill tag featuring Big Daddy and Steve Grey v Yasu Fuji and Mark Rocco. Daddy and Grey were victorious; when both Fuji and Rocco had had enough of Daddy, they simply left the ring after ten minutes of action and returned to the dressing rooms. The main supporting match should have been Jim Breaks v Alan Dennison, but injury ruled out Dennison so Jeff Kaye stepped in instead. Despite a weight advantage, Kaye was overwhelmed by Breaks' attacks to his arm and retired midway through the contest. A surprising result saw Vic Faulkner give Marty Jones a few stones in weight and come out the winner by two falls to one. Keith Haward made his Albert Hall debut when he beat the muscle-bound Johnny England by the one fall needed.

Big Daddy and Mark Rocco were in opposition again in the main event on *World of Sport* on March 29th from Walton-on-Thames. This time Daddy was partnered by Kid Chocolate, whilst Rocco tagged with Banger Walsh, but the result was the exact same as the Albert Hall. Rocco and Walsh simply left the ring after ten minutes and thus were counted out by referee Max Ward. This sort of finish became a regular occurrence both on

TV and around the halls. Jon Cortez beat Jeff Kaye by two falls to one in the opening bout, whilst Johnny Kwango beat Lucky Gordon by disqualification in the fifth round when Max Ward saw a blatant punch from Gordon land in Kwango's stomach.

Wrestling was missing from *World of Sport* on April 5th when ITV showed highlights of Larry Holmes v Leroy Jones, and Marvin Johnson v Eddie Gregory, boxing title fights from Las Vegas. As it was Easter weekend, wrestling was still shown that weekend on the Easter Monday edition of *World of Sport* filmed at Guildford. A heavyweight tag match was the highlight, with the rather random pairings of Pat Roach and Bully Boy Muir and Steve Veidor and Pete Roberts opposing each other. Roach and Muir came out on top, with Veidor and Roberts having to retire through injury. Rare appearances down south for both Gil Singh and John Cox saw them meet in the main supporting contest, with Singh winning by two falls to one. Chris Adams beat Gary Wensor in the other bout shown that afternoon.

Wrestling was back on a Saturday on *World of Sport* on April 12th with three heavyweight bouts recorded at Bradford. The first match saw British number one Tony St Clair give away several stones in weight against the Blackpool lifeguard Rex Strong. St Clair got an opening fall in the second round before a backbreaker submission in the fourth round brought the equaliser for Strong. St Clair got the winning fall in the next round with a cross press following a high guillotine leg drop to the cheers of the fans. World number one Wayne Bridges was also on the show and beat Caswell Martin by two falls to one in a match that didn't bring out his best. Like St Clair in the previous match, Bridges was seen in a better light against a rule-breaking opponent. The final match that week saw a new name to *World of Sport* (but not a new face) as Ox Brody lost by disqualification to Ray Steele. Brody had previously wrestled on TV as 'The Viking' and wrestled in the German tournaments as Dave Viking.

The second half of the Bradford show was seen the following week on April 19th, with John Quinn in the main event. Quinn's opponent was John Elijah, and his over-the-top forearm smash left Elijah unable to beat the count. Alan

Dennison continued his rivalry with Jim Breaks; after he had beaten Breaks by two falls to one, he demanded a championship match against him. This would eventually happen on the Wembley Arena show in June. The opening match that week saw a welcome return to the deaf-and-dumb star from Sheffield, Alan Kilby. Kilby had been missing for many a year from Joint Promotions' shows, apart from a rare appearance for Relwyskow and Green. He started his comeback with a one fall each draw against Honey Boy Zimba. Kilby would go on to be one of the decade's biggest stars on the Joint Promotions' circuit.

The match everyone had been waiting for, the World Heavyweight title match between Wayne Bridges and John Quinn, was filmed for *World of Sport* at Brent Town Hall in North London on April 21st, FA Cup Final day. I was lucky enough to be at the ringside accompanying Yasu Fuji, who was seconding Quinn, whilst Bridges had his son Dean Brisco with him. The atmosphere was red hot. Ninety-nine point nine per cent of the capacity crowd were supporting Bridges, with just a couple of Quinn fans who had flown in from North America to support their man. After taking an early fall, Bridges was thrown from the ring. When he reappeared he was badly cut. Referee Max Ward was forced to stop the contest and award the victory, together with the belt, to Quinn. The end of the match saw the crowd react angrily to their champion Wayne Bridges losing in such dubious circumstances. As John Quinn celebrated his victory in the ring with Yasu Fuji, and Wayne Bridges was being consoled in his corner, suddenly the Big Daddy music hit the PA and in walked Big Daddy himself. This was the announcement of the main event for the Wembley Arena extravaganza in June when Daddy would be teaming with Bridges to take on Quinn and Fuji. But it was not just Quinn and Fuji who looked unhappy to see Daddy; Bridges glared at him! Perhaps this was the moment a lot of wrestlers began to see which way the wind was blowing.

The Royal Albert Show in April took place two nights after the Wembley show and saw a match between teams captained by Big Daddy and John Quinn. The most interesting thing about the evening to me was the front cover of the evening's programme, which featured a picture of Quinn holding his newly won World Heavyweight title belt. That was some going to get it printed in less than two days. Unsurprisingly, Big Daddy and John Quinn avoided each other in the matches. Quinn knocked out Johnny Wilson in the first round, and Daddy beat Bruiser Muir who walked out in the first round. Daddy reappeared for the six-man tag finale and teamed with Chris Adams and Young David to easily beat Banger Walsh, Blackjack Mulligan and Mike Dean. The night's other single's matches saw David beat Mulligan by two straight falls. Walsh beat Ringo Rigby by count out. Pete Roberts beat Dean by two falls to one. Chris Adams beat Mick McManus by disqualification, and Brian Maxine beat Bob Anthony by two falls to one. It was a rather unsatisfactory night, with fans being denied the match they wanted to see.

The wrestling on *World of Sport* on April 26th came from the Kings Hall at Belle Vue in Manchester. The show was actually recorded on the previous Wednesday, the same night as the Albert Hall show, so star power was diluted slightly between the two. The main event between local favourite Tony St Clair and Yasu Fuji ended in an unsatisfactory no-contest verdict. Mal Sanders beat Sid Cooper, who was unable to beat the count of ten after falling through the ropes, and Jon Cortez beat Steve Peacock by two falls to one.

After a highly distinguished career, the former British Heavyweight champion Gwyn Davies made his final appearance on *World of Sport* on May 3rd, when he took on old rival Steve Veidor. This was the second half of the show recorded at Belle Vue and a rematch of the battle Davies and Veidor had fought at the Albert Hall in 1976. The match ended in a no contest; Veidor would make his final appearance on *World of Sport* by the end of the month. Also on the show were fellow veterans 'The Royals'. Their time in the spotlight was coming to an end but they still entertained the fans with all their usual moves as they beat Tally Ho Kaye and Johnny England by two falls to one. Finally, British Light/Heavyweight champion Marty Jones had a routine win over King Ben when Ben failed to beat the referee's count of ten.

The following Saturday was FA Cup Final day and *World of Sport* featured the Bridges v Quinn title match as part of the build-up to the big match.

'Ring Gladiator' Tony Rowney made a rare TV appearance on the May 17th show. Rowney was normally only seen on shows promoted by Ken Joyce, and on this occasion he was also matched with regular opponent Joyce. Tony Rowney was an unarmed combat instructor in the army as well as being skilled in the martial arts. Dynamite Kid had found this out when he bit off more than he could chew when he started some silliness with him at a TV taping back in 1977. The match with Joyce ended in a hard fought draw with Rowney's submission score equalised by a fall for Joyce in the allotted six rounds. Another match on the same programme ended with an inconclusive verdict: Mark Rocco's bout with Pete Roberts ended with both of them disqualified in the fifth round, with referee Max Ward for once unable to control either wrestler. The final match saw Young David take on Tally Ho Kaye, with David gaining a victory. Kaye was disqualified by referee Max Ward for refusing to break the hold after gaining an equalising submission in the fourth round.

Wrestling was missing from *World of Sport* on May 24th due to the home international football match between Scotland and England taking its place. In those days it was one of the very rare times a live football match was shown on TV.

As at Easter, grapple fans didn't have to wait a week for the next wrestling on ITV as there was a Bank Holiday programme on the Monday which had three bouts from Croydon. The main event was a heavyweight tag match which was part of the build-up to the main event at Wembley Arena in June. John Quinn partnered Yasu Fuji against Croydon's favourite son Steve Veidor (who was making his last ever appearance on *World of Sport*) and his partner, fellow South Londoner Lee Bronson. Referee Bobby Bear, who had only recently graduated from putting the ring up before the show to officiating, had no hope of controlling the bout. Both teams employed liberal use of illegal tactics before a piledriver from Fuji on Veidor led to the opening fall in the seventh minute. Veidor got a hugely popular equalising fall a minute or so later with a flying tackle and cross press on Fuji, despite Quinn's best attempts to break it up. The end came in the twelfth minute when Quinn's over-the-top forearm smash knocked Bronson spark-out with no hope of beating Bear's count of ten. Wayne Bridges, who had been sitting at the ringside watching the match, entered the ring and grabbed MC Fred Downe's microphone. Bridges told Quinn he had robbed him of his pride and his title, and he demanded Quinn name the day for the return world-title match. All manner of chaos reigned, with Lee Bronson holding Bridges back whilst Quinn and Fuji exited the ring.

The main supporting match on the show saw two northern-based welterweights make rare appearances at a Dale Martin show when John Naylor faced Jackie Robinson. Naylor won a very competitive match by two falls to one in the sixth round, with plenty of 'needle' in the contest at times. The winning fall came with Naylor's trademark use of the top rope to enable a sunset flip before pinning his opponent with a handstand and a folding press.

The final show of the season at the Royal Albert Hall on May 28th saw the return of a familiar old face and crowd favourite when Mike Marino made a comeback after an absence of a couple of years to take on John Quinn. Marino replaced Prince Mann Singh, Quinn's original opponent . Whether it was ring rust or simply old age. Quinn had too much artillery for Marino and he was forced to quit in the fifth round with a badly cut eye. The Royals had a somewhat routine victory over a new pairing of Lucky Gordon and Tony Rowney: Bert and Vic eased to a two straight falls win. Alan Kilby continued his comeback when he was matched with the much heavier John Elijah. Kilby showed up well before being forced to retire after an unlucky fall. Naturally the sporting Elijah refused to take the decision, so a no contest was the verdict. The Albert Hall fans' favourite, Steve Veidor, was matched against Pat Roach. Roach had lost his inclination to break the rules (or even bend them) so the result was a dour one fall each draw. Keith Haward continued his rise up the rankings with a victory, albeit by disqualification, against Bobby Barnes. Mick McMichael beat Tally Ho Kaye to complete the evening's entertainment.

May ended on *World of Sport* on the 31st with the belated arrival of 'Gridiron' Butts Giraud, who should have been in the country in February. His opponent in the match recorded at Solihull was none other than Wayne Bridges. MC Brian Crabtree said Giraud had received a telegram from John Quinn telling him to finish off Bridges. Giraud had appeared in British rings in the early seventies but he still cut a physically imposing figure and dwarfed the none-too-small Bridges. During the early stages of the match, commentator Kent Walton promoted the Wembley Arena show, saying it wouldn't be shown on TV. He also announced that details of Wayne Bridges' sanctioned title rematch with John Quinn would be given that night. Walton remarked that the referees were now working on a new instruction that they be less lenient to rule breaking and give out public warnings earlier. Referee Dave Reese adhered to the new rules and gave Giraud a public warning in the first round for using the closed fist. Giraud got the first fall in the second round when he caught a Bridges' flying tackle, then a slam and a cross press was enough for a count of three. Bridges quickly equalised in the first minute of the third when a flying butt weakened his opponent for Bridges to get the second fall of the match. The winner came in the fourth round, with Bridges slamming Giraud to the mat and pinning him for the count of three – an impressive victory. On the same show, Alan Dennison got another victory over Jim Breaks. Dennison got the winning fall whilst Breaks stood arguing with the referee after a disallowed submission. The other match saw Catweazle beat Sid Cooper by disqualification.

As usual with the summer months it didn't take much for *World of Sport* not to show wrestling; on June 7th live coverage of the schoolboy's football match between England and Scotland was shown instead.

All roads led to Wembley Arena for the second extravaganza there on June 11th. There was nothing like the hype for this show and, despite the absence of ITV cameras and not being shown on TV, the attendance was still disappointing. Talking to fellow ringsiders that night, the match the crowds wanted to see was the return for the World Title between

Wayne Bridges and John Quinn, not the tag match between Big Daddy and Bridges v Quinn and Yasu Fuji that was on offer.

The match was a complete farce and an embarrassment for such a show. The winning fall saw Bridges drag Quinn into the ring whilst Daddy chased Fuji outside the ring. Bridges then pinned Quinn for a two straight falls win despite neither him nor Quinn being the legal men in the ring. Even the fans saw the stupidity of this and left the referee in no doubt of how they felt about the match.

In the supporting matches in what was billed as a 'Chain Match' between Marty Jones and Mark Rocco turned into a strap match. A leather belt was attached to the wrists of each and the rules said the winner was the first to drag the other wrestler to each of the four corners. Jones won it on a conventional knockout instead and people wondered why the crowds started to drift away unhappy with what was being offered in the ring. The other main match saw Alan Dennison successfully make the welterweight title weight limit for his challenge to champion Jim Breaks. Dennison's diet was not in vain and he beat Breaks by two falls to one in the 9th round to become the new British Welterweight Champion. Breaks still remained the European Lightweight Champion. Mick McManus who was missing from the 1979 show appeared this time against old rival Vic Faulkner with McManus gaining victory in the fifth round when Faulkner was unable to continue.The other matches on the show saw Catweazle beat Tally Ho Kaye by disqualification. Jon Cortez give weight and a beating to Mick McMichael. Ray Steele's match with Gil Singh ended without a winner when it ended in a No Contest.The one thing that pleased the fans was when MC John Harris announced the news from the ring that everyone wanted to hear. The Quinn v Bridges return match would take place at Wembley Arena on the Bank Holiday Saturday in August which as events transpired would never happen.

Wrestling was again missing from World of Sport on June 14th with this time tennis the preferred sport to be shown.

Big Daddy was back on the small screen as wrestling returned to World of Sport on June 21st in a show recorded at Adwick Le Street. Daddy teamed up with Chris Adams against the duo of King Kong Kirk and Bruiser Muir with a confusing ending as Kirk and Muir simply leaving the ring after a barrage of belly butts from Big Daddy. An intriguing catchweight match saw Keith Haward face the much heavier Banger Walsh. Walsh was a lot better wrestler than he was allowed to be in the Big Daddy matches he usually appeared in but Haward was in a different class to him. Walsh eventually tired of Haward's superior skills and resorted to his usual rulebreaking manoeuvres. Referee Emil Poilve disqualified Walsh at the end of the fifth round for throwing Haward from the ring shortly after he had got an equalising submission. Mick McMichael beat Jackie Turpin by two falls to one in the final contest that week.

The second half of the show from Adwick Le Street was shown on TV the following week on June 28th with the main contest featuring John Quinn taking on Ray Steele. Yet another opponent fell victim to the over the top forearm smash with Steele only the latest to be unable to beat the count of ten and lose by a knockout. Brian Maxine wrestled a one fall each draw with the heavier John Elijah. Maxine's new approach to wrestling and not breaking the rules made this and most of his matches incredibly dull. Finally Bobby Barnes beat the veteran welterweight Bob Anthony when Anthony was unable to continue through injury.

Southport had it's annual TV show shown on World of Sport on July 5th with Mick McManus making his own annual journey to the Lancashire coast to appear on it. McManus faced the lightweight champion Steve Grey. McManus took the win when Grey was injured in the fifth round. The other two bouts shown were the semi finals of the Combat Challenge Shield. In the first Mark Rocco beat Mal Sanders with the pile driver in the fifth round leaving Sanders out for the count of ten. Marty Jones joined Rocco in the final when he saw off a spirited attempt by Young David to win by two falls to one in the final round of six.

The final of the tournament was held the next Saturday on July 12th with a slight upset as Mark Rocco came from a fall down to win to beat Marty Jones by two falls to one in the final two rounds. Giant Haystacks made short of work of Honey Boy

Zimba with a big splash in the second round leaving Zimba prostrate on the canvas for the count of ten. Alan Kilby continued his impressive comeback even though he lost to Mike Marino. Kilby pushed Marino all the way and it was only in the final round that Kilby conceded the winning fall.

The opening ceremony of the 1980 Moscow Olympics happened on July 19th which resulted in the wrestling on World of Sport from Catford restricted to 25 minutes and only one match shown. Luckily the match shown was a title rematch between new British Welterweight Champion Alan Dennison and the former champion Jim Breaks. Breaks went for Dennison's arm from the start with his usual illegal tactics. Dennison reversed a Breaks 'special' to get the first score with his own arm submission forcing Breaks to instantly submit. Breaks finally got the equaliser in the eleventh round when he finally got Dennison to submit from the 'special'. Both wrestlers went all out in the final round to get the win but it was to no avail. The bell ended the match at the end of the twelfth round with a one score each draw so Dennison retained the title.

It was the same the following week on July 26th with the coverage of the Moscow Olympics restricting the wrestling again to 25 minutes and a one match show. From the same Catford show as the previous week this time it was a heavyweight tag match with John Quinn once again pairing up with Giant Haystacks against Pete Roberts and Johnny Wilson. The weight difference between the teams was far too much for Roberts and Wilson to overcome and Haystacks and Quinn won by two straight falls.

Nothing ever of note ever happened during this time of the year or so we thought. But during July I heard from my fellow correspondents who I swapped news and results with that John Quinn had put in his notice to Joint Promotions and would be heading to the independent promoters to wrestle for Brian Dixon and Orig Williams. It would be the first time a legitimate top of the bill attraction had given notice since Jackie Pallo in 1974 and was just as newsworthy. With the move not only in the ring did Quinn change things but his input and ideas also helped to improve things greatly for the independent promoters. John Quinn leaving Joint Promotions really came about by accident. Quinn travelled to the bookings in his mobile home and had bumped into Brian Dixon quite accidentally several times at the Motorway Service Stations. After a while the question was posed would John Quinn be prepared to leave Joints and wrestle for Brian Dixon, Orig Williams and the other promoters not affiliated with Joint Promotions ? Alongside the wage increase offered was the offer for Quinn to become more involved with booking as he was getting ever frustrated with the way Max Crabtree was running things. Quinn accepted the offer and gave his notice in to the Joint Promotions' office.

Like most I didn't want to believe this or actually believed it had happened despite being told it was 100% definite by those in charge. Quinn's last match for Joint Promotions took place at Hanley on July 26th where he tagged with Mark Rocco to wrestle a 20 minute draw with the team of Pat Roach and Bobby Ryan. It didn't take Orig Williams long to use his new acquisition as he billed John Quinn the next night on one of his shows at Llandudno. Quinn's opponent was 'Beau' Jack Rowlands in a rematch of his infamous World of Sport debut back in 1979. On August 1st John Quinn made his debut at Liverpool Stadium for Wrestling Enterprises against Crusher Mason. Once it had been announced that John Quinn was appearing that night tickets sold like hot cakes and a capacity crowd was on hand for his debut. Brian Dixon's daughter Letitia was a member of a drum majorettes troupe and it was organised for them to accompany Quinn to the ring. The Liverpool crowd were volatile at the best of times, the sight of the majorettes with Quinn enraged the crowd and they were booed alongside Quinn. In the end several wrestlers had to be sent out to rescue the youngsters. Like most of Quinn's bouts this one ended in mayhem albeit a victory for the Canadian. He quickly followed up on the next show two weeks later when a contest with Wild Angus descended into some of the most violent scenes ever seen in a British ring.

Whilst Brian Dixon celebrated his new arrival by putting the house full signs up wherever Quinn appeared Max Crabtree had to work overtime to repair the damage done by the departure of Quinn and the World Heavyweight Title with him. Little did we know that it wasn't to be the only heavyweight champion to leave Joint Promotions. Unfortunately for Crabtree he had booked Quinn for a complete month of dates for August and now had a massive gap in the programme book to fill without anyone of comparable note to fill it with. All he could do was to use anyone available at short notice and hope that the fans wouldn't ask for refunds at the box office when they found out that John Quinn wouldn't be appearing that night. As if things couldn't get much worse for Max Crabtree a couple of weeks later the British Heavyweight Champion Tony St Clair gave notice he was leaving. St Clair had his final contest for Joint Promotions at Brighton on August 13th leaving yet another hole on the bill to fill. To rub salt into the wounds St Clair refused to lose the title before he left so two heavyweight champions were appearing for the independent promoters. Naturally St Clair's first match 'on the other side' would be against John Quinn at Rhyl in early September.

Wrestling again was missing from ITV on August 2nd as the Olympics in Moscow were coming to their conclusion.

With the Olympics having finished wrestling was back on ITV on August 9th with the usual three match programme at 4pm on *World of Sport* recorded at Bedworth. The centre piece was a match between Tony St Clair and Pat Roach. St Clair had refused to to put the British Heavyweight Title on the line so it was a non title affair. Roach won when St Clair was unable to continue after getting his leg trapped in the ropes. Keen eyed viewers with a video recorder were able see St Clair hook his leg in the rope before Roach went into throw him ! Wayne Bridges with his title rematch hopes shattered following the departure of Quinn took out his frustrations on Ox Brody with a two falls to one win in the fifth round. John Naylor beat Tally Ho Kaye who was disqualified in the sixth round in that week's opener.

A rather poor offering from Bedworth was shown on *World of Sport* on August 16th with none of the three bouts anywhere near top of the bill calibre. Johnny Kwango overcame Johnny England by two falls to one in the fifth round. Keith Haward gave a wrestling lesson to short notice replacement Tim Fitzmaurice with a two straight falls win in the fourth round.

Finally Ringo Rigby beat Manchester's Johnny South by two falls to one in the final round of six.

A rare visit to the North East was the feature of the *World of Sport* wrestling on August 23rd and a bill televised from Hartlepool. The main contest saw Big Daddy team up with Chris Adams to take on Yasu Fuji and the now renamed masked star 'The Black Baron'. Under the mask was Manchester heavyweight Kevin Cawley who had been wrestling as the 'The Masked Outlaw' for the previous few months. The Baron was given a manager in Charlie McGee and was used in the coming months as one of the replacements for John Quinn. In this match Daddy and Adams came out on top by two falls to one submission in a little over ten minutes. Mel Stuart had a fruitless long journey from Kent as he lost to Alan Kilby in the sixth round and Jackie Turpin beat John Wilkie by two straight falls in the fifth round.

Summer Bank Holiday Monday saw an extra helping of wrestling on the *World of Sport* special with three bouts from Croydon which were filmed way back on May 13th. Johnny Saint beat Zoltan Boscik who was forced to retire through injury. Marty Jones' match with Young David ended in a No Contest when David was unable to continue and Bert Royal beat Lucky Gordon by disqualification.

August ended on *World of Sport* on the 30th with the second half of the show recorded at Hartlepool. The featured match saw Jim Breaks gain revenge of sorts on Alan Dennison when the temperamental Breaks got the only fall needed to win in the fourth round. King Kong Kirk was back from his continental travels to take on Gil Singh but Kirk was sent packing by the referee who disqualified him in the second round. Steve Peacock wrestled a one fall each draw with Pat Patton in the other match shown.

During the Summer shows on the independent circuit a couple of new faces started appearing regularly and were to go on to much better things. Paul Tyrone would shortly move to Joints and the son in law of Tug Holton would be renamed as Tom Tyrone. Whilst the young Northern Irishman Dave Finlay would move over a year later and as Fit Finlay become known as one of the best wrestlers ever to grace British rings.

Wrestling was missing from World of Sport on September 6th as the European Golf Championship took its place.

One of the oddities of wrestling in Britain happened at Brent Town Hall in North West London on September 8th. It was just a normal Monday night show on the circuit but it made the national press. It was hardly the heist of the year but Brian Maxine had his British Middleweight Title belt stolen from the dressing room sometime during the evening. Mick McManus was quoted in the newspapers as saying 'Most of us had gone home when Brian's bout was on and anyone could have walked in'. The newspaper also said that the theft happened at Wembley Stadium which was a few hundred yards away from the town hall it actually happened at. The culprit was never caught.

Joint Promotions' booker Max Crabtree needed new blood to replace those who had left and looked all over the world as well as nearer home for new faces. The first new face to appear was the Red Indian star from the USA Bobby Bold Eagle who took on Mark Rocco as the main bout on *World of Sport* on September 13th in a show from Morecambe. After a considerable beating Bold Eagle was unable to continue in the 4th round and following several bruising encounters with the likes of Giant Haystacks and King Kong Kirk curtailed his visit by the end of the month and left early. Veteran heavyweight Peter Stewart had made a comeback the previous month as part of the replacements for John Quinn and on the same show he wrestled a one fall apiece draw with Ray Steele over six rounds. Honey Boy Zimba beat King Ben by knockout in the fifth round in the opening bout.

The next weekend on September 20th saw the second half of the Morecambe show. The highlight was Mike Marino taking on King Kong Kirk with Kirk going ahead in the second round with a neck lift submission. Marino reversed another attempted neck submission to gain the equaliser in the third round before the match ended in chaos in the fifth round. Marino lost his cool with Kirk's antics and sent Kirk flying outside of the ring before using his fist right under referee Ken Lazenby's nose. Lazenby subsequently disqualified both men for disobeying the rules of professional wrestling and rightly so. In a complete contrast to that match Steve Grey pinned Ken Joyce to win in the sixth round of traditional lightweight style match. Alan Kilby had another TV win when he beat Banger Walsh in the fourth round.

Wrestling was again missing from *World of Sport* on September 27th with Golf again being preferred and on October 4th it was Golf again as the Dunlop Masters tournament took the place of that weeks grappling.

The way to get around John Quinn leaving with the World Heavyweight Title was to pretend that Quinn had been stripped of the belt for failing to honour the return match contractual obligation with Wayne Bridges. Max Crabtree then set up a series of eliminators at each Royal Albert Hall show throughout the 1980/81 series with the final one to be for the vacant title. The first contender brought in was the Australian heavyweight Sharkey Ward together with his wife and manager Maori Princess Maemaeroa.

The final piece of the jigsaw to reset the books after the departures of Quinn and Tony St Clair was the arrival of another foreign import and this time it was the young Japanese star billed as Sammy Lee. Lee was a protege of Karl Gotch and was sent overseas to toughen him up and give him the experience of working on the British circuit every night.

Wrestling was back on *World of Sport* on October 11th from Southend which featured the debut of Sammy Lee. Lee had the perfect opponent in Sid Cooper to be able to showcase his impressive array of moves. Lee with Cooper's help looked like an absolute superstar and those at ringside and those viewing at home couldn't fail to be impressed. Kent Walton was immensely impressed by the size of Lee's thighs amongst other things and put him over perfectly. Sammy Lee got the win in the third round when he hurled Cooper through the ropes with no hope whatsoever of beating referee Joe D'Orazio's count of ten. Lee would go on to be one of the most popular as well as one of the most skilled overseas wrestlers to be seen in Britain. On the same show a heavyweight match saw Giant Haystacks take on the Indian Prince Mann Singh. Haystacks had little difficulty in dispatching the ponderous Singh in the second round when a big splash saw Joe D'Orazio stop the contest. The final match saw a first appearance of Australian Sharky Ward who was having a tune up before his match with Wayne Bridges at The Royal Albert Hall on October 15th. Ward made a winning debut against Jeff Kaye when Kaye had his neck trapped in the top two ropes. He then forced Kaye to tap out from a neck stretch submission. Unfortunately Kaye was unable to continue in the bout but Wayne Bridges would prove a much tougher proposition at the Albert Hall.

Not all departures from Joint Promotions were wrestlers and MC John Harris left Dale Martin under somewhat of a cloud. Harris was immediately employed by Wrestling Enterprises. This gave Brian Dixon the opportunity to promote in venues previously exclusive strong holds of Dale Martin through Harris's contacts with theatre managers and council entertainment chiefs. John Harris had years of experience of working in the offices of Dale Martin and this experience was to prove vital for Brian Dixon moving forward over the next few years. This left Dale Martin short of decent MC's with the likes of the immaculate Johnny Dale well past retirement age. The Count Dracula lookalike Peter Bates started to appear more often on World of Sport as well as at major venues such as the Royal Albert Hall. Unfortunately Bates neither had the charisma or the vocabulary for the role and as a consequence the running of shows suffered.

The opening show of the season at The Royal Albert Hall on October 15th not only featured the Wayne Bridges v Sharky Ward world title series eliminator but also Sammy Lee was in action too. Bridges had little difficulty beating Ward by two straight falls inside six rounds and would face tougher challengers in the months ahead. Sammy Lee took on the much heavier Butcher Bond for his Albert Hall debut but as with Sid Cooper on World of Sport Bond was bewildered by the speed and unorthodox moves of Lee and was beaten inside seven minutes. Mick McManus took on Johnny Saint with Saint winning in the sixth round after McManus was disqualified. Injury meant Alan Kilby was missing from his match with Pete Roberts and Lee Bronson took his place. The match ended with both wrestlers failing to beat the count in the fifth round. Bob Anthony and Zoltan Boscik made rare Albert Hall appearances in their match with each other. It was Anthony who came out on top with a two falls to one win in the fifth round. Finally the big men took centre stage in a tag match with Giant Haystacks and King Kong Kirk taking on the Lancashire duo of Peter Stewart and Jack Rowlands both of whom had recently made comebacks to Joint Promotions. Kirk got the first fall before Stewart got an equalising fall on Haystacks in the ninth minute. Rowlands was unable to beat the count after a big splash from Haystacks and the win went to Haystacks and Kirk.

The Royals tag team had returned to regular appearances for Joint Promotions and were featured on *World of Sport* on October 18th which was the second half of the show recorded at Southend. The Royals' opponents in the match were regular foes 'The Rockers' Pete LaPaque and Tommy Lorne in a match seen on many occasions on the circuit. Although both Bert and Vic were very much now in the veteran stage of their careers they were still able to do all the moves the crowd loved and LaPaque and Lorne were perfect foils for them. Faulkner got the winning fall on LaPaque in a little over twenty minutes. Wayne Bridges had an easy win over Lee Bronson. Bronson did surprise Bridges with an equaliser in the third round which only made Bridges go all out for the win which came within a minute of the restart. Finally Bobby Barnes and Chris Adams wrestled a bad tempered one fall each draw over six rounds. Rather than accept a draw Barnes stupidly challenged the judo blackbelt Adams to a judo throws match to decide the winner. Naturally Adams won although Barnes did make him sweat for the ten throws to nine victory.

Wrestling was again missing from *World of Sport* on October 25th when coverage of the WBA Heavyweight Title boxing match between Mike Weaver and Gerrie Coetzee from Sun City took its place.

The *World of Sport* wrestling on November 1st was taped back on May 25th with the main event between Yasu Fuji who had long departed from Britain back to the USA and Pete Curry. Fuji finished off Curry in the third round with his 'Banzai Drop' which left Curry unable to continue. Curry had also departed Joint Promotions by this time and he was back on the independent circuit. A return match from the Brent Town

Hall show seen in May between Mark Rocco and Pete Roberts was also shown although most viewers would have forgotten why a return match was being screened. This too ended without a winner with both wrestlers scoring one fall each in the allotted six rounds. The other match that week saw Marty Jones take on Butcher Bond over six rounds. The underrated Bond got the first fall in the third round pinning Jones with a reverse double knee. Jones equalised in the fifth round with a folding press and that is how it ended with a one fall each draw.

Controversy and newsworthy events never seemed to be too far away in the Autumn of 1980 and the arrival of American star Chris Colt only added to them. Colt was already notorious in the USA with his thick make up, safety pins in his face and multi coloured ring attire. Billed here as 'The American Dream' it looked like Colt may cause problems for Max Crabtree and Joint Promotions when his debut on *World of Sport* on November 8th was deemed not fit to be shown on TV by the ITV authorities. Colt's match on the show at Lincoln was with Mick McMichael which McMichael won by disqualification. The exact details are only known by those in attendance and a tape of the match is amongst the holy grails for wrestling fans. With the Colt match binned the coverage of the other two matches had to be padded out to fit the fifty minutes broadcast time. The first saw a rather dour , slow paced heavyweight match with Pat Roach beating Peter Stewart by two falls to one. The second match that week saw Big Daddy in tag action partnered by Sammy Lee against King Kong Kirk and Sharky Ward. Daddy was accompanied by what seemed to be hundreds of kids into the ring with partner Lee somewhat lost in the throng. When the action eventually started Lee got the first fall with a victory roll over Ward in just under three minutes before stunning Kirk with several arm drags on the much bigger man. Daddy took over from Lee with a big splash on Kirk to complete an impressive two straight falls win.

The following week on November 15th saw the second half of the Lincoln show screened. The first bout was a wrestling master class with Keith Haward taking on Jon Cortez over six rounds. Neither wrestler could be described as a showman but they were both superb technical wrestlers who were also great friends. Haward got the first fall in the second round with a folding press before Cortez equalised in the next round with a double leg nelson. Both wrestlers gave their all over the next three rounds to gain a winner and bragging rights. It wasn't to be and the sixth round finished with a one fall each draw. Afterwards Jon Cortez told MC Brian Crabtree that Haward was 'out of this world', had been a professional for less than a year and wanted to wrestle him for the sheer joy of doing so.

The main attraction was slightly different to that with an anything goes , over the top rope heavyweight Battle Royale. The contestants were Giant Haystacks, The Black Baron, Banger Walsh, Johnny Wilson, Beau Jack, Honey Boy Zimba, John Cox and TV newcomer Bull Pratt. Pratt was amongst a number of new heavyweights that Dale Martin had brought in to replace the departed John Quinn, Tony St Clair and others. Other new names included Steve Hammer and Izzy Van Dutch who neither lasted very long but at least Van Dutch went on to fame and fortune as one of 'The Gladiators' on the popular Saturday tea time ITV show. Not surprisingly Haystacks was favourite to win the Battle Royale unless something surprising took place. Immediately all the other wrestlers tried to eliminate Haystacks without success before the big man threw out Jack. Zimba next eliminated Pratt with Zimba himself following swiftly with the Baron. Cox threw Walsh out leaving the final three of Cox, Johnny Wilson and Giant Haystacks. It took a matter of seconds as Haystacks eliminated Wilson and Cox together to win this inaugural event which went on to become a regular feature of wrestling on TV in 1980's. The final bout saw Gil Singh beat John Elijah by two falls to one in a routine heavyweight contest.

Perhaps it wasn't the best idea looking back to book Chris Colt in a tag match against Big Daddy at the Royal Albert Hall on November 19th. Colt entered the ring that night accompanied by blues singer Joe Cocker to the music of AC/DC and tag partner the Black Baron together with his manager Charles McGee. Colt had spent the afternoon drinking around various London venues with Cocker and was in no fit state to wrestle. For once Big Daddy's entrance with his partner Steve Grey looked understated and most fans there looked on in bewilderment at the sight of it all. It all started well for Colt when a spectacular top rope move gained the opening fall on Grey but then it all fell apart big time. Steve Grey was totally aware of what was going on with Chris Colt swaying unsteadily on the top rope so when Colt fell off it Grey was perfectly placed for Colt to land on him to get the fall. Colt who was obviously in no fit state to perform whether it be under the influence of drink thanks to his afternoon session with Joe Cocker or drugs lurched around the ring or just laid on the ring apron for the rest of the match in a state of oblivion. With Colt no longer being able to participate in the match Big Daddy and Steve Grey made easy work of The Black Baron for perhaps one of the more bizarre wins of Daddy's wrestling career. One curiosity that took place during the evening was when a former member of the Dale Martin ring crew Dougie Allen who was now wrestling for the independents threw leaflets from the balcony to those sitting on the floor below. The leaflet announced that John Quinn was now wrestling for Wrestling Enterprises and would be defending the title for them and that Bridges's title attempt was irrelevant. It's fair to say that this didn't go down too well and when Allen tried the same trick at Chatham a week or so later some of the wrestlers on the bill took matters into their own hands. Allen suffered a broken arm and the leaflets were quickly destroyed.

On the same Albert Hall show Wayne Bridges was victorious in the second of the world title series eliminators when he beat the Antiguan Caswell Martin. European Lightweight Champion Jim Breaks lost to old rival Jon Cortez by two falls to one. Immediately afterwards Cortez slapped in a demand for a title match. Alan Dennison and Mark Rocco took part in a heated and rather bad tempered match which ended with Rocco being disqualified in the fifth round. Pat Roach overcame the challenge of Prince Mann Singh with the winning fall coming in the sixth round. The show closer saw Keith Haward beating Sid Cooper in another bad tempered contest with both wrestlers being issued with two public warnings as Haward registered a two straight falls win in the fourth round.

After the show Max Crabtree immediately sacked Chris Colt to nobody's surprise but as ever Brian Dixon saw an opportunity and took over his contract. The independents didn't have the same scrutiny that Joint Promotions did and billing him as 'The man banned from TV' did wonders at the box office. The first night with Chris Colt for Brian Dixon was another eventful episode. After a quiet journey home from a show at Southampton Dixon dropped Colt off at one of the lodgings used for wrestlers at Rock Ferry on The Wirral. This was shortly after 3am, at 9am Brian Dixon had a call from Merseyside Police to say Colt was under arrest for drugs offences!

To commemorate the 25th anniversary of ATV broadcasting wrestling it was announced there would be a sixteen man tournament with the victor winning the Anniversary Trophy. The sixteen participants nominated to compete were :- Mick McManus. Jim Breaks. Steve Grey. Alan Dennison. Chris Adams. Mal Sanders. Alan Kilby. John Naylor. Young David. Little Prince. Johnny England. King Ben. Lucky Gordon. Blackjack Mulligan. Pat Patton and Tony Costas.

The first four heats were seen on *World of Sport* on November 22nd from a show recorded at Chester. At the start of the show Kent Walton was shown on screen with the trophy introducing the tournament and reminiscing about the first show seen on ITV. The first match saw Young David take on Blackjack Mulligan with David overcoming the more experienced and much heavier Mulligan with a two straight falls win in three rounds. The second heat saw John Naylor face the pre tournament betting favourite Mick McManus. Naylor shocked McManus with an opening fall after thirty seconds of the first round. McManus retaliated by constantly flouting the rules before a mistimed flying tackle from Naylor in the third round saw McManus win and progress to the quarter finals. The third match saw Tally Ho Kaye meet judo ace Pat Patton. Having suitably softened Patton up Kaye opened the scoring in the second round with a Boston Crab submission but Patton quickly equalised with a flying crucifix in the third. Kaye got the winner in the fourth round with a body slam leading to the deciding fall. The final heat saw Chris Adams take on King Ben. Unlike the first three heats both wrestlers obeyed the rule book with Adams gaining the first fall in the third round. Ben equalised with a suplex leading to a cross press in the fourth round although MC Brian Crabtree confused everyone by announcing that Adams had got the equaliser ! At the end of the scheduled six rounds neither wrestler had got the winner so the result was a draw with Adams winning the toss of a coin to go through to the quarter finals.

Next to be shown were the two quarter finals between the four winners so far with different rules applied. The winner would be the first to throw his opponent onto his back ten times. In the first of them Young David took on Tally Ho Kaye, David quickly opened up a 5-0 lead before a series of bodyslams drew Kaye level. Kaye's experience saw him win 10-8 to be the first into the semi finals. In the second quarter final Chris Adams overcame Mick McManus despite at one stage McManus holding a 9-2 lead . A mule kick or what is known as a super kick nowadays drew him level before a second super kick put McManus down for the tenth time to see Chris Adams face Tally Ho Kaye in the first semi final.

The second half of the tournament took place the following Saturday on *World of Sport* with four heats followed by two quarter finals. The heats saw Alan Kilby beat Lucky Gordon by disqualification. Alan Dennison beat Mal Sanders by two falls to one and Jim Breaks beat Little Prince by two falls to one. Whilst Steve Grey beat Tony Costas he was injured in doing so therefore he was unable to continue in the tournament. His quarter final opponent Alan Kilby received a bye into the semi final. In the other quarter final old rivals Alan Dennison and Jim Breaks met once again with the match decided again by the first to throw his opponent onto his back ten times. Breaks took exception to the rules during the contest and walked out of the ring to leave Dennison the winner and join Kilby, Chris Adams and Tally Ho Kaye in the semi finals.

The first semi final for 25th Anniversary Trophy was shown on *World of Sport* on December 6th from Walthamstow with Alan Kilby facing Chris Adams. As with Adams' first round heat against King Ben this again ended in a time limit one fall each draw with Kilby grabbing an equalising fall in the very last seconds of the sixth round. Rather than decide by a toss of a coin there would be a rematch held before the final. Also on the same programme that week was a scheduled match featuring Chris Colt against Johnny Kwango. With Colt departed from Joint Promotions he was replaced by Kurt Heinz who Kwango beat by two straight falls inside four rounds. The final match shown that week was a rematch between Keith Haward and Jon Cortez after their drawn match shown the previous month. This was another technical wrestling masterpiece but again there was no winner as Cortez was injured in the sixth round and unable to continue. Haward refused to accept the win so a No Contest was the decision.

The second semi final was shown on December 13th's *World of Sport* on the second half of the Walthamstow show. This time there was a decisive winner as Alan Dennison overcame the spirited challenge of Tally Ho Kaye who led with a fall in the fourth round. Dennison scored rapid submissions in the fifth and sixth round with his arm suspension lift to become the first wrestler into the tournament final. The match that most viewers was interested in that week was between Mark Rocco and Dynamite Kid who had recently returned to the UK for his usual pre Christmas visit. Referee Max Ward had no hope of keeping this within the rules as both Rocco and Dynamite went at it as 100mph with Dynamite suffering a badly cut forehead in the second round. Dynamite Kid got the opening fall in the third round with a sequence of diving headbutt followed by a German suplex enabling Dynamite to pin Rocco for the count of three. Unfortunately referee Ward stopped the match in the interval due to Dynamite's cut on his forehead which left him unable to continue. Whilst MC Fred Downes didn't actually announce the result it was a technical knockout win for Rocco and a great shame that Dynamite Kid had left the country before a return match could be arranged. The final match shown was the complete opposite with Johnny Saint beating Bob Anthony by two falls to one in a match full of holds , counters and reversals.

The Royal Albert Hall held its final show of 1980 on December 17th with a very good looking proposed programme. Wayne Bridges was successful in the third of the world title series eliminators when he beat the giant Irish veteran Big Jim Moran. Moran had returned to the ring especially for his chance in the eliminators but the former Gargantua was way past his prime and Bridges won with the winning fall in the sixth round. King Kong Kirk beat Honey Boy Zimba who was unable to continue in the fifth round. Newcomer Ray Victor made an Albert Hall debut against Mal Sanders but lost by two straight falls inside sixteen minutes. Another debut that night was from Kent youngster Tom Tyrone who replaced the advertised Chris Adams in a match against The Exorcist. His opponent The Exorcist was not the one who was seen in the mid 1970's and who was Clayton Thomson under the mask. This new Exorcist was Gordon Corbett, the Birmingham heavyweight who had been wrestling on the independent circuit for a few years. The Exorcist had a manageress in Miss Jamie Barrington who was in fact Corbett's wife Elaine. Barrington claimed that this Exorcist had suffered horrific injuries in a motor racing accident and the mask covered his scars whilst a special boot was needed because of leg injuries. Naturally the built up sole of the boot contained a foreign object and with the help of it Exorcist beat Tyrone by knockout in the fifth round.

Saving the best for last the main event was the new Albert Hall favourite Sammy Lee tackling Mark Rocco fresh from his win on TV against Dynamite Kid. After four exceptional rounds full of action rarely ever seen in a British ring Rocco got an equalising submission on Lee who had led through a fall in the second. For refusing to break the submission hold the referee disqualified Rocco and so Lee was the winner. Rocco argued with the officials about the decision for so long the wrestlers for the evening's closing match were on their way to the ring with Rocco still there. Unluckily for Rocco one of the participants was Dynamite Kid who was still angry about the cut head loss in the TV match the previous weekend. With Rocco still refusing to leave the ring after an impromtu discussion the evening's closer became a tag match. Rocco partnered Dynamite's opponent Tally Ho Kaye against Dynamite Kid and Sammy Lee who welcomed the chance for another crack at Rocco. Although lasting only ten minutes this has to be one of the best matches seen in a British ring with some of the moves years if not decades ahead of their time. Even Tally Ho Kaye who was more of the traditional British wrestler played his part in the match and the result of the match a two straight falls win for Dynamite and Lee in ten minutes does not do it justice. Unfortunately matches at the Albert Hall weren't taped unless the ITV cameras were there for *World of Sport* which they weren't that night so there remains no film of it.

The pre Christmas *World of Sport* on December 20th naturally featured Big Daddy in a show from Leicester. Daddy dressed as Father Christmas entered the ring alongside his partner Kid Chocolate whilst their opponents Butcher Bond and Banger Walsh waited patiently. In a match lasting barely five minutes Chocolate was eliminated after two minutes after being knocked out by Bond. Daddy therefore had to carry on alone as Chocolate was stretchered from the ring. Daddy equalised with body slam and big splash on Bond before Walsh was finished off with the double elbow drop. The opening match between Jackie Robinson and Jackie Turpin ended early when both wrestlers were counted out in the second round. The 25th Anniversary Trophy was also decided that week with first the semi final rematch between Alan Kilby and Chris Adams which was decided via the ten throws route with which Kilby won by ten throws to nine. Therefore the final saw Kilby take on the much lighter Alan Dennison and it was Alan Kilby who came out on top when he pinned Dennison in the final round to lift the trophy.

The last *World of Sport* of 1980 was the second half of the Leicester show broadcast on December 27th. For a holiday period edition it was a poor offering with the advertised main event of Giant Haystacks v Lee Bronson not happening. Instead of Bronson being dwarfed by Haystacks he instead dwarfed the much smaller John Wilkie and the match ended with Wilkie unable to beat the count of ten in the fourth round. Mick McManus took on old rival Billy Torontos in the other feature match with McManus coming out on top in the fifth round. The third match featured a solid but uninspiring six round heavyweight draw between Pete Roberts and Caswell Martin.

A rather down beat way to end the year after all the excitement of the previous few weeks.

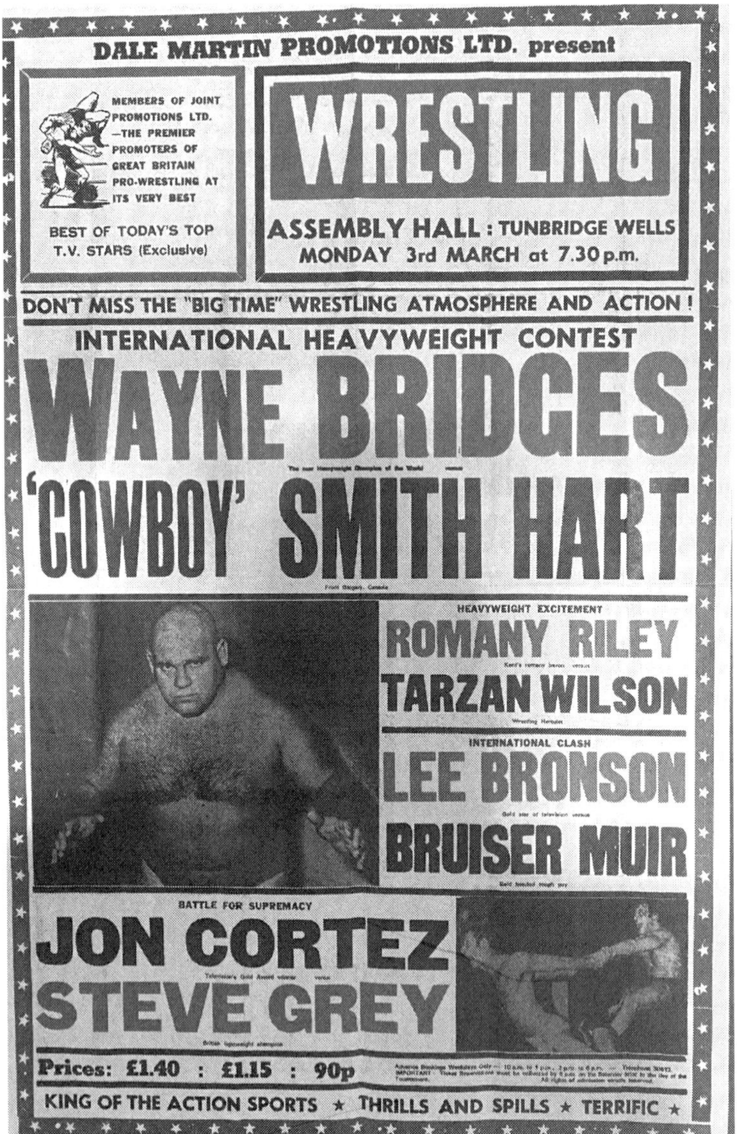

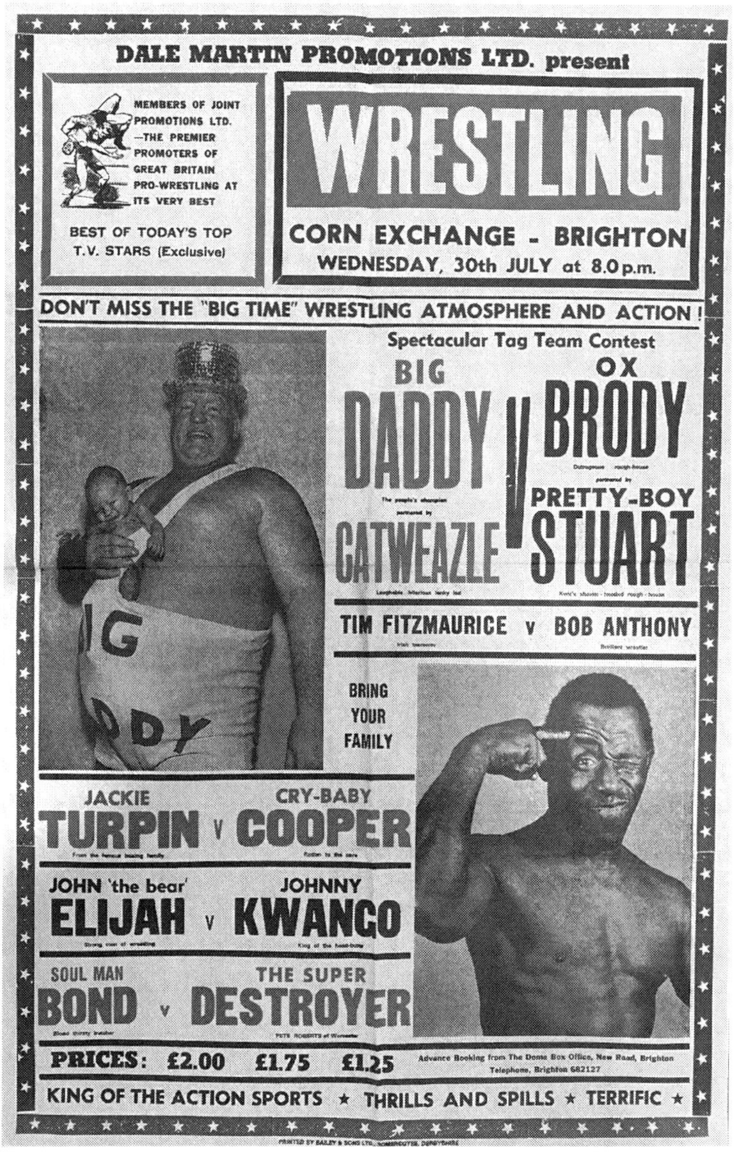
DALE MARTIN PROMOTIONS LTD. present
MEMBERS OF JOINT PROMOTIONS LTD. —THE PREMIER PROMOTERS OF GREAT BRITAIN PRO-WRESTLING AT ITS VERY BEST
BEST OF TODAY'S TOP T.V. STARS (Exclusive)
WRESTLING
CORN EXCHANGE - BRIGHTON
WEDNESDAY, 30th JULY at 8.0 p.m.
DON'T MISS THE "BIG TIME" WRESTLING ATMOSPHERE AND ACTION!
Spectacular Tag Team Contest
BIG DADDY
partnered by
CATWEAZLE
v
OX BRODY
partnered by
PRETTY-BOY STUART
TIM FITZMAURICE v BOB ANTHONY
BRING YOUR FAMILY
JACKIE TURPIN v CRY-BABY COOPER
JOHN 'the bear' ELIJAH v JOHNNY KWANGO
SOUL MAN BOND v THE SUPER DESTROYER
PRICES: £2.00 £1.75 £1.25
Advance Booking from The Dome Box Office, New Road, Brighton
Telephone, Brighton 682127
KING OF THE ACTION SPORTS ★ THRILLS AND SPILLS ★ TERRIFIC ★

DALE MARTIN PROMOTIONS LTD. present
IN CONJUNCTION WITH NUNEATON & BEDWORTH BOROUGH COUNCIL
MEMBERS OF JOINT PROMOTIONS LTD. —THE PREMIER PROMOTERS OF GREAT BRITAIN PRO-WRESTLING AT ITS VERY BEST
BEST OF TODAY'S TOP T.V. STARS (Exclusive)
WRESTLING
CIVIC HALL : High Street : BEDWORTH
FRIDAY, 12th DECEMBER at 7.45 p.m.
DON'T MISS THE "BIG TIME" WRESTLING ATMOSPHERE AND ACTION !
International Heavyweight Clash
Psychedelic, Must be seen to be believed, is he the Ninth Wonder of the World ? The Amazing
AMERICAN DREAM
"Ronald" of Hollywood Versus
THE SUPER DESTROYER
PETE ROBERTS of Worcester
CLASH OF YOUNG STARS
STEVE CASEY
Versus
RICKY JAMES
DM
ACTION AND EXCITEMENT
YOUNG DAVID
JOHNNY SOUTH
HEAVYWEIGHT BATTLE
'BULL' PRATT
Versus
PETE CURRY
Admission £1.65 : £1.40
Advance Bookings: CIVIC HALL BOX OFFICE Phone: Bedworth 311661
ALL RIGHTS OF ADMISSION STRICTLY RESERVED
KING OF THE ACTION SPORTS ★ THRILLS AND SPILLS ★ TERRIFIC ★

CHAPTER 2 - 1981

The New Year started with a departure to North America and it wasn't as predicted Young David although he would go later in the year. It was Chris Adams who left to seek fame and fortune stateside and that's something that he did achieve.

In the ring the first *World of Sport* of 1981 was on January 3rd from Burnley with three decent looking matches to watch. In the first Pat Roach took on Ray Steele and with Roach not on a 'going day' the match dragged into the sixth round before Steele was unable to continue after receiving a 'Brumagen Bump' finisher from Roach. Next up Sammy Lee took on Blackjack Mulligan and yet again Lee bewildered his opponent with his speed and moves. Even Mulligan's attempts to rough Lee up with punches and foul moves were futile as Lee eased to a two straight falls win with a knee drop leading to a cross press in the second round to seal the win. The third match saw Marty Jones tackle bitter rival Mark Rocco once again with Rocco getting the first fall in the third round. Jones equalised in the fourth with a folding press surprising Rocco who was attempting a fall of his own. With both wrestlers going all out for the winner even the ring suffered with a broken ring board causing problems before the bell for the end of the sixth round signalled a one fall each draw.

The Franco-Russian giant Le Grand Vladimir had arrived in the country for his contest with Wayne Bridges at the Royal Albert Hall as part of the world title series eliminators and was having a warm up bout on the second half of the Burnley show. This was shown on January 10th edition of World of Sport and Vladimir easily defeated his opponent John Cox who was unable to continue in the third round. The Royal Brothers were also on the show and as per usual Bert and Vic's teamwork was no match for their opponents Sid Cooper and John Wilkie who despite their finest rule bending tactics lost by two straight falls inside ten minutes. In the other match shown Peter Stewart beat Johnny South who failed to beat the count in the fifth round.

The wrestling shown on *World of Sport* on January 17th for some reason came from a show recorded at Catford the previous July. Someone must have found the footage in a cupboard and decided to show it. It wasn't worth it as it was a particularly poor show with Mick McManus beating Kid Chocolate by two falls to one. Terry Rudge wrestled a six round draw with Len Hurst and Billy Torontos pinned Kurt Heinz.

Le Grand Vladimir was back on *World of Sport* on January 24th from Wolverhampton. For some reason he was booked in a tag match against Big Daddy, not what you really want your main event at the Albert Hall the following Wednesday to be doing. Vladimir's partner was Mel Stuart and Daddy was with Sammy Lee. Vladimir even had ring entrance music with Boney M's 'Rasputin' accompanying him and Stuart to the ring. Of course Daddy and Lee entered to the strains of 'We shall not be moved' whilst a rather overexcited woman at ringside flicked 'v signs' at Vladimir. Once the action eventually started Daddy locked up with Vladimir but the giant Russian soon tagged in partner Mel Stuart who was rag dolled around the ring by Daddy before Lee joined in. Vladimir had the ringsiders seething with fury as he attacked Lee with all manner of strength holds including a public warning for clamping a sleeper hold on his opponent. Daddy got the first fall on Vladimir with a slam and big splash before Lee got the winner for a two straight falls win with the knee drop and cross press combination on Stuart in under seven minutes. The other matches shown that week saw the match between Bobby Barnes and Pat Patton end in the fifth round when both were counted out. Wayne Bridges beat Romany Riley in a heavyweight contest by two falls to one in the fifth round.

The first show at the Royal Albert Hall was held on January 28th with a rather nondescript bill on offer. The main event saw Wayne Bridges meet Le Grand Vladimir in the latest world title series eliminator. Even though Vladimir was much the bigger, Bridges had youth on his side and eventually he wore down Vladimir for a two falls to one victory. The Royal Brothers had a rather boring match against The Rockers who they had met on numerous occasions in the past. Once again Bert and Vic were the winners by two straight falls. A new face on the bill not only to the Albert Hall but Joint Promotions was Frank Cullen. He had made his name wrestling on the independent circuit mainly in North Wales for Orig Williams and elsewhere for Brian Dixon. Cullen was in at the deep end on his debut being matched with Pete Roberts and whilst Cullen showed up extremely well it was Roberts who won the match. Cullen who Max Crabtree renamed as Chic Cullen departed shortly after for world travels including a stint in Canada at Stampede Promotions. The match of the night saw Jon Cortez continue to press for a title match against Jim Breaks. This time Cortez beat the European Lightweight Champion by two straight falls. Alan Kilby faced a set back to his title ambitions when he was forced to retire through injury against Marty Jones and to complete the night Gil Singh defeated Terry Rudge.

The second half of the Wolverhampton show was screened on *World of Sport* on January 31st with five matches lined up for the fifty minute broadcast. First up were the heavyweights with King Kong Kong Kirk tackling 'Tarzan' Johnny Wilson in his leopardskin print ring attire. Kirk with a strange tuft of hair on the side of his head was in one of his bad moods after a barrage of postings and dropkicks from Wilson in the early seconds of the match. A back elbow from Kirk in the second round left Wilson in danger of being counted out by referee Jeff Kaye. As the count reached eight Kirk decided to land a guillotine elbow drop onto his prostrate opponent quickly followed by another. Kaye had no option but to disqualify Kirk and declare Wilson the winner and as MC Brian Crabtree announced the verdict he landed another elbow drop before telling Crabtree to get his brother (Big Daddy) out there. Next up was an eliminator for the European Mid/Heavyweight Title held by Mike Marino who was presented to the crowd by Brian Crabtree before the match started. Alan Kilby who was rewarded for winning the 25th Anniversary Trophy by his place in the match and he was taking on Scottish veteran Tom Dowie who hadn't been seen much on TV or even South of the Border recently. Kilby overcame the dubious tactics of the Scotsman to come from a fall behind for a two falls to one victory in the seventh round and the opportunity of the title match with Marino.

The rest of the show was a lightweight tournament featuring four of the best English lightweights around at this time. It was a shame that the matches were too short to them justice. Johnny Saint beat Jackie Robinson by the one fall needed in just over four minutes. Steve Grey pinned Bobby Ryan in just under four minutes to go through to the final against Saint. After the scheduled ten minutes neither Saint or Grey had got the required score to win so referee Jeff Kaye awarded the decision on points to Grey.

In something of a surprise the next challenger for Wayne Bridges in the world title series eliminators would be the long haired Scotsman Wild Angus who had spent the last couple of years or so wrestling overseas or on the independent circuit. Angus's first match back for Joint Promotions was improbably as a late notice subsitute at Bristol. Ringsiders there that night were shocked to see him walk out and opponent Peter Wilson wished he hadn't as he took a beating before losing to two straight submissions.

The first show in February on *World of Sport* was on the 7th recorded at Aylesbury. It should have featured the return of Red Indian Bobby Bold Eagle but he was delayed on his journey. His place was taken by Clive Myers who had returned to Joint Promotions after a couple of years on the independent circuit. The bill that week was a three a side team match and six man tag finale with the team of Clive Myers, Young David and Mick McMichael facing the team of Mal Sanders, Lucky Gordon and Steve Peacock. In the first singles match Sanders wrestled a one fall each draw with David in five excellent rounds of wrestling. Mick McMichael beat Steve Peacock by scoring the only fall of the match in the fourth round and Clive Myers beat Lucky Gordon who failed to beat the count in the fourth round after Myers had sent him flying outside of the ring. In the six man tag the win went to Myers, McMichael and David by two straight falls inside twelve minutes with in the end Sanders turning on his two team mates in frustration at their rule breaking. Bobby Bold Eagle eventually returned to the country a week later than scheduled but again he ended his visit early and was gone by the end of the month.

Sammy Lee was back in action on *World of Sport* on February 14th in the second half of the Aylesbury show where his opponent would be Johnny England. England went the same way as Lee's other opponents. A bewildered England unable to cope with the speed and surprise of Lee's moves simply left the ring in the second round and lost by count out. Before the match had actually started Mick McManus entered the ring and grabbed the microphone from MC John Curry and challenged Sammy Lee to a match. Curry translating for Lee said he was happy to accept the challenge. Frank 'Chic' Cullen made his *World of Sport* debut on the same show against John Elijah. In a sporting contest the heavier Elijah won the match in the fifth round when a backdrop from Elijah sent Cullen flying over the top rope with a heavy landing into the first row of ringsiders. The other match saw Jon Cortez continue with his campaign for a European Lightweight Title match when he took on Jim Breaks again. With the score one each going into the final round of six it seemed that Breaks had finally beaten Cortez when he pinned him but Breaks needed to tug on Cortez's leotard to do so. Commentator Kent Walton went mad and demanded referee Max Ward speak to him and to tell Ward what had happened. Walton admitted what he had done was strictly against the rules for commentators and he 'would be shot' for doing so but he couldn't abide by seeing Breaks cheat his way to the win. Breaks denied doing anything illegal but Max Ward took the word of Kent Walton and disqualified him. Breaks then told Walton to keep 'his fat mouth out of it' whilst aiming a sly kick at Jon Cortez. Two brilliant wrestlers in their own way delivering a match that had the crowd red hot throughout.

The Mike Marino v Alan Kilby match for Marino's European Mid/Heavyweight Title was featured on *World of Sport* on February 21st on a show recorded at Bury. Before the title match though it was time for another chapter of the Mark Rocco v Marty Jones rivalry with a stipulation that it would be a twenty minute time limit, no rounds and one fall to win. Both wrestlers again went off at 100mph with plenty of dubious moves employed by both. Funnily referee Kashmir Singh only issued one public warning, to Rocco, during the contest. As the match entered the final minute with still no score both wrestlers got ever desperate to get a winner but to no avail with Jones delivering a pile driver on Rocco just as the bell rang to his immense frustration. With neither wrestler able to get the winner it was a time limit draw and no doubt another return match had to be signed. The title match was up next and for me it was quite a sad sight watching Mike Marino now wearing a tee shirt under his leotard and not looking that well. Kilby got the opening fall in the fourth round with a nice reversal enabling him to pin the champion. The bout ended in the sixth round when Kilby fell between the ropes whilst attempting to throw Marino and there was no hope of the match continuing. Mike Marino therefore retained the title and generously offered Kilby another crack at the championship. Last up saw Giant Haystacks taking on Jack Rowlands who was a short notice replacement for Rex Strong. A backdrop and splash in the second round gave Rowlands no hope of beating referee Kashmir Singh's count of ten and another easy victory for the giant.

The much anticipated Sammy Lee v Mick McManus match was featured on *World of Sport* on February 28th in the second half of the Bury show. First match shown saw John Naylor beat fellow Wigan resident Kenny Hogan by the one fall needed in the fifth round in what was a very bad tempered contest. The crowd went crazy as Sammy Lee made his way to the ring to take on Mick McManus for the main event of the afternoon. As soon as the bell rang for the first round McManus was using punches to try and subdue the speed of Lee. In the second round Lee accidentally dropkicked referee Kashmir Singh. McManus thought he had won, Singh instead signalled the action to continue. After receiving a barrage of kicks McManus decided he had had enough and made his way from the ring to gift Sammy Lee another win. The final match was a rematch of the Wolverhampton tournament final between Johnny Saint and Steve Grey. This time there would be a twenty minute time limit with still the one fall needed for victory. After twenty minutes of brilliant technical wrestling it was up to referee Dave Reese to award the win this time to Johnny Saint via a points decision.

The Royal Albert Hall show on February 25th saw the much anticipated Wayne Bridges v Wild Angus world title series eliminator and things didn't go to plan for Bridges. He was unable to cope with Angus's tactics and after one rule breaking move too many from Angus he pushed referee Max Ward out of the way and proceeded to batter the Scotsman. Referee Ward had no option but to disqualify Bridges but he also disqualified Angus for his part in the fracas. Of course this led ringsiders puzzled as to what would happen next in the series of eliminators without a winner of this contest. The man who was scheduled to meet the winner in March was 'Mighty Yankee' Steve Di Salvo from Wisconsin, USA and he tuned up for the match with a quick win against Lee Bronson. There was one problem with Di Salvo and it was noticable that he wasn't actually able to wrestle and needed some extra time in the gym before he was ready. Big Daddy and his new regular partner Sammy Lee easily beat the team of Lee Sharron who had recently returned from the independent scene and his partner Banger Walsh. Both Sharron and Walsh had had enough of Lee's speed and Daddy's heavy artillery and walked out after 10 minutes.

Other matches on the Albert Hall show saw Alan Dennison's match with McMichael ending early in the usual McMichael technical disqualification spot. As was seen numerous times McMichael accidentally caught Dennison in his genitals as he was falling leaving Dennison in no fit state to continue. Young heavyweight Tom Tyrone had his father in law Tug Holton at ringside to cheer him on against Caswell Martin. It was no disgrace for Tyrone to lose to the much more experienced Antiguan by two falls to one in five rounds. Finally the show closer saw judo ace Pat Patton beat the musclebound Johnny England in a strange way. England thought he had knocked out Patton in the third round and was already strutting his way back to the dressing room as the referee counted Patton. But Patton rose at the count of nine and despite England running back to the ring failed to do so by the count of ten. The win went to Patton despite vociferous protests from England.

This was something of a boom period for attendances for Joint Promotions with Big Daddy still drawing big crowds and the likes of Sammy Lee and Wayne Bridges were also putting a considerable number of backsides on seats each night. It wasn't just Joint Promotions though as John Quinn was packing the houses out for Wrestling Enterprises and other independent promoters. He successfully defended his World Title against Steve Veidor at Southampton in an action packed 11 rounds and defeated local hero Neil Sands at Ipswich in a similar match that had the crowd on their feet willing their man to victory. Tony St Clair was still chasing that elusive shot but continued to impress in his new surroundings including victories over the likes of Quinn in non title matches and Steve Young.

The start of March was somewhat quiet with wrestling missing from *World of Sport* on March 7th as snooker was shown instead.

The outcome of the Board of Control's decision about the Wayne Bridges and Wild Angus match at the Albert Hall was waited with interest. They decided to have them have a rematch on the March Royal Albert Hall show and postpone the Steve Di Salvo eliminator till April.

Wrestling was back on *World of Sport* on March 14th from Derby with Big Daddy in action. Bobby Bold Eagle was his partner against the team of Wild Angus and Bull Pratt. Angus had his eye on the Albert Hall rematch so was happy to give Bold Eagle a pasting before letting Pratt be the recipient of the big splash from Daddy which gave him and Bold Eagle the win. Alan Dennison beat 'Rocker' Pete LaPaque by two falls to one in the fifth round of the opening match whilst the final match saw a one each draw over six rounds between Ray Steele and Gil Singh.

The Royal Albert Hall show on March 18th featured the much anticipated rematch between Wayne Bridges and Wild Angus in the next world title series eliminator. The rematch was another epic encounter with Angus at times looked to being able to derail the Bridges run of victories. Unfortunately Angus fell from the ring in the 5th round and was unable to beat the count thus Bridges progressed again after his hardest task to date. In other action Jon Cortez finally got his title match against Jim Breaks for his European Lightweight Title. In another match that had the crowds at the edge of their seats Breaks lost his title to Cortez in a thrilling contest. Cortez reversed the Breaks's special submission to get the champion to submit himself in the 8th round for the winner. In the nominal main event Pat Roach and Giant Haystacks' bout ended in a No Contest in the 3rd round when the one of ring boards seemed to break. After an inspection by referee Joe D'Orazio he had to stop the match and declare the inconclusive verdict. Bobby Bold Eagle was scheduled to face Mick McManus but with the Red Indian already departed for the USA his place was taken disappointingly by Johnny Kwango. McManus and Kwango were now in the fourth decade of facing each other having first fought in the 1950's and it would have been nice to have seen a new face get a chance. McManus picked up a routine victory with the winning submission in the fifth round. The prize for the winner of the Clive Myers v Steve Grey contest was a place in the knockout tournament on the April Albert Hall show and it was Myers who came out the winner in an excellent wrestling match in the sixth round. Finally the night ended with Billy Torontos meeting old rival Sid Cooper and beating him by two falls to one in the fourth round to send everyone home happy.

On the independent scene they saw the return of a familiar face who had been missing from action for over two years. Kendo Nagasaki with this time the mask back on made a comeback from his extended injury lay off and he targetted the imposter King Kendo in a series of tag matches for Wrestling Enterprises. Also on the tag scene the colourful Adrian Street teamed up with 'American Dream' Chris Colt in a team that had ringsiders howling with derision and seething with anger at their unruly antics.

Back on the TV screen the March 21st edition of wrestling on *World of Sport* came from Ashington in the North East of England, better known as the home town of Bobby and Jackie Charlton. It featured 'Mighty Yankee' Steve DiSalvo's TV debut having been deemed ready now to take his chance. The strange thing was this was actually a rematch of a match taped at Derby and should have been seen before this one. The match at Derby ended with a referee bump in the second round which ended the contest but this wasn't actually shown until October.

This time Roberts was the winner when DiSalvo was disqualified in the fourth round. On the same week Tally Ho Kaye had a win over Kid Chocolate in the fifth round whilst Clive Myers' match with Young David was halted in the sixth round when David hurt his back. Myers refused the win so a No Contest verdict was recorded. This was Young David's last appearance on World of Sport before he departed to Canada to link up with Dynamite Kid in Calgary and the eventual formation of 'The British Bulldogs' tag team.

The other half of the show from Ashington was shown on March 28th with the advertised bill in that week's TV Times changed at short notice. The rematch for the European Mid/Heavyweight Title between Mike Marino and Alan Kilby was cancelled with Marino unavailable. Kilby took on Blackjack Mulligan and a rather uncompetitive win for Kilby inside of three rounds. The rematch between Kilby and Marino in the end never happened. The other scheduled featured match advertised in TV Times should have been a handicap match between Giant Haystacks and The Royal Brothers. In what must have been a printers error as Haystacks was at Worthing that night so Bert and Vic took on the team of Lee Sharron and King Ben. Despite Ben and Sharron's best attempts with numerous rule bending moves Bert Royal got the winning fall in the sixteenth minute with a folding press on Sharron. The final match shown that week saw an upset with European Middleweight Champion Mal Sanders defeated by Keith Haward in a non title match. Haward got the winning fall in the final round and straight away was pressing for a title match.

After his easy victories over the likes of Mick McManus and Johnny England shown on *World of Sport* recently Sammy Lee stepped up in levels on the April 4th broadcast when he faced Mark Rocco. In a show recorded at Hemel Hempstead Lee beat Rocco although it was via disqualification when Rocco was sent to the dressing room in the third round. Lee had already scored the opening fall in the second round. Wayne Bridges had a hard fought win over Terry Rudge on the same show with a two falls to one victory in the sixth round. Jackie Turpin and John Naylor wrestled a one each draw over six rounds in the show opener.

The second half of the show from Hemel Hempstead was broadcast on *World of Sport* on April 11th with a solid rather than exciting look to it. Butcher Bond beat Tom Tyrone by two falls to one in the fifth round with Bond relying on his experience and skills rather than breaking the rules to win the match. Wild Angus replaced King Kong Kirk against Caswell Martin and a back submission in the fifth round gave Angus the win. Afterwards Giant Haystacks made his way to the ring to announce he would be forming a tag team with him and they would be targeting Big Daddy. The other match that week saw the new European Lightweight Champion Jon Cortez replace Bobby Bold Eagle to take on Bobby Barnes and it was Cortez who won by two falls to one in the sixth round.

The April 18th *World of Sport* saw the wrestling come from Leicester and an advertised team match between a team captained by Big Daddy against one captained by Giant Haystacks. The first match saw John Elijah who had replaced Alan Kilby represent the Daddy team against Tony Francis who was on the Haystacks' team. Elijah got the winning fall in the seventh round following a body slam and cross press and first point to the Big Daddy team. Next up saw Giant Haystacks himself face Johnny Wilson. Haystacks took a couple of rounds to wear down Wilson with strength holds before a mistimed flying tackle gave Haystacks the chance to land the big splash on him. The referee Dave Reese didn't even bother to count and stopped the match as Kent Walton winced at the commentary desk. The final match saw Big Daddy take on the large but limited Anaconda and as Daddy made his way to the ring Haystacks hadn't left there from the previous match. Banger Walsh was also out there for some reason. A belly butt from Daddy sent Haystacks flying out of the ring whilst Kent Walton announced they would be meeting on the FA Cup Final day World of Sport. Daddy finished off Anaconda with the double elbow drop in the first round to leave Daddy's team with a two to one lead after the first three matches.

With it being Easter Weekend grapple fans were treated to an extra edition of wrestling on *World of Sport* from Guildford on Easter Monday April 20th. This was advertised as an Easter Egg Cup knockout tournament. The contestants were Jim

Breaks, Zoltan Boscik, Steve Grey and Johnny Kidd who was making his TV debut. The semi finals saw Breaks beat Kidd with Breaks working over Kidd's arm before clamping on the 'Breaks Special' submission in the third and swiftly again in the fourth round for a two nil win. In the other match Steve Grey beat Zoltan Boscik by two falls to one in the sixth round to set up the final with Breaks. The final was to be decided over a twenty minute time limit with first fall winning and to many's surprise it was Breaks who got the winner in the fifth round. Breaks then proceeded to celebrate loudly in the ring with his Easter Egg Cup.

Finally 'Mighty Yankee' Steve DiSalvo got his chance in the world title series eliminators at The Royal Albert Hall on April 22nd. Even with his extra wrestling tuition DiSalvo was way out of his depth against Wayne Bridges and it was a rather easy night for Bridges who won by two straight falls inside three rounds. Wayne Bridges' next challenger Professor Adiwasser had already arrived in the country and was matched at the Albert Hall on this show against Pete Roberts. Adiwasser had been a frequent visitor to these shores in the 1960's but looked a lot different now. The bespectacled wrestler in the judo suit was now clad in all black ring attire complete with a mask. Even with the mask there was no doubt over his identity when he made his way to the ring. Roberts seemed certain to give the Professor a real test so it was a surprise when Roberts was the victim of Adiwasser's sleeper hold in the fourth round. With the sleeper hold being banned in Britain the contest had to be called a No Contest as Adiwasser had revived his opponent as soon as he was called to by the officials. A British style heavyweight match up between Ray Steele and Peter Stewart ended in the sixth round when Stewart was injured. The sporting Steele refused to accept the win so it ended in another No Contest on the night.

The night's knockout tournament saw Mark Rocco dismantle the lighter Clive Myers in the first semi final with a submission ending matters in the fifth round. In the other semi final Marty Jones defeated Caswell Martin by two falls to one in the sixth round of a technical style match. Of course the final would be anything but a technical wrestling match with once again Rocco and Jones throwing everything at each other. Perhaps a little surprisingly Rocco gained the one fall needed to win in the eighth minute. The show ended with Alan Kilby defeating Albert Hall debutant Tony Francis by the only fall required in the tenth minute.

The team match from Leicester continued on *World of Sport* on April 25th with Pat Patton gaining another win for the Big Daddy team when he beat Colin Bennett by two falls to one in the sixth round. Another point went to Daddy's team when the much lighter Alan Dennison defeated the Lancashire heavyweight Johnny South. Dennison much weakened from a South piledriver sent an onrushing South over the top rope and outside of the ring. South failed to beat referee Dave Reese's count and so an unlikely victory went to Dennison. With Big Daddy's team already winning by four points to one the last match had little meaning to it but Peter Stewart completed a five points to one win for Daddy and his team when he defeated opponent John Cox. A flying tackle and cross press from Stewart in the fifth round pinned Cox for a two falls to one win in the match. Apart from the wrestling the most notable thing about the show from Leicester was MC Brian Crabtree's magnificent , skin tight but with flared legs, yellow cat suit he wore in the ring. Crabtree amongst other things was indeed a fashion icon and the fans loved him for it.

May started with the sad news that Sammy Lee had to return home to Japan. It was announced that he went back due to a family bereavement but he actually went back to wrestle in his home country. Therefore his place on the big FA Cup Final *World of Sport* show was cancelled and the proposed line up would have to be changed. The first part of the Walthamstow show was screened on May 2nd with Lee's replacement Little Prince taking on Tally Ho Kaye in a match shown here instead of the following week. A clumsy six round draw between the two had mutterings of discontent from the ringside fans who were missing Sammy Lee. Professor Adiwasser had an easy win over Lancashire's Kenny Hogan with this time the sleeper hold being deemed legal when Hogan was put to sleep with it in the second round. Marty Jones defeated King Ben in the final match with a routine two falls to one win in the sixth round.

As it was Bank Holiday weekend there was an extra helping of wrestling on the holiday Monday with two matches featured in a bill from Guildford. The first bout saw Mick McManus take on Clive Myers in a match best remembered for an incredible bump from Myers. In the fourth round with Myers leading by a fall in the second round McManus sent him flying over the top rope. Myers cleared the top rope by a foot or so and actually landed in the third row of the ringside fans with the match immediately stopped by referee Max Ward. The other match saw Wild Angus face Honey Boy Zimba and in a slightly less exciting finish Angus got the winner in the fifth round forcing Zimba to submit with a backbreaker hold.

The FA Cup Final *World of Sport* show on May 9th had two matches featured across two time slots in the broadcast. First up was a European Middleweight Title defence by champion Mal Sanders against the former amateur star Keith Haward. Haward who had only been in the pro ranks for a little over one year had beaten Sanders in a televised non title match in March so demanded a chance to win the title belt. After six rounds of superb action the challenger came out on top and Sanders sportingly put the belt around the new champion's waist.

The main event at 210pm saw Big Daddy and Alan Kilby take on the fearsome pair of Giant Haystacks and his new ally Wild Angus. The children in the audience flocked around Daddy as he and Kilby made their way to the ring whilst Haystacks and Angus waited for them. Haystacks had his personal manager 'Kangaroo Kid' Ken Else with him, hopefully Else's wig would stay on his head this time. In the match Haystacks & Angus went to town on the much smaller Kilby but eventually their persistent rulebreaking taxed referee Max Ward's patience and he disqualified them after Haystacks had delivered a 'splash' to Kilby's legs. In the mayhem after the match had ended Big Daddy threw down the challenge for a no holds barred, winner takes all solo match with Giant Haystacks at Wembley Arena in June.

World of Sport was back to normal on May 16th with the usual three matches in the 4pm time slot. The opening match from Croydon saw Tom Tyrone beat Banger Walsh who was disqualified in the fifth round. Jim Breaks continued his fine run of form when he repeated his victory over Steve Grey in the Easter Egg Cup with another win. The 'Breaks Special' arm submission in the sixth round was enough to see Grey submit instantly and Breaks win by two submissions to one fall. Finally in a heavyweight match Pete Roberts conceded several stones in weight to take on Pat Roach. With the score one fall each in the fourth round Roberts attempted a crotch hold for a body slam on Roach. Roberts' back gave way and referee Joe D'Orazio was forced to stop the contest and award the win to Roach.

Wrestling was missing from *World of Sport* on May 23rd as the England v Scotland Home International football was shown instead.

One of the more bizarre wrestling shows of the 1980's happened on Sunday May 24th when Dale Martin put on a show at the Reading Waterways Festival. A three match programme took place on a barge in the middle of the River Thames. Frogmen were positioned by the barge in case of any of the wrestlers taking an unscheduled dip in the river. As if things couldn't get any more strange the police were involved when Sid Cooper was involved in a fracas as he left the barge following a loss against Billy Torontos. A 15 year old boy accused Cooper of head butting him leaving him bleeding and bruised around his left eye. Eventually the police arrested Cooper a few weeks later and he was charged with assault causing actual bodily harm. Cooper was found guilty at Reading Magistrates Court in March 1982 and was given an absolute discharge with £10 compensation to the lad and £76 costs. According to Cooper's evidence he was attempting to 'gee up' the crowd in the final match of the programme by stating he would jump in the river if he lost to Torontos. When he did lose he had no intention of doing it and as he told the magistrate if he had said he'd cut his throat if he lost nobody would expect him to do it. As Cooper was attempting to make his way back to the dressing room on a nearby double decker bus the crowd started to push and jostle him and Cooper said he simply 'bonked' the kid by accident.

There was an extra *World of Sport* shown on Bank Holiday Monday May 25th with two matches from Battersea shown on it. Neither of them really warranted staying indoors on a holiday to watch. In the first Wayne Bridges had an easy win over Bill Bromley who failed to beat the count in the third round. In the other Alan Dennison beat Jackie Turpin by two falls to one in the sixth round.

The final Royal Albert Hall show of the 1980/81 season was held on May 27th and should have featured the final world title series eliminator between Wayne Bridges and Professor Adiwasser. Before the show it was announced that Bridges had already qualified and would meet the North American representative Jim Harris who was billed as the Negro World Champion 'The Mississippi Mauler'. This took the edge off of the Bridges v Adiwasser match at the Albert Hall and it was Bridges who won by two falls to one in the seventh round with Adiwasser unmasked afterwards to reveal the familiar features of Frenchman Gaby Calderon. Jim Harris showed the Albert Hall crowd what he was about with a two round knockout win over Johnny Wilson. The Bridges v Harris title match promised great things. Gil Singh made a welcome appearance in London when he beat King Kong Kirk by disqualification in the fifth round. With Sammy Lee back in Japan his place against Mick McManus was taken by new European Middleweight Champion Keith Haward. Haward surprisingly beat McManus by two falls to one in round five. The winning fall came about when McManus was distracted by the referee. In what promised to be a wrestling classic the clash between World No.1 Johnny Saint and new European No.1 Jon Cortez instead descended into a thoroughly bad tempered affair. Rather than use his immense mat skills Cortez decided to add a little too much aggression instead. Despite receiving two public warnings he still held Saint to a one fall each draw over the six rounds time limit. The show closer saw former European Middleweight Champion Mal Sanders looking to get his career back on track against long reigning British Champion Brian Maxine but his run of misfortune continued. Sanders injured his knee in the fifth round and was unable to continue but Maxine sportingly refused the win so a No Contest verdict was the order of the referee.

Next stop would be Wembley Arena on June 18th for the annual extravaganza with Big Daddy v Giant Haystacks in the long awaited final showdown topping the bill. Two title matches announced also had fans anticipating great contests with the already mentioned Bridges v Harris heavyweight affair plus Mark Rocco's attempt to win the vacant World Heavy/Middleweight title against Sammy Lee. Some of us though were doubting that match would actually go ahead with Lee still having contractual obligations to fulfill in Japan.

Wrestling again was missing from *World of Sport* on May 30th with the Dunlop Masters Golf shown in its place.

The final wrestling shown on *World of Sport* before the Wembley Arena show was on June 6th as the schoolboy football match between England & Scotland was shown on the 13th instead. The show on the 6th from Croydon not only featured the usual three bouts but also an in ring segment between Giant Haystacks and Kent Walton to promote the Wembley match with Big Daddy. Walton was normally never shown on the TV screen, just the back of his head at the commentary desk at ringside. Haystacks towered over Walton and when asked his weight said it was now 39st but at Wembley Arena it would be 43st or even more ! The giant then straightened an iron horse shoe to show exactly what he would do to Big Daddy on that evening at Wembley. The wrestling on the show saw Gil Singh beat TV newcomer Abe Arbuckle by two falls to one in the fifth round. Professor Adiwasser brought his British trip to an end when his sleeper hold put opponent Johnny Wilson out in the fourth round. Finally King Kong Kirk took on fellow Yorkshireman Ray Steele and it was thought Steele would give Kirk plenty to think about. This wasn't the case as an impressive guillotine neck drop on Steele in the second round led to the first fall and with Steele's neck still injured Kirk gained the winner with a neck submission in the third round.

The third and what would be the final Wembley Arena extravaganza took place on June 18th, a Thursday night this time. The top of the bill was the Big Daddy v Giant Haystacks in the solo match that people had been waiting three years or more to see. On the evening of the 18th all roads led to North

West London and it was a shame that there was far from a full house in attendance. The crowd was bigger than the 1980 show but a long way from the numbers that packed the venue in 1979. The main event saw Big Daddy accompanied by the former wrestler and now a vicar Reverend Michael Brookes make his way to the ring a firm favourite. Giant Haystacks appeared from the dressing room looking bigger than ever and his seconds were usual tag partner Banger Walsh and Anaconda. Haystacks started the contest very strongly and for a moment I thought a shock result was in order. Referee Freddie Green took a bump and in the melee afterwards Haystacks missed a splash which allowed Daddy to take control. After a couple of hefty belly butts Haystacks was reeling against the ropes. Big Daddy seized his opportunity and bundled him over the top rope. Haystacks landed on a ringside table and there was no chance that he would beat replacement referee Dave Reese's count and to the fans delight Daddy was victorious. It was actually a better match than I thought it would be, at least Haystacks got in some offensive. The excitement of the fans made it as good as the Quinn match two years earlier.

Wayne Bridges's year long pursuit to reclaim the World Heavyweight Title finally ended after a titanic nine round contest with Jim Harris. The Londoner stood victorious after being presented with the belt by sixties heavyweight star and Father of Mark Rocco Jim Hussey. It was a brutal, hard hitting match, way different to the usual British heavyweight matches seen and it totally engrossed the crowd. Bridges opened the scoring with a flying tackle leading to a cross press in the fifth round. Harris retaliated with various nefarious tactics which were quite legal in the American rings but not here. The equaliser came when Bridges misjudged a flying tackle which Harris turned into a knee drop and easily pinned him in the 7th round. With the score one fall each the contest entered the ninth round of the scheduled twelve. In it Bridges reversed a back breaker attempt and pinned Harris with a folding press to once again become the World Champion. After the match Harris announced his intention to stay in this country and try and get another title shot.

The other vacant title match ended in disappointment for Mark Rocco as firstly the original opponent Sammy Lee was still in Japan. The promoters attempt to fly in Spaniard Francisco Ramirez to fight Rocco ended in failure. It was said an air traffic controllers strike scuppered the chances of the Spaniard arriving but at that time no industrial action was being taken. Rocco was left to take his frustration out on late replacement Mal Sanders who hot footed it over to Wembley after an earlier appearance that evening at Battersea. To everyones surprise Rocco decided to wrestle the whole match within the rules and beat Sanders by two falls to one in five rounds. A lot of fans felt short changed with the replacement and the loss of the title match, surely a better solution could have been found ? In the other bouts The Royals in their last year as a team with Bert shortly to retire had their major show swansong when they defeated the pairing of Bobby Barnes and Sid Cooper by the best of three falls in an entertaining fifteen minutes. Unfortunately the rest of the card featured three matches that seemed out of place on a big show. Gil Singh beat Pete Roberts by two falls to one in the fifth round. Terry Rudge wrestled a bad tempered draw with Alan Kilby over six rounds. Peter Stewart retired injured in his match with Ray Steele but the Yorkshireman refused to accept the verdict so a No Contest was called.

Big Daddy finished the month in front of several thousand fans at the annual open air spectacular at the St.Helens Rugby League ground on Merseyside on June 27th. Daddy teamed up with judo ace Pat Patton against old foe Giant Haystacks and King Kong Kirk. Daddy and Patton emerged victorious when once again Haystacks and Kirk had enough of the action and simply walked away from the ring in less than 9 minutes to the fans anger and disappointment. Sammy Lee was still missing and his place against Blackjack Mulligan was taken by Bernie Wright who won easily by two falls to one in the fifth round. Alan Kilby beat a newcomer from Manchester in Studs Lannigan again by two falls to one in the fifth round. Bert Royal was in singles action when he took on heavyweight Johnny South and beat him by two falls to one in the sixth round. Finally Jim Breaks was disqualified in the sixth round in his match against Kid Chocolate when he refused to release his 'Breaks Special' after Chocolate had submitted.

The Wembley Arena show was featured on *World of Sport* on June 20th with the Big Daddy v Giant Haystacks match and on the following week on June 27th the Wayne Bridges v Jim Harris contest was amongst the attractions.

The wrestling on *World of Sport* on July 4th was cut back to two matches with the European Cup Athletics taking away the usual 4pm start. In the first of them Marty Jones defeated the heavier Butcher Bond by two falls to one in the sixth round. The second match saw World Lightweight Champion Johnny Saint faced the veteran Ken Joyce. Saint won in what was an exhibition of mat wrestling by two falls to nil in the fourth round.

July saw more international arrivals, two more American Heavyweights landed in the UK to join Jim Harris. 'Cowboy' Rick Hunter and 'Bulldog' Bob Brown, both well known to British fans who kept an eye on the North American scene. Unfortunately Brown was only booked for a week or so to take part in some England v USA challenge tournaments but Hunter would stay for a few months. The controversial Japanese star Yasu Fuji returned to these shores but this time was signed to wrestle on the independent shows.

The second half of the show recorded at Shrewsbury was shown on *World of Sport* on July 11th which featured Jim Harris and his attempt to secure a title rematch against Wayne Bridges. Harris faced Honey Boy Zimba and destroyed the Sierra Leone native in less than three rounds. Zimba was unable to continue after Harris' version of a big splash which was delivered after momentum from a rope run. A similar beating happened to Tom Tyrone in his match with King Kong Kirk, for once Kirk wrestled within the rules but was still able to win. The Kent youngster Tyrone was unable to beat the count in the fourth round. The opening match saw an inconclusive ending with both Jackie Turpin and Pat Patton failing to beat the count after a hip toss from Turpin saw both wrestlers fall through the ropes.

Sammy Lee eventually returned to the UK halfway through the month but only stayed for a couple of weeks before leaving for Japan again and this time he didn't return. Lee was still being billed on the show's posters right the way into September with their no chance of him appearing. The right to change the bill was in small print on every poster but it still felt misleading.

Sammy Lee's final appearance on *World of Sport* would be on July 18th in a show taped at Morecambe. Intriguingly his opponent would be Jim Breaks with a packed crowd at the seaside venue firmly behind Lee. Lee got the first fall in the second round with a folding press but Breaks equalised in the third. Referee Ken Lazenby was distracted trying to give Lee a public warning and Breaks took advantage. He pulled Lee's hair to drag him to the mat where a cross press gave him the fall. Lee won the match in the fourth round with another folding press enough for the victory but Breaks had given him one of his hardest fights in Britain. The show's first match saw John Naylor defeat Bernie Wright in a fine wrestling match by two falls to one in the fifth round. The final match was an international heavyweight match with American Rick Hunter in his World of Sport debut against King Kong Kirk. Hunter had his limitations exposed in the match and it was only when Kirk got himself disqualified that Hunter was able to win. It was a very underwhelming TV debut for Rick Hunter and it didn't endear himself to the fans who preferred to boo and jeer the American visitors not feel sorry for them.

Mark Rocco was back on *World of Sport* on July 25th taking on King Ben in the second half of the Morecambe show. The powerful Ben was a match for anyone and he stunned Rocco with a flying head butt followed by a body slam and cross press to open the scoring in the second round. In a match fought at a frantic pace Rocco equalised with a back breaker submission in the fourth round. A Boston Crab saw Ben submit in the fifth round to give Rocco the win. During the match Kent Walton announced that the long running saga with the vacant World Heavy/Middleweight Title would be resolved on *World of Sport* on August 29th. It would be Plan C with this time Mark Rocco would be facing the Frenchman Joel De Fremery for the championship and belt. Other bouts seen that week saw Pat Roach finish off Romany Riley with the 'Brumagen Bump' leaving Riley unable to continue. Whilst six rounds of superb wrestling between Clive Myers and Keith Haward ended in a draw with each wrestler scoring one fall.

August started on *World of Sport* on the 1st with a bill recorded at Wembley with Jim Harris in action. Harris' opponent Ray Steele was unable to continue for the sixth round. After attempting a crotch hold and body slam Steele's back gave way. It was an unfortunate ending with Steele leading and giving Harris plenty to think about. Luton's youngster Johnny Kidd made his second appearance on World of Sport with another tough assignment after his debut against Jim Breaks. This time Kidd stood in as a late replacement to tackle World Lightweight Champion Johnny Saint and it was no disgrace that Kidd lost by two straight falls in the fourth round. The show opener saw Alan Dennison defeat Johnny England in a battle of the strong men.

The other half of the Wembley show was screened on August 8th with Wayne Bridges facing American visitor Rick Hunter in a non title match. In an uneventful match Bridges won by two falls to one in the eight rounds and there would be no clamour for Bridges to defend the World Heavyweight Title against Hunter. A clash of lightweight champions saw British champion Steve Grey take on the European champion Jon Cortez. In an absolute classic neither wrestler had scored a fall in the first five rounds so any score in the last round would win the match. The match ended in a win for Cortez in unfortunate circumstances when Grey got his leg caught between the bottom two ropes and was unable to continue. The opening match that week saw Johnny Wilson gain a quick win over Lee Sharron in the second round although it was a painful one with Sharron disqualified after a low blow.

Wrestling on *World of Sport* on August 15th was shortened to only thirty minutes due to athletics from Zagreb being shown as well after 4pm. The show from Newton Aycliffe's main match saw a new masked face for TV viewers in Kamakaze who wore multi coloured ring attire as well as a mask. Kamakaze and his partner Ron Marino were replacements for Sammy Lee. Lee who once again had departed back home to Japan was billed in a handicap '2 v 1' match against both of The Rockers. Kamakaze had an impressive array of moves but the victory for him and Marino came with The Rockers being disqualified after fifteen minutes. There was also time for an unadvertised match which saw Rick Hunter beat John Elijah by two falls to one in the sixth round.

The French challenger for the World Heavy/Middleweight Title Joel De Fremery arrived mid August for a couple of weeks acclimatisation. The first thoughts that whilst he was a superb technical wrestler he had neither the power or speed to upset Mark Rocco's title aspirations.

Three more bouts were shown on *World of Sport* on August 22nd from Newton Aycliffe. The main match saw another win for Jim Harris this time against John Cox who he knocked out in the second round. London based middleweights Mal Sanders and Jan Curtis had a long journey to the North East for their match. Former European champion Sanders beat TV debutant Curtis by two falls to one in the fifth round. Finally Alan Kilby continued to impress when he beat the much heavier Johnny South who failed to beat the count in the sixth round.

Monday August 24th saw the wrestling world reeling from the news of the death of one of the all time greats Mike Marino. Marino was travelling to Folkestone for that venue's bill with Mal Sanders when he felt unwell. He was taken to hospital in Ashford and on the way home Sanders collected him after he self discharged. On the way up to London he had a convulsive attack and died by the roadside. It was later found that Marino was suffering from leukaemia. Mike Marino was liked by everyone, his colleagues in the ring, the officials and all the fans who he always had time for to give them an autograph or a friendly chat.

Mark Rocco eventually became the World Heavy/Middleweight Champion on the August 29th *World of Sport* broadcast. In a show from Southport Rocco overcame the French challenger Joel De Fremery to claim the vacant title. As many of us thought De Fremery didn't have the power or the speed to halt Rocco's relentless attacks. The finish came in the eighth round after a great suplex was followed by a pile driver which left De Fremery with absolutely no hope of beating the count. The celebrating Rocco was joined in the ring by his father Jim Hussey as MC Gordon Pryor proclaimed him to be the new World Heavy/Middleweight Champion. On the same bill Mick McManus beat the youngster Johnny Kidd who yet again had another tough TV assignment. McManus was in the last few months of his illustrious career and liked to go on first or second on the bill so he could be on the way home as soon as possible. In the latter days Mick McManus wouldn't wrestle at weekends as he preferred to go out dancing on a Saturday night with his wife and he wasn't averse to not showing up if it didn't suit him to go somewhere. On the way back home from Southport McManus told his travelling companion as well as opponent that night Johnny Kidd he was booked at Bournemouth the following night against Brian Maxine but wouldn't be going. Sure enough the results show he was missing on the South Coast that nightThe other match shown that week saw Marty Jones defeat Len Hurst by two falls to one in the sixth round.

Wrestling was missing from *World of Sport* on September 5th with the European Open Golf Championship from Hoylake in its place.

Wrestling was back on September 12th with the second half of the Southport show screened. The main event was a heavyweight tag match with the 'Terrible Two' as that week's TV Times called them of King Kong Kirk and Bruiser Muir against Ray Steele and Scarborough's Tommy Hanson who was making a rare appearance not only on TV but away from his local area. The much heavier Kirk and Muir took the win with a submission in the sixteenth minute sealing a two to one win. In a battle of heavyweight contenders Pat Roach beat India's Gil Singh when Singh couldn't continue in the sixth through injury. The show opened that week with a win for Mick McMichael over Tally Ho Kaye who was disqualified in the fifth round.

September saw the start of the new Winter season and some new faces and a return of an old favourite. First to enter the fray was Dave 'Fit' Finlay , the young Ulsterman who had impressed on the independent circuit for the last couple of years or so and was quickly impressing the fans who saw him for the first time. Another youngster who switched to Joint Promotions from the independent circuit was Birmingham's Steve Logan. He was no relation to the Brixton iron man of the same name though. Chris Adams returned to the country after a successful last few months in the USA and was wrestling better than ever on his return. Another wrestler making a return was the former Maurice La Rue from Australia who had been away for several years. He was now known as 'Wild' Red Berry and had a lot more colourful look about him. Like the previous September there also various departures to the independent promoters, surprisingly one of them at the end of the month was the American Rick Hunter who was only a couple of months into a tour here for Joint Promotions. To be fair he was not that popular with the fans and his dour, clean wrestling style didn't go down too well. Two newly crowned champions also switched sides, Jon Cortez and Keith Haward who both took their European Title belts they had won earlier in the year with them too.

There was no wrestling shown on *World of Sport* for the next three weeks with a combination of snooker, golf and finally darts being show in the 4pm slot instead.

The first Royal Albert Hall show of the season took place on September 16th with a lot of the new faces on show. Steve Logan got a win on his Albert Hall debut although it was via disqualification when his opponent Bobby Barnes was sent back to the dressing room in the 6th round. Alan Kilby wrestled a one fall each draw with Rick Hunter who was seeing out his final few contracted dates. In the top of the bill match Big Daddy and Jackie Turpin defeated the colourful new team of 'Mississippi Mauler' Jim Harris and 'Wild' Red Berry. It was a relatively easy win for Daddy and Turpin with a big splash on Harris in just under ten minutes that sealed the victory. Chris Adams freshly returned from the USA immediately set his sights on new world champion Mark Rocco with a non title match on the bill. In the match of the night both wrestlers gave a non stop performance before a fall from the ring in the fourth round left Adams unable to continue. Another Albert Hall debutant was Hampshire lightweight Mickey Sullivan who took on British Lightweight Champion Steve Grey. Sullivan acquitted himself well despite losing by two falls to one in the sixth round. Finally the show closer saw another Albert Hall debut, this time from Fit Finlay who gave opponent Len Hurst all the trouble he wanted. It was music for Hurst's ears when Finlay's over enthusiasm and disregard for the rule book led to the Ulsterman being disqualified in the sixth round.

September ended with more tragedy when Billy Torontos died in the dressing room at Peterborough straight after a match with Blondie Barratt. Torontos had been rushed to hospital after suffering a heart attack but the doctors were unable to save him.

Mark Rocco had vacated the British Heavy/Middleweight Title after becoming world champion so the promoters decided to hold a tournament to find a new champion. The four wrestlers invited were Alan Kilby, Bobby Barnes, King Ben and Steve Casey. Casey was a surprising name as he had never appeared on TV before and rarely wrestled outside of his local Lincolnshire/East Midlands area. The two semi finals were shown on *World of Sport* on October 10th in a show from Nottingham. In the first King Ben had an easy win over Steve Casey with the Lincolnshire lad failing to beat the count in the fifth round. The other semi final was much more of an even affair with pre tournament favourite Alan Kilby facing a tough battle against the far more experienced Bobby Barnes. In a tremendous tussle Kilby got the first fall in the third round before an equaliser for Barnes in the fifth set things up nicely for the final round. Alan Kilby got the deciding fall to set up a meeting with King Ben for the vacant title which would be seen on TV in a few weeks time. Unbelievably Sammy Lee was still being advertised by the promoters with him long gone from here and there being no chance of him wrestling on the bill. Therefore Lee's place in the top of the bill tag match with Big Daddy was taken by Steve Grey. They took on the team of Red Berry and Banger Walsh. The match lasted a little over ten minutes with firstly Walsh finished off by Daddy's double elbow drop and then Grey pinned Berry with a flying tackle followed by a cross press.

The second show of the season at The Royal Albert Hall on October 14th was meant to contain the first defence by Mark Rocco of the World Heavy/Middleweight Title. His opponent was to be Bert Royal which was an uninspiring choice anyway and with Royal injured the world title match was cancelled. The advertised bill was then switched around and Rocco ended up meeting old rival Marty Jones in a non title match. With Rocco at the top of his form since winning the world title it was a surprise when Jones won the match and an even bigger surprise that it was by two straight falls inside five rounds. Although it was a disappointment that the title match was cancelled this contest more than made up for it. It was a bloodied Jones who straight after the final bell demanded a title match. The other main event was a heavyweight tag match with Giant Haystacks teaming up with the masked King Kendo, the cheap rip off copy of the original Kendo Nagasaki. Their opponents were Wayne Bridges and Pete Roberts who won the match with Haystacks disqualified for attacking Roberts. This left Bridges to get a winner against Kendo in less than seven minutes. With Marty Jones' original opponent Honey Boy Zimba also missing on the night a replacement match saw Albert Hall debuts for Johnny Kidd and Steve Casey. It was Kidd who came out on top with a winning fall in the seventh round. The show opener saw Tom Tyrone beat Johnny South to record his first Albert Hall win with a two falls to one success in the sixth round. Butcher Bond wrestled a one fall each draw with Lee Bronson whilst the final match saw former amateur star Jan Curtis beat Sid Cooper by disqualification in the third round.

It was back to February on October 24th with the *World of Sport* wrestling coming from Derby on a show filmed eight months previously. Obviously it was out of sync with current happenings with Peter Stewart beating Tom Tyrone in the opener by two falls to one in the sixth round. Stewart had retired from the ring by the time this was shown. Another wrestler long gone from Joint Promotions when this was shown was 'Mighty Yankee' Steve Di Salvo whose match finished in the second round with a referee bump utilised to hide Di Salvo's limitations at the time. The final match and yet another heavyweight contest saw Pat Roach defeat Caswell Martin by two falls to one in the sixth round of an unexciting, slow paced affair.

The final of the tournament for the vacant British Heavy/Middleweight Title was decided in a match shown on *World of Sport* on October 31st. In a bill filmed at Preston Alan Kilby won his first title when he overcame the challenge of

King Ben in the ninth round. Jim Breaks took advantage of an accidental injury to his opponent Kamikaze in the fifth round to record a victory. Finally that week Jim Harris had an easy win over Tom Tyrone when he knocked out the youngster in the second round.

The old adage that bad things happens in threes came true when it was announced at the end of October that one of the all time greats and five times winner of the Royal Albert Hall Trophy Tibor Szakacs had died after a long fight against cancer.

The start of November saw Dynamite Kid return home for his usual pre Christmas visit and this time he brought with him a young Canadian Bret Hart who was the younger brother of both Bruce who had wrestled here in 1977 and Smith who was here in 1980.

Chris Adams got another chance against Mark Rocco in a non title match shown on *World of Sport* from Croydon on November 7th. Adams came up short once again with the match halted in the fifth round with Rocco's piledriver giving Adams no chance of beating the count. With Rick Hunter gone from Joint Promotions, Johnny Wilson replaced him against Giant Haystacks. He must have wished he hadn't bothered as he was flattened by Haystacks in a couple of rounds. A lively show opener that week from Croydon saw TV debutant Steve Logan take on Jackie Turpin with the former boxer winning by two falls to one in the seventh round.

The next weekend's wrestling on *World of Sport* on November 14th saw an eight man knockout tournament for the 'Mike Marino Memorial Shield' which was held at Marino's local Croydon venue. The eight wrestlers nominated to contest the tournament were :- Mal Sanders, Sid Cooper, John Naylor, Jan Curtis, Kid Chocolate, Blackjack Mulligan, Johnny England and Pat Patton. The whole tournament was fitted into that week's show which meant seven matches so there was a five minute time limit for all matches bar the final. The heats saw Pat Patton beat Johnny England via referee's decision after neither wrestler scored a fall. Mal Sanders beat John Naylor again by referee's decision. Sid Cooper beat Jan Curtis by submission and Kid Chocolate pinned Blackjack Mulligan. The semi finals saw Sanders pin Patton and Cooper beat Chocolate by a stoppage to line up a Mal Sanders v Sid Cooper final. Fought over a more traditional eight rounds and the best of two falls etc. Mal Sanders fittingly lifted the trophy when he pinned Sid Cooper in the sixth round for the winning fall.

The November Royal Albert Hall show was held on the 18th with Big Daddy topping the bill in tag action with Jim Harris in the opposing corner for the second time in three shows at the venue. This time Daddy partnered Alan Kilby with Harris going for the heavy artillery with King Kong Kirk teaming with him this time. Another predictable result when Daddy and Kilby gaining the win when Harris and Kirk were counted out in just under eleven minutes of the match. The main supporting contest saw crowd favourite Wayne Bridges take on King Kendo who had failed to impress at the Albert Hall in the previous month's tag match. In another uncompetive match Kendo walked away from the ring in the fifth round to hand the victory by count out to Bridges. Mal Sanders fresh from winning the 'Mike Marino Memorial Trophy' was advertised to take on King Ben but with Ben injured Sid Cooper stepped in instead. In something of an upset Cooper beat Sanders with the winning submission in the sixth round for what was unbelievably his first ever win at the Albert Hall. Ringo Rigby had a routine win by two falls to one over Lucky Gordon in the sixth round. Alan Dennison's match with youngster Steve Logan ended in a No Contest when Logan was unable to continue in the seventh round. Finally regular late substitute Jan Curtis took the place of Kamakaze to face Blackjack Mulligan and won by two falls to one in the fifth round.

A heavyweight tag team tournament was the feature of the wrestling on *World of Sport* on November 21st on a bill from Leamington Spa. The four teams were Big Daddy and Alan Kilby, Jim Harris and Red Berry, King Kong Kirk and Bull Pratt (Pratt replaced Kirk's advertised partner Bruiser Muir) and Len Hurst and Honey Boy Zimba. The semi final's saw Daddy and Kilby beat Kirk and Pratt by disqualification in the tenth minute whilst Harris and Berry beat Zimba and Hurst by two falls to one in the tenth minute. In the final Daddy and Kilby beat Harris and Berry inside of six minutes to win the tournament. A preliminary match saw Brian Maxine wrestle a one fall each draw with John Elijah over eight rounds.

Wrestling was missing on November 28th with the Gymnastics World Championships taking its place. It was the same the following week on December 5th with this time darts on instead.

There was a sad occasion on December 5th with the final ever show held at the famous old Kings Hall at Belle Vue in Manchester. This was the North's premier venue and much drama had happened here over the years. Belle Vue had long since seen its heyday and now the Kings Hall was to be demolished. Promoters Best Wryton put on a star studded bill to mark the occasion but perhaps the biggest surprise on the night was the appearance of John Quinn alongside one of Belle Vue's most hated villains of the past Jack Pye. Naturally Big Daddy topped the bill when he partnered Alan Kilby to beat King Kong Kirk and Tony Francis. Dynamite Kid and Mark Rocco fought each to a standstill before both failed to beat the count in the 5th round. Marty Jones beat Bret Hart and Johnny Saint beat Jackie Turpin amongst other highlights on the night.

The last Royal Albert Hall show of 1981 took place on December 9th with Marty Jones successfully making the World Heavy/Middleweight Title weight limit for his clash with the champion Mark Rocco. After Jones' two straight falls win at the October show the fans were confident of a new champion and Jones took the lead with the first fall in the 5th round. Rocco wasn't going to surrender his title lightly though and after Jones missed a dropkick in the 9th round Rocco got an equalising submission. From then on Rocco piled on the pressure and quickly gained a winning submission in the next round to retain his title. Dynamite Kid was also on the bill but his match with Caswell Martin was somewhat of a let down and the fans became a little restless at the lack of action at times in an eight round draw. Bret Hart faced his toughest test in the UK when he squared up to Pat Roach and found it all too much when he was knocked out in the fourth round by Roach's finisher 'The Brumagen Bump'. Surprisingly Steve Grey beat World Lightweight Champion Johnny Saint by two falls to nil and of course Grey then wanted a match for the title. Mick

McManus and Jackie Turpin were both disqualified when their match turned into fisticuffs galore and the former boxer Turpin even donned the boxing gloves to teach the veteran rule breaker a lesson. Alan Kilby sent the fans home happy beating Johnny South by two falls to one in the fourth round in the show closer.

A surprising turn events happened on *World of Sports'* wrestling coverage on December 12th, this was the second half of the bill taped at Leamington Spa. The three matches saw Marty Jones beat late replacement Peter Wilson by two falls to one. Ringo Rigby beat Lucky Gordon by two falls to one in the fifth round in a lively show opener. The most interesting contest billed that week was between crowd favourite Wayne Bridges and his sometime tag partner Pete Roberts. Bridges got an opening fall in the second round before a swift equaliser for Roberts in the third round. Things then got interesting and as commentator Kent Walton observed some 'needle' started creeping in. It came to a head in the fifth round with Roberts on the floor and as he attempted to rise to his feet Bridges continually kneed him. In the end the referee disqualified Bridges to much surprise. Wayne Bridges was never a clean cut, good guy in the ring all the time and he seemed to lose his cool with wrestlers like Mike Marino and Pete Roberts. Even on the rare occasions before this Bridges did make a superb 'villain' and he was about to prove this in the months going forward.

The final wrestling of 1981 on *World of Sport* happened on December 19th with a bill taped at Oldham. Regular opponents judo expert Pat Patton and loud mouth Johnny England wrestled a six round one fall each draw in the opener. An international heavyweight match saw India's Gil Singh tackle Canada's Bret Hart with the much more experienced Singh winning by two falls to one in the sixth round. The last contest saw a non title match between Mark Rocco and Dynamite Kid which only lasted four rounds but as with their other matches was a feast of action rarely seen on TV. Dynamite's flying headbutt from the top rope not only subdued Rocco for the winning fall in the the fourth round but astounded those watching it.

Dynamite Kid got a chance at Mark Rocco's title at Hanley on the same day as the World of Sport match was shown December 19th. This match had a twist as the loser would have his head shaved. It was Dynamite who had a free haircut when he was knocked out in the fourth round. Also on the same bill Chris Adams returned home to the UK for Christmas and fitted in a few matches at the same time. This time he beat Lucky Gordon by two falls to one. After a couple of bouts at the start of the following week Dynamite Kid and Bret Hart headed back home to Canada in time for Christmas.

Wrestling Enterprises also finished off 1981 strongly thanks to their burgeoning array of international heavyweight talent. The likes of John Quinn, Tony St Clair, Rick Hunter and Yasu Fuji together with established stars like Count Bartelli, Crusher Mason, Steve Young, Steve Veidor and Dave Taylor as well as youngsters like Spaniard Enrique Marquess had a series of hard hitting and entertaining matches that packed the crowds in. The other change for Wrestling Enterprises was that they had started to use more of old Joint Promotions strongholds like Leeds Town Hall, Northgate Arena in Chester and the Preston Guildhall as well as using halls that Dale Martin had exclusive use of for years.

Perhaps this was the last golden era of British wrestling as there would never be such an array of global talent to be seen or would there be as many shows on offer at the various halls in the months and years ahead.

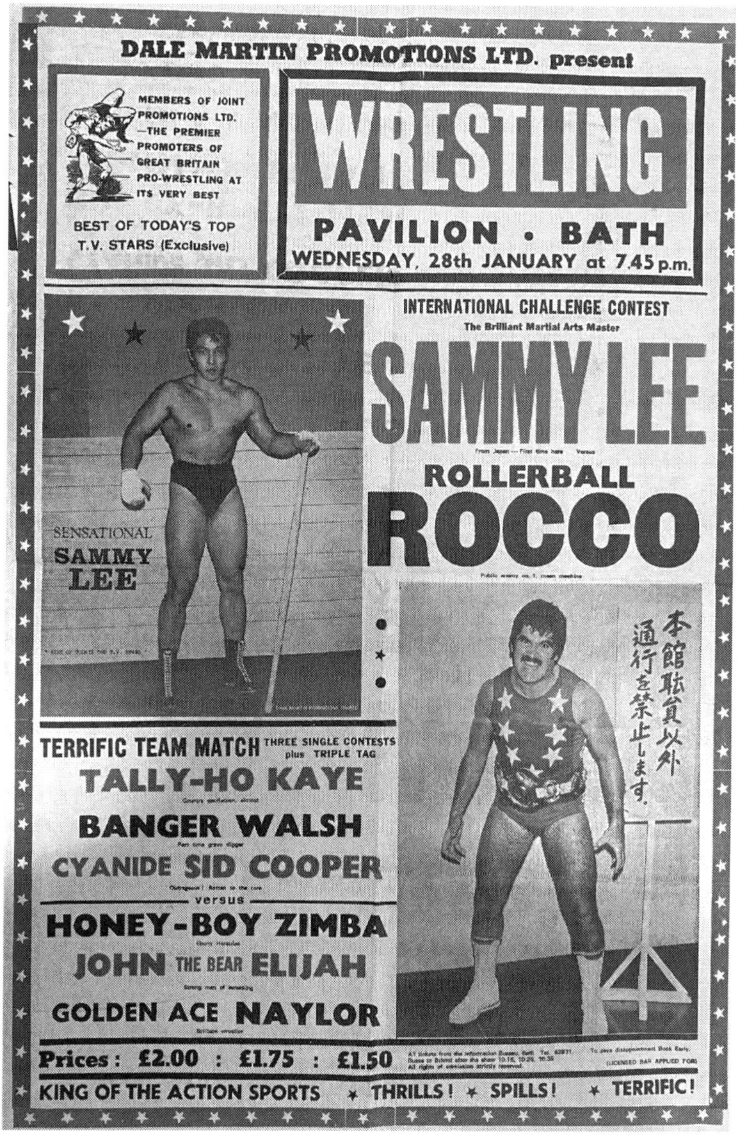
DALE MARTIN PROMOTIONS LTD. present
MEMBERS OF JOINT PROMOTIONS LTD. —THE PREMIER PROMOTERS OF GREAT BRITAIN PRO-WRESTLING AT ITS VERY BEST
BEST OF TODAY'S TOP T.V. STARS (Exclusive)
WRESTLING
PAVILION • BATH
WEDNESDAY, 28th JANUARY at 7.45 p.m.
INTERNATIONAL CHALLENGE CONTEST
The Brilliant Martial Arts Master
SAMMY LEE
ROLLERBALL
ROCCO
SENSATIONAL
SAMMY
LEE
本館職員以外
通行を禁止します。
TERRIFIC TEAM MATCH THREE SINGLE CONTESTS plus TRIPLE TAG
TALLY-HO KAYE
BANGER WALSH
CYANIDE SID COOPER
versus
HONEY-BOY ZIMBA
JOHN THE BEAR ELIJAH
GOLDEN ACE NAYLOR
Prices: £2.00 : £1.75 : £1.50
KING OF THE ACTION SPORTS ★ THRILLS! ★ SPILLS! ★ TERRIFIC!

WRESTLING ENTERPRISES OF BIRKENHEAD, MERSEYSIDE PROUDLY PRESENT

GUILDHALL, SOUTHAMPTON
★ WRESTLING ★

DOORS OPEN 7 p.m | **THURSDAY, 19th MARCH** | **COMMENCING** 7.45 p.m.

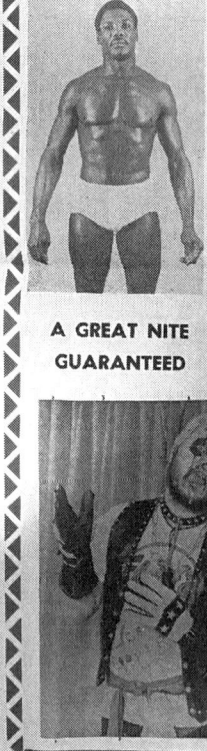

TAG THRILLER

ROLO & KATU BRAZIL
South American tag champions

JIM MOSER
Martial arts expert
&
JAMAICA KID
Fast and clever

A GREAT NITE GUARANTEED

AMERICAN DREAM MACHINE
versus
NEIL SANDS
Golden boy of the ring

Mike BENNETT
Action guaranteed
versus
Ace Riccardo
All out for victory

DAVE TAYLOR v. LEN HURST

FANTASTIC BOUT
KENDO NAGASAKIE
The masked mystery star
versus
COUNT BARTELLIE
Stylish wrestler

Seats £1.75 £1.50
The Promoters reserve the right to change the bill without prior notice

BOOKING AT BOX OFFICE:
GUILDHALL, Southampton
or at door on evening

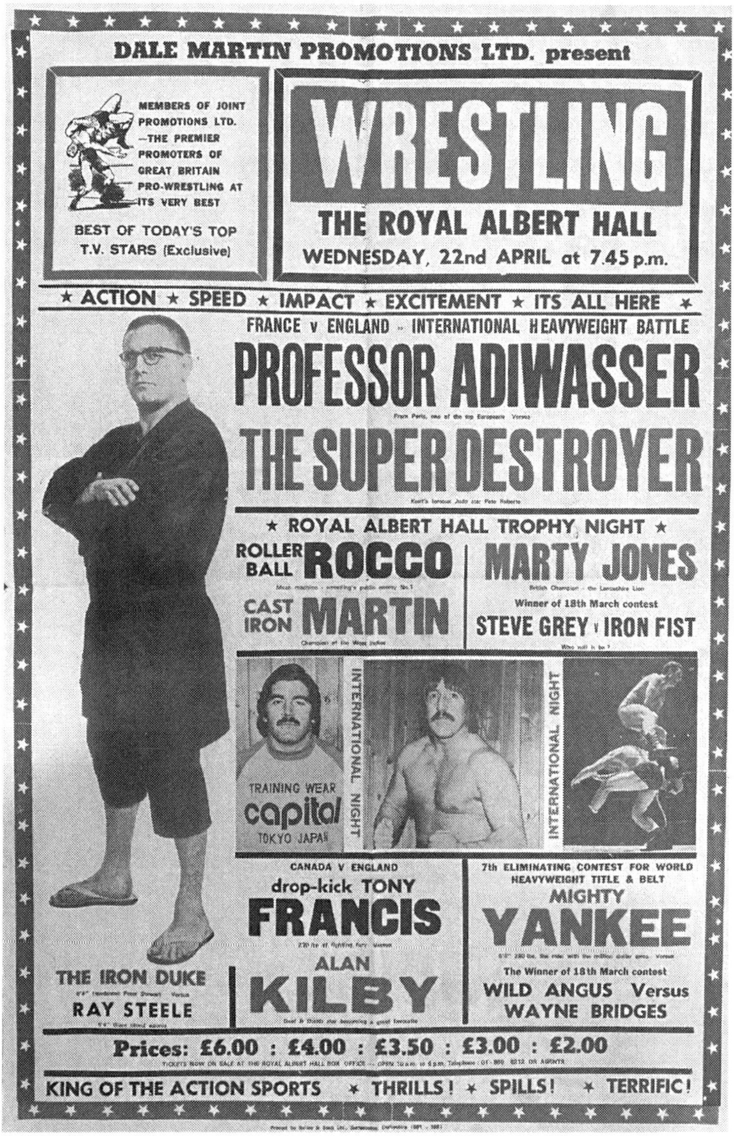
DALE MARTIN PROMOTIONS LTD. present
MEMBERS OF JOINT PROMOTIONS LTD. —THE PREMIER PROMOTERS OF GREAT BRITAIN PRO-WRESTLING AT ITS VERY BEST
BEST OF TODAY'S TOP T.V. STARS (Exclusive)
WRESTLING
THE ROYAL ALBERT HALL
WEDNESDAY, 22nd APRIL at 7.45 p.m.
★ ACTION ★ SPEED ★ IMPACT ★ EXCITEMENT ★ ITS ALL HERE ★
FRANCE v ENGLAND - INTERNATIONAL HEAVYWEIGHT BATTLE
PROFESSOR ADIWASSER
THE SUPER DESTROYER
★ ROYAL ALBERT HALL TROPHY NIGHT ★
ROLLER BALL ROCCO
CAST IRON MARTIN
MARTY JONES
Winner of 18th March contest
STEVE GREY v IRON FIST
INTERNATIONAL NIGHT
TRAINING WEAR
capital
TOKYO JAPAN
INTERNATIONAL NIGHT
CANADA V ENGLAND
drop-kick TONY
FRANCIS
ALAN
KILBY
7th ELIMINATING CONTEST FOR WORLD HEAVYWEIGHT TITLE & BELT
MIGHTY
YANKEE
The Winner of 18th March contest
WILD ANGUS Versus
WAYNE BRIDGES
THE IRON DUKE
RAY STEELE
Prices: £6.00 : £4.00 : £3.50 : £3.00 : £2.00
KING OF THE ACTION SPORTS ★ THRILLS! ★ SPILLS! ★ TERRIFIC!

DALE MARTIN PROMOTIONS LTD. present
MEMBERS OF JOINT PROMOTIONS LTD. ...THE PREMIER PROMOTERS OF GREAT BRITAIN PRO-WRESTLING AT ITS VERY BEST
BEST OF TODAY'S TOP T.V. STARS (Exclusive)
WRESTLING
COLSTON HALL • BRISTOL
THURSDAY, 9th JULY at 7.45 p.m.
DON'T MISS THE "BIG TIME" WRESTLING ATMOSPHERE AND ACTION !
U.S.A versus GREAT BRITAIN TEAM CHALLENGE
MISSISSIPPI MAULER
WAYNE BRIDGES
The new Heavyweight Champion of the World
BULLDOG BROWN
Heavyweight star just arrived from U.S.A.
LEE BRONSON
COWBOY RICK HUNTER
SUPER DESTROYER
COWBOY
RICK HUNTER
BULLDOG BROWN
KANSAS CITY U.S.A
JAN CURTIS v SUPERSTAR SANDERS
JOHNNY KWANGO v WILDMAN WILKIE
Prices : £2.00 : £1.75 : £1.40 : £1.00
KING OF THE ACTION SPORTS ★ THRILLS ! ★ SPILLS ! ★ TERRIFIC !

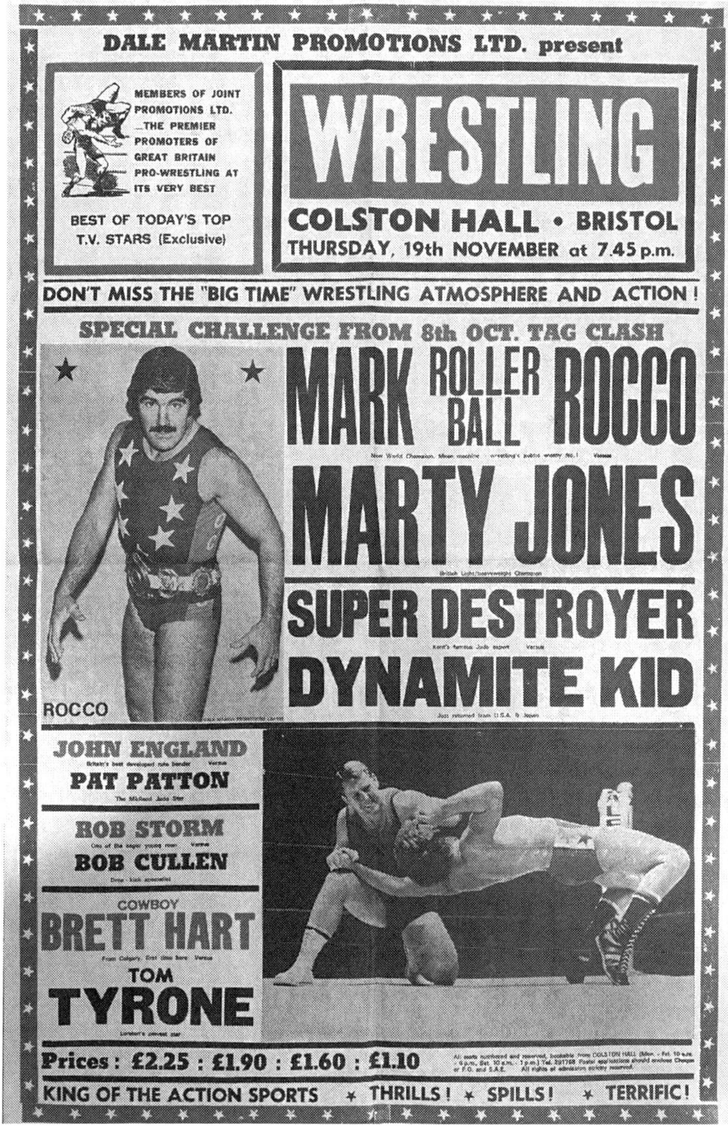
DALE MARTIN PROMOTIONS LTD. present
MEMBERS OF JOINT PROMOTIONS LTD. ...THE PREMIER PROMOTERS OF GREAT BRITAIN PRO-WRESTLING AT ITS VERY BEST
BEST OF TODAY'S TOP T.V. STARS (Exclusive)
WRESTLING
COLSTON HALL • BRISTOL
THURSDAY, 19th NOVEMBER at 7.45 p.m.
DON'T MISS THE "BIG TIME" WRESTLING ATMOSPHERE AND ACTION!
SPECIAL CHALLENGE FROM 8th OCT. TAG CLASH
MARK ROLLER BALL ROCCO
MARTY JONES
SUPER DESTROYER
DYNAMITE KID
ROCCO
JOHN ENGLAND
PAT PATTON
ROB STORM
BOB CULLEN
COWBOY
BRETT HART
TOM
TYRONE
Prices: £2.25 : £1.90 : £1.60 : £1.10
KING OF THE ACTION SPORTS ★ THRILLS! ★ SPILLS! ★ TERRIFIC!

CHAPTER 3 - 1982

The start of the New Year saw Kung Fu return to Joint Promotions after an absence of over three years wrestling on the independent shows. Kung Fu was a particular favourite of mine ever since I saw him on World of Sport with the mask on and then even more when I saw him live. I even went as far as to join his fan club. The fan clubs were a strange concept where someone, even Brian Dixon ran one in his fan days, would run a fan club for their particular favourite wrestler. For whatever it cost, you'd get a photo, a badge, a monthly newsletter with dates of forthcoming appearances as well as results and the odd programme or handbill thrown in. Out of all them Kendo Nagasaki's was the best as Gorgeous George himself wrote the newsletters and they were a very interesting read. The loss of Kung Fu from the independent scene was tempered by some departures from Joint Promotions. After a long injury absence Brian Maxine left although without the title belt that was stolen and he wasn't that much of a loss to Max Crabtree's roster. Mid card heavyweights like Romany Riley and Lee Bronson also crossed over but as the number of nightly bills started to decrease the number of wrestlers needed on Joint Promotions' books was starting to lessen.

Wrestling returned to *World of Sport* on January 2nd after the Christmas break with the second half of the Oldham show shown. The highlight was a heavyweight knockout tournament with the participants being Giant Haystacks, Pat Roach, Wild Angus and Ray Steele. First match up though saw Johnny Saint wrestle a six round draw with Vic Faulkner in an excellent match. The first tournament semi final saw Giant Haystacks tackling Ray Steele who was about half his size. The ending came after three minutes with Haystacks disqualified, Steele had attempted a flying tackle and Haystacks had punched him in the stomach. Referee Dave Reese immediately disqualified the big man and Steele progressed to the final but didn't look in any shape to do so. The other semi final saw Pat Roach meet Wild Angus with Roach reaching the final with a winning fall in the ninth minute. The final between Roach and Steele was a slow paced , rather boring match won by Roach with a 'Brumagen Bump' weakening Steele for the winner in the twelfth minute.

The first show of the new year at the Royal Albert Hall took place in the first week on January 6th. The advertised main event was Big Daddy and Kung Fu versus the pairing of Giant Haystacks and a newcomer from the USA billed as the American version of Haystacks called The Baby Blimp. The reality though was completely different the wrestler under the mask turned out to be Blackpool heavyweight Tony Francis. Either the real Blimp didn't arrive or was meant to be Francis all the time, whichever it was it was a let down for the fans. The match itself was another let down with Haystacks & Blimp walking out from the ring after a little over 10 minutes of action. After his surprise defeat to Sid Cooper at the November Albert Hall show Mal Sanders locked horns again with him. Sanders won but Cooper pushed him all the way with the winning fall not coming until the final round. Chris Adams had a lively bout with Bobby Barnes winning by disqualification in the 5th round. Up and coming young heavyweight prospect Tom Tyrone had perhaps the best result so far of his career when he held the long haired Scots giant Wild Angus to an eight round draw and youngsters Steve Logan and Johnny Kidd had a fine wrestling match with Logan winning by two falls to one in the 5th round. The fans left happy when Catweazle won the final match of the evening when he beat Mel Stuart by straight falls inside three rounds.

Although nothing had been announced regarding the World Mid/Heavyweight Title previously held by Mike Marino an eliminator for the now vacant title was shown on *World of Sport* on January 9th. The show filmed at Catford the previous November saw Marty Jones meet Bret Hart. Jones opened the scoring in the fifth round with a folding press. Hart who was adopting a surprisingly aggressive style testing referee Max Ward's patience at times. Hart equalised in the sixth round with a cross press after a pile driver. The winner came in the eight round when Jones rolled up Hart for another folding press and a step further in his quest for world title honours. As for Hart he was booed from the ring and it would be a further eight years until he returned to the UK as a 'WWF superstar'. The rest of the show that week comprised of a knockout tournament with Jim Breaks, Alan Dennison, Johnny Kidd and Jackie Turpin taking part. In the first semi final Jim Breaks beat Alan Dennison whilst in the other Jackie Turpin beat Johnny Kidd with both matches decided by the one fall. In an upset Turpin won the trophy with a two falls to one win over Breaks.

The long awaited World Heavy/Middleweight Title match between Mark Rocco and Dynamite Kid was shown on *World of Sport* on January 16th. By the time it was finally screened it was well out of sync as it had been taped at the end of November the previous year. The match was another excellent, hard hitting, fast paced contest although watching some of the bumps and moves knowing what happened to both in their later lives does bring a different aspect to it all now. This match ended in the fifth round when Dynamite Kid went to suplex Rocco and both went out of the ring over the top rope taking heavy falls. Referee Max Ward immediately halted the match and with Dynamite having left the country we were deprived of a rematch. The rest of the show that week which was the second half of the Catford bill compromised of a team match between in one corner The Rockers with Sid Cooper against a trio of Steve Grey, Mal Sanders and Steve Logan. The singles matches saw Sanders beat Lorne, Grey beat Cooper and Logan beat LaPaque. The six man tag finale saw Sanders, Grey and Logan complete a clean sweep when they beat Cooper and The Rockers by two falls to one.

The Wayne Bridges v Pete Roberts feud kicked up another notch on the January 23rd edition of *World of Sport*. Roberts this time won by two straight falls in the fourth round. Bridges was outraged by the result and afterwards went straight to Kent Walton's commentary desk to complain. As he did so he made the famous 'Who have you ever beaten comment ?' to Roberts who had the easiest comeback of all time to say 'I've just beaten you !'. Wayne Bridges was a superb villain at this time and Roberts was the perfect foil for him. Also shown that week on the bill from Aylesbury was Mick McManus who was in the final few months of his in ring career. McManus this week took on the much heavier Len Hurst. As was usually the case McManus let his temper get the better of him and after throwing Hurst out of the ring referee Joe D'Orazio disqualified him. The final bout that week was a rather dull heavyweight match with Butcher Bond wrestling within the rules for a change against Caswell Martin and the result was a one fall each draw at the end of the scheduled six rounds.

It was back to Aylesbury the following Saturday on *World of Sport* on January 30th for the second half of the bill taped there. It wasn't a week to remember with three matches but not a main event calibre one amongst them. Tom Tyrone beat Bruiser Muir by two falls to one in the fifth round. The bout between Alan Kilby and Johnny Wilson ended in the seventh round in a messy way with both of them getting tangled up in the ropes with neither able to continue. Finally Ringo Rigby beat Banger Walsh who failed to beat the count in the fifth round.

Shortly after it was announced that Pete Roberts would get his title shot against Wayne Bridges on the February show at the Royal Albert Hall. A triple World Title Match main event would see Bridges v Roberts, Mark Rocco defending the World Heavy/Middleweight Title against Kung Fu and after his win over Johnny Saint in December Steve Grey would get his chance to win the World Lightweight Title.

The end of January saw Kung Fu cut short his Joint Promotions' commitments to head stateside to wrestle for the Stampede territory in Canada and went out on a high at Queensferry in front of a crowd of 2500 when he beat Mark Rocco by disqualification in the 6th round. Chris Adams also finished up his brief visit and headed back to the USA and for Adams this was the last time he wrestled in the UK.

The *World of Sport* wrestling on February 6th was the second half of a show from Preston that had been recorded back in October and forgotten about till now. The first match between Mick McManus and Alan Dennison ended with both disqualified at the end of the fourth round. Dennison went beserk after McManus had cheated to get an equalising fall and the referee sent both of them back to the dressing room. A hard hitting heavyweight encounter saw Marty Jones defeat Johnny

South by two falls to one in the sixth round with a double arm reversal from Jones pinning South for the winner. The final match that week should have been and was advertised beforehand as a match between King Kong Kirk and Wild Angus. The match wasn't shown and was replaced by a contest filmed at Newton Aycliffe last August in which Pete Ross beat Sid Cooper by disqualification. At the time it was said the reason the Kirk v Angus match had been binned was Kent Walton made a cock up with the commentary. MC Brian Crabtree confirmed a short while after that this was indeed the case. The Kirk v Angus match was eventually shown on TV as part of the much missed 'The Wrestling Channel/Men & Movies' old *World of Sport* shows. For two such renowned 'bad guys' they both wrestled to the rule book for much of the time which was quite a surprise. Kirk got the first fall in the fifth round with a body slam followed by a cross press, Angus got the equaliser in the sixth round after suplexing Kirk. With the match scheduled for six rounds therefore it was a one fall each draw. Kent Walton's mistake was that when the timekeeper rang the bell for the second round Walton said it was the 'start of round three'. As the timekeeper then announced the start of round three Walton said it was the start of the fourth and so on which made you wonder why somebody didn't notice it during the match.

A heavyweight Battle Royale was the featured attraction on *World of Sport* on February 13th in a show from Lincoln. The eight heavyweights competing were Big Daddy, Jim Harris, King Kendo, Tony Francis, John Cox, Mel Stuart, Mike Dean and Johnny Wilson. It wouldn't need a clairvoyant to know who would win and indeed Daddy threw out Harris to claim the prize. Kid Chocolate wrestled a draw with Tally Ho Kaye in the opener. Also on show that week an interesting teacher v pupil contest when Ken Joyce took on one of his protege's Johnny Kidd. Joyce was more often seen as a referee these days. Kidd surprised Joyce in the fourth round with the first fall with a folding press and a bridge to secure no escape. Joyce showed his experience with a reverse double knee folding press to gain an immediate equaliser in the fifth round. Joyce got the winner in the seventh round with a double arm reversal in what was an intriguing match and a superb exhibition of technical wrestling. Afterwards MC Brian Crabtree announced that this was Ken Joyce's final ever match on TV, twenty six years after his first.

The triple world title show at the Royal Albert Hall on February 17th rather fell apart, despite plenty of publicity including Kent Walton giving it a mention on the previous Saturday's *World of Sport*. The first problem including for me was that the South East of England was embroiled in a railway employee's strike which meant that there were hardly any trains running, especially after 9pm. This meant I gave the show a miss as it was being taped for World of Sport and a few regular attendees couldn't make it either. The next problem was that Kung Fu had left for Canada at the beginning of the month and nothing had been announced before hand so his title match with Mark Rocco was cancelled. Kung Fu's replacement for a non title match instead turned out to be somebody very few if any of the crowd had heard of in the shape of Scottish youngster Steve McHoy. It turned out that McHoy was the son of Wild Angus and had already wrestled in the German tournaments. In the match Mark Rocco made McHoy look like a superstar with McHoy an unlucky loser in the fourth round. He was a fall in front but attempting a flying tackle on Rocco he was thrown over the top rope by his opponent and failed to beat referee Max Ward's count. It was certainly a great way to introduce a new name and Steve McHoy or Steve Casey as he was also known would be one of the top British heavyweights of the 1980's. The advertised Battle Royale included four solo matches with Butcher Bond beating Bull Pratt by two falls to one in the fourth round. John Elijah beat Big Bertha also by two falls to one in the fourth round. Caswell Martin was injured when falling from the ring against Marty Jones and the verdict was a No Contest. Finally Alan Kilby beat Banger Walsh by disqualification in only two rounds. With Caswell Martin unable to compete in the over the top rope event Marty Jones eliminated the other six participants to win it.

The much anticipated World Heavyweight Title match between Wayne Bridges and Pete Roberts saw Bridges accompanied by friend and business partner Prince Kumali whilst Roberts had the crowd firmly on his side. Roberts opened the scoring with the first fall in the sixth round with Bridges already having received a public warning in the previous round. Bridges got an equaliser with a submission in the ninth round before the end came in the eleventh round. Roberts had drop kicked Bridges from the ring , Bridges climbed back inside the ropes with a cut head. Roberts turned to the referee expecting him to take a look at the blood but instead Bridges took advantage of his distracted opponent and pinned him for the winner. There had been no announcement about the final match of the night which should have been the third title match with Johnny Saint defending his World Lightweight Title against Steve Grey. Instead Grey jumped into the ring and announced he had a lung infection and would be unable to wrestle so in a non title match local boy Jan Curtis stepped into face Johnny Saint. Saint won in the third round when Curtis was unable to continue but a lot of fans were upset by the loss of two of the three advertised title matches. By the end of the year the venue was dead. The word afterwards was that Johnny Saint had handed in his notice to Joint Promotions and was off to wrestle on the independent circuit for Brian Dixon and Orig Williams and had refused to drop the title at the Albert Hall.

Brian Dixon and his Wrestling Enterprises promotion held their own big show in London the following night on February 18th at another famous old venue The Alexandra Palace or 'Ally Pally' as it's better known. Amongst the highlights that night Tony St Clair beat John Quinn by two falls to one. Keith Haward retained the European Middleweight Title when he beat JJ Pallo. Jon Cortez beat Clive Myers to retain the European Lightweight Title and Yasu Fuji beat Steve Veidor who was unable to continue through injury.

Promoter Max Crabtree introduced a new concept for the wrestling on *World of Sport* on February 20th from a show recorded at Burnley. Team matches had been a regular item both on TV and around the halls with Big Daddy usually captaining a team against a team of villians but the personnel on each time varied with no set line up. This time Crabtree made up a four man team called 'The Jets' who were formed of the captain Tom Tyrone, Alan Kilby, Pat Patton and Steve Logan. They all wore matching vests and had a number from 1-4 on them to denote who they were. The opposing team at Burnley consisted of Bill Bromley, Blackjack Mulligan, John Wilkie and Bernie Wright, hardly the most inspiring a line up. The rules stated there would be four solo matches followed by two tags and it was hardly a surprise that 'The Jets' won by 5-0. Tyrone beat Bromley by two falls to one in the fifth round. Kilby beat Mulligan by two straight falls in three rounds. Patton beat Wilkie by countout in the third round and Logan wrestled a one fall each draw with Wright. The tags saw Tyrone and Kilby beat Bromley and Mulligan inside five minutes and Logan and Patton beat Wilkie and Wright in a minute less.

The following week on February 27th saw the second half of the Burnley show on *World of Sport* with Mark Rocco v Kung Fu as the main event. The show had been taped three weeks ago which is why Kung Fu was there although fans who had been at the Albert Hall might have wondered what was going on. Rocco had Charlie McGee in his corner for this one but didn't really need any advice or assistance. Kung Fu got the first fall in the third round with a flying tackle from the top rope followed by a cross press, Rocco got an immediate equaliser in the fourth round with a single leg Boston Crab forcing an immediate submission from Kung Fu. The winner of another excellent match came in the sixth round with Kung Fu missing a flying tackle and immediately Rocco hoisted him up and delivered a piledriver followed by a cross press. The other main match was a challenge match between Giant Haystacks and Pat Roach after they had an argument during the knockout tournament at Oldham. Haystacks got the first fall in the first round with a splash as Roach attempted to lift the big man. Roach got the equaliser straight away in the second round with a flying tackle knocking Haystacks off his feet and Roach covering him for the count of three. The match then descended into chaos with referee Jeff Kaye thrown across the ring as he attempted to separate them and he had no option but to disqualify them both. Catweazle beat Sid Cooper by two falls to one in the fifth round in the other contest shown.

The Yamaha Organs Snooker tournament replaced the wrestling on *World of Sport* on March 6th.

The wrestling was back on *World of Sport* on March 13th with an interesting show to say the least from Hemel Hempstead. The first bout saw the return to Britain of Young David who in the year or so he had been in Canada had bulked up considerably and was now a good couple of stones heavier. His opponent Fit Finlay who was also making a return to the ring after a hiatus of a few months. This was an eliminator for Mark Rocco's World Heavy/Middleweight Title. Finlay won by two falls to one with the winning fall coming in the final round of an impressively hard hitting match. Next up was the TV debut of a wrestler who was advertised as being the bigger brother of Sammy Lee called Kwik Kik Lee. He was in fact Akira Maeda a young Japanese heavyweight who had been sent here to learn the British style. Maeda went on to be one of the all time greats of Japanese wrestling but in his match here against Ireland's Lucky Gordon he was hardly extended. Gordon failed to beat the count in the second round to give Lee an easy win. Final match was the rare sight of Big Daddy in a singles match rather than a tag when he took on Jim Harris. In a bout lasting less than three minutes Harris failed to beat the count after a double elbow drop from Daddy. Harris' British tour came to an end a week later at Cleethorpes in a match with Kwik Kik Lee where he suffered a broken ankle and was forced to return home to the USA. After his return home and fully recovered Jim Harris was renamed Kamala and went on to be one of the stars of the WWF in the late 1980's. Harris passed away earlier this year.

The March show at the Royal Albert Hall was cancelled due to the BBC wishing to televise the professional debut of boxer Frank Bruno on its 'Sportsnight' programme. Usually the BBC taped the boxing on a Tuesday night and broadcast it on a Wednesday but due to the hype for Bruno they wished to show it on the same night so wrestling fans were left disappointed and having to wait for April.

The Jets team were back in action on *World of Sport* on March 20th from Hemel Hempstead with this time facing a team made up of Jim Breaks, King Kong Kirk, Ray Robinson and Johnny England. This time the match was made up of two solo matches with Tom Tyrone beating Kirk who was disqualified in the fifth round. Alan Kilby beat Robinson by two falls to one in the fifth round. The tag match saw Pat Patton and Steve Logan wrestle a twenty minute time limit draw with Breaks and England.

The *World of Sport* show on March 27th featured matches from the February Royal Albert Hall show including Mark Rocco v Steve McHoy.

Other matches from the Albert Hall were shown on April 3rd with the Wayne Bridges v Pete Roberts title match the main attraction.

The action was just as good on the independent scene through March with John Quinn and Tony St Clair meeting in ladder matches on several bills as well as Quinn successfully defending the World Heavyweight Title against St Clair at Preston at the end of the month. Preston was a surprising venue for Wrestling Enterprises to promote at as for years it was a Best/Wryton stronghold and was used for several TV tapings there. What had happened was that Joint Promotions had begun to cut the number of shows they were presenting and it gave Brian Dixon the opportunity to book his promotion there on the vacant dates. The other factor was that during the this period the financial recession really began to hit peoples finances and treats like a night at the wrestling had to be forsaken. The posters at the time advertising the night's bill even had on them in large words 'Forget the recession come and have a good night out'.

April started strongly on the independent scene with World Lightweight Champion Johnny Saint making his debut for Wrestling Enterprises with a win against JJ Pallo at Hinckley. There was a wide range of decent lightweights at this time so Saint had plenty of good opponents such as Jackie Robinson, Mike Jordan and Jon Cortez to be matched with. The next night Saturday April 3rd saw Wrestling Enterprises put their first show on at the historic Victoria Hall in Hanley, the venue where Kendo Nagasaki unmasked Count Bartelli.

The *World of Sport* show on April 10th saw a title change screened with British Lightweight Champion Steve Grey losing his title to Jim Breaks. A dramatic ending saw Breaks getting the winning fall in the twelfth and final round. That week also featured the TV debut of Crusher Brannigan from the USA and he had little trouble in beating Len Hurst who was unable to continue after submitting in the third round. Kwik Kik Lee bettered his two round win over Lucky Gordon a few weeks ago in the final bout that week when his opponent Ed Wensor was counted out in the first round.

The Royal Albert Hall got back on track on April 14th with a strong line up to compensate for missing the March date. Top of the bill was a tag match featuring Big Daddy and Tom Tyrone taking on Giant Haystacks and Bruiser Muir, Muir replaced the injured Jim Harris. Ten minutes of action later Daddy and Tyrone were the winners by two falls to one and for once Haystacks remained in the ring till the winning fall was decided. Kwik Kik Lee's quality of opponent went up a notch as he was billed against Mark Rocco and Lee's inexperience told as Rocco gave him quite a beating until he went too far in the 3rd round and got himself disqualified. Crusher Brannigan continued to impress and looked like Wayne Bridges would have a fight on his hands if the American decided to challenge for the Londoner's World Heavyweight Title. This time Brannigan beat the Yorkshire Heavyweight Ray Steele who was unable to continue for the 5th round after Brannigan's speciality move the 'Widowmaker'. The rest of the card featured The Jets in action with Tom Tyrone busy with Big Daddy the other trio took on Alan Dennison, Fit Finlay and King Ben. Pat Patton's match with Ben ended with both counted out in the fourth round. Finlay surprisingly to many at ringside beat Alan Kilby by two falls to one in the fifth round. Dennison beat Steve Logan by two falls to one in the sixth round before the concluding six man tag saw The Jets beat their opponents in a little over eleven minutes.

The *World of Sport* show on April 17th from Bolton should have featured a rematch between Wayne Bridges and Pete Roberts but with injury ruling out Bridges it was Young David who stepped in to face Roberts. The match ended in the fourth round with David unable to continue after taking an incredibly high backdrop. Roberts sportingly refused to accept the win so MC Brian Crabtree announced the result to be a No Contest. Other matches that week saw Vic Faulkner beat Sid Cooper by disqualification whilst Ray Steele wrestled a one fall each draw with Steve McHoy.

The second half of the Bolton show was screened on April 24th with the first match featuring two wrestlers making their TV debuts. Phil Johnson better known as 'Grasshopper' thanks to his resemblance to the character in the TV series 'Kung Fu' took on Dave 'Lightning' Lawrence. Both wrestlers came from the East Midlands area and only recently had made their Joint Promotions debuts too. The match ended in a one fall each draw over the usual six round time limit. The main event saw both of the two new heavyweight arrivals face each other with Crusher Brannigan taking on Kwik Kik Lee. Lee got the first fall in the second round with a slightly messy cross press following a flying tackle. The restart was delayed with one of the ring boards broken and viewers saw referee Jeff Kaye amongst others trying to fix it. Brannigan equalised with a powerslam in the third round before making a complete mess of a dive off of the top rope when he tripped. He then went back for a second attempt in which he was successful but was disqualified for doing so. Afterwards Brannigan grabbed MC Brian Crabtree's microphone to throw out a challenge to Big Daddy. The final match that week saw the return of Johnny Powers who had been overseas for a few years to face Gil Singh and it was Singh who got the one fall needed to win.

The May 1st show on *World of Sport* went back to January and the second half of the show recorded at Lincoln. Chris Adams who had long since left to go back to the USA beat Ed Wensor by two falls to one. Johnny Saint who was now wrestling on the independent circuit beat Jackie Turpin again by two falls to one and Jim Breaks beat Mick McMichael who was unable to continue after submitting to a 'Breaks special' submission hold.

May started with a bang on the independent circuit when Tony St Clair finally was able to claim the World Heavyweight Title. He beat the champion John Quinn by two falls to one in the 15th round at Hanley on May 8th. St Clair had had several unsuccessful attempts at the title over the previous year or so but this time he was successful in an epic encounter that had the fans on the edge of their seats throughout. Around this time

Wrestling Enterprises announced in one of their event programmes that the British Heavyweight Title held by Tony St Clair was now the Open Heavyweight Title and able to be challenged for by any wrestler and not just British or naturalised British citizens. This saw the end of the linear history of the original Lord Mountevans' British Heavyweight Title and it's open title replacement would going forward to these days be the 'Superslam' Title as fought for on All-Star Promotions shows.

For Joint Promotions though it was time to say goodbye to Mick McManus when he retired after a bout against his old rival Catweazle shown on *World of Sport* on May 8th. It had been obvious for a while that McManus was cutting down on his dates and the amount of travelling that he did each night and it was the perfect opportunity to go out on. The ring was a lot worse off for his absence although he went on to work for Dale Martin in the office in an administrative role. Unfortunately he didn't go out with a win as the match ended in a draw with Catweazle getting a submission in the fourth round before McManus equalised with a single leg Boston Crab in the fifth. After the match there was a ten bell salute for him before an interview was shown of him backstage with Jim Rosenthal. As they shared a glass of champagne McManus reminisced about his career and it was a good way of marking the occasion. Other matches shown that week from Bedworth saw Fit Finlay defeat Marty Jones by two falls to one to start the feud that would last all through the rest of the 1980's. In the opener Mal Sanders defeated TV newcomer Johnny Apollon by the only fall needed.

The wrestling on *World of Sport* on May 15th was restricted to one match although it was for the World Heavyweight Title with Pete Roberts getting his rematch against Wayne Bridges. One of the best feuds in British wrestling in recent years ended with Bridges once again retaining the title as a result of a two falls to one win in the ninth round.

The final show of the season at the Royal Albert Hall was held on May 19th with some interesting matches on the bill. In quite an upset Kwik Kik Lee defeated Wayne Bridges by two falls to one in the sixth round of a non title match. Bridges unlike his matches with Pete Roberts wrestled entirely within the rules and explained afterwards it was Roberts that caused him to lose his temper. Roberts himself was featured in the other main event when he met American challenger Crusher Brannigan in what turned out to be a superb, action packed match. Roberts got the first fall in the third round before Brannigan who was bleeding profusely from a cut head knocked out his opponent with the 'Widowmaker' back elbow drop from the top rope in the fourth round. After his upset win against Marty Jones on World of Sport on May 8th Fit Finlay got a crack at Jones' British Light/Heavyweight Title on this bill. In another excellent match Finlay got the first fall before Jones eventually equalised in the seventh round before a winning fall in the ninth. Pat Roach took on Bill Bromley who made Roach work surprisingly hard for his two straight falls win in the fourth round. Grasshopper and Dave Lawrence made their Albert Hall debuts against each other and as with their recent TV match once again it ended in a one fall each draw. Finally Len Hurst took the place of Steve McHoy who had departed to wrestle on the continent against Skull Murphy and Hurst got the win when Murphy was disqualified in the third round.

May 22nd was FA Cup Final day on *World of Sport* with wrestling restricted to just the one match shown at 1230. Naturally this featured Big Daddy who partnered Kwik Kik Lee against Crusher Brannigan and Banger Walsh. Walsh was a late replacement for the advertised Skull Murphy. Murphy formerly known as Steve Young had returned to Joint Promotions recently and after doing a few Big Daddy tags decided he didn't want to do anymore. There wasn't even any ring walk shown Dickie Davies went straight to Kent Walton for the first bell. The winner came with a big splash from Daddy on Brannigan in just under nine minutes of an underwhelming cup final match.

Steve Grey regained the British Lightweight Title in his contracted return match against Jim Breaks at Croydon on May 25th. Like the first match at Wolverhampton this one too went down to the wire but unlike the previous encounter this time it was Grey who got the winning fall in the 12th round to begin another reign as the champion.

Wrestling was missing from *World of Sport* on May 29th with the England v Scotland football match shown live in its place.

The start of June saw another bombshell with the news that Mark Rocco had given his notice into Joint Promotions and would be in the future wrestling for the independent promoters notably Orig Williams and Brian Dixon's Wrestling Enterprise's promotion which was rapidly increasing the number of dates they were presenting wrestling on. For some they saw it as a conspiracy theory with Rocco not happy about wrestling Big Daddy or other such rumours that passed around ringside. Although there was truth to that and a lot of wrestlers were becoming frustrated with the way things had become dependent on Big Daddy. It was a lot simpler though, Rocco as a professional sportsman was offered more money to switch sides as well as creative input and Max Crabtree refused to get into a bidding war. Over the last year or so Rocco was doing increasingly more wrestling in places like Japan and the USA but it was a surprise Max Crabtree didn't do more to keep him. Mark Rocco did prove to be a big loss to Joint Promotions and a great asset to the likes of Brian Dixon and Orig Williams. Rocco went on to become a close friend to Dixon outside of the ring as well and was one of the few wrestlers who when a show didn't draw as big a crowd as expected refused to take the full money for that night. The strange thing after Rocco's departure was that when venue managers enquired as to where Mark Rocco was and why he wasn't wrestling there anymore they were told by Joint Promotions he had retired. This came to light a couple of years later when Brian Dixon accompanied by Rocco went to a conference of entertainment managers and executives at Bournemouth and they were told by some of the delegates that they were told he had retired when they asked what had happened to him.

Mark Rocco's last big show for Joint Promotions was their return to Liverpool Stadium on June 11th, by now both sides were starting to do tit for tat promoting putting on shows at the other's venues. Suitably Rocco's opponent was Marty Jones and they had a typically lively and hard hitting match which Jones won by two falls to one in the 6th round. Naturally Big Daddy was on top of the bill duty for such a big show and he teamed with Kwik Kik Lee to defeat Giant Haystacks and Crusher Brannigan in just under eleven minutes.

Wrestling was missing on *World of Sport* on June 5th with the schoolboy's football match between England and Scotland being shown.

On June 12th the Dunlop Masters golf replaced wrestling and to complete a fourth week without any grappling on *World of Sport* the Poland v Cameroon World Cup football match was shown on June 19th.

Wrestling returned to TV on June 26th with the second half of the show taped at Bedworth in May. After the absence it would have been nice to have seen a better bill than what was put on with another dour heavyweight match between Pat Roach and Caswell Martin topping the bill. Roach won when Martin was unable to continue. Johnny Wilson beat Bruiser Muir by disqualification in the fifth round after a low blow whilst Tally Ho Kaye beat the masked Kamakaze who was forced to retire through injury.

The Jets team had another outing on *World of Sport* on July 3rd on the bill from Croydon which had been shown on FA Cup day. This time the team opposing them consisted of Bobby Barnes, Sid Cooper, Studs Lannigan and John Elijah. Tom Tyrone beat Elijah by the one fall needed in the fifth round of the first singles match. Alan Kilby beat Lannigan again by the only fall needed this time in the third round. A lively tag finale saw Barnes and Cooper beat Pat Patton and Steve Logan by two falls to one in a little over eighteen minutes.

Southport had it's annual visit from the *World of Sport* cameras with the first half of the show shown on July 10th. As usual with the Southport show a knockout tournament was featured with the four contestants being Alan Dennison, Mal Sanders, Johnny England and King Ben. The semi finals saw King Ben beat Mal Sanders by two falls to one in the sixth round and Alan Dennison beat Johnny England with the winner coming for Dennison in the fifth round when his arm suspension submission forced England to quit. The final ended early when Ben was unable to continue in the first round through injury so Dennison won the trophy. A bonus bout to fill the time saw the popular Grasshopper beat Blackjack Mulligan with a double leg nelson for the only fall needed in eight minutes.

The second half of the bill from Southport was shown the next week on July 17th and featured the debut of a brand new tag team. Fit Finlay and Skull Murphy had now teamed up to form 'The Riot Squad' and in this TV debut they faced Kwik Kik Lee Myers and Clive Myers. Finlay and Murphy won by the only fall scored in the twenty minute time limit. After the last few years of tag team wrestling on Joint Promotions consisting of Big Daddy and partners disposing of various cannon fodder it was nice to see tag matches taken seriously again. Also seen that week was Pat Roach who beat Tom Tyrone by two falls to one in the sixth round and John Naylor beat Bernie Wright again by two falls to one in the sixth round.

By the middle of July all the weekly summer season shows around the country were in full swing although some of the previous Dale Martin strongholds like the Pier Pavilion at Worthing were now being promoted by Wrestling Enterprises whilst Jackie Pallo had taken over the shows at Hastings Pier. Whilst there were still many shows held at the coastal venues it was nothing like the heydays of the 1960's with a combination of overseas holidays and the recession putting paid to the number of people going on British holidays like they once did.

Giant Haystacks teamed up with Crusher Brannigan to form a mighty combo for the main event on *World of Sport* on July 24th from Hatfield. Their opponents were Ray Steele and Steve McHoy who were dwarfed by them. A combination of quick tags followed by dropkicks was enough for Steele and McHoy to take the first fall with a flying tackle from McHoy flooring Brannigan for the count of three. A figure four powerlock from Brannigan on McHoy brought about an immediate submission equaliser a couple of minutes later. A back drop from Haystacks with his full weight landing onto the unfortunate Steele ended the match in the eleventh minute with both Steele and McHoy being assisted back to the dressing room. An international heavyweight match saw Gil Singh take on Terry

Rudge with Singh getting the winning fall in the sixth round with a cross press following a body slam. Vic Faulkner made a by now very rare appearance on TV when he faced Kid Chocolate. Faulkner came out on top with a folding press in the fifth round sealing a two falls to one win.

The second half of the Hatfield show was seen the next week on July 31st with the featured match between Jim Breaks and Jackie Turpin. Instead of rounds this was fought over a fifteen minute time limit with still two falls or submissions etc. needed to win. Turpin got the opening fall in the ninth minute when he surprised Breaks with a folding press before Breaks equalised less than two minutes later when the 'Breaks special' forced Turpin to submit. The winner came in the final minute when Turpin again caught Breaks by surprise and rolled up Breaks for the count of three. Also seen that week was Steve Grey beating Tony Costas in the sixth round whilst the crowd's favourite Catweazle wrestled a one fall apiece draw with Bobby Barnes over six rounds.

August 7th on *World of Sport* saw the second half of the show filmed at Wolverhampton back in April shown. The highlight of the show being a defence of the British Heavy/Middleweight Title by Alan Kilby against Fit Finlay which ended in the eighth round with both wrestlers unable to beat the count. A rather dull international catchweight contest saw Caswell Martin defeat King Ben by two falls to one in the fifth round. The final bout that week was a tag match between two of The Jets Steve Logan and Pat Patton against Alan Dennison and Mick McMichael. The match ended in fifteen minutes when McMichael accidentally caught Logan in his nether regions and was immediately disqualified by referee Dave Reese. This was the ending seen many times around the halls and also on TV.

Three matches from Bridlington were on offer on *World of Sport* on August 14th with the highlight being another match between Marty Jones and Pete Roberts. A suplex followed by a cross press in the third round saw Roberts get the first fall but Jones equalised in the fourth round with a double arm nelson. With neither getting a winner in the next two rounds it ended in a draw. Gil Singh recorded a two straight falls win over Bill

Bromley whilst King Kong Kirk got the only fall needed to beat John Cox in the other bouts shown.

World of Sport continued it's tour of English seaside venues on August 21st when Southend was the venue for the wrestling. As per last week's show from Bridlington the show consisted of three heavyweight bouts. The first of them saw a TV debut for 'General' John Raven. Raven having recently joined Joint Promotions had been a stalwart on the independent circuit for a few years usually known as Ripper Raven. Now adopting the persona of an American General, Raven marched to the ring in his uniform carrying a swagger stick to face opponent Peter Wilson. Wilson was no match for Raven who won with the only score needed when Wilson was forced to submit in the third round. Steve McHoy beat Butcher Bond with a reverse double arm pinfall bringing the winner in the fourteenth minute of fifteen minute time limit match. Finally in a lively match up with plenty of 'needle' Kwik Kik Lee beat Skull Murphy. Murphy was dropkicked over the top rope in the fifth round and failed to get back into the ring by the completion of referee Peter Szakac's count of ten.

The other half of the Southend was shown the next week on August 28th with the highlight being a return match between Catweazle and Bobby Barnes after their drawn bout from Hatfield a few weeks ago. This time there was another inconclusive finish as the normally affable Catweazle was disqualified for illegal use of the bucket. Barnes had gained an equalising submission in the fifth round and after releasing the hold had attacked Catweazle from the rear. An incensed Catweazle then hit Barnes on the head with his bucket. Referee Max Ward had no option but to disqualify him but he also disqualified Barnes for being the instigator. Also shown that week was Clive Myers taking on the muscular Johnny Apollon with Myers far greater experience and skills being too much for the youngster who went down by two straight falls in the sixth round. The opening match between Johnny Wilson and Banger Walsh ended in the second round when Walsh was disqualified by Max Ward for punching Wilson in the stomach.

There would be no wrestling shown on *World of Sport* for three weeks now as on September 4th the European Open golf was shown whilst on September 11th saw the European Athletics Championships screened in it's place.

The start of September saw the new season starting for the town and city venues and Max Crabtree's idea to pep up interest was to bring in midgets from the USA. Midgets hadn't been featured on Joint Promotions' bills for a few years but had always been a regular sight on the independent scene. Four midgets were booked to arrive , Haiti Kid and Carolina Kid v Ivan the Terrible and Little Boy Blue was the intention. For one reason or another which didn't become apparent only Haiti Kid and Carolina Kid actually turned up. Plans were hastily rearranged into singles matches with Haiti Kid taking on Carolina Kid and others into tag matches with the likes of Steve Grey, Sid Cooper, Tom Thumb and Catweazle.

Some other new faces appeared on Joint Promotions' bills as a result of the training school run by Pat Roach. He had advertised in the event programmes for individuals who wished to be trained by him and many took him up on the offer. The giant red haired Scrubber Daly was perhaps the best known of the trainees and he quickly took on the mantle of a Big Daddy opponent and went on to wrestle on TV on many occasions. Other graduates from the school included Andy Blair who would become a regular Big Daddy tag partner and Scott Conway who perhaps became better known for being the owner of 'The (South Eastern) Wrestling Alliance' promotion. Apart from the Pat Roach trainees Joint Promotions also had a lot of other newcomers come in, some did well others disappeared without much trace. Amongst the newcomers were Johnny Apollon who had recently been seen on World of Sport, Paul Britton who was the son of MC & referee Peter Jaye, 'SAS' Regan who claimed to be a former member of the special forces, heavyweight John McGuiness, another heavyweight from Essex Dick Stevens whilst at the other end of the weight scale Tom Thumb was now appearing for Joint Promotions. Thumb who had often wrestled under his real name Neil Evans for the independent promoters quickly became much beloved of the fans. Another new face coming from the independents was Dave George who had also wrestled on the holiday camp circuit for many a year. Jim Moza also returned to the Joint

Promotions after quite a few years away to complete quite a fresh looking roster for the new season. Amongst the departures from Joint Promotions to the independents was Johnny Kwango who was now sixty two and had been mainly refereeing for the past few months. On the independent circuit he was back wrestling and having made his debut in 1952 was well past his best but still popular with the fans.

The first Croydon show of the season on September 14th had the first title change of the new season when Fit Finlay became the new British Heavy/Middleweight Champion. Finlay beat the champion Alan Kilby in the ninth round to finally win a belt after several failures against both Kilby and the British Light/Heavyweight Champion Marty Jones.

Wrestling was back on *World of Sport* on September 18th with Skegness being the next seaside venue to host the show. The main event saw Big Daddy team up with Steve Logan to face the team of General John Raven and the masked Red Devil. The Red Devil resplendant in all red gear including the mask turned out to be the standard Daddy opponent and not a genuine threat. Daddy sealed the two straight falls victory with a big splash on the Red Devil in under seven minutes. Afterwards Daddy ripped off the mask to reveal the familar features of Lincolnshire heavyweight Bill Clarke who was better known under a different mask as King Kendo. Jackie Turpin was rewarded for a fine run of form including his televised victory over Jim Breaks with a shot at Steve Grey's British Lightweight Title. Unfortunately for Turpin he was unsuccessful with Grey winning by two falls to one to retain the belt. The other match shown that week was an international heavyweight affair with Steve McHoy beating Jim Moza by the one fall needed to win.

Grapple fans would again find wrestling missing from *World of Sport* after this show for another four weeks in what was a real barren time especially for those unable to go to shows in person. A few years ago such treatment would have caused viewers to become incensed and write to their MP's and such but now nobody seemed bothered. In the 1960's wrestling was even shown on ITV on a Sunday afternoon at 4pm if something else was shown on the Saturday but 1982 saw only one week of wrestling seen in seven shows.

On September 25th the Bob Hope Classic golf was shown, on October 2nd it was the International Open snooker and on October 9th it was the European Open golf that replaced wrestling.

The first Royal Albert Hall show was held on September 22nd and a most lacklustre affair it was. There was hardly any publicity for the show with no posters up outside the venue or on the usual fly posting sites. Even worse there were only five bouts advertised instead of the usual minimum of six contests. The two main events were the midgets in a tag match which obviously was never going to happen and the Riot Squad team of Fit Finlay and Skull Murphy taking on the team of Kwik Kik Lee and Clive Myers which at least promised to be decent. On the night there was a poor attendance with plenty of empty seats but if you fail to promote a show what do you expect? The first match saw Mal Sanders taking on one of the new faces in Johnny Apollon. Sanders came out on top with a winning submission in the fifth round. The next match was the one I was looking forward to the most with Finlay and Myers against Lee and Myers. They had had a tremendous twenty minute match shown on *World of Sport* back in July and the rematch promised to be just as good. In a huge disappointment the win went to Finlay and Murphy with Finlay getting the winning fall over Lee in just seven minutes of the match. It was a total let down and baffling that Max Crabtree would book such a poor match at the venue. The match before the interval saw Scotland's Steve McHoy meeting West Indian Jim Moza, the only problem being that the fans in attendance had seen the exact same match shown on World of Sport the previous weekend. As per the TV match McHoy won with his winning fall coming in the eight and final round.

After the interval the midgets were on show with Carolina Kid beating Haiti Kid in the fifth round, the accent was far more on comedy than wrestling with referee Joe D'Orazio playing the stooge on more than one occasion. As a one off it was fine to see but the novelty soon wore off. The final match of the night saw another match recently seen on *World of Sport* with Bobby Barnes again taking on Catweazle. After two inconclusive endings this time there was a winner with Barnes getting the winning fall in the final rounds much to the ringsiders disapproval. This was the second Albert Hall show of 1982 that had been a big let down and no wonder attendances were falling rapidly there.

Alan Kilby regained the British Heavy/Middleweight Title from Fit Finlay at Southend on October 6th in a non televised show. Kilby got the winning fall in the eighth round of a very hard fought match to reclaim the belt he had lost the previous month.

The October Royal Albert Hall show was held on the 13th with a heavyweight tag match advertised as the main event. Giant Haystacks and King Kong Kirk were booked to take on Ray Steele and Tom Tyrone although on the night it was changed to Haystacks and Bruiser Muir against Steele and Johnny Wilson. Steele got an early fall on Muir but Haystacks soon targetted Wilson and a big splash on him brought the equaliser. This was swiftly followed by the winning submission from Haystacks on Wilson in a little under nine minutes of action. There were also two championship matches on the programme with the first of them seeing Steve Grey put his British Lightweight Title on the line against perennial challenger Jim Breaks. Grey got the first fall in the third round before Breaks got the upper hand with persistent arm weakeners. This was followed by a 'Breaks special' in the sixth round which brought an equaliser when Grey was forced to submit. The winning submission came in the eighth round but it didn't come from Breaks but from Grey who forced Breaks to quit when he applied the surfboard hold. The other title match saw the British Welterweight Champion Alan Dennison defend his title against Vic Faulkner who was now concentrating on singles matches following the retirement of brother Bert Royal. An intriguing match saw Faulkner take an early lead in the second round before Dennison equalised in the sixth round. The match had an unfortunate ending in the ninth round when a clash of heads left Faulkner unable to continue and the contest had to be stopped and Dennison still champion. Alan Kilby had an easy night of it with a two straight falls win over Blackjack

Mulligan in only three rounds whilst it only took Pete Roberts a round longer to again record a two straight falls win over Steve Logan. The final match saw two Albert Hall debutants clash with Tom Thumb taking on fellow Essex wrestler Rob Storm. Thumb was no stranger to the Albert Hall as he had been a regular attendee as a fan for many years and it was pleasing that his first match there as a wrestler ended in a win for him in just over five minutes.

Wrestling was finally back on *World of Sport* on October 16th with a show from Derby. Big Daddy was on parade as the top of the bill. Daddy was at the peak of his popularity with the British public at this time. He was a regular on various mainstream TV programmes including the Saturday morning children's show TISWAS as well as signing a contract with Fleetway publishing to bring out a children's Christmas annual. The week after on October 23rd he was due to present the first in a new series of 'The Big Daddy Saturday Show' which was going to replace TISWAS in the Saturday morning time slot. Kent Walton even made a mention of the show during his commentary during the match but for reasons unknown although health problems were rumoured he dropped out in the week and co host Isla St Clair ended up hosting it alone instead of alongside Daddy.

The match from Derby saw Daddy and partner Jim Moza face old rival Giant Haystacks who partnered Bill Bromley who replaced the advertised Scrubber Daly. After his usual impressive TV show entrance the match went the same way of all the previous Big Daddy tags. Haystacks opened the scoring in the eighth minute when a big splash flattened Moza who had no hope of beating the count. After Moza was scraped up off the canvas by the local St.John's Ambulance he was stretchered back to the dressing room leaving Daddy to fight on alone. Daddy immediately equalised when a barrage of belly butts on Haystacks led to his big splash to even the match. As per usual Haystacks quickly tagged out and an impressive powerslam from Daddy on Bromley brought the winning fall in the eleventh minute. Fit Finlay and Alan Kilby continued their feud with a non title match which ended in honours even with one fall scored each in the six rounds time limit. Wigan based wrestlers competed in the opener with John Naylor scoring the only fall needed to beat Bob Walsh to secure bragging rights around the town.

On October 23rd it was back to Skegness on *World of Sport* for the other half of the show seen a month or so back. Kwik Kik Lee continued to impress on his British tour this time in a match with Ray Steele. Lee opened the scoring in the third round with a suplex leading to a cross press before Steele equalised in the next round with a cross press himself following a body slam. The next two rounds ended in deadlock with neither wrestler able to get the winning fall so a draw was the result. The other main match saw Tom Thumb make his World of Sport debut against none other than Jim Breaks. In the opening minutes Thumb bamboozled Breaks with his speed before his opponent retaliated with his usual arm weakeners followed by punches behind referee Emil Poilve's back. Thumb got the first fall with a double knee pinfall in the second round which Breaks found plenty to complain about. Breaks straightway started the arm weakeners and immediately hoisted Thumb aloft with his 'Breaks Special' to equalise in the match. Despite Thumb's attempts to avoid the submission again Breaks forced him to submit in the first minute of the fourth round with the 'Breaks Special' once again. The opening bout of the show saw a countout win for Pat Patton over Sid Cooper who was too busy arguing with the ringsiders to pay any attention to the referee's count of ten.

Derby was the venue again on October 30th for *World of Sport* with the highlight being Skull Murphy facing Pete Roberts. Murphy's gator hold brought about an immediate submission from Roberts in the fourth round. Roberts got the equaliser with a suplex in the sixth round and it was Roberts who won the contest when Murphy was disqualified by referee Emil Poilve for punching his opponent in the stomach in the seventh round. The second heavyweight match that week also featured a wrestler with a famous father following Roy 'Bull' Davis' son Skull Murphy in the previous match. This time the son of Wild Angus Steve McHoy took on Barry Douglas who came from a famous wrestling family himself. McHoy got the opening fall in the third round with a folding fall and an impressive wrestler's bridge. McHoy completed a fine two straight falls win over Douglas with a hip toss followed by a cross press in the fifth round. The other match between Vic Faulkner and Mick McMichael ended in a No Contest when McMichael caught his throat on the top rope and referee Jeff Kaye immediately called a halt as McMichael bled from his mouth.

November 6th saw the *World of Sport* cameras at Adwick Le Street for a Battle Royale. The participants were Alan Dennison, Kid Chocolate, Bobby Barnes, Eddie Riley, John Wilkie, Blackjack Mulligan, Grasshopper and Matt Matthews. The singles matches were all fought over one fall and the ten minute TV time limit saw Alan Dennison beat Blackjack Mulligan. John Wilkie v Eddie Riley ended with both counted out. Bobby Barnes beat Kid Chocolate and Grasshopper beat TV debutant Matt Matthews. Matthews was another of the rapidly expanding Derbyshire based group of wrestlers and he would go on to be matched so often with Grasshopper on the circuit that they spent more times together than they did with their wives ! The over the top rope finale was as chaotic as these events were and saw Wilkie eliminated first by Dennison. Riley threw out Matthews who was then straightaway thrown over the top rope himself by Dennison, Dennison then eliminated Chocolate, Mulligan chucked out Grasshopper and then Dennison threw out Mulligan leaving the last two to be Barnes and Dennison and in an upset it was Barnes who eliminated Dennison to win the 'King of the Ring' sash.

It was back to Bridlington on November 13th for the second half of the show filmed there back in July. Only two matches were shown this week instead of the usual three with neither of them whetting the appetite that much. Pat Roach beat Tom Tyrone by countout and Ray Steele beat John Elijah by two falls to one.

November 10th saw the next Royal Albert Hall show with Big Daddy making his first appearance of the season there in the main event. Daddy partnered Midland's judo ace Pat Patton against King Kong Kirk and Albert Hall debutant Scrubber Daly. Kirk opened the scoring with the first fall after a particularly vicious looking guilottine elbow drop on Patton.

Once Daddy made the hot tag it was all over with two falls in less than a minute for the victory. Incidentally in what must have been a first there was only one public warning issued in the match and that was for Big Daddy ! Alan Kilby put his newly regained British Heavy/Middleweight Title on the line once again against Fit Finlay with the added stipulation with a world title match for the winner. Some fans were aware that Marty Jones had won the vacant World Mid/Heavyweight Title at a TV taping the previous night at Croydon and that would be the match on offer for the winner. It was Kilby who retained his title and went forward for the world title match to be held on the December show. In a tough match Kilby beat Finlay with the winning fall in the eight round. Finlay's tag partner Skull Murphy was also on the bill where he faced a tough task against the much heavier World Heavyweight Champion Wayne Bridges. For once Murphy's aggression and nefarious tactics had no impact and in frustration Murphy caught Bridges with a punch in the champion's nether regions and was instantly disqualified. Marty Jones took on the heavier Tom Tyrone and an intriguing contest was cut short when Tyrone injured his knee attempting a leapfrog in the fourth round. Mal Sanders took on Gary Wensor who replaced Clive Myers who had gone to the USA to defend his arm wrestling championship. Sanders had an easy night beating the aggressive Wensor by count out in the second round. Johnny Kidd replaced John McGuinness to face Johnny Apollon and Apollon beat Kidd in the evening's show opener by two falls to one in the sixth round of a sporting encounter.

Croydon was the venue on November 20th's *World of Sport* with the feature being the semi finals of a tournament to crown the holders of the 'Top Tag Team' belts. For once this seemed a brilliant idea by Max Crabtree to get away from the emphasis on Big Daddy for tag matches and utilise some of the excellent teams that Joint Promotions had on their roster. Unfortunately it was a concept that just drifted away into nothing like 'The Jets' team wrestling had done. The four teams in the tournament were Fit Finlay and Skull Murphy, Alan Kilby and Steve Logan, Johnny and Peter Wilson & Kwik Kik Lee and Clive Myers. The first semi final was Finlay and Murphy v Kilby and

Logan with Finlay getting the first fall with a Samoan drop leading to an easy cross press. Kilby equalised with a flying knee to Finlay's head followed by a body slam and cross press two minutes later. It was Skull Murphy with his gator hold that brought an immediate submission from Steve Logan to send Murphy and Fit Finlay into the final after fifteen minutes. The second semi final would be between the Wilsons and Lee and Myers and would be a more slower paced match. Lee got the first fall over Peter Wilson with a suplex and cross press in the ninth minute. Johnny Wilson got the equalising fall on Lee a couple of minutes later following a body slam. Surprisingly it was the Wilsons who won the match when Peter Wilson sent Clive Myers flying over the top rope. Myers went over Kent Walton's head too as he landed at the ringsiders feet with no hope of beating referee Max Ward's ten count. Myers's bump was reminiscent of the one he took from Mick McManus a year or so earlier in a TV match and such a move was an accident waiting to happen. So the final to be shown the next week would be between 'The Riot Squad' Fit Finlay and Skull Murphy and Johnny and Peter Wilson and Finlay and Murphy would be overwhelming favourites to win the new belts.

The November 27th wrestling on *World of Sport* was a stacked show with not only the final of the 'Top Tag Team' title to be decided but finally the vacant World Mid/Heavyweight Title would be decided too. With the show coming from Croydon again there was a brief glimpse of Mal Sanders taking on Steve Grey with Grey getting the only fall needed to win in the third round. The vacant World Mid/Heavyweight Title would be between British representative Marty Jones and the French contender Bobby Gaetano. Fans who attended to Royal Albert Hall show on November 10th already knew who won as Marty Jones had paraded his newly won belt there when it was announced the winner of the Fit Finlay v Alan Kilby match would be the first challenger. Even so it was a cracking match to watch with Jones coming from behind to score the winning fall in the eighth round. Marty Jones achieved well deserved world champion status and it also gave Joint Promotions a new world champion to promote. The final match shown was the tag title match between Fit Finlay and Skull Murphy and Johnny and Peter Wilson. To nobodies surprise it was Finlay and Murphy who won the belts with Murphy's gator hold on Peter Wilson sealing a two nil win in just under nine minutes. Former heavyweight wrestler Charlie Green came into the ring to present the new belts but unfortunately nothing much was done with the titles and the concept died a death.

Wrestling was missing again from *World of Sport* on December 4th with darts shown in its place.

After a quiet time Jackie Pallo tried to get back on track with a big show at the Royal Concert Hall in Nottingham on December 7th, a 2500 capacity venue. It was an incredibly ambitious show but the six match bill was more like a tribute to the 1960's with a Les Kellett v Pallo himself match topping the programme plus the likes of Ricki Starr and Johnny Kwango appearing as well. It wasn't a success and it was the last major show Pallo put on until he tried a comeback with his WAW television shows at the end of the 1980's.

The next night on December 8th saw the final show of the year at the Royal Albert Hall and like the September show there only five matches on the bill. The top of the bill featured Marty Jones putting his newly won World Mid/Heavyweight Title on the line against Alan Kilby. Jones only needed half of the scheduled fifteen rounds to turn back the challenge of Kilby, dictating the match from start to finish. There were two tag matches on the bill as well, the first saw the newly crowned 'Top Tag Team' of Fit Finlay and Skull Murphy take on the much lighter and thoroughly over matched team of Pat Patton and Jackie Turpin. Finlay and Murphy didn't even break sweat in a two straight falls win and to make matters worse Turpin finished with blood pouring from a cut forehead. The other tag match saw the American midgets in action although they had long worn out their welcome. This time they partnered a normal wrestler each with Haiti Kid partnering Steve Grey whilst Carolina Kid paired up with Sid Cooper. Grey and Haiti Kid won by two falls to one and shortly after they returned home to the USA. Keith Haward made a return to Joint Promotions and faced old rival Clive Myers in a match that ended in a hard fought one each draw over eight round and finally Mel Stuart replaced Johnny Powers to take on popular John Elijah and it was Elijah who won with a knee drop and cross press giving him the only fall needed.

It wasn't a good show, there was nothing on offer that couldn't be seen around the normal town venues. It wasn't really a surprise then when it was announced that the 1982/83 season of shows there would be curtailed and no more of the advertised bills would take place. There was a combination of reasons, the recession was kicking in and leaving working class people losing their jobs as well as inflation hitting their disposable income. With the departures of Mark Rocco and Johnny Saint earlier in the year this had deprived Joint Promotions of two World Champions and there was simply not the level of matches to be made now that could fill a venue of the size and stature of the Albert Hall on a monthly basis anymore. Other central London venues such as the Hammersmith Odeon were considered as replacements but nothing came of it and London lost its premier wrestling venue to regular shows and it would be well over a year till wrestling was featured there again.

Big Daddy was back in action again on *World of Sport* on December 11th which would be the final time wrestling was shown that year. Daddy in front of his home town fans in Halifax partnered Pat Patton against King Kong Kirk and Scrubber Daly. After the now elaborate entrance for a TV match Daddy and Patton only needed a few minutes to see off Kirk and Daly by two falls to one. The show opener between John Naylor and King Ben saw a strange ending in the fourth round. Both wrestlers shoulders were counted by referee Emil Poilve at the same time for the count of three as Naylor attempted to pin Ben with a bridge. Therefore with only one fall needed for the win the result was a draw. The final match saw old rivals Jim Breaks and Vic Faulkner face each other once again. Kent Walton announced during the match that Faulkner would be reforming the 'Fabulous Royals' tag team shortly and they would be seen on TV in the new year. In the match Faulkner got the first fall with a folding press in the fifth round before Breaks got an equaliser in the sixth round after distracting Emil Poilve. Both wrestlers continued fighting after the bell ended and as it was a six round match the result was another draw that week.

The Hofmeister World Doubles Snooker championship replaced wrestling on December 18th and as Christmas Day fell on a Saturday that ended an eventful year for wrestling in Britain.

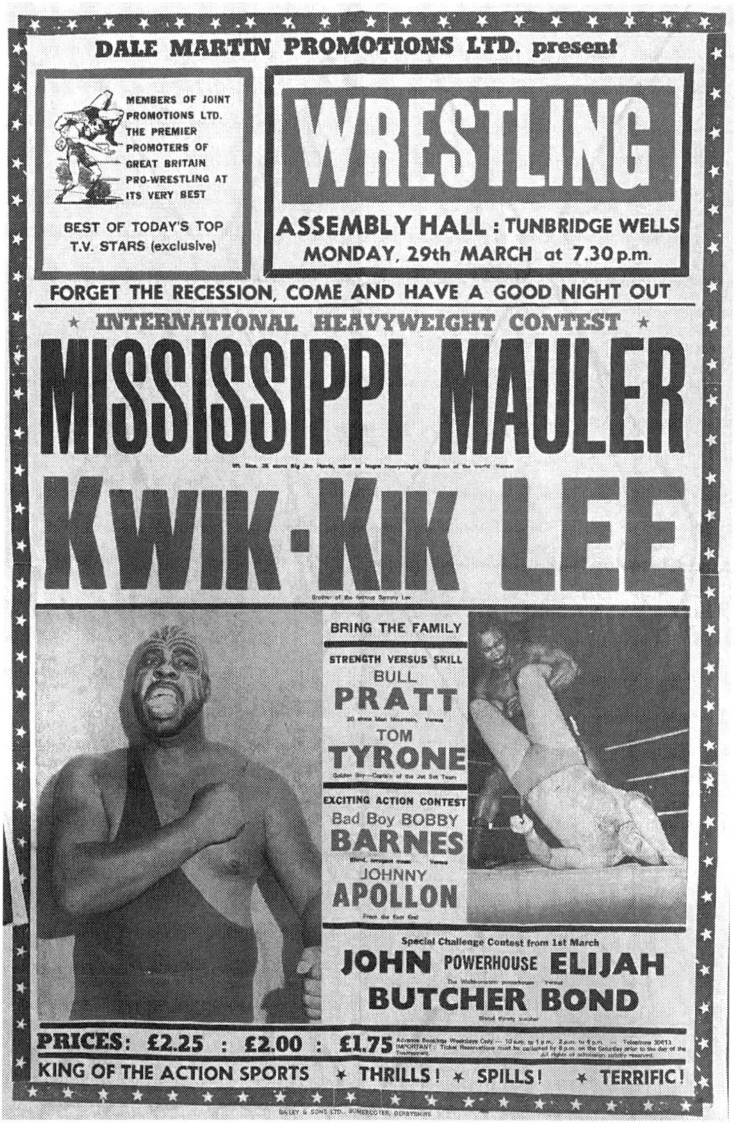
DALE MARTIN PROMOTIONS LTD. present
MEMBERS OF JOINT PROMOTIONS LTD. THE PREMIER PROMOTERS OF GREAT BRITAIN PRO-WRESTLING AT ITS VERY BEST
BEST OF TODAY'S TOP T.V. STARS (exclusive)
WRESTLING
ASSEMBLY HALL : TUNBRIDGE WELLS
MONDAY, 29th MARCH at 7.30 p.m.
FORGET THE RECESSION, COME AND HAVE A GOOD NIGHT OUT
★ INTERNATIONAL HEAVYWEIGHT CONTEST ★
MISSISSIPPI MAULER
KWIK-KIK LEE
BRING THE FAMILY
STRENGTH VERSUS SKILL
BULL
PRATT
TOM
TYRONE
EXCITING ACTION CONTEST
Bad Boy BOBBY
BARNES
JOHNNY
APOLLON
Special Challenge Contest from 1st March
JOHN POWERHOUSE ELIJAH
BUTCHER BOND
PRICES: £2.25 : £2.00 : £1.75
KING OF THE ACTION SPORTS ★ THRILLS! ★ SPILLS! ★ TERRIFIC!

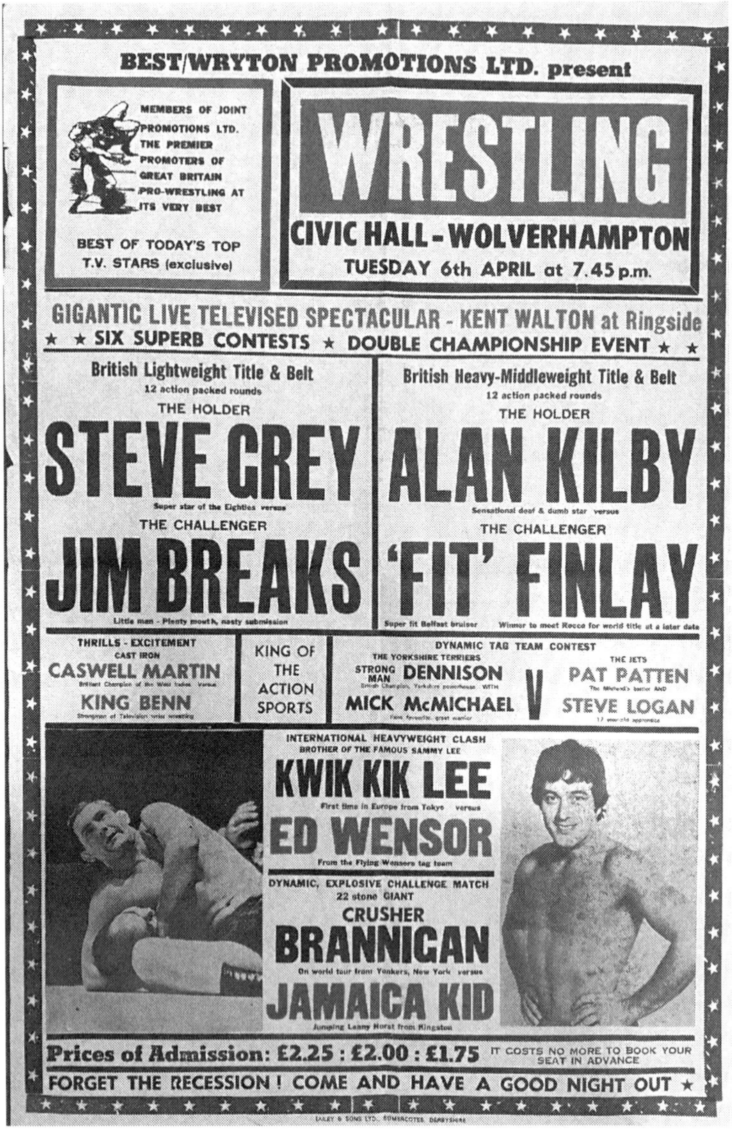
BEST/WRYTON PROMOTIONS LTD. present
MEMBERS OF JOINT PROMOTIONS LTD. THE PREMIER PROMOTERS OF GREAT BRITAIN PRO-WRESTLING AT ITS VERY BEST
BEST OF TODAY'S TOP T.V. STARS (exclusive)
WRESTLING
CIVIC HALL - WOLVERHAMPTON
TUESDAY 6th APRIL at 7.45 p.m.
GIGANTIC LIVE TELEVISED SPECTACULAR - KENT WALTON at Ringside
SIX SUPERB CONTESTS ★ DOUBLE CHAMPIONSHIP EVENT
British Lightweight Title & Belt
12 action packed rounds
THE HOLDER
STEVE GREY
Super star of the Eighties versus
THE CHALLENGER
JIM BREAKS
Little man - Plenty mouth, nasty submission
British Heavy-Middleweight Title & Belt
12 action packed rounds
THE HOLDER
ALAN KILBY
Sensational deaf & dumb star versus
THE CHALLENGER
'FIT' FINLAY
Super fit Belfast bruiser
Winner to meet Rocco for world title at a later date
THRILLS - EXCITEMENT
CAST IRON
CASWELL MARTIN
Brilliant Champion of the West Indies versus
KING BENN
KING OF THE ACTION SPORTS
DYNAMIC TAG TEAM CONTEST
THE YORKSHIRE TERRIERS
STRONG MAN DENNISON
British Champion, Yorkshire powerhouse WITH
MICK McMICHAEL
V
THE JETS
PAT PATTEN
STEVE LOGAN
INTERNATIONAL HEAVYWEIGHT CLASH
BROTHER OF THE FAMOUS SAMMY LEE
KWIK KIK LEE
First time in Europe from Tokyo versus
ED WENSOR
From the Flying Wensors tag team
DYNAMIC, EXPLOSIVE CHALLENGE MATCH
22 stone GIANT
CRUSHER
BRANNIGAN
On world tour from Yonkers, New York versus
JAMAICA KID
Jumping Lenny Hurst from Kingston
Prices of Admission: £2.25 : £2.00 : £1.75
IT COSTS NO MORE TO BOOK YOUR SEAT IN ADVANCE
FORGET THE RECESSION ! COME AND HAVE A GOOD NIGHT OUT

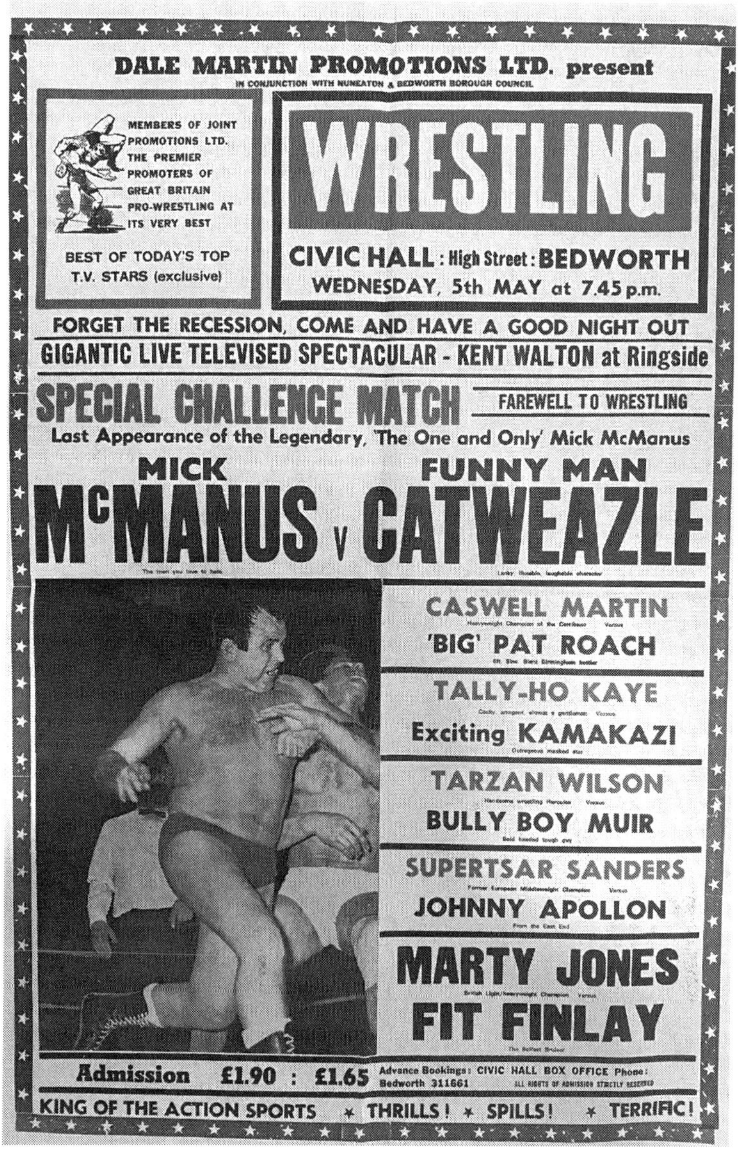

DALE MARTIN PROMOTIONS LTD. present
IN CONJUNCTION WITH NUNEATON & BEDWORTH BOROUGH COUNCIL
MEMBERS OF JOINT PROMOTIONS LTD. THE PREMIER PROMOTERS OF GREAT BRITAIN PRO-WRESTLING AT ITS VERY BEST
BEST OF TODAY'S TOP T.V. STARS (exclusive)
WRESTLING
CIVIC HALL : High Street : BEDWORTH
WEDNESDAY, 5th MAY at 7.45 p.m.
FORGET THE RECESSION, COME AND HAVE A GOOD NIGHT OUT
GIGANTIC LIVE TELEVISED SPECTACULAR - KENT WALTON at Ringside
SPECIAL CHALLENGE MATCH
FAREWELL TO WRESTLING
Last Appearance of the Legendary, 'The One and Only' Mick McManus
MICK McMANUS v FUNNY MAN CATWEAZLE
CASWELL MARTIN
'BIG' PAT ROACH
TALLY-HO KAYE
Exciting KAMAKAZI
TARZAN WILSON
BULLY BOY MUIR
SUPERTSAR SANDERS
JOHNNY APOLLON
MARTY JONES
FIT FINLAY
Admission £1.90 : £1.65
Advance Bookings: CIVIC HALL BOX OFFICE Phone: Bedworth 311661
KING OF THE ACTION SPORTS ✶ THRILLS! ✶ SPILLS! ✶ TERRIFIC!

CHAPTER 4 – 1983

With New Years Day falling on a Saturday and a full programme of sport to cover on *World of Sport* wrestling was shown in the usual 4pm slot. The show came from a new venue for the cameras, Haslingden in Lancashire. The first bout shown was an international heavyweight contest with Tom Tyrone taking on Len Hurst with only one fall needed for the win. In a minor upset Hurst got the winner in the third round with a cross press following a body slam. The rest of the show was a four man knockout tournament with Steve Grey, Sid Cooper, Tally Ho Kaye and Jackie Turpin competing for the prize. The first semi final saw Jackie Turpin tackle Tally Ho Kaye. Turpin surprised Kaye with a flying tackle to win in the final round to be the first into the final. It was Grey who went on to meet Turpin when he beat Cooper by two falls to one in his semi final. The final was fought under special rules with the winner the first to throw his opponent to the mat twenty times. It was Jackie Turpin who won by twenty throws to seventeen to claim the tournament prize.

By now the TV taping schedules were all over the place. The usual filming timetable for *World of Sport* would be to film somewhere in the week then show the first half the Saturday after followed by the second half of the show the following week. Now shows were broadcast in any kind of order with some months after they were recorded. As was the show screened on January 8th as it was back to Adwick Le Street for the second half of the show there filmed two months ago. The first match shown saw a TV debut for Saxon Brooks against Dave Lawrence. Brooks a young lad from the judo scene with a far from impressive physique. He was a light/heavyweight in build and was another of the stable containing opponent Lawrence, Grasshopper and Matt Matthews amongst others. It was Brooks who got the winning fall in the third round with a folding press. This was Lawrence's last appearance on TV and he disappeared from the ring shortly afterwards. Despite getting quite a push including being named 'Young Wrestler of the

Year' Brooks' professional wrestling career lasted less than a year.

The main match was Gil Singh facing Pete Roberts with Singh opening the score with a cross press in the second round. The restart was delayed after one of the ring boards was found to be broken. Once the action commenced again Roberts equalised in the fourth round with a body slam and cross press of his own to the polite applause of the fans. Singh was injured during the process and was very slow to start the fifth round but did so. Despite his injured leg Singh got the winning fall when he caught a Roberts' flying tackle and slammed him to the mat before covering him. MC Brian Crabtree announced the result before saying it was the one of hardest fought matches he had seen in the ring but the bout was fought in near silence with only quiet applause from the fans in attendance. Finally that week Ireland's Lucky Gordon took on Pat Patton and from the start Gordon was using the clenched fist much to commentator Kent Walton's disgust. Gordon got a submission with a back breaker in the third round to open the scoring before Patton rolled him up for the equalising fall in the fourth round. It was Patton who got the winner in the final round with a flying crucifix enough to put Gordon on the ground to cover him for the count of three.

Wrestling was missing from *World of Sport* on January 15th as the snooker classic from Warrington was shown at 4pm instead.

Halifax was the venue for the wrestling on January 22nd with three interesting matches lined up. The first being Alan Kilby v Honey Boy Zimba. The most interesting thing about the first round was Zimba continually arguing with a woman at ringside and he had more to argue about when Kilby won the match. In a clumsy match it was Kilby with a sort of suplex powerslam who got the only fall needed in the third round. Next up saw Marty Jones face Skull Murphy in a TV time limit of twenty minutes but still with two falls needed to win. In a bad tempered match both of them shunned the rules with Jones getting a public warning for an impressive cannonball from the top turnbuckle. With the match still scoreless after twelve minutes Jones seemed to slip on the canvas. Kent Walton thought that there was water on it from the previous bout. With Jones unable to continue referee Jeff Kaye decided to abandon the match and call it a No Contest. Last contest that week saw the youthful exuberance of Fit Finlay against the experienced Jim Moza. Finlay got an early fall before one of Moza's trademark dropkicks in the fourth round led to the equaliser. It was Finlay who got the winning fall in the final round with a Samoan drop after Moza had missed another dropkick.

The wrestling on *World of Sport* on January 29th came from Walthamstow and featured three heavyweight matches. The first of which saw Steve Logan who had matured into a fully grown heavyweight take on the colourful Magnificent Maurice. Maurice had returned to Joint Promotions after a few years away on the continent and also appearing on the independent circuit. Although it was Maurice who thought he had got the winning submission in the seventh round it was Logan who got the win as referee Joe D'Orazio disqualified Maurice for not releasing the hold when told to. The main match was Giant Haystacks against Kwik Kik Lee. Lee was approaching the end of his successful British tour and would shortly return home to Japan. Lee was unable to finish off with a win as Haystacks's weight advantage was too much to cope with. Following a missed flying tackle Lee was flattened by a big splash to end the match. The other heavyweight match on the show saw Ray Steele beat Butcher Bond who replaced Steve McHoy with the one fall needed in the fourth round.

The first shock of 1983 was Wayne Bridges giving in his notice to Joint Promotions and leaving to wrestle on the independent circuit. As with the other champions beforehand Bridges also took his 'World Heavyweight Title' with him. This led to an intriguing situation of there now being two 'World Heavyweight Champions' on the same circuit. It would take a couple of years for the title situation to be rectified but by 1985 Wayne Bridges was considered to the U.K. version of the World Heavyweight Champion. Before Bridges left Joint Promotions his next challenger from overseas was booked to be Bad News Allen from Calgary. Allen was a regular on the Stampede Promotions circuit and undoubtedly would have been a match worth seeing. The only thing we ended up seeing was

Allen's name and picture on the advertising posters for a month as his tour was cancelled.

A familiar name started to appear on the advertising for the shows towards the end of January, The Royals. It wasn't though the team that had been one of the fans favourites throughout the sixties and seventies that of Bert Royal and brother Vic Faulkner. This time it was Vic Faulkner who had returned to full time wrestling after a period of sporadic appearances after the retirement of Bert Royal in 1981. Faulkner was teaming with Junior Royal, who was in fact John Savage a young protege of Ted Betley following in the footsteps of Dynamite Kid and Davey 'Boy' Smith.

Another familiar face appeared on *World of Sport* on February 5th with the Dynamite Kid making a flying visit back home but he only had time to fit in the one match at Walthamstow. Dynamite was accompanied on the trip by Bruce Hart who came to the ring with him. With Mark Rocco no longer available Dynamite was matched with Marty Jones and their match was a cracker. For some reason Dynamite had forgotten the British rules and tested referee Joe D'Orazio's patience at times. Jones got the first fall in the third round with a small package after which Dynamite attacked him. He finally got the equaliser in the sixth round when he launched a flying head butt off the top rope and pinned Jones as a result. It was Jones who got the winning fall though in the seventh round when he reversed a folding press to roll up Dynamite Kid for the count of three. This new attitude of Dynamite Kid certainly angered the crowd at ringside but it would be the last time he wrestled for Joint Promotions. A new masked star appeared for the first time on TV that week, Battlestar who was billed as coming from the 'continent'. As soon as Battlestar entered the ring to face opponent Mick McMichael there was a familiarity about him. The minute the first bell rang and Battlestar locked up with his left handed style it was obvious it was Leeds heavyweight Barry Douglas under the mask. It was the masked man who won when McMichael was forced to submit in the third round when a lifted back hammer was applied. The final match saw 'Top Tag Team' title holders Fit Finlay and Skull

Murphy defeat 'The Jets' pairing of Tom Tyrone and Skull Murphy in the sixteenth minute.

The wrestling on *World of Sport* on February 12th came from Leamington Spa and was a very underwhelming show. The first match saw Johnny Wilson defeat Johnny South with the only fall needed in the second round. The second match was fought over the TV time limit of twenty minutes with no rounds and was between Ringo Rigby and King Ben. Ben got the first fall after a suplex in the thirteenth minute with Rigby equalising four minutes later with a roll up catching Ben unaware. With neither wrestler managing a winning fall in the four minutes left the result was a draw. It was announced during the match by Kent Walton that both Rigby and Ben would be part of the tournament to decide the new British Light/Heavyweight Champion after it was relinquished by Marty Jones. The other two wrestlers announced to be part of the tournament were Fit Finlay and Alan Kilby. The final match that week was a catchweight match with Clive Myers taking on the much heavier Pete Roberts. Roberts got the first fall in the third round with a double arm reversal before Myers equalised in the fifth round with a reverse double leg nelson. It was Roberts who won a superb technical match in the seventh round with a folding press. Yet again a sporting match was fought in near complete silence from the fans barring polite applause at the end of each round or when a fall was scored. People's appreciation for pure wrestling contests was beginning to wane.

The new Royals tag team were amongst the attractions of the second half of the Leamington Spa show screened the next week on *World of Sport* on February 19th. As part of a six man tag match Vic Faulkner and John Savage tagged with none other than Big Daddy against a team comprising of Battlestar, Banger Walsh and Blackjack Mulligan. With all manner of mayhem going on in the ring it was Faulkner who got the first fall in the ninth minute after a flying tackle and cross press on Battlestar. It was Daddy who finished off the match in the thirteenth minute with the double elbow drop on Walsh who had no chance of beating the count. Young David, Davey 'Boy' Smith made a quick visit home from North America and was matched against Bernie Wright who himself was on a short trip home from Canada. Five years on from when they first met on *World of Sport* both had grown significally and were now fully blown light or mid/heavyweights with the power to match. It was Smith who came out on top of this one with the winning fall coming in the final round. Johnny Kidd continued his run of tough TV matches in the final contest that week when he faced Mal Sanders. Despite a bright showing from Kidd it was Sanders who got the one fall needed to win in the fourth round with a perfect wrestlers bridge securing Kidd's shoulders to the mat.

The aforementioned tournament to decide the vacant British Light/Heavyweight Title was shown on *World of Sport* on February 26th from Harrogate. The first semi final was between Fit Finlay and Alan Kilby. Kilby was the British Heavy/Middleweight Champion but making the weight limit of 13st 5lbs was proving ever more difficult. The match had hardly warmed up when Kilby injured his shoulder in the fourth round and was unable to continue. The second final was a rematch between Ringo Rigby and King Ben of the drawn bout seen a couple of weeks previously. It was Rigby who pinned Ben in the third round for the only fall needed to win to progress to meet Finlay in the final. The final was fought over the championship time limit of twelve rounds and back to two falls etc. needed to win. Fit Finlay with his Samoan drop got the first fall on Rigby in the final seconds of the third round. Rigby with a flying tackle from the top of the cornerpost floored Finlay in the fourth round for the equalising fall. With the match perfectly poised it ended in the fifth round with Finlay attempting a second Samoan drop both wrestlers fell out of the ring over the top rope. Neither wrestler managed to beat the referee Roy Harding's count of ten to get back into the ring so it was a double count out result and a rematch would need to be held.

Snooker took the place of wrestling on *World of Sport* on March 5th.

Wrestling was back on *World of Sport* on March 12th from Oldham with the rematch for the vacant British Light/Heavyweight Title between Fit Finlay and Ringo Rigby the featured match. This time there was a winner and it was Fit

Finlay who came out the winner of a tremendous tussle when he got the winning fall in the eight round and so became the new British Light/Heavyweight Champion. The opening match that week saw King Kong Kirk beat John Cox with the guilottine drop enabling Kirk to get the winner in the second round. The other match shown saw Alan Dennison beat Jackie Turpin by two falls to one with a Boston Crab gaining the winning score for Dennison in the fourteenth minute.

Oldham was the venue on March 19th's *World of Sport* for the second half of the show recorded there. The first match saw Caswell Martin beat Steve Logan with the winner in the fifth round. Next to the ring was Giant Haystacks for his match against Steve McHoy with the contest scheduled for eight three minute rounds. For some reason timekeeper Terry Needham rang the bell after five minutes had been completed of the first round and not the required three. All that meant was two extra minutes of punishment for McHoy by Haystacks. The match was all over in the second round when an elbow drop from Haystacks left McHoy writhing in agony and the contest was stopped. As MC Brian Crabtree delivered the verdict Haystacks grabbed the microphone from him and demanded to see Crabtree's brother Big Daddy. Naturally Daddy came down to the ring , as he did so Haystacks swiped out at Brian Crabtree and left him knocked out on the canvas. As soon as Daddy got into the ring Haystacks fled whilst elsewhere Crabtree was carried back to the dressing room and Kent Walton was getting quite excited with it all. Big Daddy was at the show for the presentation of the 1982/83 Top Personalities of the Ring awards. The winners of the awards were :- The 'Most Popular Personality' won by Big Daddy. The 'Outstanding Champion' was won by Marty Jones. The 'Most Unpopular Personality' was won by Giant Haystacks. The 'Outstanding Newcomer' was won by Saxon Brooks and the 'Outstanding Tag Team' was won by Fit Finlay and Skull Murphy. On an eventful week the final contest shown was a tag match between the 'New Royals' Vic Faulkner and John Savage v 'The Rockers' Pete LaPaque and Tommy Lorne. Brian Crabtree with a nice, big plaster over his eye had recovered from being hit by Giant Haystacks to do the introductions. It was Savage who got the winning fall for the Royals when LaPaque mistimed a move off of the ropes and Savage who had a simple task to get a cross press.

After the thrills and spills of the Oldham show it was back to more mundane fayre on March 26th when the *World of Sport* cameras were at Aylesbury for the regular three bouts. Match number one saw John Naylor against Johnny Apollon. It was Naylor who got the only fall needed to win in the third round when he folded up Apollon for the count of three. The first of two heavyweight matches saw Terry Rudge take on Pete Roberts over the twenty minute TV time limit. In a typical British style heavyweight match Roberts got the first fall following a side suplex in the eleventh minute. In a match with the odd hint of needle and bad temper Rudge equalised in the sixteenth minute. With only four minutes left neither wrestler could obtain the winner so referee Peter Szakacs declared the match a draw. The other heavyweight match was between Pat Roach who had recently been filming for the new ITV series 'Auf Wiedersehen Pet' and Magnificent Maurice. Maurice brought out the best in Roach and forced him to work during the match instead of his usual coasting. Maurice got the first fall following a cannonball splash directly onto Roach in the fourth round. A now fired up Roach quickly equalised with a back drop leading to a cross press in the fifth round. It was Roach who got the winning fall in the seventh round when a hefty body slam led to a cross press which Maurice had no hope of kicking out from.

Jim Breaks finally dethroned Alan Dennison and regained the British Welterweight Title in a non televised match at Croydon on March 29th. Breaks got the winning fall in the ninth round and commenced loud celebrations. But it was Dennison who had the last laugh and reclaimed the title in his mandatory rematch at Cheltenham on April 25th. With the Royal Albert Hall shows now a distant memory plenty of title matches and changes were now happening on town and city shows away from the cameras or the usual publicity.

After the No Contest match shown on TV back in January Skull Murphy had successfully lobbied for a title match against World Mid/Heavyweight Champion Marty Jones and this was shown on *World of Sport* on April 2nd. This was the second half of the show recorded at Aylesbury and it was Jones who caught Murphy in a small package in the fourth round who scored the first fall. Jones was left with a bloodied forehead in the sixth round following a clash of heads which referee Max Ward deemed to be accidental. The match ended in the eighth round when Murphy punched Jones in his stomach right in front of Ward who instantly disqualified the challenger. The preliminary match that week saw Jim Moza take on Dave Duran. Duran the son of Harry Palin was making his TV debut. The bout had a quick ending when a back drop from Moza sent Duran flying over the top rope and taking a heavy landing amongst the ringsiders. There was no chance Duran could continue but the sporting Moza refused to accept the win in those circumstances so a No Contest was recorded. Finally in a routine international heavyweight match Tom Tyrone tackled Caswell Martin. It was Tyrone who got the winner in the final round with a folding press amongst much excitement from Kent Walton.

Eight of the lighter wrestlers lined up at Bedworth on *World of Sport* on April 9th for a knockout tournament. The participants were Jim Breaks, Pat Patton, Sid Cooper, Clive Myers, Steve Grey, Mick McMichael, Mal Sanders and Grasshopper. The four preliminary matches saw Mick McMichael beat Mal Sanders. Jim Breaks forced Grasshopper to submit with his 'Breaks special' in the third round. Steve Grey beat Clive Myers and Pat Patton upset Sid Cooper with a winning fall in the very first round with a crucifix. The first semi final saw Mick McMichael face Jim Breaks. Breaks let his temper and his big mouth get the better of him and referee Peter Szakacs disqualified him for dissent. The other semi final between Pat Patton and Steve Grey ended with neither wrestler scoring the fall needed to win in the five minute time limit. So it was down to a referee's decision and it was Patton who was awarded the verdict. The final ended in a one fall each draw with Patton getting the first fall in the sixth minute with a folding press surprising McMichael as he came off of the ropes. McMichael equalised two minutes later when a reverse suplex enabled him to pin Patton for the count of three. With no winner there would have to be a rematch to decide who would win the magnificent trophy.

On April 16th the wrestling shown on *World of Sport* was the second half of the show recorded at Haslingden the previous December. In a show without anything too exciting to report the first match saw Catweazle who was flitting between Joint Promotions and the independents take on Mel Stuart. After a round of the usual comedy it was Catweazle who got the winner in the second round with a folding press. After the antics of Catweazle in the first match things got serious in the second contest with Clive Myers facing Keith Haward with neither wrestler known for any comedy. It was Myers who got the first fall in the third round after a suplex before Haward levelled things in the fifth with a cross press after a hip toss. Neither wrestler got the winner in the sixth round so it was a hard fought one fall each draw. Finally Pat Roach took on Colin Joynson in which Roach got the first fall after weakening Joynson with a knee drop in the third round. Joynson got the equaliser after a body slam in the fifth round which took Roach by surprise. Roach got the winner straight away in the next round with a mighty body slam turned throw followed by a cross press .

On April 23rd the wrestling on *World of Sport* came from Harrogate and another show shown out of sequence as it was recorded back in February. The preliminary match saw John Naylor pinning Kid Chocolate with a double knee hold for the winning fall in the third round. Jim Breaks beat Steve Grey in a non title match by two falls to one and afterwards demanded a chance at Grey's British Lightweight Title. At the time the match was shown Breaks was still British Welterweight Champion thus causing confusion for those fans who attended the shows live. Finally there was another outing for the ' New Royals' when they took on Bobby Barnes and Tally Ho Kaye. Referee Roy Harding had his work cut out keeping order during the match and it was young John Savage who got the first fall on Bobby Barnes in the fifteenth minute. Barnes got his revenge on Savage when he forced him to submit to a Boston crab in the nineteenth minute. With only a minute left of the scheduled twenty minutes there was no time for either team to get a winner so Harding's decision was a draw.

The final show of April on *World of Sport* came from Colne which again had no obvious highlights with two rematches on the bill. Steve McHoy repeated a win over Barry Douglas. Whilst the trophy rematch between Mick McMichael and Pat Patton ended inconclusively once again this time in a No Contest. Finally King Kong Kirk beat Tom Tyrone who was unable to continue after Kirk had dropped the guillotine elbow on his neck.

The Jim Breaks title merry go round continued on *World of Sport* on May 7th when he beat Steve Grey to win the British Lightweight Title on a bill from Colne. Breaks who had defeated Grey in a non title match shown two weeks ago and this time with the belt at stake he beat Grey with the 'Breaks special' sealing the victory. Also featured was the build-up to the annual FA Cup Final World of Sport show. In what was rather a squash match two masked newcomers called 'The Masked Marauders' beat the far lighter pair of Colin Bennett and Eddie Riley by two straight falls. Afterwards their mouthpiece and manager of the Marauders , Charlie McGee issued a challenge to Big Daddy and a partner to take them on. That grapple fans is your FA Cup Final wrestling to be seen on May 21st.

Marty Jones' brief reign as World Mid/Heavyweight Champion came to an end at Croydon on May 10th at the hands of Fit Finlay. During the course of the bout Jones accidentally drop kicked referee Freddie Green. Whilst Green was lying stunned on the canvas Finlay trapped Jones by the leg in the ropes and aimed kick after kick at the helpless champion. Upon seeing Green struggle to his feet Finlay released Jones and immediately extracted a submission on the injured leg to take the title. Despite the controversial ending the result stood as the referee's decision at the time was final.

May 14th was back to Bedworth on *World of Sport* for the second half of the show recorded back in March. The preliminary match saw the hirsute Asian wrestler Little Prince take on the uncomprising John Wilkie. With only the one fall needed to win it was Little Prince who got the winner with a crotch hold and slam followed by a reverse double knee hold in the second round. Fit Finlay and Alan Kilby had yet another TV match with a rematch of the title tournament match where Kilby was unable to continue. With a twenty minute TV time limit it was Kilby who got his revenge when Finlay missed a flying headbutt and immediately submitted from a single Boston crab. Finally Pat Roach took on Ray Steele and in a dull, one paced match both wrestlers scored one fall in the six allotted rounds so a draw was the result.

The FA Cup Final on May 21st had special significance for me this year as my team Brighton were in the final for the very first time. After accepting the challenge of 'The Masked Marauders' Big Daddy had decided his partner would be Kid Chocolate for the bout held at Basildon shown during the build-up to the big match. It was nice to see both MC Peter Bates and the seconds wearing both teams rosettes and scarves when they introduced the teams. With no resemblance at all to a serious wrestling match, the Marauders who Kent Walton claimed not to know who they were but they came from Belgium took the early Big Daddy barrage before Chocolate tagged in. The big Marauder got the first submission with a Boston crab on Chocolate in the sixth minute. Once Daddy made the hot tag it was soon over with a big splash on the big Marauder to get the equalising fall followed by the double elbow drop on the smaller Marauder for the win in the ninth minute. Both Marauders fled the ring before they could traditionally unmask after the defeat but it was no secret to the fans that they were Scrubber Daly and Lucky Gordon. As the Marauders were fleeing King Kong Kirk entered the ring to challenge Big Daddy but to no avail as Daddy sent Kirk flying over the top rope with Charlie McGee following him for good measure.

The wrestling on May 28th came from Bradford and featured Steve Grey's return match with Jim Breaks for the British Lightweight Title he had lost three weeks ago on TV. This time Breaks's temper once again let him down and he was disqualified so once more Grey was the champion. The opener that week saw Johnny Kidd have yet another tough match in front of the cameras when he took on Vic Faulkner. Despite another good showing from Kidd it was Faulkner who got the winner with a reverse double arm fall in the third round. The final match saw King Kong Kirk destroy Johnny Wilson when the guillotine neck drop brought about an immediate end to the match as Wilson writhed around the ring clutching his throat. An interested spectator watching the match was Big Daddy and afterwards he accepted Kirk's challenge to a solo match.

June started on a bright note for Marty Jones when he regained the World Mid/Heavyweight Title from Fit Finlay at Croydon when the champion submitted to Jones's new powerlock submission hold. A titleless Finlay accompanied by Pete Roberts took his wounded pride to Japan for the Summer months. Giant Haystacks headed overseas as well whilst up and coming Birmingham youngster Steve Logan headed to Canada to hone his skills on the Stampede circuit.

Wrestling was missing on *World of Sport* for the first two Saturdays in June with Golf replacing it on the 4th and the schoolboy's football shown instead on June 11th.

After the two blank weeks wrestling returned to *World of Sport* on June 18th with a bill from Derby. The main event was advertised in that week's TV Times as being Alan Dennison defending his British Welterweight Title against Steve Grey who had recently regained the British Lightweight Title. Unfortunately Dennison was an absentee so he was replaced by Pete LaPaque in a non title match. Grey got the first fall in the third round with a neat folding press before LaPaque levelled the match in the fifth round when he forced Grey to submit. Grey got the winner though when he forced LaPaque to submit this time with the surfboard in the seventh round. The opener that week saw Ringo Rigby beat Lucky Gordon with a folding press that looked very near the ropes for the winning fall in the fifth round. The other match was a catchweight contest with the TV time limit of twenty minutes between Pete Roberts and Keith Haward which ended in a one fall each draw. Roberts reversed a whip to get a folding press in the thirteenth minute before Haward equalised with a folder himself in the seventeenth minute.

Grapple fans were disappointed on June 25th as wrestling was missing from *World of Sport* when the Dutch 500cc motor bike race was shown.

Wrestling was back on *World of Sport* on July 2nd from Stockport and the highlight should have been the lumberjack challenge match between Big Daddy and King Kong Kirk but Kirk had departed for the continental tournaments. For those backstage the highlight of the show was when former wrestler Hans Streiger who lived locally turned up for a 'discussion' with Big Daddy and Max Crabtree but was ushered away before any damage was done. Kirk's replacement in the lumberjack match turned out to be the bigger of the Masked Marauders who again was accompanied by Charlie McGee. The match if you could call it that lasted just over two minutes before Daddy knocked out the Marauder and afterwards ripped off the mask to reveal to nobodies surprise that it was Scrubber Daly. Perhaps it would have been more entertaining if it had been Hans Streiger taking on Big Daddy in the match ? The opening match saw the ever unpopular Sid Cooper take on 'Fireman' Colin Bennett who entered the ring in his uniform complete with bright yellow helmet. With only one score needed it was Cooper who got the winner in the fourth round with a single leg Boston crab after Bennett had mistimed a drop kick. A heavyweight match saw Tom Tyrone take on Colin Joynson which ended in an eight round draw with Tyrone's fall in the seventh round equalising Joynson's fall in the fourth.

Instead of the second half of the Stockport show on July 9th on *World of Sport* it was the second half of the Bradford show recorded in May instead. The highlight of the week was a tag match between Fit Finlay and Skull Murphy against Marty Jones and Clive Myers which ended in a one each draw after twenty minutes of frenzied action. Alan Dennison beat Rick Wiseman by the only fall needed and Alan Kilby beat Saxon Brooks with a side slam followed by cross press in the fifth round for the deciding fall. Afterwards Kent Walton told us that we would be seeing more of Brooks no question about it but in fact we didn't, that was the last time he was seen.

The second half of the Stockport show was shown on July 16th with the main match featuring Crusher Brannigan who had returned to Britain for the Summer season. He made short work of his opponent Johnny South with South failing to beat the count after Brannigan's elbow drop from the corner post landed on him. Pat Patton beat Banger Walsh by disqualification in the third round whilst Tally Ho Kaye beat Eddie Riley with the winning submission coming in the sixth round.

Also happening on July 16th was wrestling returning to Belle Vue in Manchester but this time it would be held in the Cumberland Suite. This was a lot smaller venue than the historic King's Hall which held five thousand or so and in it's heyday was packed each Saturday night. Regular Saturday night shows were held in the Cumberland Suite for the rest of 1983 but with crowds not as big as anticipated wrestling again departed from Belle Vue.

The 'Top Tag Team' titles were up for grabs on July 23 on *World of Sport* in the other half of the Derby show seen a month before. The four teams fighting it out were the 1982 winners Fit Finlay and Skull Murphy, Marty Jones and Clive Myers, Honey Boy Zimba and Len Hurst & John Naylor and King Ben. The first semi final saw Finlay and Murphy taking on Zimba and Hurst. It was Finlay who opened the scoring in the seventh minute with a Samoan drop on Hurst followed by a cross press for the first fall. Hurst levelled the match with a cross press after a high back drop had weakened Murphy in the seventeenth minute. There was to be no upset as Murphy got the winning fall a minute later after Zimba was distracted. The other semi final between Marty Jones and Clive Myers and John Naylor and King Ben was a lot more sporting and Jones got the first fall in the sixth minute when a wrestler's bridge secured Naylor's shoulders to the mat for the count of three. Ben equalised after flying headbutt stunned Myers enough for an easy cross press in the eleventh minute. Myers though got the winner with a reverse double leg nelson in the thirteenth minute to send him and Jones through to the final. The two teams in the final had already wrestled a draw recently on TV and the final of the tournament ended the same way. Finlay got the first fall in the twelfth minute with yet again the Samoan drop weakening Jones for the count of three. Jones got the equaliser when he clamped Finlay into the powerlock for an immediate submission with only a minute left of the match. Despite both team's best efforts in the final minute neither of them could get a winner so there would need to be a rematch.

World of Sport on July 30th recorded at Woking saw two newcomers amongst the three matches. The first of them was Paul Britton who took on the veteran Cypriot Tony Costas in that weeks preliminary contest. In a one fall match it was Costas who got it with a double leg nelson in the second round. After that contest which was fought to silence from the fans they were put through the mill again when Ray Steele and Gil Singh wrestled a scoreless twenty minute time limit draw. The other TV newcomer was the Ulsterman Rocky Moran who had been a stalwart for Brian Dixon , Orig Williams and other promoters in his native country for quite a while. Therefore it was a surprise to see him appear for Joint Promotions. At least he started with a bang as his TV debut saw him challenge Alan Kilby for the British Heavy/Middleweight Title. Kent Walton actually announced that this was only his second appearance on TV but in fact the first televised match for Moran hadn't yet been shown on TV. Moran got the first fall in the third round when he pinned Kilby after a body slam. Kilby immediately got the equaliser in the next round with cross press following a suplex. The end came in the seventh round when Moran missed a flying head butt from the top of the corner post which left him with a cut forehead. Referee Peter Szakacs had no option but to stop the contest and declare Kilby the winner much to Moran's frustration.

Another wrestler made his *World of Sport* debut the following week on August 6th which was the second half of the bill recorded at Basildon back in May. Jack Regan introduced in his first TV match as a former SAS soldier took on Sid Cooper in that week's opener. To nobodies surprise Cooper got the one fall required in the third round after a body slam weakened Regan. A middleweight match fought over twenty minutes with no rounds saw old rivals Mal Sanders and Keith Haward face each other again. With both wrestlers on their best behaviour for once it was Haward who got the winning fall following a body slam in the eighteenth minute. The final match saw Ringo Rigby making a rare TV appearance when he beat Bobby Barnes by two falls to one.

Wrestling was missing from *World of Sport* on August 13th when the World Athletic Championships from Helsinki was shown instead.

The *World of Sport* cameras made their annual trek to the North East coast for the show from Bridlington screened on August 20th. A rather awkward opener between Little Prince and Steve Casey which saw neither's styles mesh was won by Prince by in the fourth round with an arm lever submission. A heavyweight match saw Barry Douglas overcome a three stone or so weight disadavantage to beat John Cox by two falls to one.

The bout that the packed crowd had all come to see though was the tag match between Big Daddy and Pat Patton & King Kong Kirk and Banger Walsh. Kirk had recently returned from the continent which forced him to miss the intended lumberjack match with Daddy earlier in the summer. Kirk and Walsh had teamed up with manager Charlie McGee. Walsh had a rugby skull cap on as well as wearing a full rugby kit instead of the traditional ring attire. It wasn't only Walsh who sported daft head gear as McGee was sporting a tin foil helmet at ringside for the duration of the match. Kirk got the first score when Patton was counted out after a neck drop followed by a mighty body slam saw him fail to beat the count of ten. Daddy as per the rules of the match then had to carry on alone as MC Gordon Pryor instructed Kirk and Walsh. Daddy swiftly equalised when once again the double elbow drop gave Walsh no chance of beating the count. Before the match could restart with Daddy v Kirk Giant Haystacks who had recently returned from Canada appeared at ringside and gave us the usual spiel of hunting down Daddy everywhere he went. The match finally restarted or didn't as Kirk then left the ring and joined Haystacks in going back to the dressing room and Kirk was counted out by referee Peter Szakacs to leave the crowd happy.

The small town of Swadlincote in Derbyshire was the venue for *World of Sport* on August 27th with a tag match the feature. It was the rematch for the 1983 'Top Tag Team' titles between Marty Jones and Clive Myers & Fit Finlay and Skull Murphy. Both team's styles meshed very well and yet again it was an exceptional tag match. This time the match was scheduled for thirty minutes so hopefully there would be a conclusive ending to the match. The early minutes saw both teams feeling each other out but once Jones and Finlay squared up in the ring it upped a gear. As the action heated up referee Jeff Kaye issued a public warning to Finlay and Murphy before they softened up Myers with various tactics most of which were illegal. Finally Jones made a hot tag and after a couple of brutal face down drops he easily folded up Finlay for the first fall in the fifteenth minute. Once the match restarted it carried on at its fast pace with the Jones and Finlay rivalry being a sub plot within it especially when Jones sent Finlay flying into his partner Murphy on the apron. Murphy seemed to have Jones at his mercy when he hoisted him aloft ready for a pile driver but Jones reversed it and delivered it to Murphy instead. With about six minutes left Finlay took a crazy bump missing a flying head butt from the top of the corner post and as Jones attempted a flying tackle both wrestlers went flying over the top rope. Neither could make it back inside the ropes before the count of ten. With the Jones and Myers team already one fall ahead and both teams suffering a knockout therefore it was Marty Jones and Clive Myers who were the new holders of the 'Top Tag Team' titles. Very little was heard of them going forward as a team as Jones concentrated on his feud with Fit Finlay for the World Mid/Heavyweight Title. For me the match was a four star rating. It would have been a five star if the finish hadn't been so complicated it needed explaining by Kent Walton.

Keith Haward easily dispatched opponent Kurt Heinz in the opener with a brutal looking German suplex onto the back of Heinz's neck which gave him no chance of continuing and Haward was declared the winner by knockout. The other match saw local lad Grasshopper wrestle a one fall each draw over eight rounds with Kid Chocolate. The match was cut short after Chocolate equalised in the sixth round so the tag match could be shown in its entirety.

Wrestling was missing from *World of Sport* on September 3rd when the European Golf Open was shown. Whilst on September 10th coverage of the previous night's boxing title match between Aaron Pryor and Alexis Arguello was on instead.

The second half of the Swadlincote show was shown on September 17th as wrestling returned to *World of Sport* with a four man knockout tournament for the Silver Plate as its feature. The first semi final saw Jim Breaks face Rick Wiseman in a ten minutes duration match with the first fall etc to decide. In the last minute after a series of weakeners Breaks finally applied the 'special' to which Wiseman immediately submitted. The second semi final was between Alan Dennison and Eddie Riley which was won by Dennison when he folded up Riley with a double knee hold for the the count of three in the ninth minute. The final was fought over fifteen minutes this with the usual two falls etc to decide with old adversaries Breaks and Dennison fighting it out. Dennison got the first fall in the eighth minute with a simple folding press before Breaks equalised with the exact same move which caught not only Dennison but Kent Walton by surprise in the eleventh minute. The fifteen minutes time limit was reached before either wrestler could get the decider. Referee Emil Poilve had to choose the winner and it was Alan Dennison who got the nod much to Jim Breaks's fury. Referee Poilve explained it was the fact that Breaks got two public warnings that was decider and the Mayor of South Derbyshire presented Dennison with the splendid Silver Plate.

The fans at the Colston Hall in Bristol on September 29th saw the debut for Dale Martin of a young sixteen old named Danny Collins. Collins met regular job guy Adrian Finch and they wrestled a one fall each draw over six rounds. It was hardly a foretaste of things to come but from there on Collins had a rocket strapped to his backside and had a push that even the likes of Dynamite Kid hadn't got when he started out.

It would be four weeks before the next wrestling was shown on *World of Sport* with golf shown on September 24th. October 1st saw the Jameson International snooker tournament shown and on October 8th more snooker was shown at 4pm much to the fan's anger.

Big Daddy was the attraction when wrestling returned to *World of Sport* on October 15th on a bill from Crewe. Daddy and partner Alan Kilby beat the team of King Kong Kirk and Bruiser Muir with the usual barrage of belly butts and flops to the fore. Pete Roberts beat Len Hurst in a heavyweight tussle by two falls to one with a double arm nelson sealing the victory in the eighth round. The other match was a quick look at Alan Dennison beating Tally Ho Kaye by the only fall needed.

Wrestling again was missing from *World of Sport* on October 22nd with darts this time being shown at 4pm. It's a good job there was no social media in the 1980's as I'm sure there would have been a massive twitter campaign over wrestling being taken off of TV nearly every week.

Jim Breaks once again became British Welterweight Champion on October 25th in another non televised match at Croydon. In a very heated match the 'Breaks special' once again proved the difference between him and the champion Alan Dennison. On the same bill Alan Kilby was incredibly lucky to keep hold of his British Heavy/Middleweight Title against Mal Sanders. Kilby was injured missing an attempted pinfall and was unable to continue. Surprisingly his opponent Sanders declared he didn't want to become champion in such a manner and refused to accept the win.

Wrestling once again returned to Liverpool Stadium on October 28th with Wrestling Enterprises presenting an eight man knockout tournament. A high class list of wrestlers competing saw Mark Rocco, Johnny Saint, Kung Fu, Brian Maxine, Johnny Palance, Mike Jordan, Mike Bennett and Rob Brookside battle it out. Rocco beat Maxine in the final to win the tournament.

Keith Haward defended his European Middleweight Title against King Ben when wrestling was back on *World of Sport* on October 29th. Ben got the opening fall in the fifth round following a crutch hold and slam with Haward equalising in the eight round with a double arm suplex and an awkward looking pin. Haward retained his title and the belt in the tenth round with a German suplex this time securing Ben's shoulders to the mat for the winning fall. With the title match going ten rounds there was only time to show one more bout on the bill from Croydon and that saw Clive Myers beat Steve Grey by two falls to one in the sixth round.

An interesting line up of three bouts was shown on *World of Sport* on November 5th as wrestling returned to Crewe for the second half of the bill taped from there. The top match was an intriguing battle between Giant Haystacks and Crusher Brannigan who had fought as partners in tag matches on the circuit. Haystacks dwarfed the far from small Brannigan as referee Jeff Kaye issued his pre match instructions which would be ignored anyway. Kent Walton spent the early minutes worrying whether the ring would hold up to their combined weight and hoping they didn't come over the rope to where he was sitting. Haystacks got a public warning in the first round for continually striking Brannigan as he was on the ropes as Brannigan tried to retaliate but his blows had no impact on the big man. Haystacks got his second public warning as he dished out a series of head butts which cut Brannigan's forehead wide open. Jeff Kaye stopped the match in the second round with blood pouring down Brannigan's head and fearing he had a concussion awarded the victory to Haystacks. The second main match saw the Marty Jones and Fit Finlay rivalry ramp up a few notches as they met in a non title contest. Finlay took the lead in the fourth round after catching Jones mid air and the Samoan drop led to the first fall. Jones equalised with the powerlock submission in the fifth round after a couple of knee weakeners left Finlay tapping immediately. With one round left it was Finlay who won the match when Skull Murphy distracted Jones from ringside. After trapping Jones leg in the ropes Finlay quickly got the winning submission from a Boston crab. As MC Brian Crabtree delivered the result Finlay challenged Jones to put his title on the line against him.

Grapple fans didn't have long to wait till they saw the match as the following Saturday on November 12th on *World of Sport* Marty Jones accepted the challenge in a show from Leeds. Before the title match was shown Vic Faulkner took on Rocky Moran in a twenty minute time limit opener. Despite his advancing years Faulkner hadn't lost any of his skills or indeed any of his popularity with the crowd in attendance. Moran though got the first fall with a body slam followed by a cross press in the seventh minute. Faulkner won the match when Moran was counted out after falling from the ring in the twelfth minute although the ever sporting Faulkner tried to refuse to accept the decision. The rest of the programme was the World Mid/Heavyweight Title contest with champion Marty Jones defending against Fit Finlay. Not only was this the best contest I saw on TV in 1983 it was easily in the top five of best matches I saw in the decade. Not many wrestlers had the conditioning or fitness to wrestle at the pace they did for the forty minutes or so the fifteen round match lasted. Finlay was accompanied to the ring for the first time by Princess Paula , his real life wife and one of the best lady wrestlers around in Paula Valdez. Amazingly the match went scoreless for the first ten rounds before Finlay got the first fall in the eleventh round. Jones got his first public warning as his attempts for an equaliser got ever urgent. Finlay got his second public warning in the fourteenth round after getting his first in the eighth. The story of the last couple of rounds was Jones continually trying to weaken Finlay's leg and attempting to apply the powerlock submission. Eventually time ran out and the bell sounded at the end of the fifteenth round with Finlay still ahead through his fall in the eleventh round. As a result of this Fit Finlay was the new World Mid/Heavyweight Champion amidst great celebrations from him and Paula as Jones stood there in shock. One of the rare times I'd give a match a five star rating with the two brilliant wrestlers in action, a perfect story told throughout leading up to Jones's desperation to get an equaliser to retain his title.

There was more drama the following week on *World of Sport* on November 19th with the second half of the Leeds show. The opener saw Pete Ross face Elvis Jerome, Jerome was had also wrestled as Dave Cameron and The Godfather. The match ended in the fourth round with neither wrestler able to beat the count of ten after the usual both wrestlers going over the top rope spot after a flying tackle. The second match saw local favourite Gil Singh tackle Colin Joynson with the honours going to Singh by two falls to one in the seventh round. The final match was advertised in that week's TV Times as Jim Breaks v John Naylor but with Naylor unavailable his place was taken at short notice by Danny Collins. It was Collins much to Breaks's anger who got the first fall in the second round after which Breaks got a public warning for attacking the youngster in his corner. It didn't take Breaks long to get an equaliser though as a couple of arm weakeners followed by the

'Breaks special' was enough to see Collins submit. The minute's rest between rounds was not enough for Collins to recover and as soon as the bell for the fourth sounded Breaks immediately applied the 'special' again for the winner.

The second half of the Woking show recorded back in June popped up on *World of Sport* on November 26th. The main event was a tag match with the Wilson Brothers, Johnny and Peter taking on a weird combination of John Elijah and Butcher Bond. TV was the best selling point available for wrestling so why would you want to go to a live event at your local hall after watching seventeen minutes or so of this match ? Technically it was sound but entertainment wise it was rotten. It was a very slow paced match with strength hold after strength hold interupted by the odd throw or move off the ropes. Even Bond fought within the rules instead of livening it up with some rulebreaking. Bond got the first fall in the eight minute with a hip toss followed by a cross press over Johnny Wilson. The same two were involved in the equaliser with a suplex from Wilson leading to another cross press in the eleventh minute. Peter Wilson got the winner in the seventeenth minute when he reversed a back breaker attempt from Elijah to pin him with a folding press. Another match on TV fought to near silence throughout with just a smattering of polite applause at the end. Even MC Peter Bates was annoying with him continually announcing the Wilsons as the 'Popular' Wilson Brothers when there was no reaction to them whatsoever from the fans. Incidentally this was the final time Bates was seen as the MC on TV, his aloofness to the fans and his lack of charisma or oratory never improved in the five years he was doing the job. At the least the main supporting match that week got the crowd going with Bobby Barnes facing Mal Sanders and it was Sanders who got the win with Barnes being disqualified in the final round. The preliminary match saw the TV debut of 'Chesterfield' Ray Smith who took on fellow Derbyshire wrestler Grasshopper and it was Grasshopper who got the only fall needed in the third round.

Also on November 26th Marty Jones got a semblance of revenge against Fit Finlay when he relieved Finlay of his

British Light/Heavyweight Title in a championship match at Belle Vue that evening.

December saw the arrival of another two brothers from the Calgary based Hart family with this time Owen and Ross making the trip across the Atlantic. Owen was just over eighteen at this point but he showed great potential in his matches during the month or so he was here. The duo alternated particpating in solo matches or as the 'Calgary Cowboys' tag team and they quickly became firm favourites of those in attendance.

The first two *World of Sport* wrestling shows in December featured a team match taped at Kidderminster with Big Daddy captaining one team whilst Giant Haystacks captained the other. On the December 3rd show Lucky Gordon for the Haystacks team beat TV newcomer Andy Blair with a piledriver ensuring Blair failed to beat the count in the fourth round. Alan Kilby for the Daddy team faced Johnny Apollon with the winner for Kilby coming from a powerslam and cross press in the sixth round. Giant Haystacks made it two-one for his team when knocking out Ray Steele in the third round with his guillotine neck drop.

On December 10th Pat Patton for the Daddy team made it two wins each when he beat John Wilkie by two falls to one with a flying tackle getting the winning fall in the sixth round. Next up saw Big Daddy make it three-two to his team when he slung opponent Scrubber Daly through the ropes after only a minute or so of the match and Daly failed to make it back to the ring in time. Alan Dennison for Daddy's team then made it four-two in the final singles match when his opponent Steve Speed tumbled out of the ring and was unable to continue. Dennison tried to refuse to accept the win but due to the rules of the match was not allowed to. Finally it was time for the six man tag team finale with Big Daddy joined by Alan Kilby and Pat Patton to take on Giant Haystacks who was accompanied by Scrubber Daly and Lucky Gordon. It was Haystacks who got the first fall when a big splash on Patton left him no chance of beating the count which then left Daddy and Kilby to go on alone. Daddy soon equalised with a big splash of his own on Daly followed by a cross press. It was Kilby who got the

131

winner with a suplex on Gordon followed by another cross press in the ninth minute. So the result of the tournament saw Big Daddy's 'TV All Stars' defeat Giant Haystacks's 'Wrecking Crew' by five wins to two.

Wrestling was missing from *World of Sport* on December 17th as the Hofmeister World Doubles snooker was on at 4pm. On Christmas Eve there was no World of Sport broadcast at all. The Adam Ant 'Prince Charming Revue' followed by the film 'Jason and the Argonauts' was shown instead.

The final *World of Sport* of the year on December 31st saw Fit Finlay make his first televised defence of the World Mid/Heavyweight Title but it wasn't against Marty Jones. Finlay was keeping Jones waiting for his mandatory rematch and instead defended the title against Chic Cullen. Cullen had been something of a globetrotter since his brief spell wrestling for Joint Promotions during the winner of 1980/81. As well as many appearances on the UK independent circuit he had made quite a name for himself wrestling in Canada for Stu Hart's Stampede Promotion. It was a measure of how much Finlay had improved as a champion that he beat Cullen without too many problems. The winning fall came yet again by way of the Samoan drop after Cullen had a nasty looking landing from the top corner post onto his neck. With Princess Paula at ringside encouraging her man it looked like they would make a formidable combination to anyone. The other match shown saw Pat Roach who now was also being shown on prime time ITV playing the part the of Bomber a former wrestler in Auf Wiedersehen Pet take on Pete Roberts. As part of his introduction in the show Roach was seen wrestling Roberts which was great publicity for wrestling in general. In this match Roach used his weight and height advantage to take the win by two falls to one.

So 1983 ended with the usual drama both inside and outside the ring but the worrying aspect was the decline in the numbers of paying customers going to the shows and the cutback in terms of shows each night.

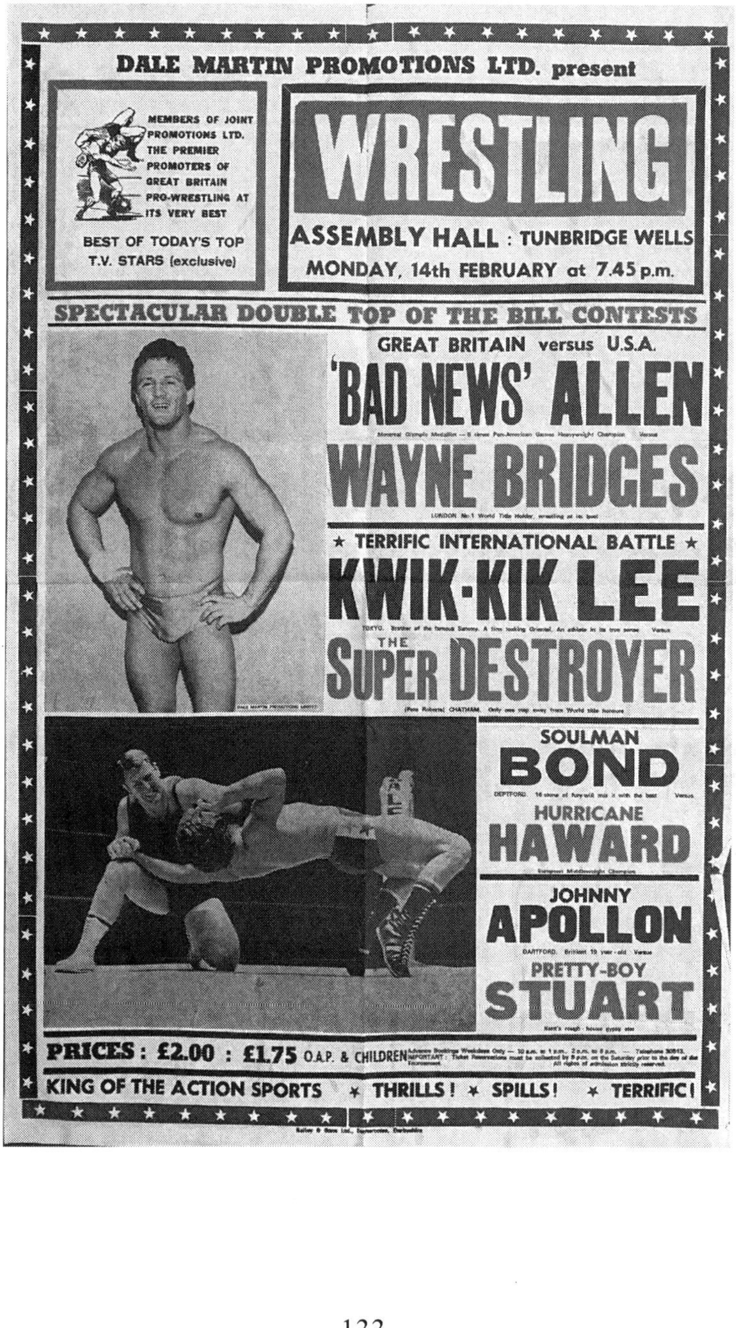
DALE MARTIN PROMOTIONS LTD. present
MEMBERS OF JOINT PROMOTIONS LTD. THE PREMIER PROMOTERS OF GREAT BRITAIN PRO-WRESTLING AT ITS VERY BEST
BEST OF TODAY'S TOP T.V. STARS (exclusive)
WRESTLING
ASSEMBLY HALL : TUNBRIDGE WELLS
MONDAY, 14th FEBRUARY at 7.45 p.m.
SPECTACULAR DOUBLE TOP OF THE BILL CONTESTS
GREAT BRITAIN versus U.S.A.
'BAD NEWS' ALLEN
WAYNE BRIDGES
★ TERRIFIC INTERNATIONAL BATTLE ★
KWIK-KIK LEE
THE SUPER DESTROYER
SOULMAN
BOND
HURRICANE
HAWARD
JOHNNY
APOLLON
PRETTY-BOY
STUART
PRICES : £2.00 : £1.75 O.A.P. & CHILDREN
KING OF THE ACTION SPORTS ★ THRILLS ! ★ SPILLS ! ★ TERRIFIC !

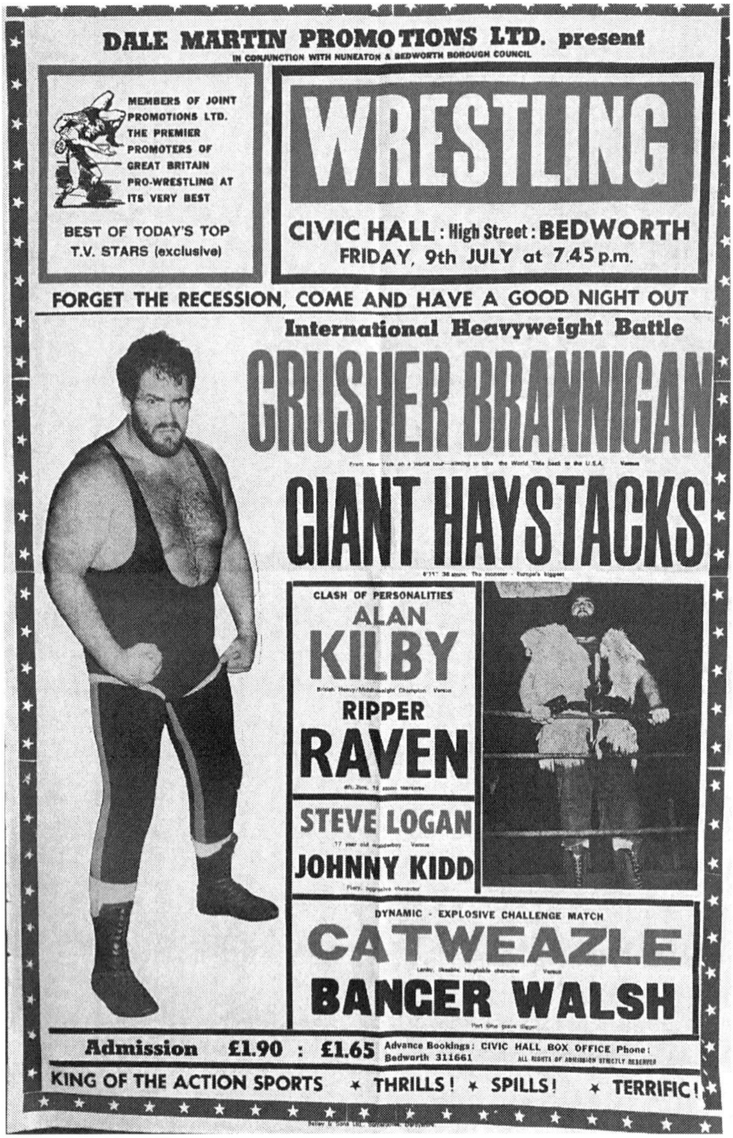

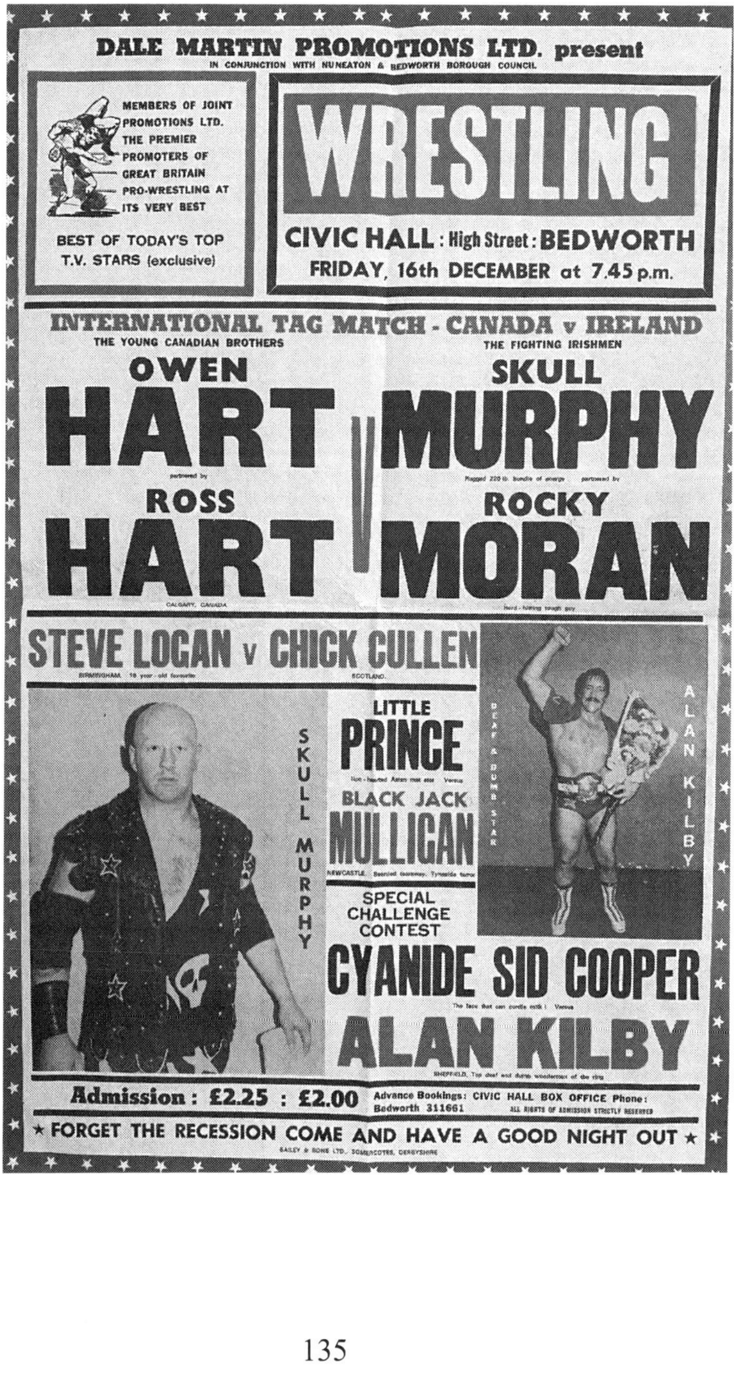

DALE MARTIN PROMOTIONS LTD. present
IN CONJUNCTION WITH NUNEATON & BEDWORTH BOROUGH COUNCIL
MEMBERS OF JOINT PROMOTIONS LTD. THE PREMIER PROMOTERS OF GREAT BRITAIN PRO-WRESTLING AT ITS VERY BEST
BEST OF TODAY'S TOP T.V. STARS (exclusive)
WRESTLING
CIVIC HALL : High Street : BEDWORTH
FRIDAY, 16th DECEMBER at 7.45 p.m.
INTERNATIONAL TAG MATCH - CANADA v IRELAND
THE YOUNG CANADIAN BROTHERS
OWEN HART
ROSS HART
v
THE FIGHTING IRISHMEN
SKULL MURPHY
ROCKY MORAN
STEVE LOGAN v CHICK CULLEN
SKULL MURPHY
LITTLE PRINCE
BLACK JACK MULLIGAN
DEAF & DUMB STAR
ALAN KILBY
SPECIAL CHALLENGE CONTEST
CYANIDE SID COOPER
ALAN KILBY
Admission : £2.25 : £2.00
Advance Bookings: CIVIC HALL BOX OFFICE Phone: Bedworth 311661
★ FORGET THE RECESSION COME AND HAVE A GOOD NIGHT OUT ★

Chapter 5 – 1984

The first *World of Sport* of 1984 on January 7th featured the Hart brothers making their TV debuts in the second half of the Macclesfield show. Perhaps Ross Hart drew the short straw as he was booked to wrestle Marty Jones. The bigger Jones gave Ross something of a tough introduction to British wrestling with Jones winning when one of his dropkicks landed on Hart's jaw in the third round and he was unable to beat the count. Owen Hart was matched with Steve Logan who himself had only recently returned from Canada and wrestling for Stampede Wrestling himself. Logan got the first fall in the fourth round with a cross press although Kent Walton remarked it looked suspiciously like Logan's feet were under the ropes. Hart got the equaliser in the fifth round with an acrobatic leap off of the top cornerpost which caught Logan by surprise and Hart rolled him up for the folding press. Neither wrestler was able to get a winning fall in the final round so a draw was the verdict of an excellent contest between two great prospects. The other contest screened that week was a tag match between the now regular pairing of Bobby Barnes and Sid Cooper & Ringo Rigby and John Naylor. The result was a one fall each draw over the twenty minute time limit.

Wrestling was missing from *World of Sport* on January 14th with the European Figure Skating championship taking its place.

There was a quick exchange of the World Lightweight Title starting on January 18th at Bath when Jackie Robinson upset the champion Johnny Saint with a two falls to one win to become the new title holder. Unfortunately Robinson's joy didn't last long as Saint regained the title the next night at Hastings.

Wrestling was back on *World of Sport* on January 21st with three bouts recorded at Guildford. The first of which saw Banger Walsh tackling Steve Kelly. Kelly hadn't been seen on TV for nearly four years and had spent the intervening period on the independent circuit. For once Walsh displayed his impressive wrestling skills with no foul moves whatsoever. Walsh was rewarded when after a body slam he got the only fall needed to win in the third round. Danny Collins continued his apprencticeship with a match against Tally Ho Kaye. Kaye along with Sid Cooper were renowned for getting the best out of an opponent and was the perfect match for Collins. Collins got the first fall with a sunset flip and a double leg nelson in the fifth minute much to Kaye's surprise. Kaye equalised with a leg suspension submission in the eleventh minute after many weakeners. Kaye who had already received two public warnings from referee Peter Szakacs and tested his patience once too often. After being dropkicked through the ropes by Collins, Kaye returned to the ring where he was back dropped and covered by Collins. Whilst Szakacs administered the count Kaye delivered a low blow to the youngster to break up the fall and was immediately disqualified. With less than six months ring experience Collins was already a firm favourite with the fans and his ring work was also developing at a rapid rate. The last match that week saw Jon Cortez make a rare TV appearance where he was meeting old rival and long time friend Keith Haward. At the start Kent Walton made the sensible suggestion that wrestlers should wear different colour trunks to make identification of them easier but it was an idea that never bore fruit. It was Haward who won a very good technical contest although slightly on the dull side by two falls to one. The strange thing about the contest was that Kent Walton continually stated that Keith Haward was the European Middleweight Champion which he was when the match was recorded back in December but in real time he was the former champion. Mal Sanders had regained the belt he lost to Haward back in 1981 when he beat the champion by two falls to one at Croydon on January 17th.

There was the sad sight in January of Les Kellett and Johnny Kwango still wrestling well into their pensionable age on a bill at Grays on January 23rd. Both won with Kellett beating Mel Stuart and Kwango beating Mike Bennett albeit by count out.

The final *World of Sport* wrestling for January on the 28th saw two heavyweight matches shown that had been recorded back in October at Croydon. The first of which was a very lively one between Gil Singh and Terry Rudge. For some reason both wrestlers lost their cool early on and the match developed into something resembling a bar room brawl rather than a wrestling match. It was Singh who got the first fall in the third round with a hip toss and a cross press which seemed to upset Rudge even more. Rudge equalised with a cross press in the fifth round after weakening Singh with a boot to the stomach. Referee Peter Szakacs would have been fully entitled to disqualify both wrestlers as the foul tactics continued apace and Kent Walton was appalled at the spectacle and wondering aloud what was going on ? In the end it was Singh who got the winner in the seventh round with a folding press. Despite the lack of wrestling and the total disregard of the rule book by either wrestler it was a hugely entertaining fight and something rarely seen on TV. The other match shown was a rather less hectic affair as Pat Roach coasted to a two falls to one win over Tom Tyrone in the sixth round.

    Fit Finlay made his second televised title defence on *World of Sport* on February 4th in a show televised from Worcester. Before the title match was shown Giant Haystacks was in action when he took on the very much lighter Caswell Martin. For a round and a half Haystacks either clubbed Martin around the ring or put on neck weakeners before Martin attempted a brief period of offence. It didn't last long as a posting from Haystacks weakened Martin before he was thrown over the top rope. Martin had no hope of continuing and another uncompetitive win for the giant. Finlay's second defence of the World Mid/Heavyweight Title was against old rival Alan Kilby with the former champion Marty Jones left awaiting his rematch. Finlay again accompanied by Princess Paula continued his fine run of form as champion when he defeated Kilby by two falls to one but he still wasn't so keen to allow Jones his title shot. The final match that week saw a brief glimpse of local favourite Ringo Rigby beating Rocky Moran by the one fall needed.

    Worcester was again the venue for *World of Sport* on February 11th with Pete Roberts who was wearing a nice bright pair of yellow trunks instead of the usual black taking on Skull Murphy. Roberts got the first fall following a suplex in the third round with Murphy stalling at the restart complaining of his back being injured. Murphy got a second public warning in the fourth round for illegal use of the fist as his attempt at a sleeper hold on Roberts was broken up by the bell. Murphy then climbed onto the top of the corner post before delivering a nasty guillotine elbow drop onto Robert's neck as a set up to getting an equalising submission from his gator hold. In the interval referee Jeff Kaye was shoved aside as mayhem broke out with both wrestlers lost their cool completely trying to attack each other. Kaye disqualified both of them for such unseemly behaviour. The main event that week saw Marty Jones trying to enhance his title credentials against the recent title challenger Chic Cullen. A folding press secured by a bridge brought an equaliser for Cullen in the fifth round after Jones had taken an early lead. Jones got the winner in the seventh round with a folding press that looked to be under the ropes. The opening match that week saw Steve Grey face a late substitute with local star Steve Speed replacing Clive Myers. With only one fall needed it was Grey who got it in the second round with a folding press.

John Quinn arrived back in Britain at the beginning of February and straight away resumed feuds with both Wayne Bridges and Tony St Clair. It was against St Clair he had his first title match with. At Norwich on February 11th St Clair defended his version of the World Heavyweight Title against Quinn and with both wrestlers failing to keep their tempers in check the match ended with both disqualified. Quinn didn't have long to wait till he got another title match opportunity as on the following Monday at Slough St Clair again put the belt up against him. This time there was a definitive result as John Quinn defeated Tony St Clair by two falls to one to become World Heavyweight Champion once again.

Big Daddy was back on *World of Sport* on February 18th on a bill recorded from Winsford in Cheshire. Daddy was partnering Pat Patton against the bigger Masked Marauder and Banger Walsh who replaced the advertised team of Tony Francis and Sid Cooper. There didn't seem much point to the Marauder anymore as viewers had seen him lose and be unmasked by Daddy a few months before. Viewers had their intelligence insulted during the early stages of the match when Kent Walton remarked he didn't know who the Marauder was and had never seen him without a mask. This was a bit rich when he had commentated on him being unmasked and identified him as Scrubber Daly. The Marauder got the first fall with a cross press following a splash in the seventh minute or thought he had until referee Jeff Kaye disallowed it for Walsh's outside interference. Once Patton had made the hot tag it didn't take long for Daddy to finish the match. A double elbow drop knocked out Walsh in the tenth minute and a big splash on the Marauder a minute later saw a two straight falls win. Afterwards Jeff Kaye unmasked the Marauder revealing Daly under the mask and whilst this was going on Charlie McGee brought Tiny Callaghan in the ring as his latest hope to finish off Big Daddy once and for all. Indian power lifting record holder Mohammed Butt made his TV debut that week against Barry Douglas. Douglas got the first fall in the fourth round with a flying tackle before Butt equalised with a crotch hold and slam followed by a cross press in the sixth round. The last two rounds were scoreless so it was a one fall each draw and a terribly slow match that didn't make entertaining viewing. The other match shown saw Steve Logan beat the much lighter Mick McMichael in a catchweight contest by the only fall needed.

 The big news the following week was the announcement that wrestling would return to the Royal Albert Hall after a hiatus of more than a year. In shades of 1980 and the mishandling of the John Quinn v Wayne Bridges title rematch disappointment it felt that way again. Instead of having the Fit Finlay v Marty Jones World Mid/Heavyweight Title return match as top of the bill instead they were shoe horned into a tag match instead. Big Daddy would partner Jones against Giant Haystacks and Finlay. Unlike the last few shows at the Albert Hall there was a very decent bill including two title matches. Jim Breaks would defend the British Welterweight Title against teenage wonder Danny Collins and Alan Kilby would put his British Light/Heavyweight Title on the line against Chic Cullen. Four heavyweight matches completed the bill with Pat Roach taking on Skull Murphy. Steve Logan versus Prince

Mann Singh. Pete Roberts would meet a former independent circuit regular Rasputin and 'Mighty Scot' Drew McDonald a recent Joint Promotions debutant would face Ray Steele.

Jim Breaks and Danny Collins warmed up for their proposed title match at the Royal Albert Hall when they were part of an eight man knockout tournament shown on *World of Sport* on February 25th from Winsford. The other six wrestlers joining them in the tournament were Pete LaPaque, Jack Regan, Sid Cooper, Eddie Riley, Rick Wiseman and Mal Sanders. The first round heats saw LaPaque beat Wiseman via a points decision after a time limit draw. Collins also beat Cooper by referee's decision after another draw. Breaks beat Sanders by way of the 'Breaks special' getting him the one score needed and Riley beat Regan by the only fall required. The semi final's saw Collins beat LaPaque when the Leicester man failed to beat the count when falling out of the ring and Breaks beat Riley in the other semi when two 'Breaks specials' sealed a two nil win. The final saw Breaks' temper once again let him down and with Collins already leading by an early fall Breaks antagonised referee Brian Crabtree once too often and got himself disqualified.

February saw not only a new design for the posters advertising each Joint Promotions' show but a famous name disappeared with Best/Wryton Promotions no more. Each show run by Max Crabtree would be under the Dale Martin name no matter where in the country it was held. Dale Martin continued with its Brixton office before downsizing to Streatham High Road before everything moved up to Leeds a couple of years later. That move left the Joint Promotions' organisation now only consisting of Dale Martin, Relwyskow & Green and Ken Joyce's Devereux Promotion as an affiliate. In truth the territory days of British Wrestling had dissapeared when Max Crabtree had started the booking for the whole country. To me this was another reason for the downfall of the sport and its problems. When I first started watching wrestling on TV and live in the mid seventies each promoters bills and matches were different and used their own rosters. Wrestlers would be brought in for a week at a time from the other promoters. People like Mark Rocco, Big Daddy, Giant Haystacks or The

Royals would come down to London and stay there whilst doing a week or so on Dale Martin bills. Although the traffic in the reverse direction wasn't so much apart from the likes of Mick McManus and Steve Logan. Without looking at a venue on the poster it was easy to tell which promoter's bill it was. For example Dale Martin would have traditional matches of the like seen since the fifties and sixties with hardly any type of gimmick matches, their idea of something special was a tag match. Whereas Best/Wryton in the Midlands/North West of the country would have all kinds of gimmicks like ladder matches and street fights especially at Belle Vue. Relwyskow & Green again were completely different, they shunned the gimmicks but also had their own roster of wrestlers which they would use alongside those of the other promoters who they had booked at that time. During the early eighties and as the decade carried on it became increasingly hard if you took the venue off the poster to know exactly which town that bill was to be held at. The same bouts were booked all over the country and so it became stale. Seeing the same matches night after night on Joint Promotions' bills was another reason why the crowd numbers around this time started dropping off even more.

There was a blank week for wrestling on March 3rd when the Yamaha Keyboards International Masters snooker tournament was shown instead at 4pm.

There was an interesting double header on *World of Sport* on March 10th with wrestling shown from Rotherham. First up was a special challenge match between Jim Breaks and Danny Collins and once again it was Collins who came out victorious and also £500 richer as part of the match's stipulation. Fit Finlay made a third televised defence of his World Mid/Heavyweight Title in the other match, this time it was Steve Logan challenging. As Brian Crabtree did the introductions Marty Jones was parading a large 'Finlay is a fake' banner at ringside but he most certainly wasn't and proved it in this match. It was thought that Logan would give Finlay a tough test but it wasn't to be as Finlay got the first fall in the third round with a cross press following a side suplex and recorded a two nil victory in the seventh round with a nasty looking leg lock to which Logan immediately submitted. Marty

Jones was back with his banner but Finlay grabbed it from him and ripped it up as an excited Princess Paula gave her man a kiss.

An example of how much 'heat' Fit Finlay and Princess Paula were generating amongst the fans at ringside happened at Derby at the end of February. Finlay was making a title defence against Ringo Rigby. An enraged fan threw a coin at Finlay which missed and hit Rigby instead leaving him with a nasty looking cut above the eye. The match had to be stopped and Rigby's only consolation was getting another opportunity at Derby on March 19th.

There were only two bouts shown on *World of Sport* the following week as well on March 17th which saw a bill from Derby screened. A heavyweight match saw Pat Roach take on 'Tarzan' Johnny Wilson in his usual leopardskin trunks but in something of a shock it was Wilson who got the first fall following a body slam in the ninth minute. Roach quickly equalised with a body slam of his own leading to a cross press in the eleventh minute. With only four seconds left of the twenty minute time limit it was Roach that got the winning fall with a hip toss and a cross press which left Wilson disconsolate. The other contestthat week saw Clive Myers and Steve Grey have yet another match on TV and yet again a draw was the result with each wrestler scoring one fall each.

All roads led to the Royal Albert Hall in London for wrestling fans for the first time since December 1982 and a decent sized crowd were entertained. The main event tag match between Big Daddy and Marty Jones & Giant Haystacks and Fit Finlay was as good as can be expected with it turning into a bloody battle as Finlay opened a nasty looking cut on Jones' forehead. Giant Haystacks got an early submission on Jones. Big Daddy got an equalising fall on Haystacks before Jones with blood pouring down his face trapped Finlay in the powerlock submission to get the winner. Chic Cullen won the British Heavy/Middleweight Title from Alan Kilby when he defeated the champion by two falls to one in the ninth round. The second title match saw a massive upset as Danny Collins at just seventeen became the youngest ever British champion when he beat Jim Breaks for the British Welterweight Title.

The ending in the fifth round was particularly controversial with referee Peter Szakacs disallowing a 'winning' submission for Breaks for illegal use of the ropes. Whilst Breaks was arguing with anyone and everyone Collins quickly swept his legs away for the winning fall.

The other matches saw a few changes as Pat Roach was away busy filming and Rasputin was still engaged on the continent so their respective opponents Skull Murphy and Pete Roberts took each other on instead. Roberts won by two falls to one of bruising encounter with tempers between the two flaring up at times. Indian heavyweight Prince Mann Singh made a return to Joint Promotions' rings but his bout with Steve Logan ended prematurely. Logan fell through the ropes injuring his ankle in the process in the third round. The sporting Mann Singh refused the decision so it was declared a No Contest. The 'Mighty Scot' Drew McDonald made an Albert Hall debut against Ray Steele and made a good impression albeit a losing one with Steele getting the one fall needed in eleven minutes. The evening's other match saw substitutes Mal Sanders and Keith Haward meet in something of a grudge match with an aggressive Haward picking up two public warnings before gaining a surprise two straight falls win over Sanders.

Only two bouts again were seen on *World of Sport* on March 24th with them coming from Derby. The first was a catchweight match with Chic Cullen facing Keith Haward with Haward getting a brilliant first fall when he reversed a leg hold to get a folding press in the fourth round. Cullen in turn surprised Haward by reversing a posting attempt and pinning him by way of a small package. Unfortunately the match ended in the seventh round when Haward attempted a German suplex but it was too close to the ropes and both wrestlers went tumbling out of the ring. Neither wrestler was able to continue so referee Ken Joyce's verdict was a draw. This was a superb technical wrestling match with many excellent holds, counter holds, escapes and reversals from two masters of their craft. It proved a point that done right fans would still enjoy a match such as this. In a complete opposite the other match shown was more of a street brawl at closing time as Pete Roberts once again took on Skull Murphy with yet again no decisive result as it ended with the score one each at the end of the scheduled time limit.

The final show on *World of Sport* for March on the 31st was an international tag knockout tournament which was from the second half of the bill recorded at Guildford back in December. The four teams were representing England Marty Jones and Vic Faulkner, Northern Ireland's Fit Finlay and Rocky Moran, Canada's Owen and Ross Hart & Caribbean duo Jim Moza and Len Hurst. The first semi final saw the Harts taking on Finlay and Moran and it was Moran getting the first fall with a reverse double leg pin on Owen. Owen himself got an equaliser in the tenth minute by pinning Moran by way of a German suplex and bridge. Finlay won the match for his team in the thirteenth minute when the Samoan drop saw him pin a weakened Owen Hart. The other semi final saw Jones and Faulkner beat Moza and Hurst by two falls to one to set up the final everyone wanted to see Jones and Faulkner v Finlay and Moran. The fans at ringside were loving it in the early stages as both Faulkner and Jones were on top before the nefarious tactics of Moran came into play targetting the lighter Faulkner. The double teaming of Faulkner brought the crowd to their feet before Vic made the hot tag and in came Jones. As soon as Moran missed a knee drop you know what would happen next and Jones got him in the powerlock it was an instant submission for the first score in the ninth minute. There was much stalling before Moran had to continue and despite Finlay's best attempts to break the hold Moran immediately submitted once Jones put him in the power lock again. So a two nil victory for the England team and Ken Joyce presented a lovely silver cup to Marty Jones and Vic Faulkner and no doubt there was much celebrating done on the streets of Guildford that night.

It wasn't such good news for Marty Jones away from the TV screens though. He lost a World Mid/Heavyweight Title eliminater to Pete Roberts at Croydon on March 27th putting him even further away from a title match with Fit Finlay. For once it was Roberts incurring the wrath of the referee with some over enthusiastic moves. It was all square with a fall for Jones equalised by a submission for Roberts in the fourth round when the match was stopped with Jones suffering a badly cut eye. There was also drama that night in a match involving Steve Grey and Vic Faulkner. Grey was attacked by Sid Cooper at ringside who hit him on the head with the timekeeper's bell. Cooper was furious having just been disqualified in his match with Danny Collins. Halfway through the match Grey collapsed in the middle of the ring and passed out as a result of a concussion from being hit by the bell. The match was stopped and Grey taken to a local medical facility for a check up.

It was only two bouts again on *World of Sport* on April 7th with Blackburn the venue. The first match saw Alan Kilby beat John Elijah by two falls to one in a contest that had been seen everywhere on Joint Promotions' shows in the last couple of years. The other match shown saw Giant Haystacks in action this time taking on Gil Singh. In his first TV appearance for a few months the big man looked even bigger and his mood quickly darkened when he saw Big Daddy sitting front row wearing a colourful red and yellow striped blazer. Daddy was accompanied by twenty or so children from a local special needs school. Singh did his best to throw Haystacks out of the ring whilst Haystacks argued with Daddy. An elbow drop to Singh's nether regions brought instant disqualification for Haystacks in the second round. Haystacks then sent referee Peter Szakacs flying as Daddy tried to drag him out of the ring by his hair. Kent Walton had a job trying to make out what was happening.

Yet again there were only two bouts from Blackburn shown on April 14th but at least there were both storylines involved which was unlike most matches shown. The first match was for the British Welterweight Title with former champion Jim Breaks getting his return match against Danny Collins. As usual Breaks started with the arm weakeners early in the bout as well as constantly shouting to both Collins and the fans at ringside. Breaks picked up his first public warning from referee Peter Szakacs for dissent in the third round. Breaks got the first fall in the fourth round with a folding press after catching Collins by surprise as Szakacs called a rope break. Collins equalised in the sixth round with another folding press much to Breaks's protests as he said Szakacs didn't count to three. To add insult to injury he got his second public warning for attacking Collins in the interval. The match came to a controversial ending in the seventh round after Collins delivered a perfect dropkick to Breaks. As Collins stood up he accidentally clashed heads with referee Szakacs leaving both of them stumbling around very groggy. Breaks as ever straight away took advantage and applied a Boston crab on Collins but Szakacs tapped Breaks on his back to signal the end of the match. Breaks thought he was the champion again but in fact the match had been stopped with Szakacs not able to continue. The verdict of a No Contest was delivered by Brian Crabtree as Collins was carried from the ring whilst Breaks threw the mother of all temper tantrums in the ring. The other match shown saw Marty Jones get his hands on Fit Finlay but only in a non title contest. Jones won but it was only due to Finlay leaving the ring to walk back to the dressing room. A count out win was a hollow victory and left Jones no nearer a title match.

World of Sport on April 21st from Lichfield saw an absolutely horrible tag match screened from Lichfield. Big Daddy was partnering Roy Scott against the duo of Tiny Callaghan and Lucky Gordon. It was full of blown spots and botches galore. Not something that was worthy of being seen on TV. The other two matches saw a one each draw between Ray Steele and Tom Tyrone & Caswell Martin beating Steve Logan by the only fall needed. It wasn't a week's wrestling to dwell on or to remember.

Clive Myers ended the reign of Mal Sanders as European Middleweight Champion at Croydon on April 24th. It was unusual due to the fact that Myers had thrown out any semblance of sportsmanship and used foul tactics which gained him two public warnings before he gained a winning fall. Afterwards Myers apologised for his behaviour but said that he had never held a title and was determined not to fail this time. Also on the same night Marty Jones suffered another defeat at the hands of Pete Roberts whilst an intriguing match between Bobby Barnes and Tally Ho Kaye unsurprisingly ended with both disqualified.

A Northern Ireland v Scotland match was the feature of the wrestling on *World of Sport* on April 28th. First match saw Jack Shirlow for Northern Ireland meeting Drew McDonald for

Scotland in a battle of TV debutants. McDonald got the first score with a Boston crab submission in the third round with Shirlow equalising immediately with a body slam followed by the usual cross press in the first minute of the fourth round. It was Shirlow who got the win for Northern Ireland when McDonald was disqualified in the fifth round by referee Dave Reese for a blatant punch to his opponent's stomach. The second match saw Chic Cullen for Scotland take on Rocky Moran for Northern Ireland. Cullen took the lead in the fourth round with a reverse knee drop setting up Moran for a folding press. Moran equalised with a cross press after weakening Cullen with a suplex to set up the final round to find the winner. Surprisingly it was Moran who had unexpectedly wrestled within the rules throughout who got the winner with a hip toss followed by a folding press to give Northern Ireland an unassailable two nil lead. The final match saw Andy Blair for Scotland trying to get a consolation win against Northern Ireland's Sean Doyle who was billed as Rinty Doyle in that week's TV Times and who was in fact Johnny Howard better known as Rasputin. Doyle outweighed Blair by at least five stone and was making a TV debut as a match with John Cox recorded at Blackburn hadn't been shown. The much more experienced Doyle made short work of Blair with a back breaker getting the first submission in the second round before a pile driver finished off Blair in the next round. So it was Northern Ireland who won the match by an impressive three nil.

After the controversial ending to the British Welterweight Title match shown three weeks previously on *World of Sport* Jim Breaks demanded and got another shot at the champion Danny Collins. The rematch was shown on May 5th on a show filmed at Nottingham but this time there was no controversy as Collins retained the belt as a result of a two falls to one win and Breaks was left to ponder his future. Also seen that week were the two semi finals of a knockout tournament to decide the winner of the 'Golden Gown'. In the first of them Sid Cooper had far too much experience and know how for Scottish youngster Ian McGregor who was making his TV debut. Cooper by way of a one nil win proceeded to the final where he would meet Vic Faulkner who beat Kid Chocolate by the only fall needed in his semi final.

Fit Finlay had a busy week during May when finally Marty Jones got a title match at Bristol on May 10th. First though Finlay had to deal with Pete Roberts who got his World Mid/Heavyweight Title match first at Croydon on May 8th as a result of his winning two eliminators in the previous weeks. To add intrigue to the match Marty Jones was sat at ringside doing some scouting for his big match. In the early rounds Jones baited both wrestlers even taking the microphone at one point to emphasise his words. In the sixth round Finlay got into another argument with Jones outside the ring and Roberts was keen to add to it. Whilst the three of them continued to row referee Ken Lazenby continued to count and both men were outside the ring at the count of ten. It was unclear at the time about the status of the championship but eventually it was stated Finlay was still champion. So onto Bristol on the Thursday night and yet again Jones was left frustrated with the title match ending in a one each draw after the scheduled fifteen rounds so Finlay retained the title. Finlay got the first fall in the ninth round and after a series of leg weakeners Jones finally got the equaliser in the thirteenth round with his powerlock submission hold. Despite Jones's best attempts he was unable to get a winner but at least he left Bristol in the knowledge a rematch was sanctioned to be held at Dartford on May 29th.

Marty Jones was back on *World of Sport* that weekend on May 12th when he faced old rival and fellow title contender Pete Roberts. Jones equalised an earlier Roberts fall in the fifth round with a small package but neither wrestler was able to get the winner so it ended in a draw at the end of the the scheduled six rounds. Another match that ended in a one fall each draw was the final for the 'Golden Gown' between Sid Cooper and Vic Faulkner so a rematch would need to be held. The opening match that week saw Gil Singh beat Barry Douglas by the only fall needed.

Saturday May 19th was the 1984 FA Cup Final day and wrestling had a twenty minute slot on *World of Sport* for its presentation. This year's Big Daddy special was a sort of rematch from the Royal Albert Hall match in March. Giant

Haystacks and Fit Finlay would be taking on Big Daddy and Honey Boy Zimba. I've no idea why Marty Jones wasn't booked in the match as he was in the country and wrestling at Rushden that night. In the end Zimba was replaced on the night by an even worse partner in Drew McDonald for Daddy. McDonald was seen wrestling as a rulebreaker on the circuit and had even featured in tag matches opposing Daddy. One of those things Joint Promotions seemed good at in the 1980's was doing things that didn't make sense and this was another example. Joe D'Orazio usually seen as a referee was the MC for the show and it was good to see him doing a different job which he did well. Haystacks and Finlay were of course accompanied by Princess Paula who did her best to provoke Daddy and McDonald. Haystacks got the first fall in the eighth minute after a big splash on McDonald. McDonald made the hot tag with Daddy and straightaway Daddy sent Haystacks through the ropes despite Paula's best attempts to save him. A rotten ending saw Finlay go out of the ring under the ropes after a high Daddy back drop and get counted out. D'Orazio announced both Finlay and Haystacks had somehow been counted out at the same time. On occasions such as these it seemed that a much better alternative was away from the TV screens and on the independent circuit.

Grapple fans had a blank Bank Holiday Saturday on May 26th with the England v Scotland football match being shown on *World of Sport* instead.

Marty Jones finally regained the World Mid/Heavyweight Title from Fit Finlay at Dartford on May 29th when he defeated the champion after ten tremendous rounds. The end came when after a clash of heads Jones reacted quickest and got the winning fall over the still groggy Finlay.

On the independent circuit Brian Dixon had parked the All Star Promotion's tanks on more of Joint Promotions' lawns including the Agricultural Hall at Maidstone which had significance as it was one of the original Dale Martin venues. Whilst the Agricultural Hall was not one of the more salubrious venues or the clientele were among the most refined it still had an atmosphere second to none amongst wrestling fans.

Wrestling was back on *World of Sport* on June 2nd but with only two matches shown from the Walton on Thames bill which also included the tag match shown on FA Cup Final day. The first match saw Bobby Barnes facing Alan Dennison in not only a clash of personalities but styles with only one score needed to decide things. Barnes dressed as usual in his multi coloured tights and trunks had become one of the stalwarts of Joint Promotions with the various departures to the independent circuit . An interesting match with Barnes's weight advantage nullified by Dennison's strength saw Barnes adopting the usual dubious tactics and Dennison battling not to lose his cool and retaliate. After referee Peter Szakacs had given Barnes two public warnings he was skating on thin ice and finally tested Szakacs's patience once too often in the fourth round. After punching Dennison in the stomach right in front of the referee he was disqualified. Sadly this was Dennison's final appearance on *World of Sport*. The other match shown saw Steve Grey meet in Johnny Kidd who had yet another tough opponent on TV. It was Kidd who took the lead in the fourth round with Kidd reversing a Grey pinfall attempt for one of his instead. Grey equalised a rather slow Kidd attempt at a victory roll for a folding press in the sixth round. It was Grey who won in the eighth and final round with a folding press in a match that it must have been a pleasure for Roy Harding to referee.

Marty Jones's joy at regaining the World Mid/Heavyweight Title was very short lived as Finlay invoked the rematch clause at the earliest opportunity which was at Carlisle on June 8th. With a two falls to one win Finlay was back on top of the pile holding the belt once again and Jones was facing another fight to get back into title contention.

After a blank weekend for grapple fans on June 9th with the England v Netherlands schoolboy's football match shown it was back to Walton on Thames on June 16th for *World of Sport*. Both bouts shown concerned the British Heavy/Middleweight Title. Firstly an eliminator between Alan Kilby and Mal Sanders to decide who would meet the winner of the other match which was Chic Cullen defending the title against Rocky Moran. Kilby's match with Sanders for the title opportunity was a rather dour affair which was no surprise with so much at stake. Kilby got the first fall in the second round with a basic folding press which caught Sanders by surprise. Sanders equalised in the fourth round with another folding press but it was Kilby who went on to win in the sixth round with his suplex come powerslam combination. After the bell rang Sanders sportingly congratulated his opponent Kilby. Maybe losing the match altered Sanders's mindset as he immediately gave his notice into Joint Promotions and made the switch to the independent circuit at the end of May. The Walton on Thames show was recorded on May 2nd so by the time it was shown Sanders was already appearing for Wrestling Enterprises amongst other promoters.

After his defeat to Rocky Moran as part of the Scotland v Northern Ireland team match Chic Cullen made no such mistake this time with the British Heavy/Middleweight Title at stake. Unlike the first match Moran totally ignored the rule book in his eagerness to win but it was Cullen who retained the title with the winning fall coming from a flying tackle from the top of the corner post followed by a cross press. Straight away Alan Kilby came into the ring to congratulate Cullen and set the scene for his title challenge whilst Chic Cullen was presented with his title belt by the Mayor of Elmbridge.

After successfully regaining the World Mid/Heavyweight Title from Marty Jones it was time for Fit Finlay to make a televised defence which was against Clive Myers. This was shown on June 23rd on *World of Sport* from Brierley Hill. The much lighter Myers was no match for Finlay and in the end Finlay retained his title by way of a two falls to one win. Also on the show Vic Faulkner won the 'Golden Gown' when his rematch with Sid Cooper saw Cooper get himself disqualified. Ringo Rigby beat John Wilkie by the one fall in the show's preliminary contest.

June 27th saw tragedy in the dressing room at Southport when Alan Dennison collapsed and died after a victory over Dave Duran. Dennison had gone from being hated to in the latter years of his career being beloved by the fans.

The *World of Sport* cameras moved a few miles down the road from Brierley Hill to West Bromwich for the show broadcast on June 30th. The first match saw Tally Ho Kaye defeat Ian McGregor followed by Pat Roach gaining a hard fought two falls to one win over Terry Rudge. The highlight that week was a tag match with the 'Gloucester Gladiators' Steve Speed and Danny Collins taking on 'The Rockers' with Pete LaPaque partnering Derek 'Ripper' Collins who had replaced the unavailable Tommy Lorne. This was his TV debut, Collins was a miner by trade and with the mining industry affected by the national strike he had made a comeback to the ring. LaPaque got the first fall with a folder in the ninth minute when Speed mistimed a victory roll. The muscular Speed got the equaliser in the eleventh minute after his version of the kamakaze crash weakened LaPaque and enabled a cross press. Danny Collins sealed a popular win for the 'Gladiators' with a cross press on Derek Collins in the fifteenth minute.

It was back to West Bromwich on July 7th for *World of Sport* with the other three matches filmed there. The main match saw British Heavy/Middleweight Champion Chic Cullen take on his number one contender Alan Kilby in a non title match over twenty minutes duration. Cullen took the first fall with a folding press in the eighth minute before Kilby equalised with an awkward looking version of his powerslam and cross press. With no further score it ended in a draw but hopefully with the title on the line the match may be more interesting than this one. Marty Jones had an easy time with Blackjack Mulligan replacing Skull Murphy with Jones winning by two straight falls. The opening match saw King Ben beat Ray Robinson by the one fall needed in a dull affair.

Big Daddy was back on *World of Sport* on July 14th from Barking as part of a tag team knockout tournament but there were two dull, slow style heavyweight matches to sit through first. Mohammed Butt's contest with Len Hurst ended in a No Contest in the third round with Hurst unable to continue through injury. Johnny Wilson wrestled a one fall each draw with John Elijah over eight rounds which would have tested the enthusiasm of the most ardent of fans. Big Daddy teamed up with Danny Collins as one team of a four team tournament and their opponents were the very much lighter Bobby Barnes and Sid Cooper. Luckily both Barnes and Cooper were such good workers they were able to make it into some sort of competitive match. It ended when they departed from the ring in the ninth minute of the contest and were counted out. Therefore Daddy and Collins went through to the final to meet the winners of the tag match to be shown the next week.

July 21st saw *World of Sport* back at Barking for the second semi final of the tag team knockout tournament with Scrubber Daly and Lucky Gordon demolishing the team of Drew McDonald and Andy Blair by two straight submissions in less than ten minutes. They would go on to meet Daddy and Collins in the final to be shown the following week. It had become noticeable in the past few months that Daly and Gordon were now the de facto opponents for Big Daddy in matches on the circuit with previous regular foe Banger Walsh being used less and less. The other two matches were fought to near silence from the fans as Steve Logan beat Peter Wilson by the one fall needed to win in the fourth round. Steve Grey's bout with Keith Haward was a nice technical match which didn't engage the fans till the finish when both wrestlers shoulders were pinned to the mat in the sixth round for a rare two falls each draw.

During July a new name appeared on Joint Promotions' bills that of Greg Gable. Gable was swiftly renamed Greg Valentine in another example of promoter Max Crabtree using names of American wrestlers with his own talent. It was soon no secret that the British Valentine was none other than Max Crabtree's son Scott.

The final of the tag team tournament between Big Daddy and Danny Collins & Scrubber Daly and Lucky Gordon was seen on *World of Sport* on July 28th as the cameras returned to Chester after quite a long absence. After the usual double teaming on Collins at the start, the youngster got the first fall with a double leg nelson on Gordon. Daddy got the winner for a two straight falls win with the big splash on Daly in just about ten minutes. Also on the same programme Gil Singh beat Rasputin by disqualification and Barry Douglas beat John Cox.

The other half of the Chester show was seen on August 4th with the highlight being Alan Kilby's challenge to Chic Cullen for the British Heavy/Middleweight Title. Their recent non title match hadn't really whetted the appetite but his was a slightly more intriguing match. Cullen retained the title via a two falls to one win. It was back to 1977 as Vic Faulkner rekindled his feud with Jim Breaks as seen back then on the Silver Jubilee show at the Royal Albert Hall. This time it was Faulkner who came out on top when once again Breaks' temper let him down and he was disqualified. The other match shown saw a slight mismatch with Fit Finlay accompanied by Princess Paula tackling the much lighter Mick McMichael. Finlay thought he had won in the third round with a neck stretch submission but it was disallowed by referee Dave Reese for not breaking the hold. It didn't matter as within seconds of the fourth round Finlay applied the same move and McMichael submitted instantly.

The *World of Sport* cameras were at Southport for their annual TV show on August 11th with a top of the bill featuring Marty Jones against the rotten King Kendo. Kendo took the lead with a body slam followed by a cross press in the eighth minute who was then joined in the ring by Fit Finlay for some reason. Jones quickly equalised with the same move of his own a minute later before Jones got the winner with a small package in the seventeenth minute. Kendo left the ring before he was unmasked as was the custom after losing but I doubt anyone really cared. The opening match saw Butcher Bond beat Bruiser Muir by disqualification in the third round for use of the fist. In a clash of martial arts styles Clive Myers beat Pat Patton by two falls to one with a double leg nelson bringing the winning fall in the seventh round.

It was back to Southport on August 18th for the second half of the show recorded there. The highlight was a super sized heavyweight tag match with Giant Haystacks and Rasputin facing Pat Roach and Pete Roberts. Rasputin was forced to do all the early work as Haystacks stood on the ring apron refusing to get involved. He finally came in once Roberts was weakened but Roach quickly made the tag. Referee Gordon Pryor had his hands full trying to keep order before Roach got the first fall with a cross press on Rasputin in the tenth minute. Haystacks evened things up with the guillotine elbow drop in the twelfth minute but with Haystacks and Rasputin continuing to attack Roberts referee Pryor decided to disqualify them. The opening match was a dour one fall affair between John Naylor and Rick

Wiseman with Naylor winning in the fourth round with a reverse double arm shoulder press. Grasshopper beat Ray Smith by two falls to one in the sixth round in the other bout shown. Grasshopper's winning fall was an impressive flying body scissors that ended with him pinning Smith with his feet.

It was announced towards the end of August that there would again be wrestling at the Royal Albert Hall in September but in a first it would be on a Saturday night, the 29th. It seemed a gamble putting on a show on a Saturday with central London not a nice place to be on a weekend night. People working in the city tended not to be around at the weekend and there were many other attractions on a Saturday going on as well. Like the March show there was a very decent proposed bill with the highlight being Otto Wanz making his Joint Promotions debut defending his version of the World Heavyweight Title against Ray Steele. Naturally Big Daddy shared top billing in a tag match partnering Danny Collins against manager Charlie McGee's latest finds 'The Bounty Hunters'. Two more title matches saw Alan Kilby get another chance at Fit Finlay's World Mid/Heavyweight Title and Marty Jones would defend his British Light/Heavyweight Title against Chic Cullen. A knockout tournament saw Greg Valentine, Sid Cooper, Bobby Barnes and Ian McGregor participating in it. Arabian champion Sheik Al Saadi would make his Albert Hall debut against Drew McDonald and Vic Faulkner would meet Steve Grey. For the available talent Joint Promotions had at the time this was a very strong bill and one I looked forward to seeing.

A Battle Royale was the attraction on *World of Sport* on August 25th from the show recorded at Brierley Hill. The singles bouts saw Honey Boy Zimba beat Blackjack Mulligan by countout when Mulligan left the ring after tiring of receiving head butts from Zimba. Lucky Gordon beat Andy Blair by throwing him straight out of the ring through the ropes and Blair couldn't beat the count. Steve Logan wrestled a one fall each draw with Rocky Moran with Moran taking the lead in the fourth round with a small package fooling Logan before Logan equalised in the fifth round with a folding press. Ian McGregor's match with Eddie Riley ended in a one fall each draw as well with a double arm from McGregor pinning Riley in the second round with Riley equalising in the fourth round with a folding press. The over the top rope finale saw Blair first out quickly followed by McGregor and Riley. Zimba and Mulligan eliminated each other leaving Logan, Moran and Gordon as the final three. Logan sent Moran and Gordon flying to become the winner in a couple of minutes or so.

September started with what seemed to be now an annual exodus from Joint Promotions to the independent circuit with two very noticeable names amongst them. Jim Breaks and Bobby Barnes departed to leave a massive hole in Joint's roster with both excellent draws as well as being instantly recognisable to the fans.

Grapple fans faced a three week absence from the sport at the start of September as *World of Sport* once again replaced wrestling at 4pm with other sports. September 1st saw a recording of the World Heavyweight Title boxing between Tim Witherspoon and Pinklon Thomas from Las Vegas. On September 8th the European Golf Championship was shown and on September 15th cricket was shown in the guise of the Silk Cup Challenge from Taunton.

Wrestling was back on *World of Sport* on September 22nd with two bouts featured from Malvern. The first of which saw Marty Jones tackle Studs Lannigan. Whilst not outright breaking the rules Lannigan was bending them at times and seemingly annoying Jones. Jones got the first fall following a body slam in the second round but Lannigan equalised in the third with a cross press after a suplex. Jones upped a gear in the fourth round and after a missile dropkick easily folded up Lannigan for the winner. The other contest screened saw Danny Collins defend his British Welterweight Title against the British Lightweight Champion Steve Grey. Since his debut a year or so ago Collins had gone from strength to strength but that run came to an end when Grey defeated him to become a double champion. Steve Grey got the winner in the twelfth and final round with a reverse double arm fall for a two falls to one victory. Afterwards Grey paid tribute to Collins and paved the way for the rematch to be held on TV. With Grey now holding the lightweight and the welterweight belts it was announced that a decision would be made on their status after the Collins rematch.

Saturday September 29th was a busy day for grapple fans with firstly two bouts from Malvern on *World of Sport* followed by the show at the Royal Albert Hall. The first of the TV bouts saw the Albert Hall heavyweight title challenger Ray Steele face Skull Murphy in a one fall match. Steele won the match when an almighty throw sent Murphy sailing over the top ropes in the third round and he didn't return before the count of ten. The other match saw Fit Finlay take on Johnny Wilson. A knee to the head weakened Wilson in the third round before a side suplex gave Finlay the opening fall. Wilson equalised with a cross press following a body slam in the fifth round. It was Finlay who won when Wilson missed an attempted knee drop and all Finlay had to do was put him in a Boston crab for the winning submission.

All roads led to the Royal Albert Hall in the evening for a stellar line up but the attendance was slightly disappointing. The CWA World Heavyweight Title match between Otto Wanz and challenger Ray Steele had a slight exhibition match feel to it as nobody gave Steele a chance of winning. Wanz through ignorance of the British rules did receive two public warnings in his two straight falls win inside six rounds but he was never troubled by Steele. There was talk afterwards of Wanz returning for another title defence but that never materialised. Charlie McGee's latest tag team 'The Bounty Hunters' turned out to be Tiny Callaghan and Lucky Gordon and a rotten match saw Big Daddy and Danny Collins beat them in just under eight minutes of a farcical contest. Fit Finlay made another successful defence of the World Mid/Heavyweight Title when his challenger Alan Kilby was counted out in the seventh round. Marty Jones made a successful defence of his British Light/Heavyweight Title against Chic Cullen when two perfectly executed small packages in the eighth and ninth round secured a two falls to one win.

Despite the big hype beforehand Arabian Heavyweight Champion Sheik Al Saadi proved to be a big disappointment in his match with Drew McDonald. McDonald was bossing the match before he disgraced himself in the fourth round by hitting referee Ken Joyce and was immediately disqualified. Vic Faulkner and Steve Grey put on a mat classic for five rounds before Grey was forced to quit following a heavy fall. Of course Faulkner refused the decision so a No Contest verdict was the order of the day. The rest of the programme was completed by a four man knockout tournament featuring newcomer Greg Valentine, as unpopular as ever Sid Cooper, youngster Ian McGregor and Blackjack Mulligan. Mulligan replaced Bobby Barnes who had left Joint Promotions and on the night of the Albert Hall show was actually wrestling for Brian Dixon on a promotion held in his home town of Maidstone. The tournament was won by Greg Valentine who beat Blackjack Mulligan by countout in the first semi final before defeating Sid Cooper in the final in a little over two minutes despite which Cooper still managed to receive two public warnings. Cooper's semi final saw him easily brush aside Ian McGregor who had no answer to the scowling Soho resident's rulebreaking tactics and ring experience.

The wrestling on *World of Sport* on October 6th was curtailed to only twenty five minutes and on at 1220 instead of 4pm. There was only time to show two bouts of an England v Scotland team match recorded at Croydon. The first of which was a horrible mess of a match that saw Drew McDonald for Scotland beat Roy Scott by two straight falls. Tally Ho Kaye for England repeated a recent televised victory over Ian McGregor. Viewers tuning in at 4pm for their weekly wrestling would have been disappointed to have seen the International Snooker tournament on then.

It was the same story the following week on October 13th with wrestling again on at 1220 with this time the World Matchplay darts tournament on at 4pm. There were a further two matches shown from Croydon from the team match with Chic Cullen for Scotland taking on Sid Cooper. It was Cullen who got the first fall in the second round with a perfect small package. Cooper who was much lighter than his opponent managed to upset Cullen with his usual nefarious tactics and equalised in the fourth round with a Boston crab submission after Cullen missed a dropkick. Cullen secured the win for Scotland in the next round with a suplex followed by a cross press. The six man tag saw Cullen joined by Drew McDonald and Ian McGregor to take on Cooper, Roy Scott and Tally Ho Kaye. Scotland secured the win with a neck lift submission from McDonald on Cooper and with Scott leaving the ring in frustration at his two partners' antics it was McGregor who got the winner by pinning Kaye in the tenth minute.

There wasn't even a twenty minute slot on *World of Sport* for wrestling on October 20th as boxing with Marvin Hagler defending his World Middleweight Title against Mustafa Hamsho was shown at 4pm instead.

Wrestling was back at its usual 4pm slot on October 27th with the start of a new concept and a new title. Eight wrestlers would compete for the 'Grand Prix' belt with the winner getting a match for the World Mid/Heavyweight Title. The eight nominated participants were John Elijah, Alan Kilby, Rasputin, Barry Douglas, Skull Murphy, Chic Cullen, Ray Robinson and Ripper Collins. The first two matches were shown this week on the bill recorded at Croydon and in the first Alan Kilby beat John Elijah. The other match saw Johnny Wilson replace Rasputin to face Barry Douglas. Wilson progressed to the semi finals with a last round winning fall coming from a folding press.

Danny Collins marked time waiting for his title rematch with Steve Grey when he took on Eddie Riley in the opener on *World of Sport* on November 3rd from Wolverhampton. Kent Walton announced that Collins would get his chance to regain the title in a match to be shown on November 17th. Collins tuned up nicely with the one fall needed in the fourth round coming from a perfect wrestler's bridge. Fit Finlay as usual with Princess Paula in his corner defeated Vic Faulkner with a submission sealing the two to one victory. The third 'Grand Prix' belt heat saw Skull Murphy face Ray Robinson and it was Robinson who took the lead with a back drop followed by a cross press in the second round. But it was Murphy who joined Johnny Wilson and Alan Kilby in the semi finals when a forearm smash on Robinson's jaw saw him counted out by referee Gordon Pryor.

Wrestling on November 10th on *World of Sport* came from the Granada Studios in Manchester with Big Daddy featured in the main event. Daddy partnered by Pete Ross took on the team of Bruiser Muir and Banger Walsh, this would be Walsh's last appearance on TV. Muir got the first submission with a stranglehold on Ross in the sixth minute. Once Ross got the hot tag and Daddy was in the ring the result was a foregone conclusion. Daddy got the equalising fall following a big splash on Muir before the double elbow saw Walsh counted out by referee Gordon Pryor for the win in the tenth minute. The show was back in the 1220 slot due to boxing being shown at 4pm with the Larry Holmes v Bonecrusher Smith title fight on its place. With only twenty five minutes alotted there was only time for one other bout and that was the final heat in the 'Grand Prix' belt. Chic Cullen took his place in final four with a two straight falls win over Ripper Collins. A flying tackle and a cross press in the second round before a side suplex and another cross press in the fifth round brought about the win.

November 17th saw the rematch for the British Welterweight Title between Danny Collins and Steve Grey as the feature on *World of Sport* coming from the Granada Studios again. The first match though was the first of the 'Grand Prix' belt semi finals between Alan Kilby and Skull Murphy. At the end of the scheduled six rounds it was one apiece with a gator hold submission from Murphy equalising an earlier fall from Kilby. Rather than go to a points decision it was announced there would be a return contest next month. Collins got back on the winning track and regained the British Welterweight Title when he defeated the champion Steve Grey in an epic encounter. It was Collins who got the first fall with a swift reversal of a Grey pinfall attempt in the fifth round. Grey got the equaliser when he reversed Collins's cross press into a folding press for the count of three. The winner came in the tenth round when Collins pinned Grey with a bridge with Grey first to congratulate the new champion. Grey's dilemma about holding the two title belts was now resolved and he dropped back down to lightweight to concentrate on defending the British Lightweight Title.

Wrestling on *World of Sport* on November 24th came from one of Dale Martin's newer venues, the Orchard Theatre in Dartford which had only been open a year or so. The 1200 capacity venue had seen a few decent shows since its opening including when Marty Jones regained the World Mid/Heavyweight Title in May and now the TV cameras were there for the first time. The preliminary contest saw the first appearance on TV of Greg Valentine who faced Sid Cooper. Valentine impressed in the contest getting the only fall needed to win with a folding press in the third round. The Big Daddy and Pete Ross combination were in action next when they faced the team of Tiny Callaghan and Scrubber Daly. The early 'highlights' saw Daddy send Callaghan over the top rope before a hefty posting for Daly even sent referee Peter Szakacs flying. The first score was a submission when after several splashes Daly got Ross to submit from a Boston crab in the seventh minute. With the usual routine as soon as Daddy made the hot tag with Ross he got an equalising fall with a big splash on Daly in the tenth minute before a winning fall with the big splash on Callaghan. Whatever is said the crowd were very much into the match and celebrated loudly at the end. The final match that week was the first 'Grand Prix' belt semi final which saw Chic Cullen face Johnny Wilson. Wilson who only entered as a late replacement got the winning fall with a cross press in the final seconds of the final round. There was a touch of controversy as Kent Walton was sure the final bell had rung before referee Joe D'Orazio had completed the count of three but the result stood.

    It was back to Dartford on December 1st when Marty Jones finally got his chance to reclaim the World Mid/Heavyweight Title back from Fit Finlay. But first the preliminary contest saw Clive Myers take on Johnny Kidd who came in as a late notice substitute. Myers got a two straight falls win inside twelve minutes but Kidd had given him plenty of problems in the contest. Marty Jones had been waiting for six months for the opportunity against Fit Finlay and he finally got his chance this week. After the early skirmishes it was Finlay who got the first fall in the sixth round. He weakened Jones with a flying knee to the head and quickly slammed him before the cross press. Jones came right back into it in the eighth round after a series of high knee drops had weakened Finlay's knees and he submitted as soon as Jones applied the power lock. The action really heated up in the eleventh round with Jones getting two public warnings to equal the two Finlay had received earlier in the contest. Strangely Jones's two public warnings came from the same move a cannonball off the top of the corner post right onto Finlay who was lying on the canvas but then the match ended with Finlay disqualified. Jones was complaining to referee Peter Szakacs about the public warnings when Finlay landed a flying knee on Jones's head but there didn't seem to be anything illegal about it. So Jones was the new champion and celebrated in the ring while a furious Princess Paula with Finlay demanded an explanation from Szakacs. Finlay even threatened MC Brian Crabtree but to no avail but with the less than straight forward finish for me it didn't rate as highly as the match at Leeds a year ago.

Wrestling was missing from *World of Sport* on December 8th when the World Doubles snooker championships were on at 4pm instead.

There were only two bouts shown on *World of Sport* on December 15th as the 4pm slot was once again taken by the snooker doubles championship and wrestling was sandwiched between horse racing from Doncaster.

The first of the matches which came from Aylesbury was the 'Grand Prix' belt semi final rematch between Skull Murphy and Alan Kilby and this time if it was a draw it would go to a points decision. It was Murphy who got the first score in the third round when the gator hold saw Kilby tap instantly. Kilby equalised with a clumsy looking attempt at a suplex followed by a cross press in the fifth round. The sixth round ended with the score still one each so it was up to referee Peter Szakacs to decide and surprisingly he gave the verdict to Murphy. The other match shown saw Ian McGregor face Eddie Riley in a match that had been seen in nearly every hall on the circuit for the past few months. Riley won by two falls to one with a reverse folding press in the seventh round of a surprisingly entertaining match.

Another example for those who say wrestlers never get hurt happened on December 20th at Stockport when Scrubber Daly was seriously injured in a Big Daddy tag match. Daly was partnering Drew McDonald against Daddy and Ray Steele in the main event when he was pulled over the top rope during the match. Daly crashed onto his head and lay motionless with a suspected broken back which gave the emergency responders a hefty problem in how to take care of near 30st wrestler. Eventually ten men had to help doctors and nurses get Daly to the local hospital where fortunately he was found to be not seriously hurt.

Three more bouts from Aylesbury were shown on the pre Christmas *World of Sport* on December 22nd. The first of which was Ringo Rigby taking on a fresh face to TV from Northern Ireland, Billy Joe Beck. With just the one fall needed to win it was Rigby who got it with a botched attempt at a crucifix rectified by a folding press in the second round. The other two matches broadcast were both heavyweight contests. In the first of them Tom Tyrone met Terry Rudge. It was Rudge who got the first submission with an arm lever that had him perched across Tyrone's shoulders in the thirteenth minute. That in fact was the only score of the contest which meant Rudge was the winner. Finally in one of those matches that seemed to be on every show Len Hurst faced Butcher Bond. Hurst took the lead with a cross press in the second round before Bond levelled with a cross press of his own following a suplex. Hurst got the winner in the sixth round with another cross press this time following a body slam.

Outside the ring December had descended into chaos with promoter Max Crabtree making a right mess of the World Mid/Heavyweight Title. It was announced that Marty Jones would be making his first defence of his newly won title at Croydon on a non televised bill on December 18th. At the same time it was also announced that Jones would be making a televised defence of his title against the winner of the 'Grand Prix' belt in the New Year. At Croydon we saw a new World Mid/Heavyweight Champion when Pete Roberts defeated Marty Jones in the seventh round. Roberts side stepped a Jones dropkick which saw him sail out of the ring and unable to beat the referee's count of ten. Roberts was presented with the belt and all those in attendance thought that at the end of 1984 finally Pete Roberts was a World Champion. Unfortunately that was not the case in a cock up of epic proportions by Max Crabtree.

The 'Grand Prix' belt final was the feature of the final wrestling of the year on *World of Sport* on December 29th from Bury. Murphy's gator hold saw Wilson submit in the fourth round for the first score but during the interval Kent Walton gave out the sad news that Murphy's father Roy 'Bull' Davis had died recently of a heart attack. Wilson finally got the equaliser with a cross press on Murphy after a high back drop so the contest ended in a one score each draw. Due to the time constraints there had to be a winner of the match and the belt so the match went into sudden death extra time of ten minutes. It was Murphy who won when once again the gator hold forced another submission from Wilson in just over a minute of the extra time. Thus Skull Murphy became the inaugural holder of a really nice looking 'Grand Prix' belt and as a result it was announced he would be taking on Marty Jones for the World Mid/Heavyweight Title early in the new year on. Which is where the problems started as Marty Jones was no longer champion having lost the title to Pete Roberts at Croydon. That week's preliminary match saw Gil Singh beat TV newcomer Al Dean by the only fall needed. The other match shown came as a result of a challenge thrown down by Sid Cooper when he lost to Greg Valentine a few weeks back. The stipulation was that for every round Valentine lasted Cooper would pay him £100. Cooper took the lead in the second round with a cross press but still had to pay £100 which wiped the smile off of his face. Valentine got the equaliser in the third round with a double leg nelson and another £100 came out of Cooper's wallet. The end of the fourth round saw another £100 go to Valentine with Cooper throwing the cash at the youngster. Cooper was disqualified for a blatant punch in the fifth round by referee Peter Szakacs and even had to pay Valentine another £100 so he left Bury a loser and £500 poorer.

ASSEMBLY ROOMS - DERBY

Frank Woodhouse Promotions present
in conjunction with Dale Martin Promotions Ltd.

WRESTLING

| DOORS OPEN 6.45 p.m. | MONDAY, 9th JANUARY | COMMENCE 7.30 p.m. |

TERRIFIC CHALLENGE WE WILL WIN AND UNMASK THIS CHARACTER STATES DADDY

BIG DADDY
Partnered by **PAT PATTON**

"We are ready for 'em and raring to go"

— versus —

GIANT HAYSTACKS
"We've beaten them once and we can beat them again" says the Giant

MASKED MARAUDER

ANDY **BLAIR** v NIPPER **RILEY**

TIGER **DALIBAR SINGH** | **JIM BREAKS**
BIG PAT ROACH | GOLDEN ACE **JOHN NAYLOR**

PRICES: £1.50 : £2.00 : £2.50 (ALL SEATED NO STANDING ALLOWED)

Tickets from Frank Woodhouse & Son, Stall 53, Eagle Centre Market, Telephone: Derby 364460 & Assembly Rooms Box Office, Derby
ADVANCED BOOKINGS MUST be collected by 7.00 p.m. on night of the show

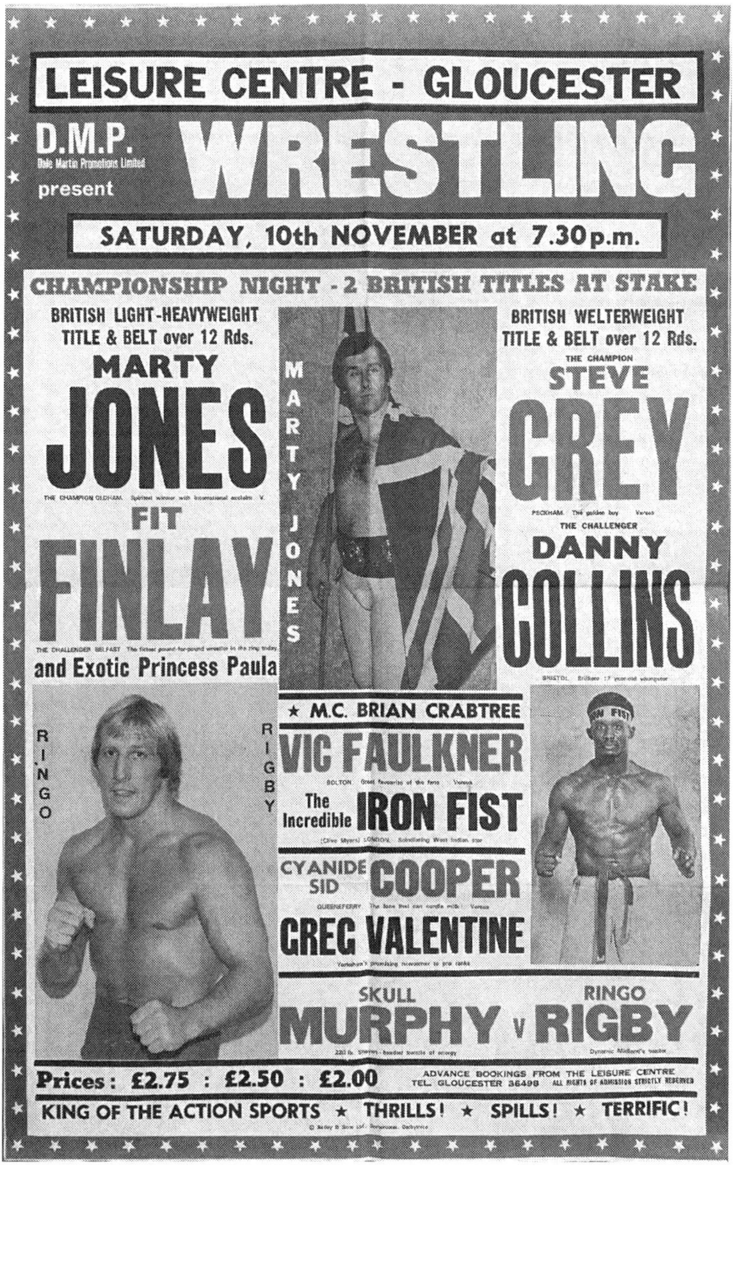
LEISURE CENTRE - GLOUCESTER
D.M.P.
Dale Martin Promotions Limited
present
WRESTLING
SATURDAY, 10th NOVEMBER at 7.30p.m.
CHAMPIONSHIP NIGHT - 2 BRITISH TITLES AT STAKE
BRITISH LIGHT-HEAVYWEIGHT TITLE & BELT over 12 Rds.
MARTY JONES
THE CHAMPION OLDHAM.
FIT FINLAY
THE CHALLENGER BELFAST
and Exotic Princess Paula
MARTY JONES
BRITISH WELTERWEIGHT TITLE & BELT over 12 Rds.
THE CHAMPION
STEVE GREY
PECKHAM. The golden boy Versus
THE CHALLENGER
DANNY COLLINS
BRISTOL.
RINGO
RIGBY
★ M.C. BRIAN CRABTREE
VIC FAULKNER
BOLTON. Versus
The Incredible IRON FIST
LONDON.
CYANIDE SID COOPER
QUEENSFERRY Versus
GREG VALENTINE
SKULL MURPHY v RINGO RIGBY
Prices: £2.75 : £2.50 : £2.00
ADVANCE BOOKINGS FROM THE LEISURE CENTRE
TEL. GLOUCESTER 36498
KING OF THE ACTION SPORTS ★ THRILLS! ★ SPILLS! ★ TERRIFIC!

Chapter 6 – 1985

The first wrestling of 1985 on *World of Sport* was on January 5th and was restricted to just one contest shown at 1220 with the Mercantile Credit Classic snooker tournament in the 4pm slot instead. The match from Keighley saw the reincarnation of the 'Martial Arts Fighters' this time consisting of Clive Myers together with newcomer Chris Bowles. Bowles had an impressive judo pedigree including competing at the Moscow Olympics but his professional wrestling career was less so and was only seen in the ring for a few months. After his ring career he returned to judo and training youngsters. He did feature in the news a good few years later when he was wrongly accused of being involved in the £53 million Securitas heist in 2006 and received damages from 'The Sun' newspaper. Their opponents in the match were 'The Rockers' who as normal were clad in their biker's gear for their entrance. Pete LaPaque got the first score with a leg submission on Chris Bowles in the tenth minute. Once the hot tag was made Myers came flying in over the top rope and got the equaliser with a folding press on Lorne although it looked to be botched. The end came when Myers pinned LaPaque with a reverse double leg nelson in sixteen minutes.

The thing that had to be cleared up was the mess Max Crabtree had made of the World Mid/Heavyweight Title with the former champion Marty Jones scheduled to defend the belt he no longer held at Keighley on January 3rd to be broadcast on World of Sport on the 12th. Skull Murphy with his 'Grand Prix' title win as part of the conditions of the victory was to meet Jones in a title match that Croydon fans had seem him lose in December. Outraged fans who had seen the title change hands in December bombarded both the office of Dale Martin Promotions and also that of London Weekend Television asking what was going on. In those days fans still took things like title matches very seriously even if the promoters didn't and to confuse things even more on January 22nd at Croydon the top of the bill would be the contracted rematch for the

World Mid/Heavyweight Title between champion Pete Roberts and challenger Marty Jones. The programme for that evening had a letter in it which read (spelling mistakes etc. and all) ....

WORLD MID-HEAVYWEIGHT TITLE

On Tuesday 18th December 1984, a proposed title match was prepared between the champion Marty Jones and challenger Pete Roberts. However an earlier negotiation for this same title was prepared in which the winner of the 1984 Grand Prix Belt eliminator being run off on television, would get a crack at the title.

As the television agreement championship took precedence over the 18th December match, this contest was made null and void. Therefore, tonight, Pete Roberts as the challenger will be contesting against the champion Marty Jones for the title and belt.

An apology from the management for this error, is forthcoming.

Dale Martin Promotiond Limited.

It was an unavoidable error that basically took the Croydon customers for fools and a business that does so will not be a successful business much longer. Incidentally Marty Jones won the match on the 22nd when Pete Roberts couldn't continue in the fifth round after Jones had applied his powerlock submission.

January 12th did in fact see the World Mid/Heavyweight Title match between Marty Jones and Skull Murphy from Keighley on *World of Sport* and after all the fuss Jones had a relatively easy time of it when Murphy was counted out. Another countout win saw John Naylor beat Tally Ho Kaye in the other bout shown.

The wrestling shown on *World of Sport* on January 19th was the second half of the show taped at Bury in December and featured the return of Mike Bennett. Bennett now was a completely changed wrestler, he had bleached his hair blond, had ditched the black trunks, boots and tracksuit for colourful ring gear including a sash he wore proclaiming him to be 'Marvellous' and handed out leaflets to ringsiders telling them that he was destined for championship honours. It was natural therefore that Danny Collins would be in his sights and it was Collins who he met in this match albeit a non title one. Bennett who won the match with a single leg Boston crab in the fourth round and immediately pressed his claims for a crack at Collins' title. The rest of the show was devoted to a four man heavyweight knockout tournament with Pat Roach, The Emperor, Drew McDonald and Ray Steele participating in it. The semi finals saw a time limit draw between Roach and Steele which Roach won by a points decision and The Emperor beat Drew McDonald by the one fall needed. The Emperor was Bill Bromley in yet another guise and regular fans knew exactly who it was wearing the mask. The final ended with both Roach and Emperor being disqualiifed so the tournament saw no winner.

Big Daddy made his first TV appearance of the year on January 26th on a show from Walsall. Daddy and partner Mick McMichael took on the team of Mel Stuart and Blackjack Mulligan , Stuart replaced Rasputin which would have made it a much more interesting match. A couple of belly butts followed by a big splash paved the way to an easy two straight falls win for Daddy and McMichael. The opener saw Jackie Turpin meet Grasshopper and with both wrestlers shoulders pinned to the mat in the fourth round it ended in a draw. The other match that week also ended without a winner as the contest between Chic Cullen and Caswell Martin ended in the eighth round with both wrestlers failing to beat the count.

The big news of the month was that Brian Dixon and his newly renamed 'All-Star Promotions' had finally got a foot in the door at the Fairfield Hall in Croydon and announced their first show there would be on February 12th. Brian Dixon had lined up a star studded bill for his first Croydon show with three world title matches as a triple main event. Wayne Bridges would defend his World Heavyweight Title against Mighty Chang , the famed Oriental stalwart of the independent scene. Mark Rocco would face the challenge of the Spaniard Mario Montez for the World Heavy/Middleweight Title and Johnny Saint put the World Lightweight Title on the line against Mal Sanders. Backing this up would see King Kong Kirk meet Dave Taylor, lightweight contenders Mike Jordan and Jackie

Robinson would meet plus a tag match with the 'Young Ones' Robbie Brookside and Wayne Martin facing the colourful duo of Tom Thumb and 'Pretty Boy' Floyd.

The second half of the show from Walsall was seen on *World of Sport* on February 2nd with Alan Kilby taking on Steve Logan for the British Light/Heavyweight Title that Marty Jones had vacated. It was Kilby who picked up another championship belt by way of a two falls to one win in the ninth round. Greg Valentine beat Lucky Gordon by disqualification in the second round and the imposing Colonel Brody beat Barry Douglas by the only fall needed in the twelfth minute. Brody had last been seen on TV a few years ago under the name of 'Magnificent Maurice' but his new military gimmick was far removed from that.

To counter the arrival of All-Star Promotions at Croydon Dale Martin scheduled a TV taping for the week before and a show featuring Big Daddy the week after. The first half of the show from Croydon shown on February 9th's *World of Sport* featured a Battle Royale with eight wrestlers under 13st competing. The first solo match saw Tally Ho Kaye take on Steve Fury from Blackpool who was making his TV debut. Kaye got the one score needed with a leg suspension submission in five minutes of the contest. Chris Bowles beat Sid Cooper by disqualification. Ian McGregor got the one fall needed to beat Johnny Kidd and Danny Collins beat Eddie Riley. It was Danny Collins who outlasted the opposition to win the over the top rope finale with Tally Ho Kaye and Sid Cooper having a falling out as Collins sent them flying out of the ring to be victorious.

The night of February 12th saw a very nervous Brian Dixon on his way to the debut All-Star Promotions show at Croydon. The nerves were not needed as it turned out to be an overwhelming success in front of a packed crowd and from now on All-Star would be on the same level if not above Dale Martin going forward in the eyes of all the fans who attended both promotion's shows. Wayne Bridges made a successful defence of his World Title against Mighty Chang. Johnny Saint's defence against Mal Sanders ended in a No Contest as did Mark Rocco's title match against Mario Montez. Mal Kirk was in Ireland so his match with Dave Taylor was replaced by Rocky Moran who had returned to 'All-Star' beating John Kenny. Mike Jordan beat Jackie Robinson in an entertaining lightweight clash and 'The Young Ones' Robbie Brookside and Wayne Martin beat Tom Thumb and 'Pretty Boy' Floyd by the one fall needed.

Wrestling was scheduled to be missing from *World of Sport* on February 16th as the Pool World Championships was on at 4pm instead. Grapple fans got lucky at short notice as the continuing arctic weather wiped out the ITV7 racing coverage and wrestling from Warrington was shown instead. Four matches were shown as part of a three a side team match, Big Daddy teamed up with Pete Roberts and Greg Valentine to face a trio of The Emperor, Drew McDonald and Scrubber Daly. The first match saw Valentine face the much bigger Daly and a big splash from Daly in the fifth round saw Valentine unable to continue. Roberts and McDonald had a hard fought one fall each draw over the scheduled six rounds. In the third match Daddy got the first fall in the first round with a big splash on the Emperor before the masked man decided he didn't fancy another one and walked out in the second round. Both Valentine and Emperor were unable to compete in the six man tag finale so it became a conventional tag match. Big Daddy and Pete Roberts beat Drew McDonald and Scrubber Daly by two straight falls in the seventh minute with a big splash on Daly by Daddy sealing the win. Incredibly the four matches were fitted into twenty eight minutes of the show just after 2pm.

There was no wrestling shown on February 23rd with The British Open snooker tournament screened and to complete another blank weekend more of the British Open snooker was shown on March 2nd. March 9th saw boxing shown on World of Sport with Stefan Tangstad's bout with Anders Eklund for the European Heavyweight Title on instead of wrestling.

It had become obvious that Joint Promotions needed some fresh talent at the top end of the card and one of the new arrivals in February was Florida based Heavyweight Scott McGhee. McGhee was the son of one of the top English Heavyweights of the 1960's and early 70's Geoff Portz and had a solid background in Florida Championship Wrestling. He was immediately given a title match for Marty Jones's World Mid/Heavyweight Title as well as several matches against the likes of Fit Finlay and Pete Roberts and was a welcome new attraction. Another newcomer or maybe a come backer to Joint Promotions was the Calgary based Heavyweight Bearcat Wright who turned out to be another wrestler returning to Joint Promotions' rings with a striking new look. Bearcat Wright was in fact Bernie Wright who had been in Canada for the past few years on the 'Stampede' circuit under the name Athol Foley the supposed son of John Foley. Wright now sported a 'Mr T' haircut and a much more aggressive style in the ring, far removed from the late 70's when he was more often than not facing Davey 'Boy' Smith in novice matches.

Bearcat Wright faced one of the toughest opponents possible when he took on Marty Jones in a contest shown on *World of Sport* on March 16th when wrestling returned after a month's absence. Unfortunately only a few minutes of the match taped at Wright's hometown of Warrington were shown and it was Jones who won with a dropkick seeing Wright unable to beat the count in the tenth minute. There was only one other match shown that week but it was a pearler as after his win over Danny Collins seen on January Mike Bennett got his chance at the British Welterweight Title held by the youngster. Collins got the first fall in the sixth round but Bennett was proving a formidable foe in the match. A neck stretch submission on Collins in the eight round saw Bennett level the contest but after already receiving two public warnings Bennett got himself disqualified by referee Jeff Kaye for kneeing Collins when he was down. Collins therefore remained the champion but not only did Bennett demand another title match he also vented his fury on referee Kaye and challenged him to a match.

Whilst things were going on in the ring more was happening outside when erstwhile Big Daddy tag team opponent Tony 'Banger' Walsh sold his story to 'The Sun' newspaper. Unbelievably or not this was front page news and under the headlines 'I slashed my face while crowd bayed for blood' , 'Big Daddy used me as a fight fall guy' and 'Family firm fix the lot' Walsh 'reveals truth about fake would of grunt 'n' groan'. Naturally the wrestlers were furious with Walsh as they were with anyone who did this and the bad feelings remained for some even up to today. Did it damage British Wrestling ? Probably not , by this time most spectators saw a Big Daddy tag match as show business more than sport and people like Walsh were just the fall guys in the spectacle. The attitude by ringsiders was more like we know that's not wrestling but this Fit Finlay match or this Mike Bennett match isn't fixed and look how hurt they are. At the end of the day there was enough wrong inside the ropes that put off paying customers so the Walsh articles were pretty much todays newspapers, tomorrows fish and chips wrapping.

    Later on in the year Jackie Pallo published his autobiography 'You Grunt I'll Groan' and he rehashed a similar story to Walsh's. A lot of the book if not most of it was rubbish, with historical facts wrong and many thought it belonged on the fiction shelf. It had a theme of being jealous about everyone else through the book whether it was Mick McManus, Big Daddy or any other wrestler who had become a bigger name than him. The person Pallo reserved most of his venom for was former Dale Martin MC and office worker Mike Judd. Judd was one of those in charge behind the scenes as well as their number one MC and Pallo says he was the reason he and his son JJ stopped working for Joint Promotions. The fact was when he left Joints in 1974 he was nearly 50 and no longer the draw at the Box Office he once was. The wrestling game needed fresh faces to revitalise what had become a tired looking top of the bill on most shows. Mike Judd in fact was quite an interesting person who had worked for Paul Lincoln before joining Dale Martin , he co-authored the book 'The who's who of Wrestling' under the name of Pam Edwards. Judd was sacked by Dale Martin in late 1978 accused of financial irregularities and was never seen or heard from again. A few wrestlers and back room boys have attempted to find out what happened to him or locate his whereabouts in the past few years but without any success.

    With the barrage of bad publicity and declining attendances the money men behind Joint Promotions decided it was time to cash in and sell up. Brian Dixon who was becoming ever frustrated in his attempts to get 'All-Star Promotions' onto ITV put together a deal with fellow independent promoter Orig Williams to buy Joint Promotions as a means to an end to get the ITV deal. Unfortunately the bid was unsuccessful and Max Crabtree bought out the consortium instead, with hindsight looking back Dixon and Williams dodged a bullet and were better off without it.

Back inside the ring it had been announced at the September 29th show that there would be another bill at The Royal Albert Hall on a Friday night this time, March 8th. As the new year progressed it seemed that this date had been quietly forgotten about and it would be another seven months before wrestling was featured there again.

Two matches from Croydon were featured on *World of Sport* on March 23rd with the first featuring the masked Emperor facing Tom Tyrone. With only the one score needed it was the Emperor who came out on top with an opposite arm lever forcing a submission from Tyrone in the third round. The other contest saw Fit Finlay with Princess Paula by his side take on a newcomer to TV 'The Black Prince' who was clad in a black judo suit. The Prince was in fact Steve Prince who would go on to be better known wearing an army uniform as 'Soldier Boy' Steve Prince. It was not a happy TV debut for Prince who was overwhelmed by Finlay and lost in the in the fifth round when he failed to beat the count after a powerslam.

It was off to Southend for the next two weeks on *World of Sport* with the show on March 30th featuring an international knockout tournament with Marty Jones, Scott McGhee, Len Hurst and Dave Duran taking part in it. The first semi final saw Marty Jones beat Dave Duran with the powerlock making Duran submit in the ninth minute. The second semi final between Scott McGhee and Len Hurst saw McGhee proceed to the final when he pinned Hurst in the eighth minute. In the final fought over a fifteen minutes time limit McGhee got the first fall in the seventh minute with a slightly obvious looking double leg nelson. Jones equalised in the eleventh minute with a folding press off of the ropes but neither wrestler got the winner before the end of the fifteenth minute so it ended in a draw. Kent Walton said that there would be a rematch but unfortunately McGhee had returned to the USA before it could happen.

April 6th saw another two matches from Southend screened on *World of Sport* with Steve Grey wrestling a one fall each draw with Clive Myers over eight rounds. The main event saw Alan Kilby defend the British Light/Heavyweight Title against Mel Stuart, Stuart had never been placed on a bill as a legitimate title contender before so it was surprising to see Kilby defend against him. To prove the point Kilby ran out an easy winner by two straight falls inside seven rounds.

The wrestling on *World of Sport* on April 13th saw thirty minutes of wrestling shown at 2.10pm with only two matches on. The first of which came from Aylesbury and had been recorded back in December between Tally Ho Kaye and Little Prince. Kaye was disqualified by referee Peter Szakacs in the third round for punching Prince in the stomach. The other contest broadcast was from Croydon and saw a surprisingly aggressive and bad tempered Keith Haward wrestle a twenty minute time limit draw with Steve Grey.

One of the new features of *World of Sport* was they had begun to show live boxing on a Saturday afternoon and on this afternoon this was the case with two bouts shown at 4pm. Sylvester Mittee defended the Commonwealth Welterweight Title against Martin McGough and Rocky Kelly fought Kostas Petrou for the vacant British Welterweight Title.

The wrestling on *World of Sport* on April 20th was cut back to only thirty minutes with continuing coverage of a speedway test match between England & Denmark on at 4pm before wrestling started at 4.15pm. The coverage from Halifax featured a tag match with 'The Riot Squad' team of Fit Finlay and Skull Murphy making their first TV appearance for a while against the team of Ringo Rigby and Steve Fury. As expected Finlay and Murphy were too much for their opponents and won without too much bother. The other match saw a rather unexciting match in which Alan Kilby beat Barry Douglas by two falls to one with the winning fall from Kilby coming in the final round of eight.

More of the show from Halifax was shown on April 27th with Jeff Kaye accepting the challenge of Mike Bennett as the main event. Bennett was furious when referee Kaye had disqualified him in his title match with Danny Collins and had demanded revenge. Unfortunately whilst still wrestling occasionally Kaye was now mainly a referee and Bennett took advantage of this. A nasty looking double arm submission gave Bennett the first score in the eleventh minute but Kaye got a submission of his own when an arm lever forced Bennett to tap in the fourteenth minute. It was Bennett that won though with his neck stretch submission following a pile driver made Kaye quit in the seventeenth minute. An international catchweight six rounder saw Chic Cullen take on heavyweight Caswell Martin. Martin got the first fall in the fourth round with a cross press following a German suplex. Cullen equalised in the fifth round with a slam followed by a cross press of his own. Neither wrestler got the winner in the last round so referee Gordon Pryor's verdict was a draw and with the winner advertised to face Marty Jones that remained undecided. The preliminary match saw Ray Steele defeat Steve Logan by the only fall required.

May 4th saw the start of the build-up for the wrestling to be seen on the FA Cup Final *World of Sport* on May 18th. The speedway was on again so there was just time for the one match and it saw Big Daddy and Mick McMichael face The Emperor and Sid Cooper. The bout had been taped at Cannock two months before and it was originally advertised as being Daddy and McMichael against The Rockers so somewhere along the line the plans were changed. A routine tag match saw Charlie McGee with The Rockers appear at ringside and Kent Walton told us that they would be taking on Daddy and McMichael on FA Cup Final day. Cooper softened up McMichael before Emperor tagged in and made McMichael submit from a neck hold submission in the third minute. Naturally once Daddy made his usual hot tag things didn't last much longer with a big splash on the Emperor for the equaliser in the sixth minute before Daddy ripped off the mask which saw him flee from the ring. McMichael then got the winning fall with a folding press on Cooper a minute later. Afterwards I remembered fondly about the days when the build-up to FA Cup Final day match meant something like the first time Big Daddy got his hands on

John Quinn in 1979 or when Wayne Bridges had his title match in 1980 with John Quinn or all the massive matches with Mick McManus, Jackie Pallo and others in the past. Now just five years later the fans were served up this load of old rubbish and it just gave ammunition to the wrestling haters at ITV.

The Rockers continued their build-up the FA Cup Final match with Big Daddy and Mick McMichael when they took on Eddie Riley and Ian McGregor on *World of Sport* on May 11th. The Rockers won by two falls to one with LaPaque getting a winning submission on McGregor in the sixteenth minute. Afterwards Charlie McGee grabbed Brian Crabtree's microphone and started a rant about what they would do to Big Daddy but I doubt anyone watching believed him or even cared. The shows preliminary match saw Bearcat Wright make short work of Pat Patton beating him in the second round by countout. The other match saw Marty Jones take on Chic Cullen and with Cullen unable to continue in the seventh round Jones sportingly refused to accept the win and so a No Contest was called.

A new British Heavyweight Champion was crowned at Croydon on May 14th, it was announced in the programme that a tournament had been held for the 'vacant' British Heavyweight Title and the final of this tournament would be held at the Surrey venue between Ray Steele and Pete Roberts. This tournament had the same authenticity of the one held by the WWF to crown their inaugural Intercontinental Champion in 1979. It was an entirely fictional series of matches that ended with Roberts and Steele to fight out the final. Steele won the title when everyone who attended the show knew the true British Heavyweight Championship was the one that Tony St Clair held when he left Joint Promotions in 1980. Since that title had been abandoned in 1982 when it was made an 'open' heavyweight title Joint Promotions might have been better served highlighting that and saying this was the true 'Mountevans Title' going forward.

There were two slots with wrestling in it on the FA Cup Final *World of Sport* on May 18th taped at Watford. One of them being the Big Daddy and Mick McMichael match against The Rockers with Charlie McGee. A terrible match ended in just over seven minutes when Daddy shoved both LaPaque and Lorne through the ropes and they were counted out by referee Peter Szakacs. The other match shown promised to be a lot better although it would have had a hard job to be worse. Danny Collins would be challenging the veteran German European Welterweight Champion Baron Von Chenok for his title. For once in a long while Joint Promotions treated the match with importance with fanfares over the PA as the wrestlers entered the ring and seconds carrying both the British and German flags. For some reason when Von Chenok was introduced a blast of 'We shall not be moved' was played. Collins took the lead in fourth round with a double leg nelson and which Kent Walton got excited about. The champion Von Chenok equalised in the sixth round when a neck stretch submission hold saw Collins tap instantly. Mick McManus jumped up to Collins' corner in the interval between the seventh and eighth round and his advice paid off as Collins won the match in the eighth with a cross press to become the new European Welterweight Champion.

Two days after the Watford show was recorded on April 25th Danny Collins was scheduled to drop the British Welterweight Title to Sid Cooper. Due to winning the European Title he was contracted to wrestle on the continent for Roger Delaporte. For some reason this change didn't happen and neither did the matches on the continent. Regardless of Collins not leaving the country another title match for Collins against Cooper was set up for May 23rd and this time Collins did drop the belt to Cooper when he was unable to continue in the 6th round. Despite losing his title Collins was booked to defend it at Bedworth on June 14th against Mike Bennett. Collins successfully defended the title he no longer held when Bennett was disqualified in the 8th round. He finally did regain the British Title when he beat Sid Cooper at Bristol on June 20th but such stupidity was unforgivable. As a keeper of records of results etc this rubbish was hard to defend and gave out the impression that the titles meant nothing anymore. Once upon a time the 'Lord Mountevans' belts meant everything in British Wrestling and title matches were often used as an excuse by promoters in the 1950's and 60's to put another shilling on the price of tickets for that night. Now Joint Promotions couldn't even bother to remember who the champion was.

A big week for All-Star Promotions started on May 20th at Slough when finally Wayne Bridges became the unified World Heavyweight Champion when he defeated John Quinn in a title v title match. The next night on May 21st at Croydon both Bridges and Quinn were in opposition again as All Star held their second show there with once again a bumper crowd in attendance. This time though it was a tag match with Bridges partnering long time Croydon favourite Steve Veidor against Quinn and Mark Rocco. To nobodies surprise the match descended into chaos and the referee was unable to restore any kind of order. The first fall went to Quinn and Rocco before an equaliser for Bridges and Veidor after thirteen minutes. Bridges and Rocco were both disqualified after sixteen minutes before the match was completely abandoned in the 20th minute. Whilst not much scientific wrestling was seen those in attendance loved every minute of it. The main supporting match saw Jim Breaks make a successful defence of his European Lightweight Title when he beat the challenger Mike Jordan by two falls to one in the tenth round. In a rematch from the first Croydon show Mal Sanders beat the maestro Johnny Saint in something of a surprise by two falls to one in the sixth round. Jon Cortez made a welcome return and showed all his skills still remained when he beat Jackie Robinson and Bobby Barnes beat John Kenny by the only fall needed to complete a fine nights wrestling.

The second part of the Watford show was shown on *World of Sport* on May 25th. The preliminary match saw Pat Roach who was riding the waves of popularity due to his role as Bomber in ITV's 'Auf Wiedersehen Pet' take on Pete Roberts with Roach getting the one fall needed to win in the fourth round. The main match saw Giant Haystacks take on both of the Wilson brothers, Johnny and Peter in a handicap tag match. A neck hold saw Peter submit in the third minute before a hefty looking guillotine elbow drop saw him counted out and an another easy win for the big man. The final match that week was advertised as being a title eliminator between Fit Finlay and Scott McGhee but McGhee had returned home to Florida so his place was taken by Roy Scott. Finlay polished off Scott with a pile driver in the fourth round where he had absolutely no hope of beating referee Peter Szakac's count of ten.

In a massive blow for Joint Promotions it was announced that due to declining ratings *World of Sport* would no longer be screened and the final broadcast would be on September 28th. The coveted 4 o'clock slot on ITV was gone and would be replaced by a stand alone show that would be broadcast on Saturday lunchtimes instead.

The Summer Season of 1985 got under way later that year with venues opening their doors later than ever more and a lot less shows than in previous years. My local venue, Hove Town Hall, abandoned their shows after only a couple as the attendances were abysmal considering Big Daddy was on one of these bills and Marty Jones v Fit Finlay was on the other it showed how much the interest in wrestling was declining. With the lack of shows it was no surprise that Joint Promotions could no longer hold wrestlers to exclusive contracts and threaten to sack them if they wanted to work for other promoters such as Brian Dixon or Orig Williams. Several new faces were on show for Joint Promotions during the Summer including the veteran Northern Irish duo Billy Joe Beck and Diamond Shondell who were both respected in the Emerald Isle and started making regular appearances on the mainland. Mike Jordan made a welcome comeback after wrestling on the independent scene for the past five or six years and 'Manxman' John Savage returned after an absence of two years. Other newcomers included the West Country duo of Richie Brooks and Jeff Kerry whilst the older brother of Danny Collins, Peter Collins billed as 'The College Boy' made his debut. One of the most surprising things about the start of the Summer season was that Joint Promotions started to advertise ladies wrestling on some of their bills with Princess Paula returning to the ring. None of the matches actually happened and were replaced by a mens match each night. The word was that the 'authorities', which probably meant the ITV executives, didn't want Joint Promotions putting on ladies bouts thereby associating themselves with it. This attitude in 1985 is quite unbelievable really as British ladies wrestling at the time was a legitimate sporting entertainment and nothing was sleazy about it. The ban still held in London and despite Brian Dixon's many efforts he was still unable to promote ladies wrestling in the capital. As I will write about later on as soon as ITV cancelled the TV contract Joint Promotions started billing ladies matches and would do so up until their demise.

Three matches from Morley in Yorkshire were shown on *World of Sport* on June 1st with Alan Kilby once again matched with John Elijah although this time they were competing for the 'George De Relwyskow Cup'. It was Kilby who claimed the prize with the winning fall of a two falls to one victory coming in the eighth round. Gil Singh beat Bruiser Muir in the third round with a flying tackle followed by a cross press for the winner. Steve Grey's match with Jackie Turpin ended in a No Contest.

The following week's *World of Sport* on June 8th saw Ray Steele make a first defence of his British Heavyweight Title against Colin Joynson from the bill recorded at Morley. Steele retained the belt with a Boston crab submission in the ninth round to seal the win. Ernest Baldwin came into the ring to present Steele with the belt afterwards. Due to athletics being shown throughout the afternoon wrestling was shown at 1220 with only time for that one contest.

The small town of Hyde just outside of Manchester was the venue for wrestling on *World of Sport* on June 15th. Hyde's main claim to fame is being where Dr Harold Shipman practised and his surgery was right opposite the town hall where the wrestling was held. The first bout that week saw Ron Marino replace Chris Bowles whose pro wrestling career had already ended and it was Marino who faced one of 'The Rockers' Pete LaPaque. Marino and LaPaque were part of the Leicester crew who travelled together and usually wrestled each other. A single leg Boston crab was enough to make Marino submit in the fourth round and the win went to LaPaque. An international catchweight match saw Len Hurst take on Keith Haward with Haward taking the lead in the fifth round with a German suplex taking Hurst down and a wrestler's bridge used to pin him. Hurst reversed a flying tackle in the sixth round to equalise with a cross press but there was no further score so at the end of the eight round the result was a draw. The final contest was a tag match with the team of Danny Collins and Greg Valentine meeting the pair of Sid Cooper and Blackjack Mulligan. This was an ideal chance for Collins and Valentine to show what they could do in a tag match without being overshadowed by Big Daddy. The youngsters impressed those watching with a two straight falls win with the first fall seeing Collins pin Mulligan in the seventh minute with a double leg nelson following a flying sunset flip from the top of the corner post. Valentine got the winning fall on Cooper in the twelfth minute with a cross press following a body slam.

Hyde again was the venue on June 22nd for *World of Sport* with the second half of the show recorded there. First match was a brief glimpse of Bearcat Wright taking on Ian McGregor with the contest having an unfortunate ending in the fourth round. Wright attempted to suplex McGregor but in doing so McGregor went out of the ring over the top rope and had no chance of being able to continue after a bad landing on the floor. Wright refused to accept the technical knockout win so it was deemed a No Contest and afterwards presenter Dickie Davies informed concerned viewers that McGregor was ok. Mike Bennett faced Jackie Turpin next in a twenty minute time limit match with Bennett now a real villain in the eyes of the fans. First fall went to Bennett in the eight minute with a cross press with Bennett proudly displaying his 'Marvellous Mike' banner to Turpin during the interval. Turpin wiped the smirk off of Bennett's face when a flying tackle followed by a cross press brought the equalising fall in the sixteenth minute. Unfortunately Turpin completely lost his cool with Bennett when the action resumed and the former boxer used his pugilistic skills to land a right hook right on Bennett's jaw. Referee Peter Szakacs had no option to stop the match but instead of being the end of the contest he told both wrestlers to resume and to respect the rules. Naturally Bennett didn't and in the final minute got Turpin to submit from a Boston crab as the crowd howled their disapproval and once again the 'Marvelous Mike' banner got an airing. The final match saw the crowd's favourite Marty Jones give away a huge amount of weight to take on Giant Haystacks. As Kent Walton noted Haystacks outweighed Jones by over 30st but Jones' speed gave Haystacks a few problems in the first round. He even attempted to hoist Haystacks over the top rope but it wasn't long before the big man was rag dolling Jones around the ring. Jones managed to last into the second round and after a series of punches to Haystacks' stomach which referee Gordon Pryor allowed Jones landed a flying tackle on his opponent. Haystacks kicked out of the pinfall attempt and in doing so sent Jones out of the ring where he was unable to continue after injuring his wrist.

World of Sport on June 29th saw wrestling once again reduced to an earlier slot with just the one match shown from Slough. Athletics was deemed to be more important at 4pm so grapple fans had to be satisfied with Fit Finlay tackling Clive Myers at 1220 instead. Myers got the first fall with a superb lean back double nelson pinning Finlay in the eighth minute. Finlay though emerged with the win when he sent Myers flying off of the top of the corner post and unable to beat the count in the seventeenth minute.

Wrestling again was shown in the 1220 slot on *World of Sport* on July 6th with a further two bouts shown from Slough. Athletics again got priority at 4pm and grapple fans had to be grateful that twenty five minutes at lunchtime was better than no wrestling shown at all. The first match saw Skull Murphy beat Alan Kilby with a gator hold forcing Kilby to tap out in the final round. In the other match Steve Grey defended his British Lightweight Title against Rick Wiseman. Wiseman had never been portrayed as being worthy of a title match, a bit like Mel Stuart in his title match against Alan Kilby a few weeks back. Grey retained with a two straight falls win in the seventh round in a match that Wiseman never looked like getting a fall let alone winning.

Athletics seemed to have taken hold of the 4pm slot on *World of Sport* on July 13th as for the third week running wrestling was relegated to 1220. Even artistic roller skating got more coverage than the wrestling this week as only one contest was shown. Big Daddy was in action though in the match recorded at Alfreton when he teamed up with Pat Patton to face Bearcat Wright and Bull Pratt. The usual combination of belly butts, double teaming by the villains followed by a hot tag and a big splash to end it would make anyone think it was scripted. Anyway a big splash from Daddy finished things off for yet another win but the crowd were loud and they enjoyed it and I dare say the lunchtime viewers did too.

Alfreton was again the venue for the wrestling on *World of Sport* on July 20th with the coverage back on at its usual time of 4pm although to be pedantic it actually started at 3.55. The first match shown was a match to decide the winner for the grandly named 'Amber Valley Industrial Development Challenge Shield'. The two wrestlers to fight for it were Greg Valentine and Lucky Gordon and it was Valentine who took the shield back home to Yorkshire as a result of a two falls to one win. The other match saw Alan Kilby defend his British Light/Heavyweight Title against Skull Murphy as a result of Murphy beating him in a non title match shown two weeks previously. This time though Murphy over did the rule breaking in his efforts to win the belt and in the end tested the referee's patience once too often and Kilby retained the title as a result of a disqualification.

Wrestling was back to the 1220 slot on *World of Sport* on July 27th with two matches from Bradford screened. Athletics was once again shown at 4pm with the WAAA Championships broadcast. Danny Collins beat Johnny Kidd by two straight falls in the first of the bouts and in the other Marty Jones beat John Savage by two falls to one.

It was announced at the start of August that there would be another show at The Royal Albert Hall, this time back on its usual Wednesday night, on October 30th. At the end of the month it was announced that it would be a 'full scale international tournament with a nine man Great Britain squad facing a star studded line up drawn from the Rest of the World in a mammoth eight bout presentation'. Remember the words 'star studded' for later on as they have never been misused so much in wrestling history. The nine members of the British team were announced as Big Daddy and naturally he was also captain, Ray Steele, Pete Roberts, Marty Jones, Fit Finlay, Alan Kilby, Greg Valentine, Mike Bennett and Danny Collins. Ringsiders waited with anticipation for the names of the Rest of the World team.

There was no athletics shown on *World of Sport* on August 3rd so wrestling was back on at 4pm with three matches from Bradford. The first match shown between John Naylor and Little Prince ended with both counted out. Next match saw Mike Bennett give away plenty of weight to take on Steve Logan over eight rounds. Although Bennett was wrestling at his local venue it was Logan who the fans were firmly behind but Bennett silenced them getting the first fall in the fifth round with a folding press. Logan finally got the equalising fall in the seventh round with a cross press after a flying tackle from the corner post. It was Bennett though that got the winner in the final round with a Boston crab that saw Logan submit instantly. Third and final contest shown saw Fit Finlay with Princess Paula in his corner as usual face King Ben. Referee Ken Joyce was forced to warn Paula for continually haranguing him and to remind her he was in charge. A surprisingly evenly fought match was still scoreless in the twelfth minute when a high flying knee from Finlay caught Ben on his temple and a weakened Ben was knocked out by a pile driver straight after.

Tag team wrestling was the feature on *World of Sport* on August 10th from Oakengates with a four team knockout tournament. As well as the tournament a catchweight match was shown between Keith Haward and John Elijah. Elijah got the first fall with a cross press in the fourth round before Haward equalised in the next round with a double leg nelson. With only one round left neither wrestler got a winner so the result was a draw. The first of the tag matches saw 'The Rockers' Pete LaPaque and Tommy Lorne take on TV debutants Richie Brooks and Jeff Kerry. Lorne got the first fall with a reverse double knee in the fourth minute over Kerry after several weakeners. Brooks got an equaliser when reversing a Boston crab attempt by LaPaque for a double leg nelson in the seventh minute of the scheduled ten minutes time limit. But LaPaque and Lorne were far too experienced and following a back drop LaPaque forced Brooks to submit from a backbreaker a minute later. The second tag match featured Danny Collins and Greg Valentine taking on a new team of Tally Ho Kaye and Blondie Barratt. The speed and agility of Collins and Valentine totally bewildered their opponents and a sunset flip from

Collins followed by a double leg nelson on Barratt brought the first fall in the sixth minute. A folding press from Valentine on Kaye with a minute of so left of the match was the winner in a two straight falls victory for Collins and Valentine. The final of the tournament saw Danny Collins and Greg Valentine take on 'The Rockers' with again a ten minute time limit. Despite plenty of double teaming and illegal tactics it was Collins with a folding press on LaPaque in the seventh minute who got the first fall. Before the match could restart LaPaque and Lorne had a discussion in their corner and simply left the ring and walked back to the dressing room. Referee Peter Szakacs had no option but to count both of them out and award the win to Collins and Valentine.

September 7th saw boxing the main feature of *World of Sport* with two hours of live coverage from 3.10pm which included Clinton McKenzie versus Lloyd Christie and Prince Rodney defending the British Light/Middleweight Title against Mike Courtney. Therefore wrestling was again back in the 12.20 slot and just enough time to show another two contests from the Oakengates bill. The two matches shown were the semi finals of a knockout tournament of which Marty Jones, Fit Finlay, Johnny Kincaid and Beau Jack Rowlands were the entrants. Rowlands hadn't been seen on TV for nearly five years and Kincaid hadn't been seen on TV for even longer. The semi finals were drawn to see Jones take on Finlay and Kincaid face Rowlands. The first match ended in a surprise with Jones losing his cool and getting himself disqualified. The second match saw Kincaid come from a fall behind to win with a folding press in final minute of the twenty minutes time limit. The final between Finlay and Kincaid would be shown the next week.

The first show of the season at the Fairfield Halls in Croydon and now the major London area venue wasn't from Dale Martin but an All-Star Promotions show. After over twenty years of holding fortnightly shows Dale Martin had curtailed their schedule to now go alternate months with the opposition. The bill on September 10th saw eight wrestlers competing in a tournament for the 'Fairfield Halls Trophy' plus there would be an international heavyweight tag match too. On the night there were a few changes and the tag match saw the team of Lee Bronson and Spinner McKenzie beat The Warlord and Shane Stevens. The first round of the tournament saw Chic Cullen beat Rocky Moran in the twelfth minute. Rob Brookside beat Brian Maxine who was unable to continue in the ninth minute. Mark Rocco pinned John Kenny in the ninth minute and Mal Sanders beat Mike Jordan in the the twelfth minute. Chic Cullen won the first semi final when he pinned Brookside in the eighth minute and Sanders lifted the roof off the venue when he beat Rocco in the other semi final albeit by disqualification in eleventh minute. Despite being hated in most venues Sanders was the fans favourite at Croydon and they all celebrated when Sanders beat Cullen in the final by two falls to one in the fourth round. ITN newscaster Gordon Honeycombe who was guest of honour and had looked bored and bewildered throughout the show was called into the ring to present Sanders with the trophy. Nowadays it would be like inviting somebody like Andrew Neil to a British wrestling show and expecting him to sit through the whole thing to present the trophy at the end of the night.

It seemed that in the final few weeks of *World of Sport* being broadcast anything rather than wrestling was being shown and on September 14th an athletics match between England and Romania was screened at 4pm instead. Wrestling once again had to make do with the 1220 slot and two matches from High Wycombe were shown. First up saw young heavyweight John Savage 'The Manxman' taking on Terry Rudge with Savage getting an early lead in sixth minute with the first fall. Savage was now a lot heavier than his days tagging with Vic Faulkner a couple of years ago and had become a fully blown heavyweight. Rudge levelled things up in the eleventh minute when a Boston crab saw Savage tap out straightaway. A second Boston crab from Rudge in the fourteenth minute saw the same result with Savage submitting and a win for Rudge. The second match was the tournament final between Fit Finlay and Johnny Kincaid with as per normal now Princess Paula being very vocal in support of her man at ringside. It was Kincaid who took the lead with a cross press in the fourth round but the lead didn't last long as following a berating from Paula who even refused Finlay his usual kiss the Ulsterman went up a gear. Kincaid missed a posting and straightaway Finlay put him in a chicken wing submission to which Kincaid gave up straight away. Unfortunately Kincaid's corner man was forced to throw the towel in as the damage to his shoulder had forced him to retire from the match. Paula was a lot happier now and celebrated by kissing her man fully on his lips.

Wrestling was missing completely from the penultimate weekend of *World of Sport* on September 21st with a rare appearance of cricket on ITV shown instead. The 'Silk Cut Challenge' tournament from Arundel was on throughout the afternoon.

ITV's flagship Saturday sport's show *World of Sport* came to an end on September 28th. Instead of going out on a high, or even showing some of the memorable moments of wrestling in the 4pm slot over the years a very low key ending was screened instead. Wrestling was again on at 12.20 with a 'Goodbye World of Sport' show seen at 4pm. Filmed at the tiny venue of the Benn Memorial Hall in Rugby which only held four hundred just two matches were shown. In the first Skull Murphy easily disposed of the much lighter Scots youngster Ian McGregor inside four rounds. In the other Alan Kilby beat Northern Irish visitor Billy Joe Beck by two falls to one in just over sixteen minutes. It was a great shame that wrestling ended on *World of Sport* in such a low key way.

The Rest of the World team for the Royal Albert Hall show was finally announced at the beginning of October alongside the big news that children would be admitted free with an accompanying adult. The star studded team we were promised were either wrestlers who had been on the circuit for years such as Clive Myers, Johnny Kincaid and Ali Shan or wrestlers nobody had heard of. The rest of the team was Diamond Shondell, the Northern Irishman who had made a decent impression during the Summer. Sheik Al Saadi who had made a few appearances of no consequence the Winter before. Digger Nolan from Australia who had recently arrived for a tour of Britain. Steve Casey a Canadian newcomer who was apparantly from Vancouver. '21st Far East Collosus' Tony 'The Brute'

Baron who was billed from Singapore but was in fact a wrestler better known on the Norfolk holiday camp circuit and the 'Far East' obviously meant Great Yarmouth not Singapore ! The final member of the team was the Nigerian Samson Ubo who as per the publicity was immensely strong but was in fact one of the worst wrestlers ever seen in the British rings. During his appearances it was like someone from the crowd had climbed into the ring and wanted to be a wrestler. He had absolutely no clue what he was doing or when he was meant to be doing it and why he was booked we will never know. Perhaps a hint that the team match format of Great Britain v The Rest of the World hadn't been thought through was that Northern Irishman Fit Finlay was in the British team and fellow Northern Irishman Diamond Shondell was in the World team.

The first show of the new ITV stand alone wrestling presentation was broadcast on October 5th in the 1230 time slot with viewers by now quite used to seeing wrestling screened at lunchtime. As per the last *World of Sport* show nothing was done to mark the occasion. The creativity at this time for Joint Promotions was running on fumes and the two bouts shown did nothing to change this, Big Daddy and Steve Grey rolled over Tiny Callaghan and Sid Cooper by two straight falls in the main event. The opener saw Pete Roberts beat Ray Steele by two falls to one in the eighth round to put in a claim for a shot at the Heavyweight Title that Steele held.

The more interesting news on the TV front was that finally after years of persistance Brian Dixon had finally got a TV deal although it was on the Screensport cable TV channel. Pat Brogan the boxing promoter from Stoke had been providing boxing for the channel and now he was asked to provide wrestling too hence him asking Dixon to book the shows they wanted. Screensport had been broadcasting for about a year and was only available in a limited number of homes. I subscribed through Granada TV rentals and Rediffusion was another company that could connect viewers. There were only five or six channels to choose from but it was a wrestling fans paradise and introduced me to the delights of American wrestling of which I quickly became a fan. Apart from All-Star Wrestling on Screensport they also showed South West Championship

Wrestling, AWA, WCCW and a bit later Stampede was on. The Sky Channel which was a forerunner of Sky One had the WWF contract and aired 'Superstars of Wrestling' every week and they screened Wrestlemania III live as it happened. As the Screensport Channel was based in Cheshire and Pat Brogan was based in Stoke all the tapings took place in that area and the first show was taped on October 19th at Hanley. The show was shown multiple times through the month with a new one taped and broadcast monthly. It was a completely new way of seeing wrestling on TV with the hosts and commentators being Vince Miller and Maxton G Beesley. Miller was better known as a Northern club circuit comic and compere. Beesley was also a comedian on the club circuit as well as being an impersonator and was best known for winning on the ITV talent show 'Opportunity Knocks'. Miller and Beesley had an obvious knowledge of the way wrestling was broadcast in the USA as their input into the way the show was presented was heavily influenced by the over the top nature of the stateside wrestling commentators and presenters rather than the rather low key Kent Walton style. Mark Rocco was a big part of the new show and his run ins with both Miller and Beesley were a continuing theme throughout each broadcast. The first show screened saw the veteran Count Bartelli build-up to his retirement bout when the beat The Warlord. Robbie Brookside beat John Kenny and in a knockout tournament Mark Rocco beat Chic Cullen in the final. Rocco beat Kung Fu in the first semi final and Cullen beat Bobby Barnes in the second. Chic Cullen had returned to wrestle for 'All-Star' and was immediately feuding with Mark Rocco in title and non title matches.

The second edition of the new wrestling show on ITV was broadcast on October 12th and it was back to High Wycombe for two more contests recorded there. The first was a heavyweight bout with Johnny Wilson facing Tom Tyrone over eight rounds. Kent Walton was in his element with two good looking boys with tremendous physiques competing. Tyrone took the lead in the fifth round with a cross press but Wilson quickly equalised with a cross press himself following a flying tackle. The match went all the way into the eighth and final round but it was Tyrone who came out on top with a double leg nelson pinning Wilson for a two falls to one win. The other match saw Mike Bennett facing Clive Myers with once again Bennett's frequent use of illegal tactics seeing his downfall with referee Peter Szakacs disqualifying him.

Rickmansworth, a small town near Watford, hosted the ITV wrestling show on October 19th with now just the two bouts as usual. The first match saw young Richie Brooks who was making a good impression with the fans in his first few months of his pro wrestling career take on the vastly more experienced Tally Ho Kaye. Following a series of weakeners it was Kaye who got the first score when a leg suspension saw Brooks submit in the third round. Brooks equalised in the fifth round with a folding press before Kaye overdid the illegal tactics once too often in the sixth round. Referee Roy Harding had already given Kaye his final public warning in the round before Kaye punched Brooks and then shoved Harding and so got himself disqualified. The other match that week saw Pat Roach take on Colin Joynson and in a routine match Roach won by two falls to one in the sixth round.

Two more matches from Rickmansworth were shown on October 26th with an international clash in the first with Australian Digger Nolan making a TV debut against Marty Jones. Jones won the match in the seventh minute when a dropkick from him landed flush on Nolan's chin and knocked him spark out. Nolan abandoned the rest of his UK tour to return home to Australia and take up a music career. The second contest saw Danny Collins make a successful defence of his British Welterweight Title when he defeated challenger Mike Jordan by two falls to one in the ninth round of an excellent match.

Wednesday night, October 30th was the night of the big Royal Albert Hall show in London with the Great Britain v The World team match. I always looked forward to attending shows there as usually something newsworthy happened or you saw a great match or two and arriving home at 1am or later was always worth it. Arriving on the 30th the first clue this wouldn't be a good night was there seemed to be hardly anyone outside waiting to get in and once inside it was no surprise as the attendance for the evening was terrible. Things went wrong from the start, the advertised format of the evening seemed to have been forgotten about and the usual in ring presentation of each team and introduction of the wrestlers with the announcement of the matches didn't happen. MC Fred Downes had trouble throughout the whole evening identifying the wrestlers he was meant to introduce and needing prompting from the referee at times just to announce a match. From the original line ups Fit Finlay was missing from the British team and the Rest of the World team were without several members of their team. Digger Nolan had left the country after seemingly having his head dropkicked into the third or fourth row of the crowd in a TV bout against Marty Jones the week before. Abdul Al Saadi despite living about two miles from the venue wasn't there. Steve Casey whoever he was didn't show neither did Ali Shan and luckily Samson Ubo wasn't there or things incredibly would have been even worse. Drew McDonald replaced Fit Finlay for the British team and Zoltan Boscik, Tony Costas and those famed foreigners Sid Cooper and Bull Pratt took the place of those missing on the Rest of the World team.

The matches ended up with Caswell Martin wrestling a one fall each draw with Ray Steele. Clive Myers also wrestled a one fall each draw against the much heavier Pete Roberts. Johnny Kincaid beat Drew McDonald. Tony Costas beat Mike Bennett by disqualification. Danny Collins beat the veteran Hungarian Zoltan Boscik who was making a comeback after an absence from the ring. Alan Kilby beat Diamond Shondell in a comedy bout before the worst of the evening's matches. Marty Jones disinterestedly dismantled the East Anglian Tony Barron before the evening's tag match where the team of Big Daddy and Greg Valentine beat the duo of Sid Cooper and Bull Pratt in a match nobody cared about. The whole evening felt very flat, I personally sat there bored most of the time and facing a two or three hour journey home afterwards wished I had stayed at home instead. For a last Joint Promotions show at the Albert Hall it was desperately sad to go out on such a low note. It seemed Max Crabtree and Joint Promotions had got lazy or maybe complacent with their guaranteed TV money revenue stream as well as Big Daddy still drawing crowds although not so big as in the past. The individual matches and bills they were putting on weren't what people wanted to see.

Just as an example of what was on offer from Brian Dixon's match making, he held a show at Leicester the same night in what was always one of Joint Promotions' strongholds the De Montford Hall. The main event saw Chic Cullen defeat Mark Rocco in seven rounds to win the World Heavy/Middleweight Title. Jim Breaks retained the European Lightweight Title when he beat the World No.1 Johnny Saint by two falls to one in the seventh round of a heated encounter. A ladies tag match saw the ever popular Mitzi Mueller team up with Gemma Best to defeat the hated Klondyke Kaye and her partner 'Big Momma' in just under twenty minutes. In the third championship match Brian Maxine kept hold of the British Middleweight Title when the challenger Johnny England was unable to continue in the 6th round. A touch of comedy saw the midgets wrestle with Mini Quinn beating Tiny Tim before the evening ended with local star John Jenkins beating John Kenny.

It was becoming obvious that the old fashioned way of presenting wrestling which had been done since the 1950's and 60's was dying out. The demographic that had been around since then were dying out and nobody was replacing them, a simple watch of wrestling on the TV showed that you rarely saw anyone aged under forty at ringside. A programme consisting of five minute rounds matches, ten minute rounds had gone in the late 70's, but with most of the five minutes consisting of two big men lying on the mat in a chin lock had become too dated. Joint Promotions were failing to go with the time and what people wanted to see which was a livelier feel to the matches. Though they had a new programme to showcase their offerings on TV Joint Promotions had not updated anything and the whole thing had a tired look about it.

Even with the new stand alone show it wasn't enough to see ITV drop wrestling and on November 2nd a womens 15km road race from Gateshead was shown instead.

The All-Star Promotions November show at Croydon on the 5th featured plenty of fireworks in the ring with a tag match as a fall out from the September tournament. The match between Mark Rocco and Rocky Moran & Chic Cullen and Mal Sanders ended up being abandoned with the bout totally out of control. There was also a title change with finally Jim Breaks getting his hands on the World Lightweight Title when he defeated the reigning champion Johnny Saint by two falls to one. Breaks' title reign didn't last long as he lost the belt back to Saint a month later at Bradford on December 9th. The rest of the bill saw Brian Maxine pin Shane Stevens to win their match. Jon Cortez beat Jackie Robinson by two falls to one and veteran comedy wrestler Kevin Conneely beat Spinner McKenzie.

Wrestling was back on ITV on November 9th with a couple of bouts from St.Helens aired. Two heavyweight matches were on the menu this week with Gil Singh taking on John Elijah as the appetiser. It was Singh who got the only fall needed to win with a cross press following a body slam in the third round. The other match saw Ray Steele make a defence of his British Heavyweight Title against Pete Roberts after his loss to Roberts in a non title match seen on the first ITV show. Steele retained his belt but only after a titanic struggle that ended with both wrestlers counted out.

There was something of a build-up going on to a feud between Big Daddy and Fit Finlay with Princess Paula as 1985 went into its last two months. A tag match was billed to be on ITV on November 16th. Daddy would partner Steve Grey against Finlay and his partner Scrubber Daly, which with Finlay and Paula involved would be a cut above the usual Daddy tags. Fit Finlay and Scrubber Daly were shown entering the ring with Princess Paula whilst Big Daddy's music played and him and Steve Grey made their entrance. With both teams in the ring an argument broke out between Daddy, Finlay and Paula and with that Finlay and Paula simply left the ring and went back to the dressing room. A solemn sounding Kent Walton announced that they were refusing to wrestle and luckily they had a stand by wrestler waiting and so enter Lucky Gordon. Everyone who had paid their money to see a match involving Big Daddy and Fit Finlay were short changed, everyone who tuned into to see the match felt let down and in the terms of 'wrestling angles' and trying to draw money all it did was get people angry, feel ripped off and not make a penny out of it. Big Daddy and Fit Finlay were already doing tags all around the country so there was absolutely no point to be made by what happened here. In the match shown on TV that week which came from St.Helens Daly and new partner Gordon went the same way as they all did as Daddy and Grey won by two falls to one.The preliminary match was between Eddie Riley and Elvis Jerome and it was Riley who got the one fall needed to win.

November 23rd saw the wrestling on ITV come from the tiny Miner's Welfare Hall in Coalville which held two hundred if that and you could still see empty seats on the TV. The show that week featured a Battle Royale which squeezed in four singles matches and the over the top rope finale. In the singles matches all over a ten minute duration Richie Brooks beat Blackjack Mulligan who was disqualified for deliberately throwing Brooks out of the ring and not allowing him back in the ninth minute. Mike Bennett took on Johnny Kidd , Bennett with his usual illegal moves overpowered Kidd and won by two straight submissions. Kidd caught his neck between the top two ropes and whilst referee Roy Harding allowed him to continue Bennett showed no mercy and a neck stretch saw Kidd submit twice in less than a minute. Danny Collins faced fellow Bristolian Jeff Kerry and a folding press with a bridge saw Collins get the first fall in the third round. Collins got the second fall in the seventh minute with another folding press this time secured by a hand stand for a two straight falls win. Lucky Gordon took on Jackie Turpin in the other singles match with Turpin taking the lead with a folding press in the second minute. Gordon equalised with a Boston crab that saw Turpin submit in the seventh minute but no wrestler was able to get a winner so it was a one score each draw. The Battle Royale ended in controversy with the final two wrestlers left, Mike Bennett and Danny Collins both exiting over the top rope together so it was decided that they were joint winners.

Two more bouts were shown on ITV from Coalville on November 30th with the preliminary match seeing Little Prince take on King Ben. The score was one fall each when in the fifth round a flying headbutt from Ben knocked out Prince but unfortunately Ben was unable to beat the count either. The main match saw Marty Jones defend the World Mid/Heavyweight Title against Caswell Martin. Jones retained the belt by two falls to one in what was a technically sound match but dull for the viewers and it failed to engage with the fans in attendance.The question that had to be asked though was how Caswell Martin, a solid 16st or more heavyweight able to make the Mid/Heavyweight weight limit of 14st 13lbs ?

The November Screensport show again featured a couple of hours of entertaining wrestling. The top of the bill was a tag match with the team of Mark Rocco and Rocky Moran defeating the duo of Johnny Saint and Mal Sanders. Count Bartelli continued his countdown to his farewell match and retirement by beating Mad Dog Wilson. Chic Cullen wrestled an excellent one fall each draw with Kung Fu and Jon Cortez beat Johnny England.

The wrestling on ITV on December 7th came from Barnsley and featured the TV debut of French wrestler Jacques Le Jacques, Jacques was here to challenge for Danny Collins' European Welterweight Title. Jacques looked more like a Red Indian than a Frenchman and indeed wrestled on the continent as Indio Apache. His opponent was Ray Crawley who despite wrestling for quite a few years was making his TV debut too. Jacques took the lead with cross press following a hip toss in the second round before he sealed a two straight falls win in the fourth round with another cross press. Afterwards MC Brian Crabtree asked Jacques to say a few words to the fans to which he did but I doubt many of the viewers or those in attendance had any idea what he said as he addressed them in French. The main match saw Tally Ho Kaye and Sid Cooper take on Greg Valentine and Peter Collins rather than brother Danny. Despite a few moves at the start Collins wasn't ready for a TV match and his inexperienced showed at times. Valentine got the first fall when he rolled up Cooper for a folding press in the seventh minute. Cooper got the equaliser when a Boston crab saw Collins submit in the twelfth minute before Kaye got a submission on Collins with another Boston crab in the fifteenth minute whilst Valentine stood helpless on the end of the tag rope. A bonus match that week saw John Savage beat Jack Rowlands with a cross press after a hip toss in the fourth round.

Another two matches from Barnsley were shown on December 14th with neither of them that interesting. Len Hurst wrestled a one fall each draw with Terry Rudge over six rounds whilst Alan Kilby beat Diamond Shondell with the mule kick setting up Shondell for the winning fall in the fifth round.

The Christmas edition of the wrestling show on ITV shown on December 21st saw Big Daddy once again in the spotlight when he partnered Danny Collins against the team of Mike Bennett and Bruiser Muir. Before the match could start we were shown footage of Daddy visiting the local children's hospital dressed as Santa Claus and giving out festive gifts. Daddy and Collins were accompanied by the local pearly king and queen to the ring whilst Bennett and Muir had Tony Francis as their manager. Once things started the usual match unfolded with Daddy sending Muir and Bennett flying before Collins tagged in and the double team and illegal tactics started. Eventually the hot tag was made and Daddy quickly launched a big splash on Muir for the first fall in the sixth minute. The match only lasted another minute and a confused ending with Bennett disqualified for punching Collins although even watching the replay Kent Walton was nonplussed as to what had happened. The show from Battersea also featured Pat Roach taking on Tom Tyrone over eight rounds and it wasn't until the final round that Roach was able to get the winning fall with a cross press.

The final wrestling of the year on ITV came again from Battersea on December 28th with Steve Grey retaining the British Lightweight Title when his challenger Mike Jordan was unable to continue in the seventh round. Pete Roberts took on the Peruvian wildman Indio Guajaro in the other match over six rounds. Guajaro was a regular visitor to the continental tournaments but this was his first time in a British ring and he had difficulty understanding referee Peter Jaye's instructions. The match turned into something of a wild brawl rather than a wrestling contest but Roberts opened the scoring in the second round with a flying tackle flooring Guajaro before pinning him. Guajaro equalised in the fourth round with a grapevine and double arm hold which saw Roberts tap out. Unfortunately Roberts was unable to continue and his second threw in the towel which made Guajaro a lucky winner as referee Jaye would have been justified in disqualifying him. MC Paul Chalmers tried to announce the winner but the Peruvian grabbed the microphone and launched a barrage of Spanish insults at the audience, the MC and his stricken opponent.

It was an entertaining end to the year of wrestling shown on TV and a year full of happenings both in and out of the ring came to a close.

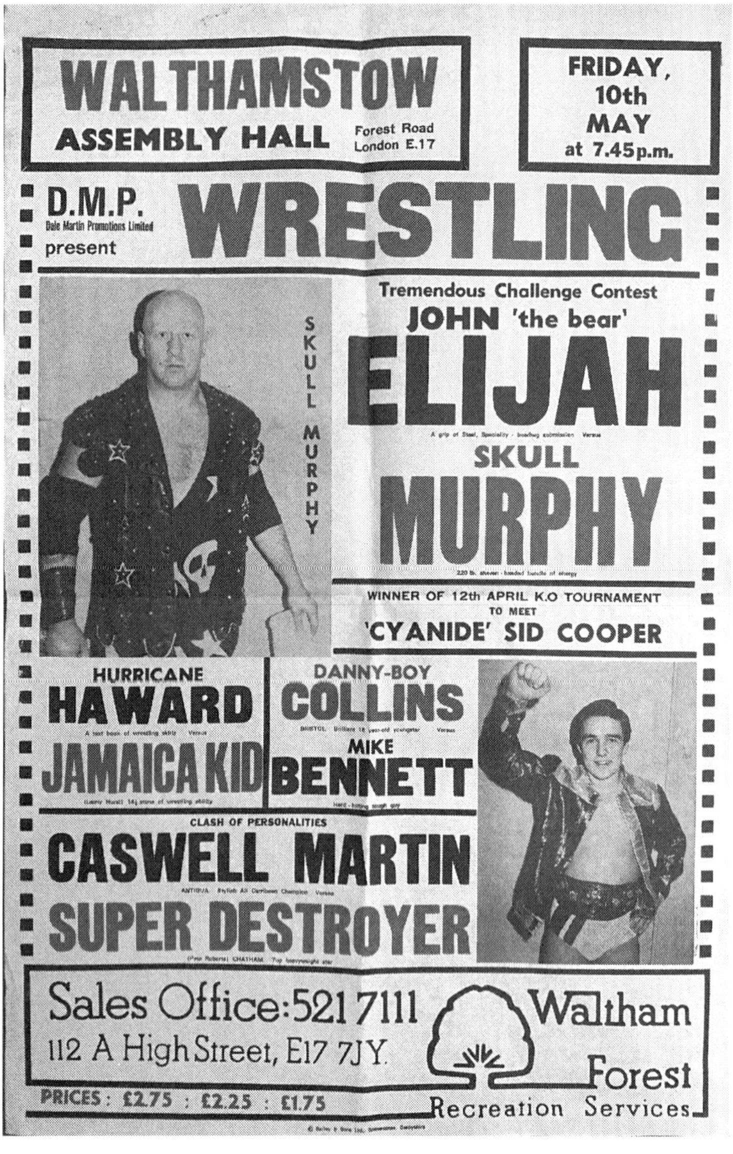

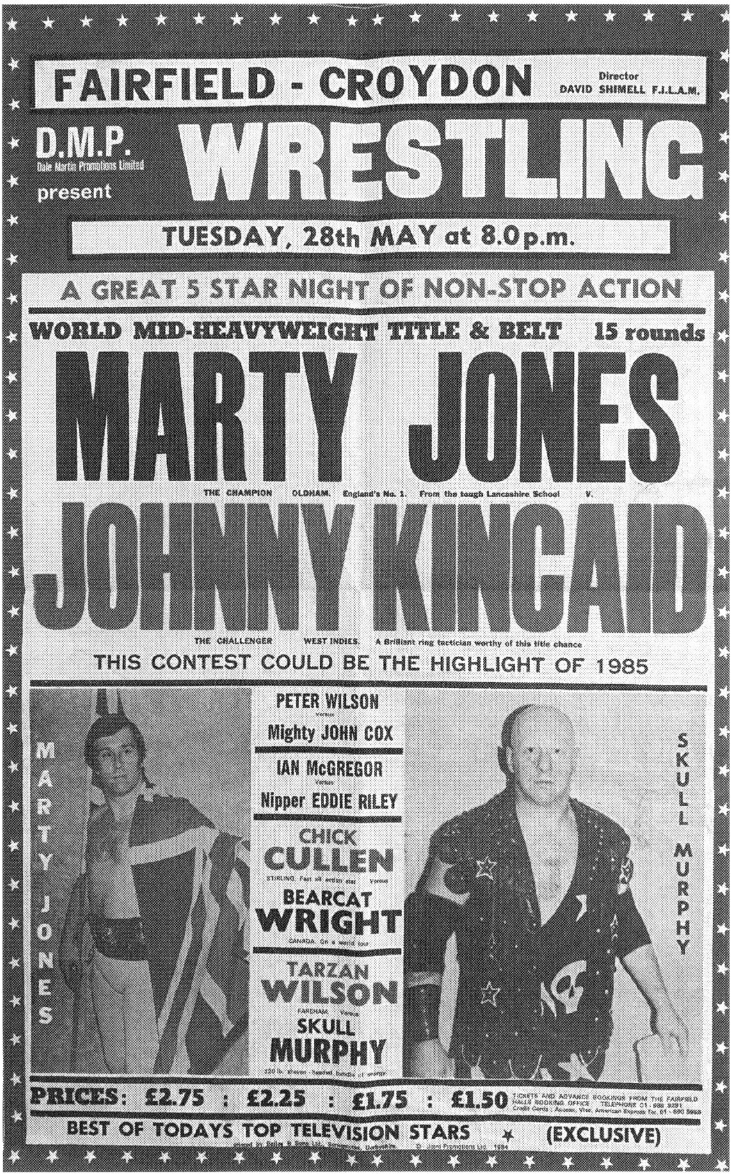
FAIRFIELD - CROYDON
Director
DAVID SHIMELL F.I.L.A.M.
D.M.P.
Dale Martin Promotions Limited
present
WRESTLING
TUESDAY, 28th MAY at 8.0p.m.
A GREAT 5 STAR NIGHT OF NON-STOP ACTION
WORLD MID-HEAVYWEIGHT TITLE & BELT
15 rounds
MARTY JONES
THE CHAMPION OLDHAM. England's No. 1. From the tough Lancashire School V.
JOHNNY KINCAID
THE CHALLENGER WEST INDIES. A Brilliant ring tactician worthy of this title chance
THIS CONTEST COULD BE THE HIGHLIGHT OF 1985
MARTY JONES
PETER WILSON
Mighty JOHN COX
IAN McGREGOR
Nipper EDDIE RILEY
CHICK CULLEN
BEARCAT WRIGHT
TARZAN WILSON
SKULL MURPHY
SKULL MURPHY
PRICES: £2.75 : £2.25 : £1.75 : £1.50
TICKETS AND ADVANCE BOOKINGS FROM THE FAIRFIELD HALLS BOOKING OFFICE
BEST OF TODAYS TOP TELEVISION STARS
(EXCLUSIVE)

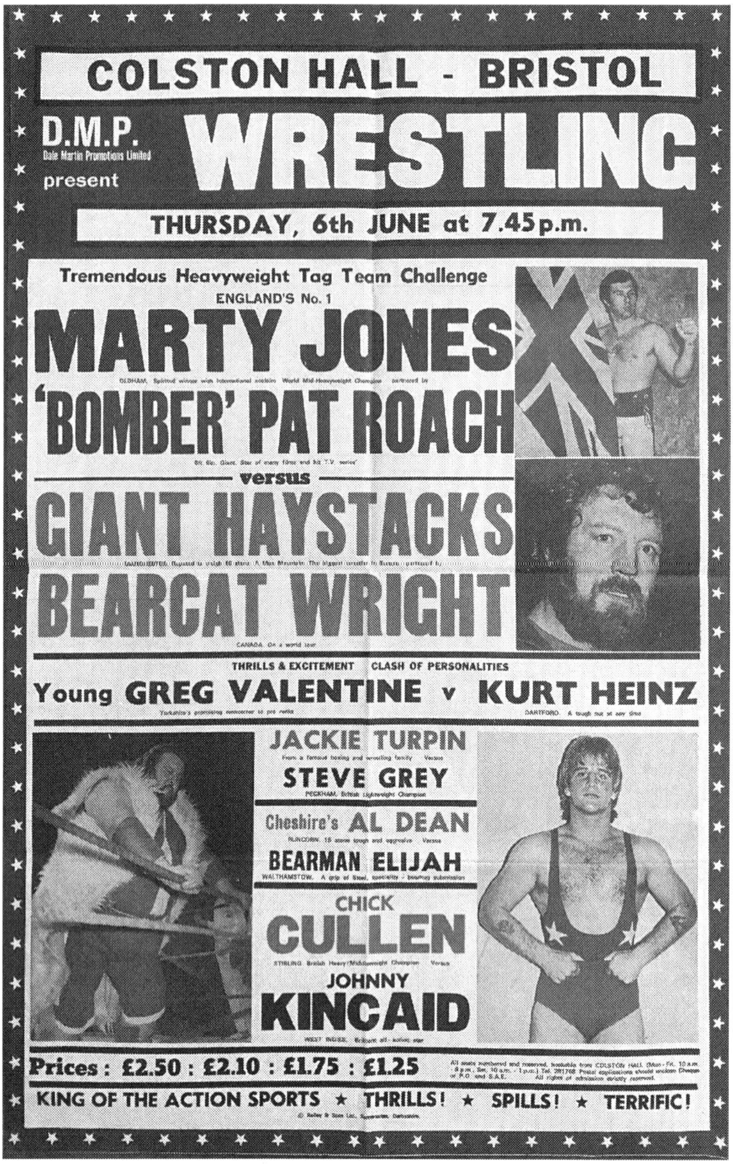
COLSTON HALL - BRISTOL
D.M.P.
Dale Martin Promotions Limited
present
WRESTLING
THURSDAY, 6th JUNE at 7.45p.m.
Tremendous Heavyweight Tag Team Challenge
ENGLAND'S No. 1
MARTY JONES
'BOMBER' PAT ROACH
versus
GIANT HAYSTACKS
BEARCAT WRIGHT
CANADA. On a world tour
THRILLS & EXCITEMENT CLASH OF PERSONALITIES
Young GREG VALENTINE v KURT HEINZ
JACKIE TURPIN
STEVE GREY
PECKHAM. British Lightweight Champion
Cheshire's AL DEAN
BEARMAN ELIJAH
CHICK CULLEN
JOHNNY KINCAID
Prices : £2.50 : £2.10 : £1.75 : £1.25
KING OF THE ACTION SPORTS ★ THRILLS! ★ SPILLS! ★ TERRIFIC!

COMMUNITY CENTRE : HEANOR

D.M.P.
Dale Martin Promotions Limited
present

WRESTLING

SATURDAY 21st SEPTEMBER at 7.45p.m.

TOP TAG TEAM CHALLENGE CONTEST OF 1985

'FIT' FINLAY
with Beautiful PRINCESS PAULA
BELFAST: The finest pound-for-pound wrestler in the ring today partnered by

SKULL MURPHY
Shaven headed 220 lb. bundle of orange

—versus—
THE CHAMPIONS

MARTY JONES
OLDHAM. World Mid-heavyweight champion.

RAY STEELE
WAKEFIELD: British Heavyweight Champion

BEST OF TODAY'S TOP T.V. STARS
BRING THE FAMILY EVERYBODY WELCOME

GRASSHOPPER
LEABROOKS. Premier Derbyshire wrestler Versus
BLACK JACK MULLIGAN
NEWCASTLE. Bearded supremacy. Tyneside terror

LITTLE PRINCE
(Mohammed Alam) PAKISTAN. Versus
KING BENN
KEIGHLEY. Finesse fencing, is there to win

THRILLS - ACTION - EXCITEMENT

DANNY BOY COLLINS
BRISTOL. Brilliant 18 year old British Welterweight Champion Versus

MARVELLOUS MIKE BENNETT
Bradford's leading title contender

ALL ONE PRICE : £2.50   ADVANCE BOOKING AT THE CENTRE
DON'T MISS THE BIG TIME WRESTLING ATMOSPHERE & EXCITEMENT

Chapter 7 – 1986

ITV's wrestling show had its first broadcast for 1986 on January 4th with three matches from Chester shown. First contest was fought under points rules with the first wrestler to throw his opponent onto his back ten times would be the winner. John Savage who now sported blond hair defeated Bearcat Wright by ten points to seven in the ninth minute with a particularly high back drop bringing the winning point. Clive Myers took on Skull Murphy in a catchweight match with both missing spectacular moves in the opening two rounds especially Myers whose flying headbutt from the top of the cornerpost failed to land. Myers took the lead in the third round with an over the top cross press pinned Murphy for the first fall. Murphy after a couple of neck weakeners on Myers evened things up in the sixth round when the gator hold saw Myers submit at once. Murphy had already received two public warnings and as Myers lay on the mat he climbed onto the corner post and landed a flying head butt onto him. Referee Emil Poilve had no hesitation in disqualifying Murphy and Myers gained a somewhat fortunate win. A bonus third match saw King Ben meet Kid Chocolate and a suplex followed by a cross press in the fourth round brought Ben the victory.

The New Year started with a bang for 'All-Star' when they presented another show at Croydon. The highlight of which was Rocky Moran who after many unsuccessful title tilts finally won the British Heavy/Middleweight Title when he defeated the champion Chic Cullen. Typically the tag match between John Quinn and 'Bonecrusher' Pat Barrett & Dave Taylor and Johnny South was abandoned with the match beyond the control of the referee. Johnny Saint retained the World Lightweight Title when he beat the challenger and long time foe Jim Breaks. Catweazle beat Bobby Barnes by disqualification and young Merseysider Rob Brookside beat Ace Ricardo by the one fall needed, Ricardo was better known on Joint Promotions as Ricky Wiseman.

Two further matches from Chester were shown on ITV on January 11th with a poor ending to the main match when The Emperor walked out of the ring and left his opponent Marty Jones fuming as he was about to unmask him. Regular opponents Ian McGregor and Eddie Riley had another outing together and the match ended in a one fall each draw.

The January *Screensport* presentation filmed at the Victoria Hall in Hanley saw the legendary Count Bartelli bow out after a career spanning over forty years. His final match saw him beat the long haired wildman Tarantula after which local favourite Bobby Ryan gave the bell a ceremonial ten rings. There was a who's who of wrestling in the ring at the end to pay their respects to Bartelli and these included The Royals, Bert & Vic, Roy St Clair, Emil Poilve, Colin Joynson, Jim Hussey, Terry Nylands and Terry Downes. Other bouts on the show saw Bonecrusher Barrett knockout John Kowalski. The popular 'Young Ones' tag team of Rob Brookside and Wayne Martin beat the 'Wild Boys' Shane Stevens and Blondie Barrett. Jon Cortez beat Jackie Robinson whilst the match between Kung Fu and The Mighty Chang ended in a No Contest.

The ITV show on January 18th from St Albans saw Danny Collins successfully defend the European Welterweight Title against French challenger Jacques Le Jacques. Collins who had Mick McManus in his corner came out on top with the winning fall coming in the eight round. Keith Haward met Little Prince in the other match that week with neither wrestler's styles meshing and it ended up being a bit of a bad tempered affair. It was Haward who got the winning fall with a body slam and cross press in the seventeenth minute with referee Roy Harding having to drag Prince away who wished to continue the match.

A four man heavyweight knockout tournament was the feature on ITV's wrestling show on January 25th coming from St.Albans again. The first semi final saw Pat Roach take on Johnny Kincaid over a fifteen minute time limit. Roach got the first fall with a knee drop weakening Kincaid for the pin in the sixth minute. Kincaid equalised when he pinned Roach after a back drop in the ninth minute. It was Roach who progressed to the final when Kincaid was knocked through the ropes and was counted out in the twelfth minute. The second semi final between Ray Steele and Gil Singh ended in a draw at the end of the scheduled fifteen minutes and referee Roy Harding awarded the points decision to Singh. The final was again over a fifteen minutes duration but this time the first fall would be enough for the win. In something of a turn up it was Singh who won the tournament when he pinned Roach with a cross press after a hip toss in just under five minutes.

Samson Ubo finally made his ITV debut on the February 1st show from Cleckheaton where he partnered Mike Jordan and Greg Valentine against the team of Mike Bennett, Bernie Wright and Blackjack Mulligan in an elimination six man tag match. Whilst not as bad as he had been around the halls on the circuit he still gave off the air of not knowing what he was doing. He hadn't grasped the process of selling yet and he would just walk away after an opponent had delivered a seemingly hard hitting punch or forearm. Luckily he was eliminated by Bennett allowing the match to continue without him. The two winners were Mike Bennett and Bearcat Wright who finally finished off Greg Valentine with a Boston crab after everyone else had been eliminated. Also on the bill Fit Finlay took on Danny Collins. This was part of a series of matches against much smaller opponents as quest for a match with Big Daddy. Of course we were meant to forget that Finlay had walked out of a match against Daddy less than two months ago and now we were led to believe Finlay together with Princess Paula were desperate for the match. The match with Collins went as expected despite the Bristol youngster putting up a fine show Finlay ended it with a vicious piledriver in the third round which left Collins unable to beat the count.

The other half of the show from Cleckheaton was shown on ITV the following Saturday on February 8th with a new name on the bill, that of Black Salem. Salem was in fact a replacement for Giant Haystacks who was missing many of his scheduled appearances as he was either on the continent, in Ireland where he was a fan favourite or in North America. Unfortunately no substitute was an acceptable enough replacement and when it was realised Black Salem was in fact George Burgess under yet another name it was another disappointment. Salem's opponent Ray Steele beat him with ease by two straight falls inside fifteen minutes. A second heavyweight match that week saw Colonel Brody face Steve Logan and it was Brody who got the winner in the seventh round with a leg lift submission for the deciding score.

February's *Screensport* show was taped at Hanley on February 8th with two title matches on the bill. In the first Rocky Moran retained his newly won British Heavy/Middleweight Title as a result of a one fall each draw with the challenger Keith Haward. The second title match saw Brian Maxine defend the British Middleweight Title against veteran Keith Martinelli. The first fall went to Maxine with a reverse double arm pinfall in the sixth minute. A referee bump with Billy Finlay incapacitated saw Martinelli take advantage with a folding press for the equalising fall. Maxine got the winning fall with a flying tackle followed by a cross press to make another successful defence and commentator Vince Miller presented him with a trophy for being Britain's longest reigning champion.

Mal Sanders beat Carl Jason by count out after a flying head butt saw Sanders only just beat the count himself. John Quinn defeated Johnny South in a tag captains contest before the tag match saw Quinn and Bonecrusher Barrett take on South and Sandy Scott. Referee Frank Casey was interviewed before the start by Maxton Beesley about his recent suspension for failing to control a match properly and he promised this time to be the strictest referee in the country. Casey's vow was worthless as he had no control at all in the match with Quinn and Barrett totally working over their opponents with double teaming and illegal moves. Scott's head was split open with blood gushing out and he was unable to continue which left South to go on alone. As the match continued a riot broke out at ringside as Barrett was attacked by fans and Quinn had to intervene. Quinn finally finished off South with a neck lift suspension which saw South submit instantly. You could not imagine seeing this sort of match on ITV.

Wolverhampton was the venue for ITV's wrestling on February 15th when Fit Finlay's next opponent in his series of matches against lighter opponents was Jackie Turpin. Turpin went the same way as Collins when he was unable to beat the count from another nasty looking piledriver in the fourth round. On the same bill that week Pete Roberts beat Barry Douglas by two falls to one in the seventh round of an excellent heavyweight match.

Even Big Daddy wasn't immune to being hurt and he was forced to miss two shows on a Scottish tour on February 18th and 19th at Inverness and Dundee. Losing your top of the bill any night caused promoters problems in not wanting to refund customers but when it was Daddy even more so. After switching the programme both nights Max Crabtree put on an extra bout each evening which featured the first appearance of Kid McCoy for Joint Promotions when he took on fellow newcomer Barry Lancaster from Teeside. Lancaster going forward would be renamed Rex Lane and appeared on TV under that name whilst featuring on Joint Promotions' bills for the next few years. Kid McCoy in the short time he was wrestling had a quite illustrious career even when the TV cameras stopped rolling. Unfortunately it all came to a grinding halt in the Summer of 1990 at an All-Star Promotions show at Worthing. McCoy was booked to partner his father King Ben in a match against Kendo Nagasaki and Blondie Barratt. Before the match Ben overheard some disparaging comments about them coming from the Nagasaki dressing room and revenge was extracted in the actual match. The aftermath saw King Ben and Kid McCoy removed from the books of All-Star to placate Nagasaki and as they were now the major promoter in Britain it left very few promoters to get regular work from so McCoy's career just fizzled out shortly afterwards.

The wrestling on ITV came from Wolverhampton again on February 22nd with a further two bouts shown from there. Steve Grey had yet another match with Clive Myers and this time Grey ran out the winner by two falls to one. In a heavyweight match Pat Roach met the military man Colonel Brody and Roach won the match by two falls to one.

Wrestling was missing from ITV on March 1st when the USA Indoor Athletics Grand Prix Final was shown at 1220 instead. The TV deal with ITV and Joint Promotions ended at the end of the year and once again Brian Dixon was in there pitching for an opportunity to get a least a slice of the terrestial

TV coverage. It would take a while though before things would progress.

The March edition of the *Screensport* wrestling show was recorded at Hanley on March 1st with five matches on the bill. Mark Rocco who had recently returned from Japan was in the top of the bill match. Rocco was booked against George Burgess AKA The Jamaica Kid although he was being seen for Joint Promotions at the time as Black Salem. As the match progressed the action was as much out of the ring as inside of it with Burgess hitting Rocco with a chair. Burgess got the first fall with a folding press with an incensed Rocco throwing his water bucket into the crowd. A pile driver from Rocco finished off Burgess who had no hope of beating referee Billy Finlay's count of ten. A contest for the Midland's Area Middleweight Title took place between the champion John Wilkie and challenger Keith Myatt. Myatt was incredibly popular with the fans at Hanley and had his manager 'Legendary Lonnie' with him at ringside. Wilkie's usual rule bending soon angered the crowd as well as referee Billy Finlay who gave him two public warnings in quick succession. Myatt got the first fall with a sort of power slam before Wilkie equalised with a cross press. Wilkie got the winning fall after a heinous low blow right into Myatt's groin and pinned him for the winner. Wilkie swaggered from the ring in celebration whilst poor Myatt limped away a defeated man. Kung Fu met Johnny Palance in the shows preliminary contest with Kung Fu winning courtesy of a reverse double arm pinfall. The mystery man Hugo Von Wallenstein took on Dave Taylor in a heavyweight match which soon got out of control with Von Wallenstein having a fall disallowed for pulling Taylor's hair. The match finally ended in a no score time limit draw. The final match of the show saw Johnny Saint beat Jim Breaks by two falls to one.

Another All-Star show at Croydon took place on March 4th with something of an upset in the main event as the smaller Mark Rocco defeated Tony St Clair when St Clair was knocked out in the 6th round. Pat Barrett beat the mystery man from the continent Hugo Von Wallenstein by two falls to one in the fifth round. Croydon favourite Mal Sanders beat the current British Heavy/Middleweight Champion Rocky Moran by two falls to one in a non title match. Other matches on the bill saw Lee Roberts v Wayne Martin end in a No Contest when Martin couldn't continue in the thirteenth minute and Bob Collins pinned Shane Stevens in the the eighteenth minute. Perhaps it was fair to say this wasn't a strong a show as previous All-Star offerings at Croydon.

Big Daddy made his first appearance of 1986 on ITV on March 8th from Hertford but before the tag match viewers had to sit through another Alan Kilby and John Elijah match. This one ended in a one fall each time limit draw. Daddy partnered Danny Collins against a 'B Team' of Mel Stuart and Bull Pratt. Needless to say Daddy and Collins won in a match seen a thousand times before.

There was another strange defence by Marty Jones of his World Mid/Heavyweight Title shown on March 15th on ITV. Kincaid was a full blown heavyweight and nowhere near the under fifteen stone championship weight limit although Kent Walton said he weighed in at 14st13lbs. A match between Jones and the 'Caribbean Sunshine Boy' Kincaid would have been far more interesting than this one with Jones retaining the title once again. Kincaid got the first fall with a reversal of a hip toss enabled him to pin Jones in the fifth round. Jones equalised with a folding press secured by a bridge in the seventh round before he got the winner with a small package in the eighth round. The other match on that week from the bill taped at Hertford saw Skull Murphy now wearing some kind of red face make up taking on Johnny Wilson. Wilson took the first fall in the third round with a flying tackle followed by a cross press. Murphy equalised in the sixth round when the gator hold got an instant submission from Wilson and with Wilson still suffering he submitted again from another gator hold as soon as the next round started.

March 22nd saw the 'Grand Prix Belt' raise its head again and this time it was for lighter weights rather than the heavier wrestlers who competed for the last version. Unlike the previous tournament which had eight wrestlers in it this one had one four so it was straight into the semi final stage. The first semi final saw Steve Logan defeat Ian McGregor by two falls to one in the 6th round. On the same show recorded at Dewsbury was the next Fit Finlay squash match this time against the very much smaller Grasshopper. In the initial stages Grasshopper with his mix of martial arts skills perplexed the Ulsterman but it wasn't long before another piledriver brought matters to an end inside ten minutes.

The second semi final of the 'Grand Prix Belt' took place on March 29th at Dewsbury again with Mike Bennett taking on Kid Chocolate with Bennett securing a winning submission from Chocolate in the fifth round. Steve Grey and Clive Myers had yet another televised match on the same show with this time Myers winning by two falls to one in the fifth round.

Before the final of the Grand Prix Belt it was announced that there would be another televised tournament, this time for the 'Golden Grappler Trophy' and again it would be competed for by wrestlers from the lighter weights. I'm not sure in which order of prestige each tournament was held but I'm sure any wrestler winning one of them would be absolutely delighted. The eight wrestlers nominated to compete for the 'Golden Grappler' were Greg Valentine, Sid Cooper, Mick McMichael, Mike Jordan, Tally Ho Kaye, Johnny Kidd, Richie Brooks and Mike Bennett. The first heat for the 'Grappler' was held on April 5th in a programme screened from Fleetwood with Greg Valentine beating Sid Cooper by two falls to one in the 6th round. In the other match shown that week Mike Bennett won the 'Grand Prix Belt' when he defeated Steve Logan in an excellent match with the winning submission coming for Bennett in the final round. Of course the first question to be asked afterwards was would Bennett be able to win the 'Golden Grappler Trophy' too and hold both of these prizes at the same time ?

The second heat for the 'Grappler' was held the following week on April 12th also from Fleetwood when the veteran Mick McMichael came out on top when his opponent the underrated Mike Jordan took a tumble from the ring in the seventh round and was unable to continue. Also on the show was Big Daddy who partnered Danny Collins against the team of The Emperor and Bearcat Wright who were accompanied by their manager Tony 'The Brain' Francis. Daddy and Collins won in the tenth minute when a 'big splash' on The Emperor finished him off. As usual the fans in attendance lapped up everything from Daddy's entrance to the finish of the match. Due to the early finish of the tag match it was time for a bonus with a heavyweight match between Ray Steele and Terry Rudge. Steele got the only fall to win with a suplex followed by a cross press in the fourth round.

The 'Golden Grappler' heats continued throughout April with the show from Dorking screened on ITV on April 19th featuring the next. This time it was the Tally Ho Kaye who beat Johnny Kidd who found Kaye's nefarious tactics too much to deal with. The winning submission for Kaye came in the seventh round and as MC Brian Crabtree announced his victory Kaye celebrated by blowing his hunting horn much to the crowd's displeasure. In the other bouts shown that week Marty Jones rolled up Tom Tyrone with a 'small package' in the third round to gain the only fall needed whilst in the other match Alan Kilby was forced to retire in his match with Fit Finlay when a leg injury proved too much for him. Kilby had trapped his leg between the ropes and after he submitted to Finlay's single Boston crab he was unable to continue.

The final first round heat for the 'Grappler' was held on the second half of the Dorking show on April 26th when Mike Bennett saw off the spirited challenge of the young Richie Brooks. A forearm smash over the top from Bennett in the sixth round left Brooks out cold with no chance of beating the count of ten and the first aiders were immediately summoned to help the youngster. In the other match screened Ray Steele's reign as the Joint Promotions' British Heavyweight Champion came to an end when Pat Roach defeated him by two falls to one to win the belt.

The April *Screensport* show saw a knockout tournament for the World Heavyweight Title although there was still some confusion as to what was the true version of the title, Wayne Bridges claimed a 'BWA' version of it. The participants were John Quinn, Tony St Clair, Johnny South and King Kendo. Quinn beat South and St Clair beat Kendo in the respective semi finals before Quinn reclaimed the belt when St Clair was unable to continue in the final with a badly cut head. Other bouts shown included Terry Rudge beating Neil Sands in a fine heavyweight match up. Mad Dog Wilson defeated Tiger Tonkin and Ace Ricardo beat the punk rocker Ziggy Zag by disqualification.

May started with the semi finals and final of the 'Golden Grappler' Tournament shown on May 3rd on ITV from Heanor. In the first Greg Valentine beat John Wilkie by two straight falls inside four rounds. Wilkie replaced an injured Tally Ho Kaye which in the end caused his retirement and the end of a fine career inside the ring. The other semi final caused confusion as Mick McMichael was to face the winner of the Mike Bennett v Richie Brooks match which was shown on TV on April 26th. The winner was Bennett who quite clearly won by a knockout and was announced as the winner yet it was Richie Brooks who was lined up to face Mick McMichael in the semi final. It turned out that Mike Bennett had left Joint Promotions and had emigrated to Australia leaving the farcical situation of each semi final containing a wrestler who had not won their quarter final. Anyway McMichael beat Brooks by two falls to one in the sixth round to progress to the final. Greg Valentine won the trophy when he beat McMichael by two falls to one in the fifth round of the final.

Without the World of Sport programme being broadcast anymore there was not the usual publicity of wrestling being on in the build-up to the FA Cup Final. The wrestling on ITV on Cup Final day on May 10th was buried away at 2.10 amongst the football coverage. Even the main event felt tired as the Big Daddy v Fit Finlay feud had not taken off as they had been meeting in tags around the country for the past few months. Daddy and his partner Danny Collins beat Finlay and his partner Scrubber Daly without too much to report.

The ITV wrestling on May 17th featured a dire England v Pakistan team match from Leeds which was only of use for insomniacs to watch late at night. Pakistan won the first two contests with Mohammed Afzal beating Blackjack Mulligan by disqualification in the fourth round and Ali Shan beating Barry Douglas by two falls to one in the sixth round. The other match ended in a draw with John Elijah's fall in the third round equalised by Mohammed Butt in the fifth round.

Two more bouts from Leeds were shown on May 24th with Clive Myers taking on fellow West Indian Caswell Martin in a catchweight contest. Martin got the first fall in the fourth round with Myers getting an equaliser in the fifth for the match to end in a one each draw at the end of the sixth round. Ray Steele beat Colonel Brody in an entertaining heavyweight scrap with Steele's winning fall coming in the seventh round.

May went out with a bang on ITV on the show shown on the 31st from Walkden. Marty Jones was booked to defend his World Mid/Heavyweight Title against the German challenger from Nuremburg, Bull Blitzer. Blitzer was in fact Steve Wright who had moved to Germany about ten years previously. I'm not sure why Kent Walton didn't recognise him and Walton even went as far to say it was Blitzer's first visit to the UK. With two of the greatest British wrestlers ever in competition it was no wonder that this was one of the best matches I have ever seen. After a quiet couple of rounds at the start it was fought at a tremendous pace most unlike the usual British style at the time. In the ninth round Bull Blitzer got the winning fall when a piledriver left a prone Jones an easy target for the winning fall. Ted Betley, the trainer of Dynamite Kid amongst others was called into the ring to present the belt to Blitzer whilst a stunned Jones sat in his corner unable to comprehend what had just happened. The show that week didn't really need another contest shown but it did and Pat Roach met Butcher Bond in it. Roach won it when Bond was counted out. It was so frustrating as a wrestling fan that one week you would have a match of the calibre of Jones v Blitzer shown on ITV and the following week it would be so bad you could barely watch it.

Screenport's May show was in the form of a Battle Royale taped in a tent at the Stoke on Trent Garden Festival. The singles matches saw Rob Brookside pin Shane Stevens. Mark Rocco knocked out Wayne Martin. Keith Haward beat Mal Sanders who was disqualified and Sandy Scott pinned John Kenny. Rocco won the over the top rope finale in an out of control manner as usual.

With the loss of names like Mike Bennett and Tally Ho Kaye to their roster it was obvious that Joint Promotions needed some reinforcements before the busy Summer season started.

One of those was a wrestler billed as Man Mountain Pitt, on the poster he was described as being 7ft 2in tall, size 17 feet and having hands like shovels. This would put him bigger than Giant Haystacks and on a par with the legendary Andre the Giant and I couldn't wait to see him live. Unfortunately he never appeared for a single billed contest, whether he ever existed or was just a figment of Max Crabtree's imagination we will never know. Another new name on the bills was the '28st Samurai', there was only an illustration of him on the poster not a photograph so nobody knew what to expect. Unlike Pitt at least he existed but as soon as I saw him live for the first time it was clear who it was behind the mask. The Samurai was the Blackpool powerhouse Rex Strong and even the most casual fan knew who it was which made wearing a mask somewhat pointless.

Mal Sanders made a welcome return to Joint Promotions as well at this time, after a couple of years on the independent circuit and with the end of the exclusivity contract clause Sanders was the first of many wrestlers who would return to wrestle for Joint Promotions again. Sanders was in the feature match on ITV on June 7th from Walkden when he faced Danny Collins. Sanders managed to drag Collins down to his level and in the end the match degenerated to such an extent that both of them were disqualified. Kid McCoy made his TV debut partnering his father King Ben in that week's other match against Mike Jordan and Rick Wiseman. Ben and McCoy were the winners with Ben pinning Wiseman in the fifteenth minute for the deciding fall.

All-Star Promotions held another successful Croydon show at the start of June with Jim Breaks making a defence of the European Lightweight Title against Johnny Kidd as the top of the bill match. Breaks retained the title by two falls to one despite a spirited attempt by Kidd to try and claim a first title in his career. World Heavyweight Title claimant Wayne Bridges beat Terry Rudge in a non title match. The young Liverpool star Robby Brookside's progress in the pro ranks was derailed when Mal Sanders beat him by two falls to one. The best wrestling match of the night should have been Keith Haward v old rival Jon Cortez but Haward forsook using his skills for a rule bending approach which tested the referee's patience to such an extent that he ended up being disqualified. The evening's tag match sent the fans home happy when the team of Catweazle and Tom Thumb defeated Shane Stevens and Carl McGrath.

Outside of the ring though there was frustration for Brian Dixon and All-Star with no further news on their attempt to get a share of the ITV deal. The problem was that all the ITV Sport's executives were tied up with The World Cup in Mexico. Some were busy in the studio in London dealing with the presentation there and others were in Central America making sure things went without a hitch.

The Samurai made his TV debut on June 14th on a show recorded at Battersea where his opponent was Tom Tyrone. I think the majority of viewers would have recognised Rex Strong as soon as he made his entrance to the ring although Kent Walton claimed to not know anything about him. A rather slow paced match saw Samurai concentrating on strength holds but Tyrone upset the odds when a flying tackled floored Samurai and he was able to pin the masked man. In the fifth round Samurai got Tyrone in a sleeper hold and refused to release him so referee Peter Szakacs disqualified him. The sleeper hold is an illegal move under the Mountevans rules which gave Szakacs no option but to send the Samurai back to the dressing room. The show's opening contest was an entertaining lightweight match between British Lightweight Champion Steve Grey and Richie Brooks over six rounds. Brooks got the first fall in the second round with a folding press secured by a wrestler's bridge. Grey got the equaliser in the fifth round with his speciality surfboard submission hold which saw Brooks tap immediately. The final round saw no further score so the decision was a draw. A bonus match that week saw Alan Kilby take on John Savage with the match ending in the sixth round in a double knockout when an attempted suplex from Kilby saw both of them take a heavy landing on Kent Walton's ringside table.

Two more matches from Battersea were seen on ITV on June 21st with Marty Jones' return match with Bull Blitzer for the World Mid/Heavyweight Title the proposed feature. The problem was that Blitzer didn't show up, the word at ringside was that Blitzer or I should say Steve Wright had some sort of problem with promoter Max Crabtree and his payback was not to show up for the return title match. Short term this left a TV taping short of a main event and the best Crabtree could do was put Barry Douglas in against Marty Jones as a substitute match for the ITV show. Long term Joint Promotions had lost another world title in similar circumstances to John Quinn's departure in 1980 and Max Crabtree had to go the similar route by declaring the World Mid/Heavyweight Title vacant and have Marty Jones compete for the vacant title. Jones beat Douglas by countout in the fifth round of the match seen on TV and the other match saw a one each draw between Ray Steele who was on TV yet again and Caswell Martin.

June 28th saw Big Daddy in televised action once more in a show recorded at Digbeth Civic Hall in the centre of Birmingham. It was one of the grand old venues of British wrestling and a place that had an atmosphere second to none. This would be the final time that wrestling would be televised from here which was a great shame. Before Daddy's match we got to see an international heavyweight match between local lad Steve Logan and Gil Singh over eight rounds. Logan got the first fall when he pinned Singh in the fourth round following a flying tackle from the corner post. Singh equalised with a leg lever submission in the sixth round despite Logan's attempts to escape. A similar move in the seventh move saw Logan submit again and Singh won by two submissions to Logan's one fall. The tag match saw The Samurai back in televised action although he was now accompanied by manager Charlie McGee. The Samurai partnered Lucky Gordon against Big Daddy and Jackie Turpin. Kent Walton tried to tell us that the Samurai was heavier than Daddy but it didn't look like it from the pictures. After the usual opening spell of Daddymania running wild the match settled down with Turpin and Gordon in the ring. Daddy received a public warning from the strict referee Gordon Pryor for some double teaming before Samurai and Gordon did some double teaming of their own. Once Daddy was tagged in it was soon over with a big splash on Samurai for the first fall in the seventh minute. Samurai then attempted to put a sleeper hold on Turpin as Pryor dished out public warnings like confetti before

Turpin got the winning fall with a crucifix pinning Gordon in the eleventh minute.

June's *Screensport* show came from Stoke with a things a little quieter than previous offerings. Johnny Kidd who had recently started to appear for All-Star but was using the name Kid Jonathan so as to not let Joint Promotions know he was wrestling elsewhere, appeared against Blondie Barratt and beat him by two falls to one. Chic Cullen beat Johnny Saint in an excellent catchweight match and Bonecrusher Barratt pinned Dave Taylor. The other match saw Maurice Hunter making a comeback but it was a losing one to Jim Breaks.

Ray Steele got his rematch for the British Heavyweight Title against the new champion Pat Roach shown on July 5th from Digbeth. Steele was unsuccessful in his attempt to reclaim the title when he was forced to retire through injury. The first contest that week saw the ever unpopular Fit Finlay with Princess Paula take on Clive Myers in a ten minute duration match. Referee Gordon Pryor was in charge for this one and once again he was tested by Finlay's illegal moves and Paula's constant dissent from outside the ring. Finlay won the match with a powerslam in the eighth minute but it wasn't the end of affairs as they were now going to fight in a best of three arm wrestling challenge match. Myers being a former world arm wrestling champion was the favourite to win this and he won the first match. Finlay looked on the brink of winning the second match but Myers reversed it for a two straight wins victory.

July 12th saw the ITV cameras go just a few miles down the road from Birmingham to Stourbridge for two matches including a six man continental rules tag match. On one team there was Sid Cooper, Mike Jordan and Eddie Riley and the other Kid McCoy, Spiderman and Ian McGregor. Spiderman was a masked wrestler in the costume of the super hero but Kent Walton spoiled it somewhat by identifying him as Ray Crawley. With the match fought over the best of five falls etc. it was Spiderman himself who got the winning fall with a folding press in the eighteenth minute for a three falls to two win. Richie Brooks continued his rivalry with Steve Grey after his drawn match from Battersea with this time completely upsetting the apple cart by beating the British Lightweight Champion by two falls to one. Straight afterwards Brooks slapped down a demand for a title match.

July 19th saw two further contests from Stourbridge shown on ITV with both at heavyweight or as MC Alec Caine introduced them they were 'evvyweight matches. The first saw Drew McDonald take on Johnny Wilson over six rounds. McDonald got the first fall with a submission in the third round after a bear hug saw Wilson tap. Wilson got a quick equaliser in the fourth round after managing to pick up McDonald and slam him for a cross press. The final two rounds were scoreless so it ended in a draw. Skull Murphy and Pete Roberts had another match on TV in the other bout shown and as per all the others things got a little out of hand. Murphy had his face make up on again and as Kent Walton commented it made him look ridiculous. The match had a stipulation that the winner would go on to face Gil Singh in a televised match next Saturday. Murphy took the first fall in the third round pinning Roberts after a body slam or he thought he had as referee Ken Joyce disallowed it for striking his opponent after the count of three. Murphy did get the first fall legally in the fifth round with a clothesline flooring Roberts and Murphy quickly following up with a pinfall. Roberts equalised in the sixth round with a cross press following a back drop on Murphy. But it was Murphy who would go on to meet Singh when in the final round he forced Roberts to submit from his gator hold. Gil Singh came into the ring to greet the winner and his opponent for next week but Murphy attacked him and tried to tear his shirt off. Singh then floored Murphy with a head butt as Peter Szakacs joined Ken Joyce in pulling them apart.

The Gil Singh v Skull Murphy match was shown on ITV on July 26th from Buxton and not surprisingly the rule book was thrown out of the window early on. Despite receiving two public warnings and several private ones Murphy refused to heed them and in the end was disqualified giving Singh the win although he would have preferred to beat him by pinfall or submission. Alan Kilby wrestled a one fall each draw with King Ben and also on the same show in a bonus match Simon Hurst made his TV debut against fellow Scunthorpe resident Ray

Robinson. Hurst had made a TV appearance on the popular 'Game for a Laugh' show when he fooled his wife when wrestling a match with Ray Steele whilst wearing a mask. After the success of that Hurst joined the pro ranks but the match with Robinson ended in a loss when he was pinned following a suplex in the second round.

Danny Collins had been turning back all challenges for his British and European Welterweight Titles all year and on August 2nd it was Mal Sanders chance for a title match. Sanders had already faced Collins in a non title match on TV earlier in the summer and with the match ending with both of them disqualified now had his chance for the title. In an entertaining match, the now very much outspoken and temperamental Sanders lost out when he landed legs astride the top rope in the eighth round and was unable to continue. This would be the last chance for quite a while to see Collins not only on TV but around the country too as he was found to be suffering from a serious illness which meant he lost a kidney. The other match shown that week from Buxton saw Clive Myers beat Zoltan Boscik by two falls to one.

The following week on August 9th saw a 'Battle Royale' tournament featured in the coverage from Bridlington. This show featured one of my favourite matches shown on the TV in the 1980's. This was one of the single matches with Bearcat Wright taking on Peter Collins who had yet to complete a full year on the circuit. Wright absolutely destroyed Collins, apart from a couple of moves Wright gave him nothing and some of the moves landed had me wincing. The definition of a squash match ended in the third round when Collins was forced to submit from a half nelson. Studs Lannigan wrestled a scoreless draw with Pat Patton over four rounds. Rick Wiseman pinned Jeff Kerry in the fourth round and Greg Valentine beat Blackjack Mulligan in the third round. The 'Battle Royale' ended with Greg Valentine being the last wrestler remaining in the ring having eliminated the other seven participants.

The second half of the coverage from Bridlington was shown on August 16th with Steve Grey defending the British Lightweight Title against Richie Brooks as the main event. Brooks had a wrestled a draw with Grey and then defeated him on TV recently so as a result pressed for this championship opportunity. The match ended in confusion in the seventh round, Grey had forced Brooks to submit in the sixth round from his trademark 'surfboard' hold. Grey immediately applied the move again but on doing so he went too far forward and ended up pinning Brooks for a winning fall but as he moved forward his shoulders were also pinned for the count of three by referee Max Ward. MC Brian Crabtree announced a two to one win for the champion Grey with his score in the sixth round and the fall in the seventh against Brooks' fall in the seventh. The first match that week saw Scrubber Daly for a change in a singles match when he took on Steve Logan. Daly outweighed his opponent by 8st or more and coupled with his illegal tactics gave Logan a tough time. Daly eventually got a public warning from referee Ken Lazenby in the third round for refusing to break the hold when asked. The match ended when Lazenby had no hesitation in disqualifying Daly for launching a flying splash on the prostate Logan seconds after a first one.

A new face to the TV screen was featured on August 23rd with Jean Le Force from Canada was matched against veteran Lennie Hurst. Le Force was better known as Rambo on the continent and went onto wrestle for the WWF in the late 90's as part of the 'Truth Commision'. Commentator Kent Walton was most taken by the Canadian and liked his impressive physique and Le Force dwarfed the much lighter Hurst. The match ended shortly after the third round when Hurst injured his back trying to lift his opponent, unfortunately we didn't get to see Le Force on ITV again. The opening match that week on the show from Borehamwood was between Tom Tyrone and John Elijah which ended in a six round draw with Elijah getting the first fall in the fourth round before Tyrone equalised in the fifth with a cross press following a double arm suplex.

It was back to Borehamwood again on August 30th with the preliminary match seeing Mike Jordan beat Spiderman by two falls to one in the sixth round. The featured contest saw Ringo Rigby who was again appearing regularly for Joint Promotions taking on Fit Finlay of course accompanied by Princess Paula who was now introduced as the 'first lady of wrestling'. Finlay got his first public warning from Peter Szakacs in the second round for using the closed fist but not before Kent Walton criticised Szakacs for his leniency. Finlay though got the first fall in the third round with a reverse double knee hold after weakening Rigby with a nasty looking flying knee to his jaw. Rigby came back in the fourth round an arm lever suspension submission after Finlay had injured his shoulder on the corner post. Paula was furious and sent her man flying after she slapped him for being so careless. Rigby tried to follow up but Finlay countered by throwing him over the top rope and then used Marty Jones' powerlock to which Rigby submitted to give Finlay the win.

The August *Screensport* show was again filmed in the marquee at the Stoke Garden Festival and this time it featured an eight man knockout tournament. The wrestlers entered were quite a mix of weights and experience, they were Mark Rocco, Pat Barrett, Chief Screaming Eagle, Butcher Bond, Steve Fury, Steve Peacock, Mad Dog Wilson and Mickey Gold. The final ended up being between Rocco and Barrett and was fought all over the tent as well as inside the ring. Referee John Harris had no hope of controlling either wrestler and in the end he was forced to abandon the match and declare it a 'No Contest'. Even as the announcements were made various wrestlers had to keep Rocco and Barrett apart as they continued to trade blows.

The ITV executives had now returned to normal duties after the World Cup and the negotiations for the new TV contract were about to be completed. One of the ITV producers Mike Archer was invited by Brian Dixon to see an 'All-Star' show at Aylesbury to see what was on offer. The first thing Archer noticed that night was the size of the bell used by the timekeeper and that was the only thing he insisted on being changed for something more larger and more of a focal point. For some reason the opening titles of the ITV Wrestling Show featured a bell as would the new programme too. With the matter of the bell concluded it would be announced that the presentation of wrestling on ITV would be rebooted in January and feature Joint Promotions as usual but the coverage would be shared with All-Star Promotions. But in a move few saw coming a show from the WWF in the USA would also be screened every two months. The WWF at this time in the UK was only available on the Sky One cable channel and apart from the hardest of the hardcore fans had no real interest here or mainstream coverage.

Big Daddy's annual seaside tour continued at Skegness with a contest shown on TV on September 6th. The first match that week saw a return between Alan Kilby and King Ben following on from their draw at Buxton seen at the end of July. This time there was a winner and it was Kilby who got the victory by two falls to one. Daddy's tag match saw him with a new partner in the shape of 'Golden Apollon' Richie Brooks taking on Drew McDonald and Sid Cooper. Daddy made his usual elaborate entrance with a young child in his arms swamped by loads of kids, Kent Walton noted that he didn't think the baby was Daddys. Once MC Ron Denbury made the introductions it was Daddy and McDonald who started but after the bodychecks and belly butts Brooks was tagged in and the normal script followed. Referee Gordon Pryor again was having a hard time keeping control of the double teaming but as soon as Daddy was tagged in he did the big splash on McDonald for the first fall in the seventh minute. As the teams waited for the restart Giant Haystacks appeared at ringside having recently returned from the continent to repeat his challenge to Daddy. Once the match restarted Brooks rolled up Cooper for the winner in a two straight falls win in the eighth minute. Haystacks then entered the ring and landed a forearm to Daddy's head which knocked him backwards. The big man demanded that Kent Walton tell all the viewers he was back and to me he looked bigger than ever but I doubt he was the 43st that Walton claimed he was now. The bonus match saw Pat Roach facing Skull Murphy in a one fall match over six rounds. Kent Walton did cause something of a shock when he told the viewers that Roach had vacated the heavyweight belt citing he was too busy with his film and TV commitments to be able to defend it on a regular basis. Walton announced the vacant title would be decided in a four man knockout tournament to be seen on ITV in the near future. During the match Murphy did his best to rile Roach but once Roach had lost his temper it was all over, following a high knee drop he pinned Murphy in the third round for the winner. Afterwards Roach took the MC's microphone to announce to the crowd in attendance as well as to the TV viewers of his decision to relinquish the title and to wish the new champion the best of luck.

The other half of the Skegness show was seen the next week on September 13th and featured a four man knockout tournament with the 'Jolly Fisherman' trophy up for grabs and a lovely piece of china it was too. The first semi final saw Greg Valentine take on Bearcat Wright over six rounds. Wright got the first score in the third round with a leg lever suspension which saw Valentine submit instantly. The early rounds were reminiscint of Wright's match with Peter Collins earlier in the summer with Wright receiving two public warnings from referee Gordon Pryor by the end of the third round. Valentine had hardly landed any blows until the fifth round when Wright missed a knee drop and Valentine rolled him up for the equaliser. A less lenient referee than Pryor would have already disqualified Wright but in the final round he was finally forced to do so when Wright punched Valentine in his stomach and then tossed him out of the ring over the top rope. The injured Valentine had to be carried back to the dressing room and Kent Walton plus all of us watching wondered how would he be able to compete in the final ? The second semi final again over six rounds was between Ray Robinson and Ian McGregor. Before the match started Walton told us that Greg Valentine would not be able to wrestle in the final due to the injuries he had received at the hands of Bearcat Wright so therefore the winner of this would win the trophy. In a far more sporting match it was Robinson who got the first fall with a cross press after a suplex floored McGregor in the fourth round. McGregor got the equaliser in the fifth round with a carbon copy move of suplex followed by a cross press. At the end of the sixth round there was no further score so who would Mr Shepherd, the Director of Entertainment for East Lindsay Council present the trophy to ? Mr Shepherd generously told MC Ron Denbury that he would ensure another trophy was made and both McGregor and Robinson would have a 'Jolly Fisherman' trophy for their mantlepiece.

The four wrestlers nominated to compete for the vacant Joint Promotions' heavyweight title were the former champion

Ray Steele, Gil Singh, Caswell Martin and a wrestler not seen in the Joint Promotions rings for over ten years Dave Taylor. The semi finals were seen on ITV on September 20th in a show recorded at Stratford on Avon, the home of Shakespeare and not normally a wrestling hotbed. Before the tournament matches we got to see the TV debut of the Zimbabwean Patrick Flyer who was taking on Pete LaPaque. Flyer came to the ring in full Zulu tribal dress whilst LaPaque had his leather biker's jacket on. Flyer got the first fall when he pinned LaPaque in the second round before LaPaque equalised when a single leg Boston crab forced Flyer to submit in the fourth round. There was no further score in the final two rounds so it ended in the draw. Flyer returned home to Zimbabwe where he was the All Nations Lightweight Champion and said to be the best professional wrestler to ever emerge from his home country. The first semi final of the tournament to crown the new heavyweight champion saw Ray Steele take on Dave Taylor with Kent Walton spouting nonsense saying Taylor had only been a pro for a couple of years when he had been wrestling for years. Steele took the first fall in the fourth round with a folding press but Taylor came back in the fifth when he pinned Steele following a suplex to make it one each with a round left. Neither wrestler could get a winner in the final round so it ended up a draw so a rematch would have to be held before the final was shown on October 18th. The second semi final saw Gil Singh face Caswell Martin with Martin surprisingly pinning Singh for the first fall in the second round. Singh equalised with a double knee hold pinning Martin in the fourth round and it was Singh who got the winner with a similar move in the fifth round.

The following week on September 27th also from Stratford on Avon saw the 'Riot Squad' tag team of Fit Finlay & Skull Murphy reunited where they were matched against a team of Red Indian Don Eagle who had just arrived for a short tour and Johnny Wilson. An entertaining match ended after a little over twenty minutes when a piledriver by Finlay on Eagle was quickly followed by the winning fall for the 'Riot Squad'. The other contest that week saw Ringo Rigby meet Studs Lannigan over six rounds. Rigby pinned Lannigan in the third round for the first fall but Lannigan immediately equalised in the fourth with a single leg Boston crab which saw Rigby submit. The winner went to Rigby in the final round in slightly bizarre circumstances when a ringsider counted to three with Lannigan on the mat but referee Emil Poilve wasn't counting. A few seconds later Poilve did count to three after Rigby pinned Lannigan with a folding press.

The September *Screensport* show featured another entertaining line up of matches filmed in the tent at the Stoke on Trent garden festival once again. The highlight saw Tony St Clair take on King King Kirk in a twenty minute time limit match with just the one fall etc. to decide the winner. Referee Mal Mason was in charge and once again the referee had problems keeping order. At one stage Kirk headbutted the referee which should have resulted in an instant disqualification but Mason was far too lenient on him. The bell rang at the end of a tremendously hard fought match with neither wrestler pinning the other so a draw was the verdict. Other matches saw Neil Sands pin Bill Bromley. Another heavyweight match saw Dave Taylor beat Shane Stevens and a tag match the revamped version of the 'Hells Angels' now consisting of Bobby Barnes and Blondie Barratt beat Rob Brookside and Johnny Kidd.

Don Eagle was in action on ITV from Southport on October 4th in a match with Steve Logan. The bout ended in the fourth round following a nasty looking fall by Eagle. The Red Indian misjudged a leap over Logan, tripped and went through the ropes with the contest immediately being halted and a 'No Contest' was the decision. On the same show youngster Kid McCoy's rapid progress through the pro ranks was halted by the wily Hungarian Zoltan Boscik. Boscik's experience was far too much for McCoy and the youngster was forced to submit for the winner in the fifth round when he was clamped into the Hungarian's speciality 'three in one' hold. The bonus match that week saw Chic Cullen pin Barry Douglas in the fourth round to win with the only fall needed.

The following week on October 11th featured three very entertaining matches from the Southport bill and the best show screened in quite a while. Roy Regal made his TV debut against Marty Jones in what could be described as very much jumping in at the deep end. Regal had made his debut for Joint Promotions earlier in the Summer and to compensate for his lack of experience was given a one fall start. The match ended in the second round when a perfectly delivered drop kick from Jones left Regal unable to beat referee Gordon Pryor's count of ten. Regal would shortly change his name to Steve Regal and go onto wrestle for All-Star Promotions before departing for the USA and worldwide fame. The second match on this week's show was between two wrestlers who hadn't been seen on ITV for quite a while, Jim Breaks and Kung Fu. To be fair there wasn't much wrestling, mostly a combination of comedy or rulebreaking by Breaks which ended in the sixth round when referee Peter Szakacs disqualified him for one punch too many leaving Kung Fu a popular winner. The final match saw quite an upset when a leg submission hold on Steve Grey gave Mal Sanders a two straight falls win over the British Lightweight Champion. Straight afterwards Sanders announced his ambition to train down to the lightweight weight limit and challenge Grey for his title.

Giant Haystacks was back on TV on October 18th from Hemel Hemsptead although it was a blink and you've missed it match as opponent John Cox was unable to continue after less than two minutes of the first round. The other match shown was the final for the vacant British Heavyweight Title between Gil Singh and Ray Steele, this match also had a special guest referee in Mick McManus. It wasn't announced how Steele had progressed to the final after his drawn match with Dave Taylor. It was another example of not thinking about the next step when a result could have been determined on the day of the drawn match. Just to complicate the picture even more the title was still undecided when both wrestlers were counted out in the eighth round and another match would have to be held.

With the announcement that All-Star Promotions would now be seen on ITV the *Screensport* shows came to an end with the October edition. The highlight of this was the first appearance of the Japanese youngster Fuji Yamada on TV. Yamada had been recommended to Brian Dixon by Mark Rocco having seen him on his Japanese tours and Dixon was quick to book Yamada for a UK tour. Much like when Sammy Lee first arrived in 1980 Yamada showed his inexperience in his early matches here but it wasn't long till he showed his great potential and of course he went on to have a long and illustrious career as Jushin 'Thunder' Liger in the Japanese rings as well as around the world. On the Screensport show Fuji Yamada partnered 'Iron Fist' Clive Myers in a Tag KO Tournament with in another team Brian Maxine and local youngster Keith Myatt. Myatt at this time is still wrestling into his fifth decade in the ring whilst his present day tag partner Blondie Barratt who was also in the tournament incredibly is in his sixth decade having made his wrestling debut in the 1970's. The other teams were John Wilkie and Chris McNeill and the aforementioned Blondie Barratt and Rocky Moran. Yamada and Myers won the tournament beating Wilkie and McNeill in the first semi final before defeating Barratt and Moran to lift the prize.

Mal Sanders having insisted he could make the lightweight title limit was given his match against Steve Grey for the British Lightweight Title on October 25th. The problem was that Sanders failed to make the weight on the night so the match was deemed to be a non title affair and even though Sanders got another win it didn't matter with the title not being up for grabs. The show from Hemel Hempstead that week also saw another Marty Jones v Pete Roberts bout with the match ending in the fourth round when Roberts injured his arm. Referee Peter Jay stopped the contest but Jones refused to accept the win so a No Contest was called.

Giant Haystacks was back in action on TV on the November 1st show from Bradford. His opponent was Tony Francis who had been called in at short notice to replace the unavailable Pat Roach. A posting, followed by a splash into the corner and an elbow drop finished off Francis in twenty eight seconds which I think must have been the quickest finish seen on UK TV. Haystacks spent more time in the ring calling out the likes of Big Daddy and stating that he was no longer 'Mr Nice Guy' than doing any actual wrestling. This was Joint Promotions latest attempt to resurrect the Daddy v Haystacks feud which had long ago passed its sell by date. The other two matches shown that week actually featured some wrestling with Alan Kilby taking on Steve Logan in the opening match over eight rounds. The match was nicely poised at one fall each when Logan was injured in the final round and Kilby wouldn't accept the win so as per usual in the circumstances a No Contest was called. The bonus contest between Eddie Riley and Mike Jordan ended in the fourth round when both wrestlers had their shoulders pinned to the mat at the same time for the count of three so a draw was the decision.

The following Saturday on November 8th again from Bradford saw another attempt to resolve the vacant heavyweight title with Ray Steele and Gil Singh having their rematch. At last we got a winner when Singh got the winning fall in the 8th round to become the new champion. The other match featured was a heavyweight tag match with the team of King Kong Kirk and Scrubber Daly taking on Bill Clarke and Lee McConnon, this was McConnon's one and only TV appearance and for Clarke it was weird seeing him instead of his alter ego King Kendo. A big splash by Daly on McConnon finished the match in ten minutes. As the winners celebrated in the ring Big Daddy together with Peter Collins interupted things throwing out a challenge for a match which would be seen on the next ITV show.

Whilst things with Joint Promotions were the same as they ever were the big change for the ITV coverage was getting closer and All-Star Promotions announced that their first TV taping would be held at Catford on November 25th. The proposed bill was a nice mix of wrestlers that hadn't been seen on TV for quite a while with some newer faces too. The two top of the bill matches were a heavyweight contest between Tony St Clair and World No.1 Wayne Bridges who had finally established his title credentials. Mark Rocco would take on fellow World Champion Johnny Saint in the other main event. Youngsters Rob Brookside and Wayne Martin would make their TV debuts in a tag match against Bobby Barnes and Blondie Barratt and Fuji Yamada would also be featured. Although this would be the first ITV show to be taped by All-Star Promotions their first show scheduled to be shown and to kick off the new coverage would be filmed on December 27th and come from the London Hippodrome with the main event being a 'Disco Ladder Match' main event between Kendo

Nagasaki and Clive Myers. At the time commentator Kent Walton was a Joint Promotions' man through and through and sceptical about the new promoters whilst naturally Joint's main man Max Crabtree did not like Brian Dixon but had to now tolerate him at the meetings they had with the ITV producers.

Big Daddy was back on ITV on November 15th in the tag match against King Kong Kirk and Scrubber Daly. It was a popular misconception that Big Daddy was on TV every week and was ruining wrestling when in fact this was only sixth appearance of the year and hadn't been seen since the start of September on the small screen. It was hardly worth the wait as Daddy and Peter Collins beat Kirk and Daly inside 6 minutes and barely worth noting the details. The first match shown saw the Asian powerlifter Mohammed Butt beat Barry Douglas with the winner in the fifth round. This was becoming the Joint Promotions tactic on their shows, put on a match like this that had the fans bored before Big Daddy came on to up the action. The third match shown was a lot more interesting as Ted Heath was back from the USA for a brief visit and lost to Greg Valentine by two falls to one in the sixth round.

Mal Sanders had finally managed to get down to the lightweight title limit of 11st and got his title chance against Steve Grey on the ITV show November 22nd from Loughborough. The Sanders diet turned out to be a waste of time as the match ended in the eighth round with both wrestlers unable to beat the count and Grey retaining his title. The other match shown that week saw Fit Finlay beat the British Heavy/Middleweight Champion Chic Cullen. Cullen was unable to continue because of an injury to his face in the eighteenth minute, afterwards Finlay naturally demanded a rematch with Cullen's title at stake.

The exclusive Joint Promotions coverage on ITV was petering out with a whimper and on November 29th it was decided that cross country athletics was more important to show than wrestling.

Wrestling was back on December 6th with three bouts filmed at Bolton, unfortunately the matches bore no relation to those advertised beforehand. First contest saw Kung Fu meet Lucky Gordon over eight rounds, Gordon replaced Rocky

Moran. Kung Fu pinned Gordon with a folding press and bridge in the fifth round for a two falls to one win. Next was the main event with Romany Riley who hadn't been seen on TV for over five years taking on the masked King Kendo. The match was a replacement for Giant Haystacks v The Emperor which would have been far more entertaining to watch than this was. This was fought over a twenty minute duration with Kendo getting the first fall with a reverse double knee hold in the eleventh minute. Riley equalised with a cross press following a slam in the sixteenth minute and that was the score after twenty minutes. The third match was a brief glimpse of Rick Wiseman beating Jackie Turpin when he pinned him in the third round.

Bolton was again the venue on December 13th with two matches broadcast, the first saw Marty Jones and Skull Murphy face each other once again on TV. Predictably there was plenty of 'needle' in the match with Murphy taking the lead in the third round with once again the gator hold forcing a submission from his opponent. Jones came back though with his speciality powerlock submission and Murphy tapped out in no time in the fifth round. Murphy blotted his copybook once more in the final round when referee Jeff Kaye disqualified him for smashing Jones' head against the ring apron. The other match was a dreadfully dull heavyweight match fought in near silence between Caswell Martin and John Elijah. Martin put the viewers out of their misery with a winning fall in the final round pinning Elijah following a flying tackle.

The pre Christmas wrestling show on ITV shown on December 20th came from Harrogate and consisted of a four man knockout tournament. The four wrestlers competing for the prize were Zoltan Boscik, Jeff Kerry, Johnny Kidd and Kid McCoy. The first semi final fought over six rounds saw Boscik face Kidd. It was Boscik who took the lead in the third round with a nasty looking leg hold that saw Kidd submit. Kidd equalised though in the fourth round with a reverse double arm that so incensed Boscik that he attacked Kidd in the interval. It was Boscik though who went through to the final when his speciality 'three in one' hold saw another submission from Kidd in the final round. The second semi final again over six rounds saw McCoy take on Kerry. McCoy took the lead in just fifty two seconds of the first round with a double leg nelson pinning Kerry for the count of three. Kerry fought back from that early set back and equalised in the in the third round with his version of the 'kamakaze crash' followed by a cross press. McCoy got the deciding fall in the fifth round with a folding press in a move off the top rope devised by John Naylor. The final between Boscik and McCoy was this time fought over a ten minute time limit with the first score winning. Surprisingly it was McCoy who got the winner with a straight arm lift which made Boscik submit in the seventh minute and first into the ring to congratulate him was his father King Ben. Ann Relwyskow came into the ring to present McCoy with the Christmas Challenge Trophy and a nice bouquet of flowers.

The final ITV show of 1986 on December 27th was the final show with Joint Promotions as the sole promoter and in a programme of finals it would be the final time that Big Daddy and Giant Haystacks would fight each other on the small screen. The opener that week was a rematch between Eddie Riley and Mike Jordan after a drawn match seen a few weeks ago. This time there was a winner although it wasn't until the final round that the match was decided when Jordan pinned Riley with a folding press secured by a bridge for the two falls to one win. The second match was a bonus bout between King Ben and Ian McGregor with the just the one fall to win. It was Ben who pinned McGregor with a cross press in the fourth round who won. Daddy and Haystacks this time fought in a six man tag with Roy Regal and Richie Brooks partnering Daddy whilst Haystacks teamed up with Charlie McGee and Sid Cooper. Seeing as the match was a complete pantomine it might as well have been Daddy and Cinderella taking on Haystacks and Widow Twankey. The bout started in the usual way with Daddy sending Cooper and McGee flying and Haystacks refusing to get involved but once Cooper had weakened Regal in came the big man. After a couple of clubbing forearms and a big splash in the corner from Haystacks Regal was counted out and he would play no further part in the match. Brooks took over against Haystacks and Brooks was soon in trouble as he was flung over the top rope landing onto Kent Walton's commentary table. Brooks finally made the hot tag and after a couple of belly butts Haystacks left the ring and Daddy pinned McGee with a big splash. Cooper was then tagged in by McGee who was pinned by Brooks seconds later with a double leg nelson in the eighth minute. As Daddy and Brooks celebrated in the ring with a children's marching band playing their drums on the outside Kent Walton asked viewers to join him next week for a whole new look for the wrestling show with some exciting new faces as well as some we haven't seen for quite a while.

234

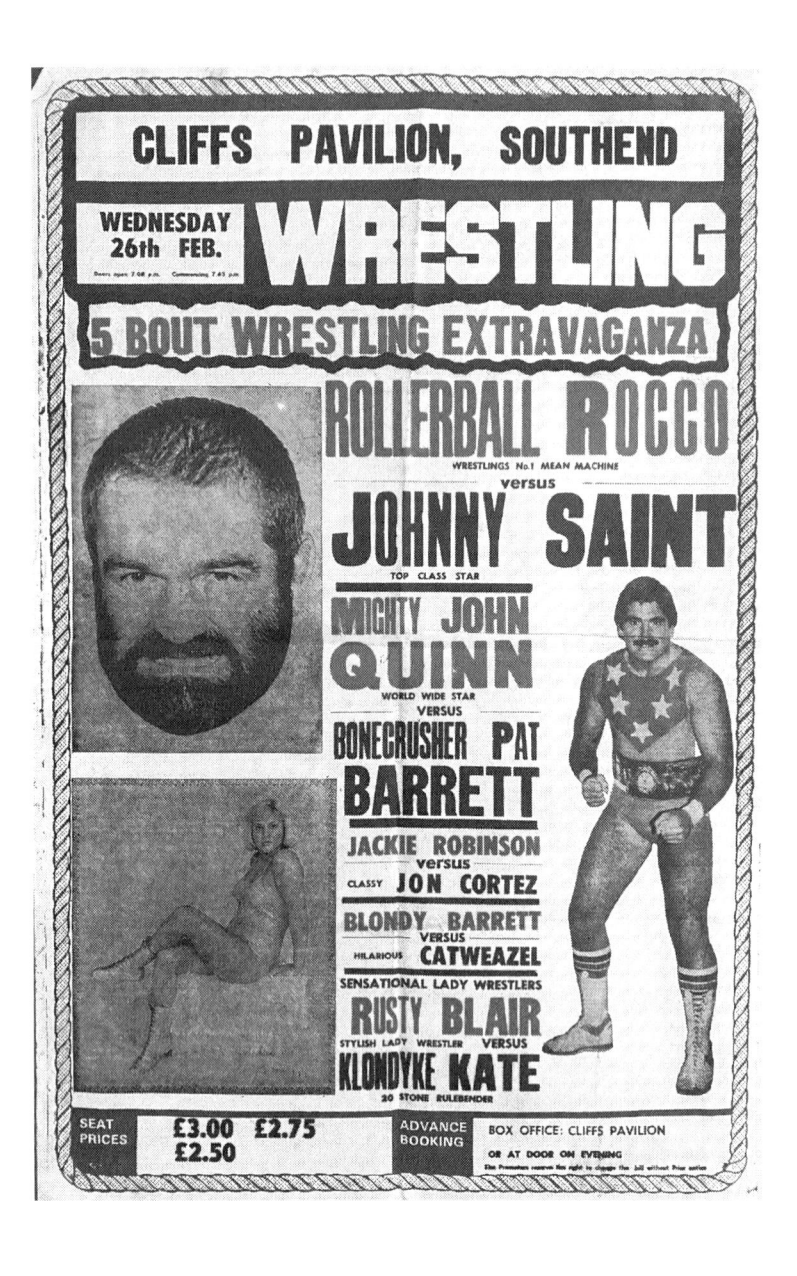

TOWER CIRCUS : BLACKPOOL
D.M.P.
Dale Martin Promotions Limited
present
WRESTLING
SUNDAY, 22nd JUNE at 7.30 p.m.
SPECTACULAR ★ TOP TELEVISION STARS IN ACTION
BOMBER ROACH
Super Heavyweight Star of the James Bond film & hit T.V. series 'Auf Wiedersehen Pet' V.
Indestructible SKULL
MURPHY
STEVE GREY
SPIDERMAN
CYANIDE
SID COOPER
KID McCOY
★ Top T.V. Stars
ALAN
KILBY
SUPER STAR SANDERS
RINGSIDE
REAR RINGSIDE
STALLS
BALCONY
CHILDREN ALL SEATS
Prices: £3.25 : £3.10 : £3.00 : £2.50 : £2.50
KING OF THE ACTION SPORTS ★ THRILLS ★ SPILLS ★ EXCITEMENT

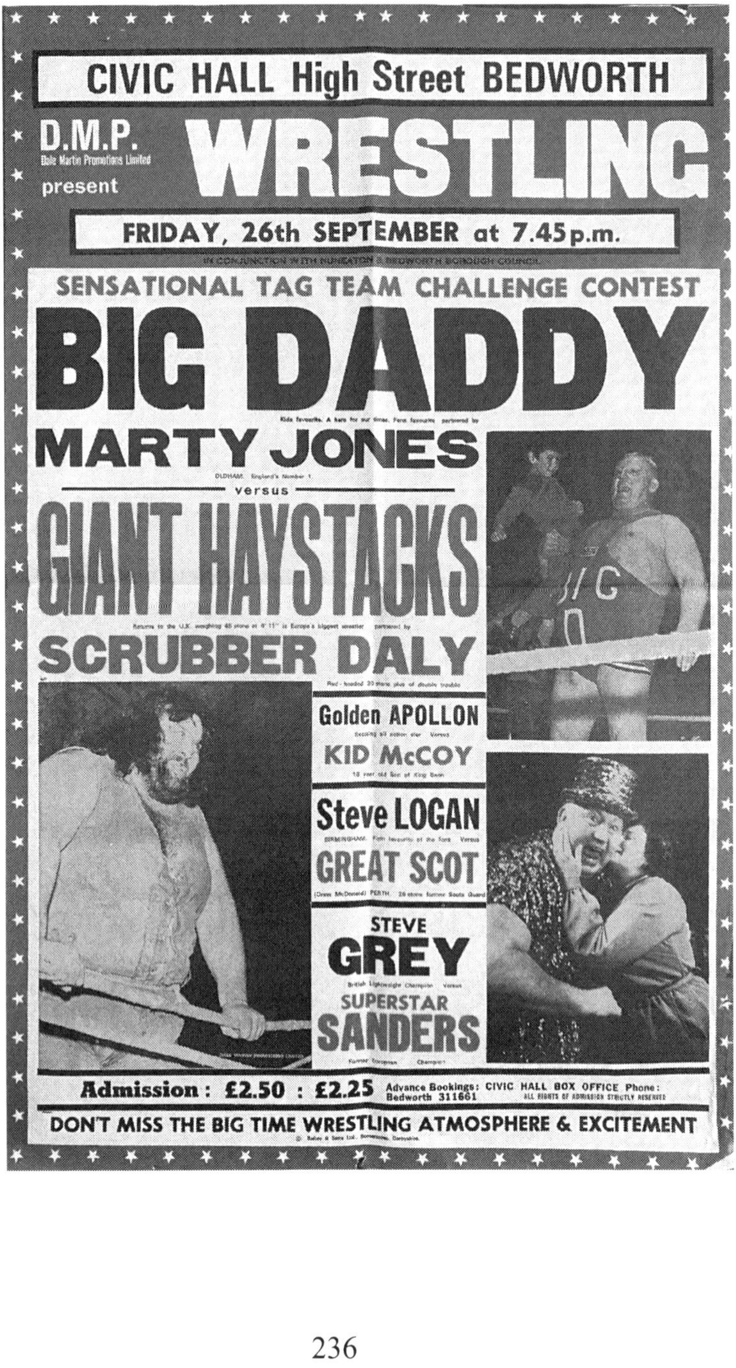
CIVIC HALL High Street BEDWORTH
D.M.P.
Dale Martin Promotions Limited
present
WRESTLING
FRIDAY, 26th SEPTEMBER at 7.45 p.m.
SENSATIONAL TAG TEAM CHALLENGE CONTEST
BIG DADDY
MARTY JONES
OLDHAM. England's Number 1
versus
GIANT HAYSTACKS
SCRUBBER DALY
Golden APOLLON
KID McCOY
Steve LOGAN
GREAT SCOT
STEVE
GREY
British Lightweight Champion Versus
SUPERSTAR
SANDERS
Admission : £2.50 : £2.25
Advance Bookings: CIVIC HALL BOX OFFICE Phone: Bedworth 311661
DON'T MISS THE BIG TIME WRESTLING ATMOSPHERE & EXCITEMENT

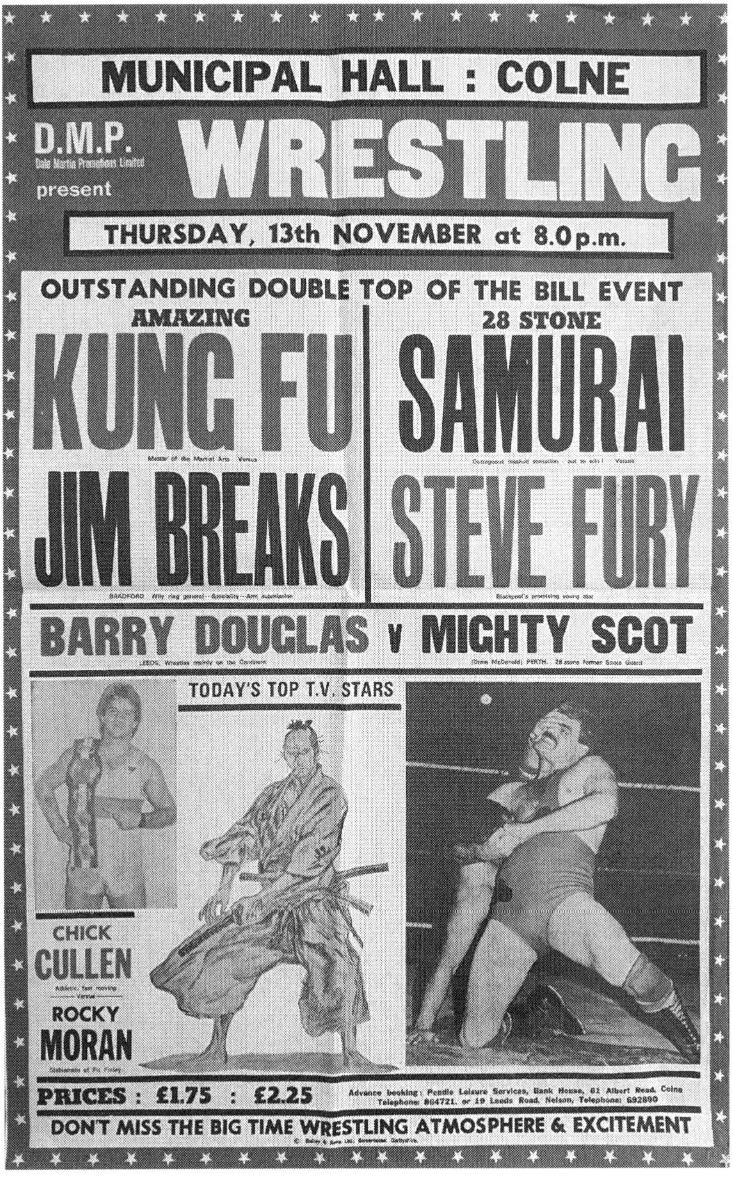
MUNICIPAL HALL : COLNE
D.M.P.
Dale Martin Promotions Limited
present
WRESTLING
THURSDAY, 13th NOVEMBER at 8.0 p.m.
OUTSTANDING DOUBLE TOP OF THE BILL EVENT
AMAZING
KUNG FU
Master of the Martial Arts Versus
JIM BREAKS
BRADFORD. Wily ring general -- Speciality -- Arm submission
28 STONE
SAMURAI
STEVE FURY
Blackpool's promising young star
BARRY DOUGLAS v MIGHTY SCOT
LEEDS. Wrestles mainly on the Continent
(Drew McDonald) PERTH. 28 stone former Scots Guard
TODAY'S TOP T.V. STARS
CHICK
CULLEN
Athletic, fast moving
Versus
ROCKY
MORAN
PRICES : £1.75 : £2.25
Advance booking: Pendle Leisure Services, Bank House, 61 Albert Road, Colne
Telephone: 864721, or 19 Leeds Road, Nelson, Telephone: 692890
DON'T MISS THE BIG TIME WRESTLING ATMOSPHERE & EXCITEMENT

Chapter 8 – 1987

After many years of letter writing , petitions and meetings All-Star Promotions finally got their chance to be seen on ITV. At 1230 on Saturday January 3rd it was their opportunity to show what they could do. It was preceeded by the popular lunchtime football preview show 'On the Ball' which did a big lead in piece for the wrestling when presenter Jimmy Greaves got into the ring to wrestle Kendo Nagasaki. The first show to be broadcast was filmed at the London Hippodrome on December 27th. Maybe it was a good thing that Brian Dixon and the ITV producers Mike Archer and John Scriminger had a long lunch before hand as the main event, the famed 'Disco Ladder Match' between the return of Kendo Nagasaki and Clive Myers turned into something of a disaster. It was Nagasaki's idea to do something different but it went horribly wrong from the start, there was no crowd in view by the ring and the camera was too far away a lot of the time. After about thirty seconds music started playing and the disco lights were flashing which shouldn't have happened till after the match had ended. Nagasaki won the match when he got hold of the golden disc that was hanging over the ring but talking to friends afterwards the general opinion was what the hell was that ? At least Nagasaki admitted in his autobiography that it was nothing like what he intended the match to be but looking back the punters who went to the shows and watched it on TV were too conservative in their tastes to like something as outlandish as that.

At least there were two traditional style contests on the bill with Fuji Yamada making his ITV debut against Stoke wildman John Wilkie. Yamada had really improved since his British arrival three months ago and Kent Walton commented that he was reputed to be even better than Sammy Lee. Yamada pinned Wilkie for the winner in the third round with a dive from the corner post following up with a cross press. The other match was the return to ITV for Mark Rocco having been in terrestial TV exile for nearly five years to take on Chic Cullen. MC John

Harris who was another returning to ITV after an absence messed up the introductions with saying it was a one fall match when in fact it was the best of three falls etc. to decide the winner. There was some wrestling for the first minute or so before Rocco's impatience took over and referee Frank Casey gave him a first public warning. In announcing it Harris also corrected his earlier mistake about the number of falls to win. Rocco pinned Cullen for the first fall in the third round after a suplex over the top rope from outside the ring following several weakeners. Cullen came back strongly in the fourth round and equalised with a cross press from a hip toss. It was to no avail as Cullen was thrown from the top of the corner post and following a pile driver Rocco pinned him with a small package for the win in the fifth round. Just like the Nagasaki match the surroundings spoilt the bout, the lighting and the camera angles as well as having hardly any fans visible did it a disservice. The only good thing was that All-Star Promotions had already recorded their next show to be broadcast and it would be back to the traditional way of doing things.

Joint Promotions had their first show of the new series the following week on January 10th which featured Marty Jones in an eliminator for the now vacant World Mid/Heavyweight Title against the elderly looking Belgian Jean Pierre Auvert. Unlike All-Star's attempt to do something different Joint Promotions were still using the same old tired formula to their shows. The only change was a quick promo by the wrestlers in the main event before the advert break, some like Mark Rocco and Americans like John Quinn were used to doing them and came across naturally whilst others struggled. It looked like they were just reading words off of a piece of card held in front of them, which of course they probably were! The first contest was a typical Joint Promotions heavyweight match over six rounds between Ray Steele and Dave Taylor. The match ended in a draw with Steele taking the first fall in the third round before an equaliser from Taylor in the fifth round. Marty Jones got back on the title track in front of his hometown fans at Oldham when he won the eliminater for the World Mid/Heavyweight Title beating Jean Pierre Auvert. Auvert took the lead in the third round pinning Jones after a clothesline weakener. Jones quickly equalised in the fourth round before the powerlock submission hold finished off Auvert in the seventh round. It was announced Jones would face the nominated North American challenger for the vacant title sometime in the future.

One thing Kendo Nagasaki said at the time was proved right the following week when the WWF had their first network TV coverage in Britain. Nagasaki had voiced what some of us were fearing, the American style and coverage made the British presentation look very dated as well as small time. From 20 000 at Madison Square Gardens to 500 or so at the Queen Elizabeth Hall in the Oldham Civic Centre. Rows of elderly British fans sitting for most of the time in silence or politely applauding whilst the American fans were youngsters or families having a night out invested in the action in front of them and noisily cheering for their favourites. The first WWF coverage was shown on January 17th and naturally featured 'The British Bulldogs' who were the current WWF Tag Team Champions. Neither Dynamite Kid or Davey 'Boy' Smith looked anything like they did in their earlier days in the UK but with their Union Jack style trunks and their muscle bound physiques they immediately got over with the TV viewers. Their match with 'The Hart Foundation' showcased both teams abilities perfectly. The strange thing is that neither Dynamite or Smith were ever top of the bill wrestlers in the UK unless they were in Big Daddy tag matches before they went to Canada but now they were legitimate superstars in the eyes of British viewers. The other featured match saw Hulk Hogan and at this time in the UK he was more known for being Thunderlips in Rocky 3 than for any wrestling exploits but you couldn't be impressed looking at him and the match with Randy Savage saw him gain thousands of new British fans.

January 24th saw the transmission of the first All-Star Promotions show to be taped back in November. The main event saw Wayne Bridges take on Tony St Clair which unfortunately ended prematurely in the fourth round when both wrestlers failed to beat referee Frank Casey's count of ten after a nasty looking collision. Fuji Yamada continued to make fans sit up and take notice when an impressive looking moonsault from the top rope finished off the vastly more experienced

Rocky Moran inside twelve minutes with the only fall needed to win. The final bout that week saw Catweazle back on ITV after a long absence to take on ITV debutant Shane Stevens. Catweazle was still loved by the fans and he went through his entire repertoire of comedy before pinning Stevens with a folding press in the third round for the winner. Stevens would be something of a pariah in the wrestling world in the latter years with various frauds and such like committed which saw him imprisoned.

Joint Promotions were back in the ITV slot on January 31st with two more matches recorded at Oldham. The first of which saw an international heavyweight match between Gil Singh and General John Raven the American military man from Lancashire. The match ended in the fourth round when a half piledriver from Singh saw Raven unable to beat the count of ten. The other contest saw Alan Kilby defend his British Light/Heavyweight Title against Andy Blair, again there was no reason or explanation given as to why Blair should get a title match. The match still fought over the traditional title match limit of twelve rounds ended as many expected with a two straight falls win for Kilby. Kilby's usual powerslam finisher ended the match in the sixth round which was fought mainly in complete silence from the fans and a smattering of polite applause at the end.

Another Joint Promotions' show was shown on ITV on February 7th with two matches from Hereford. The first of which saw Greg Valentine give lumps of weight away to face Scrubber Daly and Valentine won the match with Daly disqualified in the fifth round. The main contest saw Pat Roach taking on Steve Logan who was a replacement for John Quinn which would have been far more interesting. Roach got the first fall when he pinned Logan in the fourth round after a body slam. Roach was the winner in the sixth round when Logan was unable to continue after missing a dropkick, interestingly Roach accepted the win rather than call it a 'No Contest'. Roach took MC Roy Harding's microphone to say it taught Logan a lesson to lose the match. Roach always made a far better villain in the ring than what he had become in the latter years.

February saw the start of the 1987 version of the 'Grand Prix Belt' and after the 1986 one featured the lightweights this year's tournament went back to the heavyweights. The competition started at the semi final stage with the coverage shown on February 14th from Hereford. Tom Tyrone beat Johnny Wilson by two falls to one in the fifth round of the first semi final. The other semi final ended in controversy though. The match between Skull Murphy and Pete Roberts ended in a one fall each draw at the end of the scheduled six rounds. Roberts was declared the winner as he had only received one public warning against Murphy receiving two.

The other half of the All-Star Promotions show from Catford was screened on February 21st. The match featured the ITV debut of the 'Young Ones' tag team of Rob Brookside and Wayne Martin. Brian Dixon had spoken to commentator Kent Walton and had told him that Brookside was a great young prospect and one to note , Walton told Dixon he would decide who was good and who wasn't. That wasn't unexpected as Kent Walton had been very reluctant about the new promoters and the changes to the ITV show format. Walton did though take to Brookside and did recognise his talents going forward. For tag partner Wayne Martin who came from a wrestling family with father Johnny Lee and sister Tina Martin both wrestlers this was his only appearance on ITV. He seemed to disappear without trace shortly after before he made a comeback of sorts a couple of years later barely recognisable as he had put on about five stones in weight and was a fully fledged heavyweight. The comeback didn't last long either and nothing was heard from him wrestling wise since. Brookside and Martin's opponents in the tag were the flamboyant pairing of Bobby Barnes and Blondie Barratt whose ring attire favoured the 'Hells Angels' tag team of which Barnes was a member of many years before. The 'Young Ones' acheived victory when Brookside pinned Barnes for the winner inside eleven minutes.

The main event saw Mark Rocco who was never in a dull match taking on Johnny Saint. An excellent bout saw Saint take the lead when he reversed a Rocco piledriver to take the opening fall in the sixth round before an unfortunate ending in the next round left Rocco the victor. Saint failed to jump high enough in a leap frog and Rocco's head caught Saint full on in the nether regions. Referee Frank Casey had no option but to stop the match as Saint was unable to continue. The other match saw a clash of veteran lightweights with Jon Cortez pinning Jackie Robinson for the only fall needed.

No wrestling was shown on February 28th as the US Indoor Athletic Championships was broadcast instead. This was to become one of the reasons viewing figures declined, the 1230 slot was the next to go and the programme started to have different show times most weeks. There was no wrestling shown the following week on March 7th either but this was due to tragic circumstances. The ITV lunchtime news was extended to cover the Zeebrugge Ferry disaster and the intended wrestling programme was put back to later in the month. Wrestling was again missing on March 14th as this time it was deemed ice skating would be preferable to be shown in the time slot so it would be a four week gap before the next wrestling was on ITV.

Away from the TV screen Joint Promotions had some different faces on their bills during February, some new and some making a welcome return. A new face was a musclebound Russian called 'Red Ivan' who in fact was Richard Krupa and wrestled under the name 'Vladimir Krupa' for Stampede Promotions in Canada. Another arrival from Canada was Owen Hart who was returning to the UK after a three year absence and was the nominated North American challenger for the vacant World Mid/Heavyweight Title. In recent years Andy Robbins had become more famous for wrestling his bear 'Hercules' but now made a return to conventional wrestling and was quickly topping the bill 'North of the Border'. Finally Danny Collins was fit to resume wrestling after the illness which had cost him a kidney and several months away from the ring. After a few bouts for Joint Promotions Collins went on to work for All-Star Promotions for the majority of the time.

The start of March saw a new World Heavy/Middleweight Champion when Fuji Yamada dethroned the reigning title holder Mark Rocco at Croydon on March 3rd. Yamada came out on top in a tremendous match with the winning fall in the seventh round. Rocco was immediately demanding a return match but would be forced to wait till the end of April for his chance. Another match that night saw John Quinn beat Tony St Clair in the fifth round when the stipulation was that only a knockout would be enough to win. Catweazle pinned Jim Breaks. Steve Regal beat Shane Stevens by disqualification and Steve Fury wrestled a draw with Spinner McKenzie in the other bouts on the show.

The first of promoter Brian Dixon's two big ambitions in wrestling was to promote on ITV which he had finally achieved and the other was to be able to promote ladies wrestling in London. After another long campaign of letter writing, meetings and petitions this became a reality when it was announced that All-Star Promotions would be presenting a show at The Royal Albert Hall on Friday April 24th. It would feature Dixon's wife Mitzi Mueller in the main event of the evening. Mueller would tag with Scotland's Rusty Blair against 'The Bovver Birds' duo of Klondyke Kate and Nicky Monroe. With a supporting bill of Kendo Nagasaki, John Quinn, Tony St Clair, Fit Finlay , Johnny Saint etc hopefully it would turn out to be a better show than the last Joint Promotions' presentation there back in 1985.

Wrestling returned to ITV after the four week absence with a bill from Croydon shown on March 21st. The main event was a fantastic tag match with Mark Rocco teaming up with Kendo Nagasaki to take on Fuji Yamada and Clive Myers. Rocco finished off Yamada with a piledriver for the win in just under 20 minutes with some of their moves never seen in a British ring before. The other contest shown was the complete opposite and a technical masterpiece between Jon Cortez and Keith Haward which ended in a one fall each draw at the end of eight rounds. The strange thing was that in the newspaper TV listings the coverage listed was a WWF show which would include Hulk Hogan defending his title against Kamala and Bret Hart taking on Tom Magee in what turned out to be a fabled match. The WWF matches ended up never being seen on ITV.

The show scheduled to have been seen on March 7th was eventually screened on March 28th although it had been recorded back on January 8th. Filmed at Huddersfield it featured the start of the 1987 version of the 'Golden Grappler' trophy with Mal Sanders pinning Pat Patton in the fourth round to progress to the next round. The main event match saw newly crowned Joint Promotions heavyweight champion Gil Singh take on Giant Haystacks with Big Daddy sat at ringside. The contest ended in the second round with Haystacks disqualified by referee Peter Szakacs for an elbow drop on Singh which was the cue for Daddy to get involved in some comedy skirmishes. The other contest shown saw Fit Finlay beat the much heavier West Indian heavyweight Caswell Martin in the fifth round with a suplex leading to Finlay pinning Martin.

April started off on ITV with the final of the 'Grand Prix' belt shown on the 4th with more of the Huddersfield bill shown. Pete Roberts won the belt when he used his greater experience to just edge out Tom Tyrone with the winning fall coming in the final round from a side suplex. Big Daddy made his first ITV appearance of the year when he partnered Marty Jones against the team of King Kong Kirk and The Samurai who were accompanied by their manager Tony Francis. As Big Daddy tag matches go this was quite a good match with Jones and Kirk doing most of the work before Daddy landed the big splash on Samurai to get the winning fall. Straight afterwards as MC Brian Crabtree announced the winners the ring was flooded with loads of children wanting to celebrate with Daddy and it just showed how popular he still was. The final match that week was the second heat of the 'Golden Grappler' trophy with Richie Brooks progressing when the accidental low blow routine seen many times before from opponent Mick McMichael saw him disqualified.

Danny Collins made his comeback to ITV on April 11th against Kung Fu in a bill recorded at Stockport. Collins and Kung Fu wrestled a crowd pleasing six round draw with each wrestler scoring a fall each. Collins' equaliser coming with a slightly botched sunset flip from the middle rope in the last round. Kid McCoy was the next wrestler through to the next round of the 'Golden Grappler' trophy when he beat the far more experienced Jackie Turpin with the one fall needed in the fifth round when the youngster reversed a Boston crab from Turpin to pin him for the count of three. Finally Red Ivan made his British TV debut when he faced Barry Douglas. Ivan's physique was splendid but his wrestling not so. Luckily the match only lasted a couple of minutes before a clothes line from Ivan saw Douglas take a heavy fall from the ring onto the TV monitors and he was unable to continue. As Ivan celebrated by waving a Hammer & Sickle flag in the ring Big Daddy marched down the stairs towards him waving a Union Jack flag and for a few moments we had a flag waving contest before Daddy pushed Ivan through the middle of the ropes and outside of the ring.

Ian McGregor was final wrestler through to the semi final stage of the 'Golden Grappler' trophy on the April 18th show on ITV which was the second half of the one taped at Stockport. McGregor beat regular opponent Eddie Riley by the only fall needed in the fourth round and joined Kid McCoy, Richie Brooks and Mal Sanders in the semi finals. Another of those matches that seemed to be on TV all the time Pat Roach v Ray Steele was also on that week. Steele took the lead in the third round with a cross press after an impressive body slam on Roach. But it was Roach who had another win in front of the cameras when a forearm smash landed flush on Steele's jaw and he was counted out by referee Gordon Pryor in the fifth round. The main event saw Andy Robbins make his first TV appearance for many years against Mel Stuart. The match ended in the third round when Stuart submitted to the Robbins finisher, the 'Indian Deathlock' and was unable to take any further part in the match.

After plenty of pre tournament publicity it was time for the long awaited All-Star Promotions show at the Royal Albert Hall in London on Friday April 24th. This would be the first wrestling show held there by a company other than Dale Martin for over twenty years and had been heavily promoted both in the wrestling world and also the mainstream media had seen plenty of coverage. Despite all the publicity disappointingly the crowd was smaller than expected and like the Dale Martin Saturday show back in 1984 it seemed the London fans didn't like turning out at the weekend. Whatever the reason it was a great shame more people didn't turn out for the occasion. Eastbourne wrestler Johnny Lee, the father of young wrestlers Wayne and Tina Martin had brought his family to watch the show but ended up wrestling instead. Keith Haward had been matched to wrestle Johnny Saint but Haward was unhappy with the evening's wages as he was used to receiving a bonus when wrestling at the Albert Hall for Dale Martin so he was missing on the night. A quick swap of opponents saw Johnny Lee now face the teenager Peter Bainbridge whilst Bainbridge's original opponent Mike Jordan was now matched with Johnny Saint. Bainbridge saw off the challenge of Lee winning by the only fall required in the third round. Saint won the clash of sometime World Lightweight Champions when he beat Jordan with the winning fall coming in the sixth round. The main event was up next with the ladies finally getting their chance to wrestle at the Royal Albert Hall after many years of trying to get the Kensington & Chelsea Council as well as the hall's trustees to approve of it. Not only that it was also the farewell appearance in the ring of Mitzi Mueller after a legendary career of over twenty years but injuries had taken their toll and Mitzi was going out at the top. Mitzi Mueller partnered Scotland's Rusty Blair against the team of Klondyke Kate and Nicky Monroe. In a lively and spirited match Mitzi and Rusty came out on top by two falls to one in just over twenty one minutes to the fans delight.

At the interval it came to promoter Brian Dixon and others notice that the show was running somewhat behind its schedule and if they weren't careful they would be have to pay several thousand pounds for breaking the venue's curfew. Therefore the second half of the show had a rushed feeling about it which started with the mens main event of the evening with John Quinn and Kendo Nagasaki taking on Dave Taylor and Neil Sands. Quinn and Nagasaki won by two straight falls in the seventeenth minute. Five public warnings were issued during it which showed the rule book and sportsmanship had gone clean out of the window. Fuji Yamada's match against Chic Cullen ended in the third round with neither wrestler able to continue after a clash of heads. The evening ended with Fit Finlay meeting Tony St Clair with Finlay disqualified in the third round after receiving public warnings in the first and second rounds.

April ended with a blockbuster on the ITV show screened on the 25th as they had the vacant World Mid/Heavyweight Title match between Marty Jones and Owen Hart. Even watching it back today it doesn't fail to still impress me as a match with everything done perfectly. If I was using star ratings it would be a 5* match with perhaps Jones's title match against Fit Finlay in 1983 ,Jones v Bull Blitzer in 1986 and Mark Rocco's title matches with Fuji Yamada alongside it as worthy of that rating. Jones won the vacant title in the tenth round when he suckered Hart with a small package for the winning fall. As the belt was presented to Jones the loser Hart congratulated him on the microphone and generously put him over. A noisy and packed crowd at Bradford, a superbly crafted match between two great wrestlers showed that Joint Promotions could still put on brilliant wrestling contests when they wanted to. It was one of those weeks when the other contests got forgotten about but Alan Kilby was scheduled to face Fit Finlay but he was replaced by Colonel Brody in the opening bout. Brody was accompanied by 'his beautiful mentor' Miss Petite Fleur who for a reason not explained carried a trophy to the ring. Kilby got the equaliser in the fifth round and whilst the cameras were showing a replay he attacked Kilby and was disqualified by referee Jeff Kaye. Richie Brooks went through to the final of the 'Golden Grappler' trophy when his semi final opponent Mal Sanders was unable to continue in the third round.

Another great All-Star Promotions show was held at Croydon on May 5th with three main event contests. Mark Rocco beat Chic Cullen by two falls to one in the fifth round of another 100mph Rocco style match. Fit Finlay beat Fuji Yamada who was coming to the end of his first British tour and Tony St Clair knocked out John Quinn in the fifth round for a notable win. Also on the show Johnny Saint pinned Eddie Riley in the fifteenth minute and Tom Thumb wrestled a twenty minute time limit draw with Blondie Barratt.

Red Ivan made his second appearance on ITV on May 2nd from Bradford when he took on Andy Blair in something of a mismatch. Ivan slaughtered Blair having attacked him before the bell signalled the start of the contest. In the two minutes or so the match lasted Ivan simply threw him around the ring like a rag doll. The finish came when Ivan pressed Blair above his head before deliberately throwing him over the top rope to land heavily outside the ring. Referee Emil Poilve counted to ten and MC Brian Crabtree announced Ivan the winner by knockout. But surely the Russian should have been disqualified as such a move is forbidden under Mountevan's rules ? The previous week had seen Richie Brooks go through to the final of the 'Golden Grappler' trophy and this week it was the turn of Kid McCoy to advance to the final. McCoy beat his opponent Ian McGregor in a fine match when he pinned him in the fifth round. Finally Gil Singh resumed hostilities with Skull Murphy. Singh who was treated like a god in that area of Yorkshire and was on a par with Big Daddy in the popularity stakes. Singh got the first fall following a suplex and to add insult to injury a lady at ringside gave Murphy a piece of her mind. Like their previous matches this one started to fall apart once Murphy got the equaliser with his gator hold making Singh submit instantly. Referee Jeff Kaye totally lost control and dished out two public warnings to both wrestlers but to no avail and in the sixth round Kaye had enough and disqualified the pair of them.

Big Daddy finally got his hands on Red Ivan on May 9th but surprisingly this was shown on ITV the week before the FA Cup Final instead of as usual being part of the big match build-up. Fans around the country had already seen them square off in tag matches that featured Daddy and a partner versus Ivan and various 'Comrades' on numerous occasions. This time Daddy was back partnering Danny Collins whilst Ivan was with 'Comrade' Drew McDonald. Collins got an early fall on McDonald in the second minute with commentator Kent Walton shouting out in excitement 'he's holding him' as Collins pinned the much bigger McDonald with an assist from Daddy. A backbreaker on Collins by Ivan saw Collins submit for the equaliser before a bodyslam and a big splash on Ivan by Daddy got the winner in the ninth minute. The opener that week from Bedworth saw a rather dull match between King Ben and Ray Robinson which ended with Ben pinning Robinson in the eighth round for a two falls to one win.

The 1987 FA Cup Final day saw the ITV coverage start at 1200 with the wrestling given a twenty five minute slot at 1250.

The opening match saw Steve Logan beat Greg Valentine with the only fall needed in the second round coming from a flying tackle from the corner post. The main event was a 'Battle Royale' featuring eight heavyweights, Giant Haystacks, Pat Roach, King Kong Kirk, Scrubber Daly, King Kendo, Colonel Brody, Terry Rudge and Johnny Wilson. The final three left were Haystacks, Kirk and Roach, Roach quickly eliminated Kirk leaving him and Haystacks. Roach was attempting to remove the corner post pad when Haystacks flattened him from behind and referee Max Ward had no alternative but to halt proceedings and declare Giant Haystacks the winner.

All-Star Promotions were back on ITV on May 23rd with more of the Croydon bill shown. The main event saw the World Lightweight Champion Johnny Saint make a successful title defence against Mike Jordan. The match ended in the seventh round when after an accidental clash of heads Jordan was left bleeding profusely from his forehead. Referee Billy Finlay had no choice but to stop the match. The other contest featured saw Wayne Bridges and John Quinn meet on ITV for the first time since the epic World Heavyweight Title match in 1980. Bridges got some sort of revenge this time when Quinn was disqualified to leave him the winner.

After several weeks of excellent matches on the ITV Wrestling Show things shuddered to a halt on the May 30th edition from Broxbourne. Two championship main events were on offer the main one being Danny Collins defending his British Welterweight Title against Rick Wiseman. There was no story to this match. Wiseman was a typical 'old school' British style wrestler, he wore dark trunks and boots and his name on the bills was usually in such small print it was only fractionally bigger than the name of 'Baileys' the printers at the bottom of the card. Wiseman had had a televised championship match against Steve Grey two years previously which he lost by two straight falls and now he had another chance. As with Andy Blair earlier in the year there was no back story to the match, no previous non title victory or anything similar just that Max Crabtree decided to book this as a championship match on TV. This was just a continuation of treating titles as if they were meaningless and even more now they had reduced the matches to eight three minute rounds, way down from a few years ago with the fifteen five minute rounds time limits. Naturally Collins won the match and retained his title with the winning fall in the eighth round to the polite applause from the ringsiders who had sat silent through most of the match. The second of the title matches had a much better build to it with the British Lightweight Champion Steve Grey defending his title against the youngster Kid McCoy. McCoy had impressed greatly during his first year as a professional wrestler and having won the 'Christmas Trophy' knockout tournament was deserving of a title match. Again this match was fought under the new eight rounds time limit and with both wrestlers having a score each it ended in a one all time limit draw so Grey retained and everyone looked forward to a return match.

An interesting tag match also occured on May 30th at Cheltenham with the IWF Junior Tag Titles being fought for between the USA team of Bryan Walsh and Johnny Di Carlo and the British team of Danny Collins and local teenager Peter Bainbridge. Collins and Bainbridge won the titles but there wassn't much if at all said about the IWF Junior Tag Titles afterwards. Di Carlo went home after the match but Walsh remained in the UK and was repackaged by Max Crabtree as Bill Pearl. Crabtree paying homage to the American strongman with the same name as he did frequently when he renamed wrestlers with names better known in the USA. Bill Pearl spent most of the rest of the eighties and into the nineties as an integral part of the Big Daddy show and lined up against him with a myriad of different partners.

The second half of the Broxbourne show was screened the following week on June 6th and was very much a 'B show' in terms of talent on offer from Joint Promotions. The feature was a tag team knockout tournament with the teams of Greg Valentine and Pat Patton, Sid Cooper and Zoltan Boscik, Peter Collins and Jeff Kerry & 'The Skinheads' Karl and Kurt Heinz fighting it out. The first semi final saw the veteran duo of Cooper and Boscik progress through to the final when they beat Collins and Kerry. Cooper and Boscik had far too much experience for the West Country team. The winning submission came from Boscik with his three in one speciality in just over

11 minutes. The second semi final saw the Heinz Brothers, who were normally seen in the last bout of an evening's show being tormented by the likes of Catweazle or Johnny Kwango, make a very rare appearance on TV. The brothers were very adept to playing to the crowd through years of experience of the holiday camp circuit and proved perfect foils for Greg Valentine and Pat Patton. Valentine got the first fall in 38 seconds as he caught Kurt Heinz unaware , a submission in the seventh minute on Pat Patton by Karl Heinz brought the equaliser. A surprisingly entertaining match came to its conclusion when Valentine got the winning fall following a body slam on Kurt Heinz in just under eight minutes. Before the final we had a quick look at Johnny Kidd taking on Irish strongman Jim Fitzmaurice. This was also a rare appearance on TV for Fitzmaurice with the match ending in a draw as both wrestlers shoulders were pinned to the mat simultaneously in the fourth round. The tournament final was won by Greg Valentine and Pat Patton by two straight falls in the seventh minute of another enjoyable match with Sid Cooper's playing to the crowd being his undoing as Valentine rolled up the scowling Yorkshireman whilst he was arguing with the ringsiders.

June 13th saw All-Star Promotions back on ITV with a bill from Catford which had been recorded back on April 28th. First up was a catchweight match between Johnny Saint taking on the much heavier but inexperienced Rob Brookside. This was a fine technical match and by now commentator Kent Walton was very much singing Brookside's praises throughout the bout. The match scheduled for six rounds entered the last round with the score one fall each and as both wrestlers sought the winner a backdrop from Saint left Brookside groggy and a flying tackle followed by a quick shoulder press gave Saint the winner. The afternoon's main event was Mark Rocco's contracted rematch for the World Heavy/Middleweight Title he had lost back in March to Fuji Yamada. Referee Mal Mason making his TV debut had his hands fall even before the bout started as both wrestlers tried to start fighting before even MC John Harris had done the introductions. The match went at a tremendous pace from the very start and there was very little lull in the action. An early fall by Yamada was evened up in the sixth round by Rocco with a fall following a suplex. The seventh round saw the winning fall for Rocco after Yamada had missed a missile dropkick from the top rope which left him weakened. Rocco swiftly used a piledriver to gain the winning fall and regain the title. This was easily another five star match with Mark Rocco being the most exciting British wrestler to watch on TV at this time. As for Yamada he returned home to Japan after what was a supremely successful first UK tour.

Joint Promotions were back on ITV on June 20th from Adwick Le Street. Giant Haystacks was top of the bill when he faced Jamaica George who was a replacement for The Samurai. George was carried from the ring after a vicious elbow drop in the third round left him poleaxed. Marty Jones took on TV newcomer Axel Anderson. Jones didn't have to extend himself to beat Anderson by two straight falls in the fifth round whilst the other contest was a heavyweight match which ended in a one fall each draw between Butcher Bond and Caswell Martin.

Andy Robbins was back on ITV with more of the Adwick Le Street bill on June 27th. Robbins was matched with Ripper Raven and the match ended the same way as his encounter with Mel Stuart earlier in the year. Raven was left unable to continue after he had submitted to the Robbins' powerlock in the fourth round. After a brief bonus match which saw Ray Steele pin Dave Duran in the fourth round the main event saw a return match for the British Lightweight Title. Steve Grey was still the champion after the drawn match with Kid McCoy shown on May 30th and now McCoy had another chance. This time we had a new champion albeit fortuitously with Grey injured in the seventh round and McCoy was now the new British Lightweight Champion.

The WWF was back on ITV on an 'American Independence Day' special on July 4th. The main event was billed to be a match between the 'British Bulldogs' & the 'Hart Foundation' from Madison Square Garden but due to the Dynamite Kid being injured he was replaced by Billy Jack Haynes which lessened the interest for British viewers.

All-Star Promotions' last Croydon show of the season took place on July 7th and if anything was even better than their May show. Kendo Nagasaki took on Wayne Bridges in the main event and following a two falls to one win for Nagasaki the demands became ever louder for him to be granted a shot at Bridges' World Heavyweight Title. Fit Finlay's match with Clive Myers ended with both of them counted out whilst Chic Cullen pinned Steve Regal in the fifth round for a two falls to one victory. Rob Brookside defeated Johnny Kidd and the evening's tag match saw Blondie Barratt and Steve Peacock beat Tom Thumb and Steve Prince in the eighteenth minute.

British action courtesy of All-Star Promotions was back on ITV on July 11th with three bouts from Catford shown. The highlight being a tag match with John Quinn and Kendo Nagasaki taking on Tony St Clair and Neil Sands. The rule book was ignored throughout the match with referee Billy Finlay unable to keep control of things. Finlay eventually disqualified both Quinn and St Clair for continued use of the closed fist which left Nagasaki to finish off Sands with the 'kamakazi crash' to win the match after twenty one minutes. Fit Finlay was now wrestling regularly for All-Star and he met another newcomer to ITV Sandy Scott who was finished off by the piledriver in the fourth round. The last match saw Catweazle make his final ever appearance on ITV when he beat Mad Dog Wilson in the fourth round. The much loved Catweazle was forced to retire through illness shortly after and he sadly died of cancer in 1993.

Bryan Walsh who was now known as Bill Pearl made his Joint Promotions' ITV debut on July 18th in a match against Greg Valentine recorded at Nottingham. An interesting aspect was a promo by Pearl which was aired in the top corner of the screen as the match continued which hadn't been seen very often in the past. Pearl took some great bumps during the match flying out of the ring on several occasions before a final fall outside of the ring in the fourth round saw him counted out by referee Dave Reece. The bonus bout saw Kid McCoy take on Steve Speed with McCoy pinning Speed with a folding press in the fourteenth minute to win. The afternoon's main event saw Bernie Wright now without the daft haircut, not being known as Bearcat anymore and back to being billed from Warrington not Calgary, Canada. The Bearcat version of Wright was much more entertaining and in this match against Rasputin he was back to being the good guy in the contest. A rather one paced match came to the end in the final round with Rasputin gaining the winner from a 'camel clutch' submission.

The second half of the Nottingham show was screened on ITV on July 25th with a rarity in the first match. Ray Steele and Terry Rudge wrestled an eight round draw with neither wrestler managing to gain a fall. Whilst there might have been no falls in the match there was plenty of action with both of them landing plenty of hard looking blows. The other match screened that week was a tag match with the super heavyweight pairing of Giant Haystacks and King Kong Kirk facing the much lighter team of Marty Jones and Steve Logan. This was a strange match mired in controversy from the start, the action took nearly two minutes to start after the bell rung as Haystacks and Kirk were more concerned with arguing with everybody in sight. Jones got the first fall with a pin on Kirk following a flying tackle in the ninth minute as Haystacks tried in vain to break it up. Haystacks got the equaliser with a submission on Logan three minutes later and with the match perfectly poised at one score each chaos happened. Marty Jones landed a dropkick full force on referee Dave Reese as Kirk ducked and the match had to be abandoned on the advice of substitute referee Ken Joyce.

August began on ITV on the 1st with a show from Leicester. Both contests shown featured reappearances from wrestlers after a while away from being seen on ITV. In the first Ray Stevens wrestled a draw with Ian McGregor. Whilst in the other I'm not sure if Inca Peru had been booked or exhumed for his match with Alan Kilby. Peru had been a regular in the mid 1950's in Britain and it had been twenty years or more since he had last wrestled here. For whatever reason he was back for just this one match which was a losing effort with Kilby winning by two falls to one.

The match between Giant Haystacks and King Kong Kirk and Marty Jones and Steve Logan which had been abandoned a fortnight ago was the subject of a rematch on August 8th's ITV show. The first match shown which was from Leicester saw Gil Singh beat John Elijah by two falls to one. Gordon Prior was the lucky referee for the tag match this time with fortunately no controversy. Kirk got the first fall with a guillotine elbow drop, 'a dastardly move' as Kent Walton described it, on Logan. Haystacks landed the elbow drop on Logan in the tenth minute to finish the match. Poignantly this was the final appearance on TV by Mal Kirk but at least he went out on the winning side and was allowed to show what a good wrestler he was when given the chance.

Joint Promotions' next show for ITV was recorded at Bridlington on July 22nd and it had eight bouts on it which were shown over three weeks. The first part of it was shown on August 15th with Big Daddy making his first TV appearance since May. This time Daddy partnered Andy Blair against the former Masked Marauders now just 'The Marauders' team of Scrubber Daly and Lucky Gordon. Daddy and Blair were accompanied to the ring by drum majorettes as well as Daddy pushing a lady in the wheelchair. Whilst this was going on Gordon, who came across like a less aggressive version of Roy Keane in his promo, and Daly waited patiently in the ring. This match had been doing the rounds of all the summer venues and was a perfectly timed and executed Big Daddy tag match with Daddy's winner coming in the twelfth minute with the big splash on Daly. The other matches shown that week weren't so entertaining with an old school dour heavyweight match between Barry Douglas and Caswell Martin. It went the full eight rounds as Martin got winner in the final round for a two falls to one verdict. Interestingly the referee was Martin Warren who was making his TV debut. I had known Martin for a long time as a pen pal who I exchanged the bills and results from around the halls with. He had been a second at various Yorkshire venues for a few years and had now stepped up to be a qualified referee. Away from the ring he was also a dentist which is quite a combination of occupations. Incidentally in the days after British wrestling had finished being shown on TV he went on to become a wrestler, wearing a mask under the name of Count Von Zuppi and was a regular participant in Big Daddy tag matches. King Ben v Jackie Turpin was the bonus match shown that week with Ben the victor by two falls to one in the fifth round.

It was All-Star Promotions turn for the ITV slot on August 22nd and it was a pleasant surprise to see some old faces return after long absences and others make their ITV debuts. The first match saw first TV appearance of the fifteen year old Peter Bainbridge against fellow TV debutant Gary Clwyd. The match ended in the fifth round with both youngsters counted out after a clash of heads. Lee Bronson returned to ITV after nearly seven years away taking on Tom Tyrone who was another Dale Martins regular being seen more often now on All-Star Promotions. Tyrone got the one fall needed to win in the thirteenth minute. The main event was a tag match with the Taylor Brothers, Dave and Steve facing the heavier pair of Ian Muir and Mighty Chang. Chang had wrestled on the independent scene for many years either as Chang or under the name of Crusher Mason whose tag matches with partner Danny Lynch were well known for becoming blood baths. In the end referee Billy Finlay's patience with Chang and Muir was tested once too often and he disqualified them in the eighteenth minute.

That same weekend on August 23rd saw the tragic death of Mal Kirk whilst wrestling in a Big Daddy tag match at Great Yarmouth. Following a big splash by Daddy on Kirk he didn't respond and was taken to the local hospital but was dead on arrival. The night's MC Fred Downes was left to break the news to a stunned crowd. The news made the front pages of the national newspapers as well as the main TV news broadcasts and over the following few days a lot of bad feeling between those involved came out. Mal Kirk for a big man was an excellent wrestler, well liked by his colleagues in the ring and able to get a good match out of anyone which is why he was an ideal opponent for Big Daddy in their tag matches. He still remains much missed by his family, fellow wrestlers and the fans who he angered so much at times. As for Big Daddy the show went on and he was in action at Bridlington the next night stating Kirk would have wished that to happen. Kirk's name had to be quickly removed from the poster advertising his appearance that night and also through the following week's booked matches.

The month ended with the final of the 1987 'Golden Grappler' trophy shown on a truncated edition of the ITV Wrestling show on August 29th from Bridlington. Wrestling was only granted twenty five minutes of TV time this week as a preview of the World Athletics Championship was deemed more worthy of the other thirty minutes usually allocated for the wrestling. Like many other fans no doubt I had forgotten all about the trophy and it was back at the start of May that Kid McCoy and Richie Brooks had won their respective semi finals to advance into the final. Kent Walton told us the final had been delayed due to Brooks being injured so in the end losing semi finalist Mal Sanders was given the chance to face McCoy for the trophy. After eight rounds the score was one fall each so referee Ken Lazenby was called upon to decide the winner via a points decision which he gave to Kid McCoy.

September started with a change in time for the ITV show which had now moved from the regular 1230 slot to an hour later at 130pm which would be the start of the many changes to the broadcast time. The 130pm starting time was a lot less convenient than the 1230 start with people now unable to watch the wrestling before going out to the football, shopping or other Saturday afternoon activities.

The first All-Star Promotions show of the new season at Croydon saw a significant title change when Mike Jordan defeated Johnny Saint to become the new World Lightweight Champion. After his defeat of Wayne Bridges at the last Croydon show Kendo Nagasaki got his title match but it ended in confusion with Nagasaki walking away from the ring and losing by countout. In a night of title matches Clive Myers beat Mal Sanders by disqualification to become European Middleweight Champion again and Brian Maxine made a successful defence of the British Middleweight Title against Shane Stevens. The other contest on the bill was a heavyweight tag match which saw Dave Taylor and Neil Sands defeat Mighty Chang and Terry Rudge.

The September 5th ITV show from the Bridlington bill saw the return of Bobby Bold Eagle to the UK. His tours here back in 1980/81 were hardly a success with both visits being curtailed early when the likes of Mark Rocco were far too much for the Red Indian to cope with. He left the UK battered and bruised and it was a surprise to see him return. He was in a lot calmer waters in his match here against Pete LaPaque though. Even so Bold Eagle ended the match in agony with a low blow from LaPaque which led to his disqualification in the third round. The second match was a heavyweight contest between Colonel Brody and Ray Steele with Martin Warren refereeing. Kent Walton noted that Warren was a 'nice looking lad' and bringing up the fact once again that he was a qualified dentist. A rather slow paced match was only notable for the way it ended with surprisingly Ray Steele being disqualified. Referee Warren was trying to check on a loose rope in the corner when Brody switched a posting from Steele and sent him flying into the corner where Warren took a heavy bump. Warren instantly disqualified Steele leaving Brody a lucky winner. The stricken referee was helped away from the ring and no doubt he would be needing treatment from one of his colleagues at his day job.

The WWF was back on British TV screens on September 12th with the highlight being Hulk Hogan defending the WWF title against Cowboy Bob Orton in front of a packed crowd at the Los Angeles Convention Centre. From Madison Square Garden the Intercontinental Champion The Honky Tonk Man took on Ken Patera and tag champions The Hart Foundation defended their titles against Paul Roma and Jim Powers. The WWF hadn't really taken off in terms of popularity here yet but Vince McMahon was obviously playing the long game which would prove to be successful.

Southport had it's annual ITV recording shown on September 19th with the 'Southport Shield' knockout tournament the highlight of the broadcast. In the first semi final Skull Murphy faced Jamaica George. George took a pasting from Murphy and after submitting to Murphy's gator hold neck submission George was unable to continue for the fourth round. The second semi final saw Marty Jones take on Bernie Wright with Jones coming from behind to get the winning fall from a powerslam in the fifth round which MC Brian Crabtree described as having been a 'macho contest'. Viewers would have to wait for the Jones v Murphy final until the following week. Instead Gil Singh met Terry Rudge in the final match that week. This was easily another 'macho contest' with the Joint Promotions Heavyweight No.1 Singh coming out on top by two falls to one in the sixth round. Whilst it was a decent match to see it wasn't a patch on the brawl they had on TV back in 1984.

Three intriguing matches made up the programme on ITV for September 26th which again came from Southport. First up was a return match between Colonel Brody and Ray Steele after the controversial ending to their first match seen earlier in the month. This time senior referee Gordon Pryor took charge with the stipulation that the only way to win would be by knockout. Steele got his revenge when a dropkick from him sent Brody flying over the top rope and referee Pryor counted him out before he could return. The final of the 'Southport Shield' was up next between last week's winners Skull Murphy and Marty Jones. Jones got the one fall needed in just over six minutes to win. Count Bartelli entered the ring to present a nice looking shield to the winner Jones. Finally there was a championship match with British Light/Heavyweight Title holder Alan Kilby facing the challenge of Steve Logan. Once again the TV time limit of only eight rounds hurt the match. At the end of the eighth round it was one fall apiece so the verdict was a draw and Kilby retained his title.

All-Star Promotions was back on TV for the start of October with two matches from the bill recorded at Walthamstow. Fit Finlay accompanied by Princess Paula was in the main event against Pete Roberts. A really good match ended in the final round. The score was one each when Finlay clamped Roberts in a back hammer neck submission to which he immediately tapped out and so Finlay was the victor. The other match saw Chic Cullen take on Rob Brookside. Brookside cemented his growing reputation but ended up the loser when a dropkick from Cullen in the fourth round knocked him out. Afterwards Fit Finlay entered the ring to challenge Cullen for his British Heavy/Middleweight Title telling him to stop taking on 'little boys' and take him on instead.

An intriguing new threat to Big Daddy was the attraction on the October 10th ITV show recorded at Borehamwood. Daddy was billed to partner Andy Blair once again but this time their opposition would be a masked duo of King Kendo who everyone knew about but his partner 'The Spoiler' less so. 'The Spoiler' was accompanied by his manager Dr. Monika Kaiser who in the pre fight promo promised he would break Daddy. As soon as they entered the ring it was obvious who the 'Spoiler' was, it was Drew McDonald. Daddy's partner Blair was unable to continue after five minutes when a piledriver from the Spoiler knocked him out. Daddy then had to take on the two men alone and after delivering a 'Winston Churchill' style rallying cry Daddy saw off the Spoiler a minute later after big splash. This was followed a minute later when King Kendo walked out of the ring to be counted out. Daddy had removed the Spoiler's mask to reveal him wearing a pair of tights over his head and Daddy then pulled off Kendo's fake pony tail for no apparant reason but to make them look stupid. As he celebrated in the ring with many children Daddy was once again challenged by Giant Haystacks who had appeared at ringside but nothing was to come of it. Before the main event viewers had to sit through a horribly dull heavyweight match which saw John Elijah beat John Kowalski by two falls to one in the sixth round. Kowalski was another returner to Joint Promotions earlier in the Summer and hadn't been seen on TV for a good ten years or more.

Wrestling was missing from ITV on October 17th which was probably a good thing with the whole country trying to clear up after the 'Big Storm' had caused devastation everywhere. The ITV chiefs had decided that a recording of the Mike Tyson v Tyrell Biggs heavyweight fight was more worthy than wrestling being seen in the 130pm slot.

Steve Grey received his rematch for the British Lightweight Title as the main event when wrestling resumed on ITV on October 24th with two more bouts from Borehamwood. This time though it was Kid McCoy's good fortune to retain his title as a result of the TV time limit of eight rounds, Grey got an early lead with a fall in the fourth round, McCoy equalised in the sixth round and neither wrestler could manage a winner in the final two rounds. In the other match shown Greg Valentine ventured into the heavyweight division when he took on the long haired Irishman Rasputin. Valentine got a victory albeit by disqualification which happened after he obtained an equalising fall. As he celebrated Rasputin struck him from behind with a forearm blow which sent him careering into referee Roy Harding leaving both dazed. Once Harding had recovered he immediately disqualified Rasputin to leave Valentine the winner although maybe a tad fortunately with the Irishman being on top throughout the match.

Fit Finlay having trimmed down to the heavy/middleweight title limit received his chance against Chic Cullen for his British title as the centrepiece of the ITV show from Bradford on October 31st. A superbly fought match was locked at one fall each as it entered the eleventh round before injury forced Cullen to quit. However the victory came Finlay didn't care as he celebrated his victory with Princess Paula in the ring whilst the defeated champion Cullen was helped from the ring to receive medical attention. Due to the title match being shown in full this would be the only match on this week.

Joint Promotions were back on ITV on November 7th with two boring bouts from Huddersfield. Ray Steele v Gil Singh and Grasshopper v Matt Matthews. Not only had Steele v Singh been done to death the previous year with the title matches but was on the bills round the circuit most of the time as was Matthews v Grasshopper. The only interesting thing was Steele beating Singh by two straight falls inside five rounds. Steele had come in as a late replacement as Pat Roach didn't show up and the bill had to be changed. Watching two old fashioned slow paced British style matches on one show without anything livelier was becoming a hard watch especially as All-Star Promotions were putting on much livelier and faster paced bouts on their coverage.

The other half of the Huddersfield bill was shown the following week on November 14th with an eight man Battle Royale on offer. There were three preliminary singles bouts shown before the 'over the top rope' finale. All three were fought over a very brief three rounds. In the first match two ITV debutants met with Ivan Trevors beating Jimmy Ocean with a reverse pile driver leading to the only fall needed to win in the third round. The muscle bound Trevors was the spitting image of his father Brian Trevors the Yorkshire strongman who wrestled mainly in the 1960's. The colourful Ocean went onto be one half of the 'Superflys' tag team with partner Ricky Knight in the days after British wrestling on TV came to an end. The second match saw the crowd favourite Alan Kilby beat American based Ted Heath who was back in the UK for a short visit. Kilby was the winner in the second round when a body slam and cross press finished the match. The final preliminary match shown saw King Ben meet the man of mystery 'El Diablo'. A flying tackle followed by a cross press in the second round saw Ben come out as the winner. Diablo as was the usual custom didn't unmask after the loss but many watching on TV recognised him as Blackpool heavyweight Tony Francis. The six men then lined up for the finale along with Pat O'Sullivan and Kurt Heinz whose match was not shown but O'Sullivan picked up a rare victory when Heinz was counted out in the 3rd round. The final three left were King Ben, El Diablo and Ted Heath. Diablo was first to go when Ben threw him over the top rope with Ben trying to drop kick Heath out but as the Texas based Yorkshireman clung to the top rope Ben forced him over to win the prize.

Wayne Bridges' long anticipated World Heavyweight Title defence against Kendo Nagasaki was the feature of the November 21st ITV show recorded at Bradford. Perhaps the saddest thing about the pre match promos was seeing how frail Gorgeous George was looking but he had not lost his gift of the gab and promised Kendo would win and then go on to challenge Hulk Hogan in the USA. A very lively and vocal crowd waited for both wrestlers to make their way to the ring with MC Max Beesley , he of the Screensport TV shows, making his introductions. Nagasaki was accompanied by not only George but a young member of his fan club who was dressed identically to his idol. Referee Peter Baines certainly had his work cut out with both wrestlers going at it from the first bell. Bridges was always one of Kent Walton's favourites and he was putting him over again during this match, 'still a good looking lad' was possibly his best bit of praise. The fourth round saw Bridges get the first fall following a flying headbutt and plenty of punches which left Nagasaki dazed and weakened. Nagasaki got the equaliser with a back drop and then a cross press on Bridges in the sixth round. A controversial ending in the seventh round saw Bridges lose his title and with it his coveted belt. Bridges crashed into referee Baines as Nagasaki attempted a back drop and as a result Bridges covered the challenger but the referee was too dazed to count. As Bridges tried to revive Baines Nagasaki blindsided him, threw him to the mat and Baines was alert enough this time for the count of three. Mayhem ensued, Bridges clotheslined Nagasaki from the ring, a ringsider threw a chair into the ring and Bridges went beserk. Bridges' protests were all in vain as the new champion Nagasaki celebrated amongst his fans in the crowd. Nagasaki eventually returned to the ring with George where the new champion was presented with his belt and this was the second occasion when Bridges would lose his title in controversial circumstances.

Due to the main event being over early there was time to see Kung Fu taking on Merseyside veteran John Kenny who was making a rare appearance on TV. Kung Fu came out on top with the winning fall in the eighteenth minute of a one fall match.

An England v Scotland team match was the featured attraction of the November 28th ITV show from Shrewsbury. Andy Robbins captained a Scottish trio of him, Ian McGregor and Alex Munroe versus an English team of Barry Douglas, Bernie Wright and Dave Duran. The first singles match saw England and Dave Duran win by two straight submissions in the second and third round against Alex Munroe. Munroe suddenly reappeared out of the blue for this show. He had a few matches on 'Combat Promotions' run by Max Crabtree in the early to mid 1970's but I hadn't heard anything of him for years before he popped up on this show. The second match saw a six round draw with Ian McGregor equalising an early fall from Bernie Wright in the fourth round and neither wrestler could get the winner in the final two rounds. The final singles match saw Andy Robbins defeat Barry Douglas when he was knocked from the ring in the second round and failed to beat the count, although it looked rather like a botch. In the six man tag match finale the Scottish team sealed the win with Andy Robbins' powerlock on Dave Duran for the winning submission.

Joint Promotions had an interesting newcomer from the USA arrive during November, he was billed as the 'Mighty Yankee' although he was nothing to do with the previous version from 1981 Steve Di Salvo or the one that was on British bills in the mid 1970's. This Yankee was called Daryl Karolat and had just completed a tour of South Africa, as with many visitors to Britain he had started off his wrestling career with Stu Hart in Canada. It was said on the advertising posters he was 7ft tall but realistically he was about 6ft 8/9in but still a physically imposing man. After his short UK tour he returned to the USA where he signed with WCW as a body guard before wrestling there for a short while. He then became a successful film actor under the name Tyler Mane.

A year previously in November 1986 a Sussex entrepreneur and concert promoter called Nick Wilson bought a show from Dale Martin featuring Big Daddy to put on at my local venue The Dome in Brighton. It was a relative success and a year later he bought another show for The Dome but this time he used Brian Dixon and All-Star Promotions. He had a decent bill for his show with Mark Rocco v Chic Cullen as the top of the bill. Also on the show was Klondyke Kate v Rusty Blair as well as wrestlers like Clive Myers, Mal Sanders and Steve Grey. The final match lined up was a midgets match between Little Daddy and Mini Quinn which aped the originals match from 1979. Nobody in their right mind could surely confuse the two but that is what happened and it led to the formation of 'Premier Promotions' which thirty three years later is still presenting wrestling shows. A few days after the Brighton show there was an article in the local newspaper the 'Evening Argus' accompanied by the obligatory photo of two unhappy punters of how they were ripped off as they were expecting the real Big Daddy and John Quinn to be at The Dome and not the midgets. At this time John Freemantle who was a wrestling fan and had contibuted to 'The Wrestler' magazine in 1960's was the sports editor on the Argus . The story ran in the paper and the upshot was that the paper bought a show featuring the real Big Daddy as a fundraiser for the newspaper's Christmas charity appeal. The Evening Argus backed the first few shows and promoted them heavily in their newspaper before Freemantle eventually branched out on his own with 'Premier Promotions'.

December started on ITV from Shrewsbury on the 5th with Marty Jones defending his World Mid/Heavyweight Title against Caswell Martin in a repeat of a defence screened a couple of years previously. Put Marty Jones in with a Mark Rocco or a Fit Finlay or the likes of Steve Wright or Owen Hart and you'd guarantee a five star bout and well worth watching on TV. As with the previous Caswell Martin title match shown in 1985 this was a carbon copy and whilst technically excellent I found this sort of long drawn out match to be hard to watch without my attention drifting elsewhere. Jones retained his title once again pinning Martin with a small package in the eighth round for the deciding fall. The Mayor of Shrewsbury entered the ring to present Jones with his belt once again and the winner's bouquet of flowers. The preliminary match saw a clash of West Country rivals with Richie Brooks beating Steve Speed in the fifth round with a rather botched looking finish. Speed clearly had his shoulders off of the mat as referee Peter Jay counted three.

Big Daddy and Giant Haystacks were back on the TV screens on December 12th although in separate contests. Haystacks was in action first on the show recorded at Blackburn when he took on Scotland's Rory Campbell. Despite Kent Walton saying it was his first appearance on TV Campbell had been seen on TV in the mid 1970's under the name Bill Turner. Haystacks looked bored throughout the match , disinterestedly throwing Campbell around the ring before dropping the big elbow on him in the second round. Campbell had no chance of beating referee Gordon Pryor's count of ten. In hindsight Kent Walton's description of Campbell as being a nice lad was very much wrong as he was incarcerated in 2019 for twelve years following being convicted of rape and other charges in the period of 1980-2001. Giant Haystacks was still in the ring as Daddy and his partner Kashmir Singh made their way from the dressing room for the tag match. Singh entered the ring first where Haystacks posted him and flattened him with a splash into the corner. Before Daddy could get his retribution in Haystacks left the ring to return to the dressing room. Luckily Kashmir Singh was taped up and able to start the match against The Spoiler with manageress Doctor Monika Kaiser and his partner Rasputin. Naturally The Spoiler and Rasputin targetted the injured ribs of Singh with plenty of illegal moves before Singh could get the hot tag and bring in Big Daddy. Spoiler got the first fall when he delivered a pile driver on Singh which gave him no chance of beating referee Jeff Kaye's count of ten. The match continued with Daddy taking on Rasputin and Spoiler on his own. Within a few seconds a belly butt had sent Spoiler flying into the front row of the crowd and Rasputin had no intention of taking on Big Daddy alone so the winners were Big Daddy and Kashmir Singh. After the match Daddy officially unmasked Spoiler as Drew McDonald which most of the crowd knew anyway. There was also time for the usual bonus bout and this week it saw Rick Wiseman beat Johnny Kidd.

The Evening Argus Christmas Appeal show took place at the Hove Town Hall on December 14th and unlike the previous wrestling held there in 1985 a full house was in attendance. The show had been promoted everywhere with posters up in shops all over the town and the event mentioned every night in the local newspaper. I even had to get there early to make sure I got my ringside seat ! The show had been bought in from Ken Joyce and the only disappointment being the Mighty Yankee not turning up for his match. He had cut short his visit and had already returned to the USA. His replacement for his match with Ray Steele was King Ben which ended in a No Contest. The main event saw Big Daddy and Greg Valentine overcome the team of Drew McDonald and Rasputin to the delight of the crowd especially the large number of children in attendance. Local wrestlers Barry Cooper and Tony Grant were given a chance to wrestle before a big crowd when they contested the Sussex Lightweight Title. The evenings other attraction was the first Evening Argus knockout tournament trophy with the contestants being Kid McCoy, Steve Grey, Sid Cooper and Andy Blair. McCoy beat Cooper and Grey beat Blair to reach the final but it ended inconclusively with a double knockout verdict after both wrestlers failed to beat the count. The organisers were so pleased with the evening they announced that there would be another tournament there in January.

The last wrestling of 1987 on ITV was shown on December 19th with the following Saturday being Boxing Day. It was All-Star Promotions turn this week with the recently retired Mitzi Mueller making her TV debut as MC for the afternoon's programme. The show was recorded just down the road from the All-Star Promotions HQ in Wallasey. The first match between Pete Roberts and Dave Taylor over six rounds ended with neither wrestler gaining a fall or submission. The other match shown was a tag featuring Kung Fu and Clive Myers resuming a partnership last seen ten years or more ago against the team of Fit Finlay and Rocky Moran. A tremendously entertaining match fought at a really fast pace saw Kung Fu get an equalising fall over Fit Finlay in the very last seconds of the twenty minutes time limit to leave the result as a one fall each draw.

LEISURE CENTRE Coventry Road HINCKLEY

Presenting the Stars of Television

WRESTLING
☆ ★ EXTRAVAGANZA ★ ☆

Doors Open 7.00 p.m. | **FRIDAY, 10th APRIL 1987** | COMMENCE 7.45 p.m.

SENSATIONAL TAG TEAM CHALLENGE CONTEST

BIG DADDY
STEVE LOGAN

versus

GIANT HAYSTACKS

KING-KONG KIRK

TERRIFIC ALL SCOTTISH CLASH
ANDY BLAIR
versus
IAN McGREGOR

THE GREAT SCOT
versus
GREG VALENTINE

THRILLS & EXCITEMENT
ALAN KILBY
versus
JOHN ELIJAH

PRICES: £3.00 : £2.50 Res. : £2.00 Tiered Seating Unres.

Advance Booking from The Leisure Centre, 10 a.m. to 10 p.m. Daily. Telephone: (0455) 610011. Also available at the Door on the night

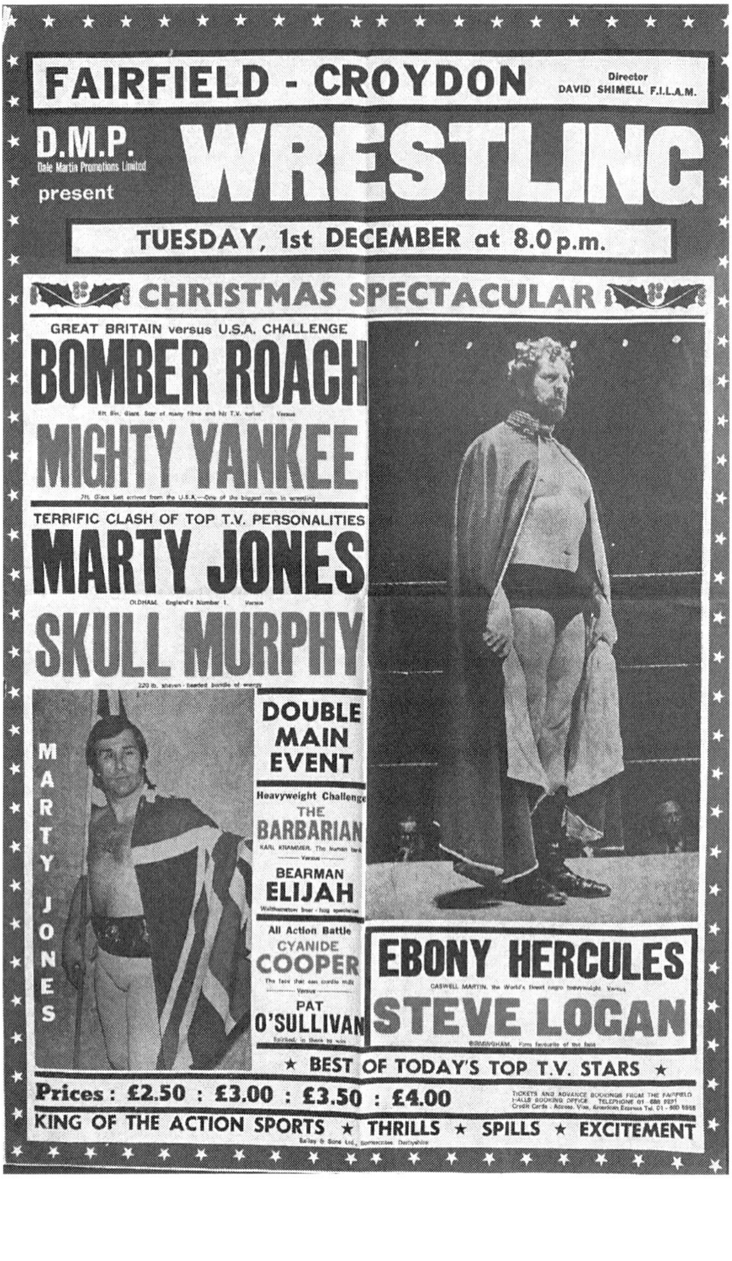
FAIRFIELD - CROYDON
Director
DAVID SHIMELL F.I.L.A.M.
D.M.P.
Dale Martin Promotions Limited
present
WRESTLING
TUESDAY, 1st DECEMBER at 8.0 p.m.
CHRISTMAS SPECTACULAR
GREAT BRITAIN versus U.S.A. CHALLENGE
BOMBER ROACH
Versus
MIGHTY YANKEE
TERRIFIC CLASH OF TOP T.V. PERSONALITIES
MARTY JONES
OLDHAM. England's Number 1. Versus
SKULL MURPHY
MARTY JONES
DOUBLE MAIN EVENT
Heavyweight Challenge
THE BARBARIAN
Versus
BEARMAN ELIJAH
All Action Battle
CYANIDE COOPER
Versus
PAT O'SULLIVAN
EBONY HERCULES
STEVE LOGAN
★ BEST OF TODAY'S TOP T.V. STARS ★
Prices : £2.50 : £3.00 : £3.50 : £4.00
KING OF THE ACTION SPORTS ★ THRILLS ★ SPILLS ★ EXCITEMENT

THE TOWN HALL · HOVE
D.M.P.
Dale Martin Promotions Limited
present
WRESTLING
MONDAY, 14th DECEMBER at 7.45 p.m.
SENSATIONAL TOP OF THE BILL INTERNATIONAL
★ HEAVYWEIGHT TAG TEAM CHALLENGE ★
ENGLAND versus THE REST
BIG DADDY
The People's Champion, partnered by
GREG VALENTINE
The teenagers' idol
VERSUS
RASPUTIN
IRELAND The mad monk partnered by
DREW McDONALD
SCOTLAND Monarch of the ring
★ MAIN EVENT ★
SPONSORED BY TVS (BRIGHTON)
BIG DADDY
Plus
Evening Argus Knockout Trophy
Six Great Contests featuring the Stars of T.V. Wrestling
MIGHTY YANKEE
GOLDEN BOY
STEVE GREY
PECKHAM
CHAMPION
KID McCOY
CYANIDE
SID COOPER
QUEENSFERRY
IN AID OF
The Evening Argus Christmas Appeal
THE BIG NIGHT OUT
FOR ALL THE FAMILY
Prices : £3.50 Adults : £2.50 Children & O.A.P. : £1.00 OFF IN ADVANCE WITH EVENING ARGUS VOUCHERS
Advance booking from Evening Argus Offices, North Road, Brighton & Church Road, Hove
KING OF THE ACTION SPORTS ★ THRILLS ★ SPILLS ★ EXCITEMENT

Chapter 9 – 1988

Little did viewers of the first wrestling show of 1988 on ITV know that this would be the last year that British wrestling would be shown on terrestial TV until well into the twenty first century. The show on January 2nd from Blackburn featured the only TV appearance of Mighty Yankee Sky Walker as he was introduced with the now usual pre match promo about limeys and destroying them. Walker took on Pat Roach who for once was looking up to an opponent. The match had warmed up nicely when in the third round the Yankee picked up referee Jeff Kaye and body slammed him heavily into the mat. This came after the referee had admonished him for his continual foul moves. Kaye had to be helped from the ring by the various officials. Ray Steele and Gil Singh met yet again in the other match shown. This time Singh's version of the heavyweight title was at stake as a result of Steele's victory on TV back in November. This was the fourth time they had met in just over a year on TV and I doubt many viewers wanted to see the match again. Singh retained the belt as a result of a two falls to one win.

Mark Rocco was back on TV on the January 9th show coming from Wallasey after an absence of six months due to various wrestling commitments overseas. His comeback opponent was Danny Collins who gave as good as he got and is now a fully grown middleweight branching into the light/heavyweight division. In the match Collins took Rocco all the way but came up a little short with the World Champion winning. The second match saw Mal Sanders chasing a shot at the British Heavy/Middleweight Title but came unstuck against the former champion Chic Cullen losing by the only fall needed.

The WWF were back on the ITV screens on January 16th with the British Bulldogs taking on The Bolsheviks. There was also a tag team title defence by The Hart Foundation against the Strike Force team of Tito Santana and Rick Martel which saw new champions crowned.

There was no wrestling shown on ITV for the next three weeks with on January 23rd a recording of the Mike Tyson fight with Larry Holmes taking over the slot. Indoor athletics was preferred on January 30th and on February 6th a 'Munich Remembered' documentary marking the 30th anniversary of the Manchester United Munich air crash disaster was shown.

The Evening Argus ran its second show at Hove Town Hall on January 19th and unlike the first one this was a show more for real wrestling fans rather than the families with the children who made up a good part of the audience in December. Encouragingly there was still a decent sized crowd for the show which saw Marty Jones retain his World Heavy/Middleweight Title when he beat Skull Murphy by two falls to one with special guest referee Mick McManus officiating. Alan Kilby defended the British Light/Heavyweight Title against Bernie Wright and came out on top by two falls to one. Johnny Kidd beat Zoltan Boscik by disqualification, incidentally the photo of Boscik putting Kidd in his '3 in 1' submission hold from the bout is still used as the Premier Promotions logo. Lucky Gordon beat Kashmir Singh and Ian McGregor beat Richie Brooks by knockout to complete a good night's wrestling. At ringside for the show were two old names from the past. The first was 'Dropkick' Johnny Peters one of the crowd favourites with his tag partner 'Dazzler' Joe Cornelius from the old Brighton Sports Stadium days .The other was the former Dale Martin MC ,the still dapper Bobby 'Now gentlemen, ladiees and gentlemen' Palmer. Palmer had lived in the Brighton area for a long time and Peters had promoted shows in conjunction with Dale Martin at the old Hove Town Hall before it burnt down in 1966. At the time the name of the promoters was 'Southern Promotions' in conjunction with Dale Martin, the name 'Premier Promotions' would come about later on.

Wrestling returned to ITV on February 13th with a bill recorded at West Bromwich back in December. The main event on the 13th showed all that was wrong with the way Joint Promotions were doing things, Big Daddy partnered by Marty Jones were taking on TV newcomers 'The Barbarians' Wolf and Karl Krammer. Karl Krammer had had a few matches in the previous few weeks but his brother hadn't so to pitch them straight in like this was a bit strange. Instead of building the new boys up into something like a threat that would draw some money somewhere down the line they were completely jobbed out with both Daddy and Jones at times treating them with contempt. Big Daddy got the first fall on Karl Krammer followed by a missile dropkick by Marty Jones on Wolf Krammer which ended the match in just over six minutes. That was the end of The Barbarians on TV as they were never seen again. As Brian Crabtree announced the verdict Drew McDonald crashed the proceedings with a large pair of garden shears to challenge Big Daddy to a hair versus hair singles match with the loser being shaved bald. Daddy of course accepted the challenge and the whole of the wrestling world awaited the match with bated breath. The other bout shown saw Richie Brooks take on Kid McCoy in a challenge match resulting from Brooks missing his chance to take on McCoy in the final of the 1987 Golden Grappler Trophy. Brooks got his revenge this time getting a winning fall in the final round of an excellent contest.

The Gala Cup was up for grabs on ITV on February 20th as the next part of the coverage of the West Bromwich show. The four participants were Greg Valentine, Rex Lane, Andy Blair and Sid Cooper. The first semi final saw Valentine take on Lane , a fall in the second round followed by a suplex leading to the winning pinfall in the fourth saw Valentine safely through to the final. The second semi final saw Blair face Cooper. This was another Sid Cooper masterpiece of a match with Blair getting the first fall with a flying tackle and cross press in the second. Cooper progressed to the final when Blair was unable to beat the count of ten following a pile driver on him. Greg Valentine won the final with the winning fall coming in the fourth round when Cooper tripped re-entering the ring and Valentine folded him up for the winner. Valentine was now able to add The Gala Cup to the Royal Albert Hall Trophy, The Amber Valley Trophy and many more trophies he had now won in his four years of being a professional wrestler.

Wrestling was missing from the ITV schedules again on February 27th with the climax of the American indoor athletics season from Madison Square Gardens deemed more worthy than the grappling.

March started with a bang to make up for the lack of wrestling on ITV in the previous weeks. The show on March 5th was recorded back at the start of January at Croydon and was an All-Star Promotions show. The first match shown was at lightweight with Mike Jordan facing Steve Grey. The match was a twenty minute time limit with the first fall winning. After 14 minutes with the match still scoreless referee Roger Brown collapsed and the contest had to abandoned. The main event saw Mark Rocco renew his tag partnership with Kendo Nagasaki when they took on Rocco's old rival Clive Myers who this time had the much heavier Dave Taylor as his partner. As with all Rocco matches it started off at an incredibly fast pace with a public warning for Nagasaki before the two minute mark for interfering from outside the ring. Rocco got his first public warning for a spiked piledriver on Myers but it was a few minutes later that the match descended into chaos. Taylor had Nagasaki in a pinning predicament which Rocco tried to break up with a knee drop from the top rope. Unfortunately Taylor saw him and moved with Rocco landing heavily on his own partner. Taylor then sent Rocco flying out of the ring before Taylor removed Nagasaki's mask who fled from the ring unmasked. Taylor and Myers were deemed winners as Nagasaki and Rocco refused to continue and then they had a massive falling out. Nagasaki blamed Rocco for being unmasked and with 'Gorgeous' George calling him a scoundrel there was now a top of the bill match to take around the country which did big business at the box office for both tags and single matches.

The first Nagasaki v Rocco match actually took place before the tag match was shown on ITV but was at Croydon so the fans in attendance would already know the story. Nagasaki won an explosive match when Rocco was counted out in the fourth round. Mal Sanders wrestled a two falls each draw with Rob Brookside when both wrestler's shoulders were pinned to the mat in the sixth round. The rest of the show comprised of a heavyweight tournament with the winner to meet John Quinn on the next show. Tony St Clair pinned Buffalo Beaney in the eleventh minute to win the first semi final and Pete Roberts beat Johnny Kincaid in the second when Kincaid was unable to continue. Those expecting a classic wrestling final were left frustrated when Roberts surprisingly adopted a far more aggressive style but to no avail as St Clair pinned him in the seventeenth minute to win.

It was back to West Bromwich for ITV on March 12th with the final two matches recorded back in December. The first match shown between Terry Rudge and Steve Logan ended in a one fall each six round draw with Rudge taking the lead in the third round with a flying tackle followed by a cross press. Logan equalised with the exact same move in the fourth round, a flying tackle followed by a cross press to gain a credible draw. The main event saw a six man super heavyweight tag match with Giant Haystacks together with Rasputin and Scrubber Daly taking on Pat Roach who partnered Jamaica George and John Elijah. With Elijah in the match commentator Kent Walton just had to mention he was a taxi driver and a paleontologist as he did for every Elijah match he commentated on. The early stages saw both Elijah and George being softened up by the opposing trio who were using the most dubious of tactics before Daly after a couple of splashes in the corner used his 'flying splash' to get the first fall on Elijah. Once Elijah tagged in Pat Roach the equaliser swiftly followed with a body slam and cross press on Rasputin in the ninth minute. The ending came in the eleventh minute when a weakened Jamaica George was the victim of the elbow drop from Giant Haystacks and he had no hope of beating referee Ken Joyce's count of ten. Whilst there wasn't much wrestling skill on offer it was always entertaining watching these kind of matches with the big heavyweights in action.

Steve McHoy made a welcome return to the ITV screens on March 19th on a show from Burnley. He had been absent for the last five years with his being on the independent circuit as well as wrestling all over the world. It was also a pleasure that Brian Crabtree had the night off and Gordon Pryor was MC for the show. McHoy had now gone back to his original wrestling name of Steve Casey and in this match he was up against Bernie Wright. The much smaller Wright surprisingly got the first fall in the third round but Casey quickly equalised in the next round. Casey got the win in the final round when he backdropped Wright from the ring and he failed to make it back inside the ropes before the count had finished. The long awaited (for some) hair v hair match between Big Daddy and Drew McDonald was the main event that afternoon although it had now turned into a tag match with Daddy teaming up with Kashmir Singh again, they also had the Rev. Michael Brooks in their corner whilst McDonald partnered Rasputin and of course Dr Monika Kaiser was in his corner too with El Diablo accompanying her. Surprisingly it was Singh who got the opening fall over Rasputin in the fifth minute with an assist from Daddy who pushed the Irishman over. McDonald got the equaliser when a Boston Crab saw Singh submit a couple of minutes later. Big Daddy got the winner with the big splash on McDonald. McDonald now had his hair cut in the ring with a local hairdresser being called in by Gordon Pryor to do the honours. As usual there was a loud and raucous crowd enjoying every moment of the match and the aftermath.

Wrestling was missing again from the ITV schedules on March 26th when International Athletics was given the time slot.

The veteran West Indian Jim Moza returned to the ITV screens on April 2nd as the next part of the Burnley show was broadcast. As with Steve Casey a fortnight previously Moza had been wrestling on the independent circuit for the past five years since he had last been seen on TV. Moza had a tough task in this comeback match against Skull Murphy. During the opening round Kent Walton made the curious comment that Murphy had made his pro debut in May 1982. Maybe he had got confused with the date Murphy had changed his ring name to Skull Murphy from his former name Steve Young ?Moza got the first fall in the fourth round with a cross press following a body slam but Murphy was too strong quickly equalising in the next round with his gator hold submission. A severely weakened Moza was soon in trouble in the final round and another gator hold from Murphy finished him off. The bill topper that week featured another defence from Marty Jones of his World Mid/Heavyweight Title this time against Colin

Joynson who was in the final throes of his great career. It was very disappointing that the championship time limit of fifteen rounds was reduced to only eight rounds which diminshed the importance of the contest. As per every Colin Joynson contest on ITV Kent Walton had to mention his nickname from the German tournaments which was 'Taschen Panzer' or pocket tank. Jones took the lead in the third round with a slightly messy looking folding press. Joynson equalised in the fifth round when he made the champion submit from a full Boston crab. Jones got the winner in the sixth round with a submission but this time not the powerlock but a Boston crab himself. Mick McManus came into the ring to present the belt back to Jones and to console Joynson after a fine although losing effort.

All-Star Promotions were back on ITV on April 9th but the time slot had moved now to a Midday start with an hour given to the show. This week was the second half of the show recorded at Croydon in January with a World Heavyweight Title eliminator for the former champion Wayne Bridges against the so called Austrian contender Baron Johan Von Schultz who was in fact Judd Harris. Harris had wrestled on TV on numerous occasions in the past but Kent Walton insisted it was his first time on TV. Bridges got the first fall in the third round with a flying tackle and crosspress swiftly followed by a winning fall in the fifth round to record a two nil victory. One of the problems with filming so far ahead of the transmission on TV was that by the time this match was shown Wayne Bridges had already regained the World Heavyweight Title from Kendo Nagasaki. Bridges had beaten Nagasaki by disqualification in a championship rematch held at Cheltenham on March 28th without the TV cameras in attendance which was a great shame.

Johnny Saint had plenty on his plate in the main event when he took on Fit Finlay of course accompanied by Princess Paula. Finlay got the opening fall in the third round but Saint equalised in the fourth round to the packed crowd's delight when he rolled up Finlay for the count of three. The weight discrepancy between the two eventually told with the much heavier Finlay getting the winner in the sixth round when Saint was forced to submit from an armbar after he had been thrown over the top rope. This was an excellent contest between two masters of their craft. The other match shown was a tag contest featuring the brothers Danny and Peter Collins against 'The Golden Boy's' Rob Brookside and Steve Regal. With no team gaining the one fall or submission needed to win this ended in a fifteen minute time limit draw.

The Golden Grappler Trophy 1988 version was on ITV on April 16th as the final part of the show recorded at Burnley. The 1987 holder Kid McCoy was looking to be the first winner to retain the trophy but had a tough looking task especially as the list of participants included his father King Ben. The other six in the line up were Richie Brooks, Ian McGregor, Blackjack Mulligan, Little Prince, Lucky Gordon and Steve Fury. The four quarter finals were shown this week and in the first of them Ian McGregor faced Richie Brooks. Brooks got the winner in the fourth round when he reversed a McGregor move to get the only fall needed to win a good contest. Next up was defending trophy holder Kid McCoy who took on the much heavier Blackjack Mulligan. Despite Mulligan employing all his old tricks he was no match for McCoy who got the only fall needed to win in the second round. Kid McCoy was an excellent young wrestler and as displayed during this match really popular with the crowds. The third quarter final saw McCoy's father King Ben meet the hirsute Little Prince. An evenly match contest saw neither wrestler gain the fall needed for victory in the five rounds so it went to a referee's decision verdict. Referee Jeff Kaye decided that Ben had done enough during the match to gain the decision and progress in the tournament. The final quarter final saw Lucky Gordon take on Blackpool's Steve Fury who was making a rare appearance on TV. Gordon was the final man through to the semi finals when he took advantage of a Fury shoulder injury to gain the winning submission in the third round.

The title stupidity reared its ugly head again when a Dale Martin Promotion at Hanley on April 16th saw World Mid/Heavyweight Champion Marty Jones booked to defend his title against John Quinn who had to be at least 20st in weight. If he was to make the title weight of under 15st he would have to cut both legs off let alone one ! On the night of the show not surprisingly it was announced that Quinn had failed to make the weight and he ended up losing to Jones by knockout in a non title affair.

The Golden Grappler Trophy tournament carried on the following week April 23rd in a bill recorded at Normanton in Yorkshire. The first semi final was between Kid McCoy and Richie Brooks which should have been the final of the 1987 version but was derailed by Brooks being injured. Yet again Brooks' trophy ambitions were thwarted by bad luck with the contest perfectly poised at one fall each and into the final round. An attempted throw by Brooks led to both wrestlers falling from the ring and neither one could beat referee Ken Lazenby's count of ten. It was left to Lazenby to make a decision to who proceeded to the final and he decided that it was McCoy who would be the first finalist. Giant Haystack's quest for men and not boys to take him on found Skull Murphy in the opposing corner in the main attraction that week. For once Murphy had the crowd supporting him. Even Murphy's liberal use of use of the fist failed to subdue Haystacks and it was all over in the second round. Murphy was unable to continue after being thrown over the top rope. He failed to beat referee Ken Lazenby's count of ten and once again Haystacks demanded a man to take him on. The other match shown saw Ray Steele beat Caswell Martin in a routine heavyweight match by the one fall required to win in the fourth round.

There is a saying in life that you should never say never and I thought I'd never see John Quinn in a Joint Promotions' ring booked by Max Crabtree again. After the rancour of Quinn's departure in August 1980 I thought all bridges had been burnt but in April 1988 he reappeared in Joint Promotions' rings again. Quinn was back on ITV for Joint Promotions on April 30th in the second half of the show recorded at Normanton. John Quinn took on Steve Casey in the main event with Quinn as usual never missing a chance to use MC Brian Crabtree's microphone to insult his opponent. Quinn took the lead in the third round when a forearm smash on Casey's jaw left him open to being pinned. Casey equalised in the fifth round when a missle dropkick weakened Quinn for a body slam and cross press to level the match. Neither wrestler could get the winner in the sixth and final round so it ended up being a draw. The bonus match that week was a throws contest with the winner the first to throw his opponent to the mat ten times. Greg Valentine won when he threw opponent El Diablo for the tenth time against five for the masked man. The second Golden Grappler Trophy semi final saw King Ben meet Lucky Gordon. Gordon took the first score in the third round with an arm submission following several weakeners both legal and illegal with referee Martin Warren being surprisingly lenient towards the Irishman. Ben got the win in the fourth round when despite missing with an attempted dropkick on Gordon he still fell through the ropes and failed to beat the count of ten. This meant the final of the 1988 Golden Grappler Trophy would be intriguingly father v son, King Ben v Kid McCoy.

The Golden Grappler Trophy final of 1988 took place on May 7th on a show recorded at the Cox Moor Woods Leisure Centre in Birmingham. The fact that it was father v son, the King Ben v Kid McCoy match had attracted a bit of interest outside of the wrestling world too. Ben took the lead in the third round when he pinned McCoy with a cross press, McCoy got the equaliser in the next round when rolled up Ben for the count of three. Ben got the winner in the sixth round when he reversed a sunset flip to pin his son and become the Golden Grappler Trophy winner of 1988. The other two matches shown that week were heavyweight affairs with firstly Gil Singh facing The Emperor. Singh got the only fall needed to win in the third round following a dropkick that connected with fresh air and a weak looking kick and body slam. The Emperor fled the ring immediately to avoid having to unmask but his identity was widely known. The final match saw local favourite Pat Roach against Colonel Brody. Brody got the opening fall in the second round with a folding press after a liberal use of illegal moves had weakened Roach. Roach quickly equalised in the third round with a cross press and then got the winner in the fifth round. A big boot to the jaw then a bodyslam enabled him to easily cover Brody for the count of three. It must be said that Brody gave Roach all he could handle in the match and Roach's growing commitments to TV and films were having an adverse effect on his wrestling career.

The FA Cup Final between Liverpool & Wimbledon took place on May 14th and as an example of the disregard or even disrespect that ITV now held for wrestling it was not part of the traditional build-up at all this year. Despite finding time for Jimmy Tarbuck and Gloria Hunniford meeting guests in the Champions Bar and other such rubbish no room could be found for even one bout.

The Golden Rose TV Festival in Montreux, Switzerland is not a place that British professional wrestling is associated with but on May 16th 1988 an event happened there which changed the sport forever. Greg Dyke had been Director of Programmes for London Weekend Television since April 1987 and it was in Montreux that he made the announcement that he was taking British wrestling off of the ITV screens at the end of the year. Dyke had also been given the job of Head of Sport for ITV and his remit was to cut costs so they were able to concentrate on bidding for live and exclusive sport for the channel such as football. His other mandate was to modernise and update the ITV programming and broaden its appeal from its mainly working class audience. Despite tensions with some of the large Northern TV franchises such as Granada Dyke decided that British wrestling as had been featured for over thirty years no longer fitted the type of viewer they were trying now to attract. Many theories were put forward why and to this day some people continue to blame Big Daddy and Max Crabtree for the decision but at the time Daddy was still the biggest draw in British wrestling and every British wrestling promoter even Brian Dixon would have booked him for their shows if they could. The WWF was a factor but it hadn't yet became mainstream as its only coverage was in the shared ITV slot at the time and a WWF taping had only been shown on four occasions since the start of 1987. The WWF in the UK really took off with Sky starting their satellite broadcasting in 1989 with all the publicity in the Murdoch owned media.

For me one of the main reasons was that if you looked at the audience on any wrestling shown on ITV and apart from when Big Daddy was on hardly any of the crowd shown would be under fifty. Young people didn't think wrestling was a 'cool' thing to watch on TV or to see live. Even the children who came to see Big Daddy wouldn't be there at the next tournament held in that hall. Wrestling was a sport or an entertainment that had a declining interest, the fanbase was dying out, it wasn't being replaced and Greg Dyke saw this and acted accordingly. The fanbase that latched onto the WWF a couple of years later were not interested at all in British wrestling or British wrestlers unless they were the British Bulldogs or Davey 'Boy' Smith in particular as Dynamite Kid had departed from the WWF by the time the Sky satellite coverage had become really popular. It hadn't been the first time ITV had attempted to remove wrestling from its screens as back in 1967 a new Director of Sport on ITV John McMillan tried to do it. McMillan had arrived at ITV from Rediffusion and his first target was to get rid of wrestling. Like Greg Dyke he wanted to use the sport's budget for things like world title boxing matches and other live sports. But that time once the wrestling fans found about his plans he was forced to back peddle immediately. Unfortunately the outcry in 1988 didn't have the same happy outcome and despite numerous campaigns, letters written and petitions Dyke refused to change his mind.

On May 21st it was time for the WWF to present another offering. Naturally the British Bulldogs were on when they beat The Conquistadors. The Ultimate Warrior defeated Harley Race. Honky Tonk Man beat Randy Savage to retain the Intercontinental Title and Jimmy Powers and Paul Roma beat Barry Horowitz and Steve Lombardi.

British wrestling was back on ITV on May 28th with a continuation of the Kendo Nagasaki v Mark Rocco feud and this time they met in a tag match. Intriguingly Rocco paired up with Wayne Bridges whilst Nagasaki had Shane Stevens as his partner. It was another splendidly chaotic tag match as usual with Nagasaki involved which referee Mal Mason had no hope of controlling. Nagasaki got the first fall in the sixth minute with a kamakazi crash weakening Bridges. Rocco then chased Nagasaki around the ring with a chair whilst Gorgeous George berated the injured Bridges. Bridges eventually tagged in Rocco who sent Stevens flying head first through the ropes in a nasty looking bump as he landed outside the ring. It was becoming very difficult to keep up with the action but Rocco equalised in the 12th minute with cross press on Stevens after a nasty looking attempt at a spiked piledriver assisted by Bridges. The winner came with Bridges pinning Stevens inside the ring whilst Rocco was again chasing Nagasaki outside of it. The most surprising thing was that despite twenty two minutes of mayhem referee Mal Mason didn't see fit to issue one public warning and commentator Kent Walton commented on his leniency. As Rocco and Bridges celebrated their win Gorgeous George returned to the ring and grabbed MC Lee Bamber's microphone and declared that they were both rubbish in a way only George could. I dare anyone to say that they didn't enjoy watching a match like that and this was the disappointing thing about the ITV decision. Brian Dixon had learnt what was good on TV and perhaps he crossed the line at times with what was acceptable to ITV but it made a really entertaining thing to watch. Also on the show Robbie Brookside added to his growing reputation with a victory against Bobby Barnes and in a hard fought show opener Dave Taylor beat Johnny South by two falls to one in the fifth round.

Sadly Mal Mason died as this book was about to be published. He will be greatly missed by every member of 'The Wrestling Family'.

Now Joint Promotions had lost the ITV contract they no longer felt compelled to not promote ladies wrestling on their bills and this time the contests advertising Princess Paula wrestling actually went ahead.

June started with the second half of the Joint Promotions' show at Birmingham on the 4th. The main contest was a continental rules tag match which took nearly as long for MC Gordon Pryor to explain what the rules were than the actual match lasted. On one side was Mal Sanders, Sid Cooper and Zoltan Boscik and on the other was Steve Grey, Johnny Kidd and Rick Wiseman. The main difference in the rules was each member of each side wore a numbered vest and instead of public warnings any transgressor of the rules would be sent to a 'prison area'. Grey was an early visitor to the 'prison' before Kidd opened the scoring with a lovely roll up of Cooper in the ninth minute. Kent Walton was most appreciative of the new rules demanding referee Jeff Kaye use it like they did on the continent all the time. Grey was sent again to the 'prison' after ten minutes for accidentally dropkicking referee Kaye and this time it was for a maximum sentence of five minutes. Cooper followed Grey to the 'prison' for two minutes with an extra minute added for dissent. Sanders got the equaliser with a submission after fifteen minutes as the extra man advantage took its toll. Grey's team got a popular winning fall in the eighteenth minute and despite the slightly confusing format but with six great workers on view it couldn't fail to be an entertaining match. The rest of the show saw the 1988 Grand Prix Belt start with Alan Kilby maybe fortuitously proceeding to the next round when opponent Steve Logan was unable to continue through injury. The final match saw a new slimmer Butcher Bond ,who Kent Walton told us had come down from 18st to now under 16st, take on Terry Rudge. It didn't take long for the 'niggle' to start and referee Max Ward had his work cut out to keep each wrestler to the rulebook. A very bad tempered match saw referee Ward disqualify Rudge in the third round for punching Bond in the stomach leaving him for once to hear the crowds appreciation.

The second Grand Prix Belt heat between Barry Douglas and Ian McGregor opened the ITV programme on June 11th on a bill recorded at Retford. Douglas took the lead in the second round when his Boston crab saw McGregor submit. McGregor rolled up Douglas in the fifth round to get the equaliser and despite both wrestler's best efforts neither could get a winning score. The contest was decided via referee Ken Joyce's points decision and it was McGregor who got the verdict. An eight man super sized heavyweight Battle Royale was the main event that week and taking part were Giant Haystacks, Marty Jones, Rasputin, Steve Regal, Rory Campbell, Colonel Brody, King Kendo and Drew McDonald. With mayhem going on all over the ring the final four wrestlers left were Regal who had shown great promise eliminating Brody with a dropkick which sent the military man flying over the top rope. Jones who was the lightest wrestler left, Rasputin and his tag partner Haystacks completed those remaining. Regal was soon sent flying by Haystacks quickly followed by Jones who daftly attempted a flying tackle on the big man. This left Haystacks and Rasputin as joint winners as they refused to wrestle each other. The show's MC Brian Crabtree climbed onto the ring apron to remind both wrestlers that there must be a winner. Proving the old saying 'If you want loyalty buy a dog' true Haystacks threw his supposed friend Rasputin over the top rope to win the prize. Rasputin was furious and he came back into the ring to challenge Haystacks to a solo match whilst Haystacks told him he didn't have any friends and 'It was no more Mr Nice Guy' once again. The third and final match that week saw a mid/heavyweight contest between Ray Robinson and Bernie Wright. Wright won a hard hitting match with the only fall needed in the second round with a hip toss followed by a cross press for the count of three whilst the loser left the ring with his nose bleeding profusely.

It was back to Retford on June 18th for the second half of the show recorded there at the beginning of April. Skull Murphy was the third wrestler to qualify for the quarter finals of the Grand Prix Belt when he beat John Elijah in the opening match. Murphy opened the scoring in the fourth round when his gator hold made Elijah submit instantly. Elijah equalised in the next when his bearhug submission saw Murphy tap and with one round left Murphy grabbed the winner. A back elbow left Elijah weakened and a quick cross press was enough to win the match. John Quinn and Steve Casey renewed their hostilities in the featured contest of the week following their drawn match shown at the end of April. Matters didn't get any better this time as referee Ken Joyce having tired of both wrestlers flagrantly disobeying the rule book decided to bring the match to an end by disqualifying both of them. The final match saw Grasshopper take on 'Chesterfield' Ray Smith who as Kent Walton told us funnily enough came from Chesterfield. MC Brian Crabtree then ruined it by introducing him from Sheffield ! Both of them were making rare appearances on TV and it was Grasshopper who got the win in the second round when a flying tackle and crosspress saw him pin Smith for the count of three.

June's ITV shows ended on the 25th with an All-Star Promotion which was the second half of the show recorded at Dewsbury back in March. First match was Fit Finlay with

Princess Paula by his side against Danny Collins. This was a lot different from the last time they met on ITV back at the start of 1986 with Collins having gone up through the weights to sit in the heavy/middleweight division now. Finlay opened the scoring with a side suplex followed by a cross press in the second round. Collins equalised in the fourth round leaving Paula furious in the corner. Former footballer and now referee Mal Mason was signalling public warnings using yellow cards including giving Collins one for dissent. The ending came in the fifth round when a clash of heads left neither wrestler being in a fit state to continue and an unfortunate ending to a contest which was warming up nicely. The second contest was introduced by MC Lee Bamber as being between two newcomers to TV in Doc Dean and Steve Prince. He was incorrect in this as Steve Prince had featured on World of Sport back in 1985 as The Black Prince when he was defeated by Fit Finlay. Bamber a former Butlins' redcoat was also making his ITV debut as the MC and apart from that minor blip has gone on to have a fine career in wrestling both as MC and referee and he is still officiating to this very day. Prince got the win with the only fall needed in the fourth round. As well as Lee Bamber still working for All-Star Promotions one of the seconds at Dewsbury Steve Barker is another who still works for them albeit promoted from carrying a bucket to compering the shows as the evening's MC. Barker also promotes his own shows under the 'Rumble Promotions' banner which started in the 1990's and has made a comeback in recent years to put shows on again. Incidentally the other second at Dewsbury Scott Conway was not only beginning to promote his own shows at the time but also wrestling for various promoters. Conway's promotion 'The South Eastern Wrestling Alliance' was later shortened to 'The Wrestling Alliance'. The promotion was one of the more prolific in the 1990's and began the trend of bringing in big name imports from America and Japan amongst other places for short tours of the UK.

The afternoon's main event was for the World Lightweight Title which again was blighted by being fought for over eight rounds instead of the customary fifteen rounds. This was the former champion Johnny Saint's chance to regain the title he had lost to Mike Jordan a few months ago back in 1987. As can be expected with two lightweights of their calibre in opposition it was full of holds and counters fought at a tremendous pace till Saint got the first fall in the fifth round. For some reason Jordan took exception to this and as Saint celebrated on the corner post he knocked him out of the ring. Referee Billy Finlay gave Jordan a public warning for this but Saint had injured his knee as he landed out of the ring and was unable to continue for the next round. Kent Walton hadn't got a clue what was going on and hadn't seen Jordan send Saint flying to the floor. Altogether this was an unsatisfactory ending to the match.

Bishops Stortford is not a place that has registered very often in wrestling history or for that matter had many shows in the past but it was the venue on June 14th for a notable event. Big Daddy locked horns with Giant Haystacks for the final time in the main event of the show there. Daddy teaming up with Greg Valentine beat Haystacks and his partner Drew McDonald to end the rivalry that had lasted well over ten years. Both wrestlers were no longer in a physical shape to do much in their matches anymore especially Daddy who had suffered ill health in the recent past and had taken to wearing a white t-shirt under his wrestling leotard to cover the effects. The Big Daddy v Giant Haystacks feud had got very stale and was well past its sell by date. Since Daddy had beaten Haystacks so comprehensively at Wembley Arena in 1981 it had really sucked any life out of their future matches. By the time 1988 had come around Giant Haystacks was seen more on his overseas travels to North America, Europe and various other places than in Britain. Daddy was more or less now carrying what was left of Joint Promotions on his admittedly broad shoulders. It was still a shame that more wasn't made of their final time in combat together.

Big Daddy was back on ITV on July 2nd in a show from the Everton Park Sports Centre in Liverpool recorded back in April. Apart from the wrestling what was noticeable throughout the show was the total lack of security around the ring and at times the ring was full of children messing about. Daddy was as usual in tag action partnering Tom Thumb against Drew McDonald and Sid Cooper. The match was all over in around nine minutes when a rather slow big splash finished off McDonald. It must be said the crowd enjoyed it especially when Daddy started singing 'She loves you, yeah, yeah' before hundreds of children invaded the ring to celebrate with their hero. The next heat of the Grand Prix Belt saw Richie Brooks go through to the quarter final when he beat TV newcomer 'Karate Kid' Chris Cougar who was based in the Isle of Man. Cougar who had been trained by Ted Betley showed up very well in his television debut and it wasn't till the final round that Brooks got the winner. The bonus match that week saw Pat Patton beat 'Gaylord' Steve Peacock by disqualification.

The following week on July 9th Greg Valentine earned his place in the Grand Prix Belt quarter finals when he beat Mel Stuart in the show opener. This was the second half of the show recorded at Liverpool and again the children invaded the ring after Valentine got the winner in the fifth round. After his betrayal by former friend Giant Haystacks in the Battle Royale shown on ITV a month or so ago Rasputin got his chance for revenge against the big man. As Kent Walton commented 'There's not much wrestling here' as after three minutes of punches and kicks Haystacks was disqualified by referee Jeff Kaye for ramming Rasputin's head into the corner post. Just to make things even worse Haystacks then floored Kaye before landing his guillotine elbow drop on him to leave the poor referee out cold. No doubt Haystacks faced a trip to the offices of the Board of Control afterwards to explain his conduct. That week's third match saw Jim Moza wrestle a one fall each draw with Dave Duran over six rounds.

Terry Rudge was the next qualifier for the Grand Prix Belt quarter finals when he beat Mohammed Afzal on the July 16th ITV Wrestling show from Walthamstow. There was 'needle' between Rudge and Afzal who was the brother of 'Little Prince' Mohammed Alam and some of the blows exchanged seemed to be of some force. The match actually ended in a one fall each draw at the end of the scheduled six rounds but the referee's points decision went to Rudge. The rest of the show featured a four man heavyweight tournament, the first semi final saw Ray Steele defeat Johnny Wilson in a slow paced match. The winner came for Steele in the fourth round after

Wilson mistimed a flying tackle amidst a ripple of polite applause from the fans at ringside. The second final saw Pat Roach with a considerable weight advantage against the now slimline Butcher Bond. This was another slow paced match with a disinterested Roach doing nothing apart from a big boot to Bond's jaw in the fourth round which sent him through the ropes and unable to beat referee Ken Joyce's count of ten. The final was more of the same old style, slow paced heavyweight wrestling with the match being stopped when Ray Steele was injured but Roach refused to take the verdict so the tournament ended without a winner. This was a change of attitude from Roach after telling TV viewers and fans in attendance he would never call a No Contest when his match with Steve Logan a year so was stopped. If only somebody would remember such details.

The 1987 Grand Prix Belt winner Pete Roberts made his entrance in the 1988 competition the following week on July 23rd on the second half of the show from Walthamstow. Robert's opponent was Mal Sanders who had thrown his hat into the ring following successive failures for The Golden Grappler Trophy amongst the lighter weights. The temperamental Sanders was in one of his moods and after initially refusing to lock up with Roberts went on to give the much heavier Roberts a hard time. It wasn't till the final round that Roberts got the winning fall with a side suplex finally seeing off the challenge of Sanders. Marty Jones made a defence of his World Mid/Heavyweight Title against the French challenger Marc Mercier in the main event that afternoon. Mercier had wrestled in this country in the early eighties for Brian Dixon and he was the son of Guy Mercier. Mercier actually took the lead in the fourth round when a slick reversal led to him pinning Jones. It wasn't till the penultimate round that Jones was finally able to subdue the energetic French challenger when a double arm suplex enabled Jones to gain the winning fall. This would be the last time that Marty Jones made a televised defence of the World Mid/Heavyweight Title. There was also time for a bonus match with John Elijah pinning Mohammed Butt in the second round to win it.

July ended with an All-Star Promotion's show from Bedworth on the 30th. The first match saw the TV debut of the teenager from Cheltenham Peter Bainbridge who faced a tough test against Jim Breaks. Bainbridge took the lead in the third round with a roll up off the ropes to pin Breaks but he had no answer to the 'Breaks special' arm submission for a quick equaliser early in the fourth round. With Bainbridge's arm still weakened he was an easy target for Breaks once more and he was forced to submit again in the fifth round. Clive Myers and Steve Grey met for another match seen on TV. Whilst both were great wrestlers it became a feature of frustration that a bout seen on TV on umpteen occasions in the past would once again be screened instead of showcasing something different. Grey won by two falls to one in the seventh round. The afternoon's final match saw Rob Brookside and Steve Regal take on 'The Road Warriors'. This wasn't the American team of the same name but a British version consisting of Dave Duran and Jimmy Munroe. This would be Munroe's first appearance on ITV but he had been around for years before on the independent circuit and was an accomplished wrestler as well as being known as a legitimate tough guy. Brookside and Regal got the win after twelve minutes with a reversal off the ropes enabling Brookside to pin Duran.

The final heat for the Grand Prix Belt kicked off the ITV coverage for August on the 6th with a show recorded at Radcliffe. The contest saw Luton's Johnny Kidd going up in the weights as per Mal Sanders to try his luck amongst the heavier wrestlers. Kidd's opponent was the masked 'Mr X'. Kent Walton professed not to know who was under the mask but in fact it was Durham's 'Farmer's Boy' Pete Ross. Mr X got the win when he put Kidd to sleep with the sleeper hold and as Walton commented that hold is illegal in Britain. For some reason referee Jeff Kaye deemed the move to be legal so the win stood. Mr X therefore joined Pete Roberts, Alan Kilby, Greg Valentine, Terry Rudge, Ian McGregor, Richie Brooks and Skull Murphy in the quarter finals. The main event that week should have been the return match from the trophy final at Walthamstow between Pat Roach and Ray Steele but Roach was unavailable so regular stand by Barry Douglas took his place. Steele got the win with a fall in the seventh round. The final match promised a lot more action as former World title holder Mike Jordan who had recently lost the title to Johnny Saint took on British Lightweight Title Kid McCoy. The only shame was that the match was scheduled for only fifteen minutes and it ended in a time limit draw with both wrestlers scoring one fall apiece.

The second half of the Radcliffe show was screened on August 13th with the big guys in the main event. Giant Haystacks was now tagging with Scrubber Daly after his falling out with Rasputin. They took on Jamaica George and Ali Shan who was a late replacement for Caswell Martin. I think it was obvious to anyone who watched who the winners would be but at least the team of George and Shan got the opening fall when Ali Shan pinned Scrubber Daly following a flying tackle. That was as good as it got with the flying splash from Daly on Shan getting the equaliser. The win came when Haystacks finished off Jamaica George with the guillotine elbow drop in the tenth minute. There must have been easier ways for George to make a living rather than being on the end of the elbow drop night after night on the circuit. The show opener between Steve Casey and Gil Singh was warming up nicely with the score at one fall each when in the fifth round referee Jeff Kaye was knocked out of the ring. Singh had attempted a flying tackle on Casey but Kaye had got in the way and went flying through the ropes. The contest unfortunately had to be stopped and a No Contest verdict declared. The final match saw Johnny Saint take on the 'Mighty Atom' Carl McGrath who was another ITV debutant but had been wrestling for many years on the independent circuit. A highly entertaining lightweight match saw Saint win in the fifth round when he folded up McGrath for the count of three.

After a gap of seven years Mark Rocco again faced Marty Jones on ITV on the August 20th show from Bedworth. Jones had become the latest Joint Promotions' star to wrestle for All-Star Promotions so it was time for another chapter in their long standing rivalry. Before the match Rocco proved not only was he the best wrestler in the country but his pre match promo delivery was top drawer too. Both wrestlers were so keen to get on with things they didn't even wait for the bell to start attacking each other. Jones took the first fall in the third round after Rocco had started the round trying to strangle his opponent with his towel. The equaliser came immediately in the fourth round when a pile driver left Jones an easy touch for a fall although Rocco could well have left him there for the count of ten. The match fell apart in the fifth round with both wrestlers losing their cool completely and referee Frank Casey disqualifying both of them. A bloody Rocco then demanded an extra round with Jones without a referee which of course Jones agreed to. It was surprising the ITV authorities allowed this to be shown. The extra round lasted about twenty seconds as Jones threw Rocco over the top rope and they then brawled their way back to the dressing room. The afternoon's opening contest saw Danny Collins take on a late replacement Blue Buchanan who was actually the son of Princess Paula and making his ITV debut. Collins won a keenly fought match in the seventh minute when a pile driver left Buchanan out for the count. Buchanan had time for a quick shower and to get the car ready for him and Mark Rocco as they were also in the main event tag match at Leicester the same night which was about a ten mile drive away. The final match that week saw another ITV newcomer in Alan Gregg take on Eddie Riley which Riley won by two falls to one in four rounds.

The Grand Prix Belt quarter finals started on ITV on August 27th on a Joint Promotions' show recorded at Dartford. The first heat saw Ian McGregor getting his revenge for his defeat at the hands of Richie Brooks in the Golden Grappler earlier in 1988 by getting the one fall needed to progress to the semi finals. The other quarter final shown that week saw an upset as Terry Rudge gave Ian Muir a seven stone advantage but still got the one fall required to beat him in the fourth round. For some reason it was never announced Muir replaced Alan Kilby in the tournament. The afternoon's main event saw Big Daddy in action partnering Pat Patton against Rasputin and Anaconda. Daddy was still suffering from a recent bout of Bells Palsy and it was a sad sight watching him on the show. Naturally Daddy and Patton came out on top when Daddy sent latest cannon fodder Anaconda out of the ring to land on Rasputin with both of them being counted out. This was not one of British wrestling's finest hours. At the end of the broadcast Kent Walton informed the viewers that next week's show would now move to be screened at 135pm going forward and only be on for forty minutes.

The other two Grand Prix Belt quarter finals were held at the new time of 135pm on September 3rd which came from Dartford again. Greg Valentine took on Mr X in the first of them. Valentine went through to the semi finals when Mr X was unable to beat referee Roy Harding's count of ten following a dropkick that landed right on his chin. The final quarter final saw the 1987 winner Pete Roberts take on Skull Murphy. Roberts marched to the ring proudly wearing his 'Ribera Steakhouse' jacket as befitting a wrestler who had appeared in Japanese rings many times. In a hard fought contest Murphy got the winning submission in the fifth round with the Gator Hold submission or so he and the viewers thought. Referee Roy Harding had other ideas and decided to disqualify Murphy as he had dropped Roberts onto the top rope neck first seconds earlier. It was a shocking decision by Harding and a rotten way to end the match. So it was Pete Roberts who joined Greg Valentine, Terry Rudge and Ian McGregor in the final four of the Grand Prix Belt tournament.

The start of September saw a new departure for televised wrestling in Britain. The All-Star Promotions' show at Croydon on September 6th would be filmed for a video release. This would be the first time it would be done in this country and it was a novel idea to try and get around the loss of the ITV Wrestling show. The only problem is that in those days it was still expensive to buy a video cassette, they cost around £10 and only lasted an hour or so. The strange thing was despite this being an All-Star Promotions' show it was Mick McManus who put his name to the venture and so the 'Mick McManus World of Wrestling' was born. It must be said that McManus had become very friendly with promoter Brian Dixon but rather than having Kent Walton as commentator it was the young MC Lee Bamber who shared the duties with McManus at the commentary table. The first match saw Fit Finlay accompanied by Princess Paula take on Danny Collins in a return from their inconclusive match seen on ITV back in June. This time there was a winner as Finlay got the deciding fall in the sixth round although it needed an assist from Paula who gave Collins a shove as he attempted to pile drive her man.

A lightweight tournament between Johnny Saint, Mal Sanders, Clive Myers and Steve Grey was up next. The first semi final saw Saint and Myers go to a time limit no fall draw with Saint winning the toss of a coin to go to the final. The second semi final saw Grey beat old rival Sanders with his surfboard submission in the eighth minute. The final ended in a no contest when Grey ducked a flying tackle from Saint who instead sent referee Mal Mason tumbling through the ropes. The main event was a tag match with Kendo Nagasaki and Skull Murphy facing the team of Pete Roberts and American newcomer Steve Adonis. Adonis replaced the advertised Wayne Bridges who regrettably was forced to retire from the ring earlier in the Summer after injuries had finally caught up with him. Nagasaki had his usual entourage with him headed by Gorgeous George with Lloyd Ryan in attendance too. As with every Nagasaki match chaos reigned with the fans furious at his antics with one angry lady throwing a traffic cone into the ring. The end came with the Nagasaki 'Kamakazi Crash' seeing off Adonis in just over sixteen minutes for the winning fall. In 1992 Joint Promotions did a similar straight to video show recording but that was released over three separate cassettes which made it an incredibly expensive way to watch it.

By now it seemed every Joint Promotions' show recorded for ITV had to have Ray Steele on it and the Bridlington show which was shown on September 10th was no exception. Steele's opponent was Pat Roach for the long awaited rematch and this didn't deliver a winner either as the score was one fall each at the end of the allotted six rounds. The other match shown was the first semi final of the Grand Prix Belt between Pete Roberts and Terry Rudge. For such a prestigous prize the time limit of ten minutes and one fall to win was ridiculous. Despite both wrestler's best efforts neither of them was able to get a winning fall in the ten minutes allowed and it was left to referee Peter Szakacs to give a verdict on points. Szakacs announced he was unable to make the decision so MC Gordon Pryor announced that there would have to be a return contest.

Wrestling was missing from the ITV schedules on September 17th as various films were shown in the different regions instead. It was the same for the following two Saturdays as wrestling was not shown with films again shown during the afternoon. The Olympics were being shown on 'Grandstand' on BBC at the time but it didn't seem like a good reason to not show wrestling on ITV for three weeks.

Wrestling was back on ITV on October 8th with the second half of the show recorded at Bridlington under the Relwyskow & Green banner. The main match was the second semi final for the 1988 Grand Prix Belt between Greg Valentine and Ian McGregor. The match was again a ten minute time limit with one fall to win. Unlike the Pete Roberts v Terry Rudge semi final we got a winner. Valentine won the match when a dropkick sent McGregor flying through the ropes in the seventh minute and the Scotsman failed to get himself back inside the ring before referee Ken Lazenby completed his count of ten. Greg Valentine was therefore the first finalist for the belt and we awaited the rematch between Pete Roberts and Terry Rudge to decide the other. This is where it all ended though, there was no rematch on TV or on the circuit. With there only being two more shows recorded by Joint Promotions for ITV that was the end of the Grand Prix Belt and it wasn't mentioned again. The other two matches shown that week saw the outspoken Mal Sanders take on Clive Myers which was an entertaining affair to watch. Sanders was once again in one of his unruly moods. He tested referee Peter Szakacs' patience once too often in the fifth round and was disqualified. Sanders had used the bottom rope to assist him put a single leg Boston crab on Myers. Szakacs having seen this immediately sent Sanders back to the dressing room. Danny Collins met Steve Grey in the final contest that week with Collins a lot more experienced and notably heavier than when they last met on TV. Unfortunately we only saw a couple of minutes of it as the match was joined in progress at the start of the fourth round and after two minutes Grey attempted a flying tackle on Collins and in doing so both went over the top rope with neither of them able to continue.

One of the more infamous British wrestling angles took place on the ITV Wrestling Show on October 15th on an All-Star Promotions' show recorded at Bedworth. The main event was a tag match between Kendo Nagasaki and by now regular partner Blondie Barratt accompanied by Gorgeous George, Lloyd Ryan and Status Quo drummer John Coghlan. Their opponents were 'The Golden Boys' Steve Regal and Rob Brookside with the match starting with the usual stalling from Nagasaki before things livened up. An impressively high back drop on Brookside by Nagasaki followed by a cross press gave Nagasaki and Barratt the opening fall. The equaliser came when a missile dropkick from the top rope by Brookside on Barratt led to Barratt failing to beat the count of ten which meant he was no longer able to take part in the match for the third session. So Nagasaki had to take on Brookside and Regal on his own, after a nice spot of double teaming and quick tags Brookside unmasked the weakened Nagasaki. Nagasaki then stared at Brookside apparently putting him into a trance then instructing him to attack his partner Regal. A weakened Regal was then finished off by Nagasaki's 'Kamakazi Crash' for the win amongst cries of surprise by Kent Walton. The ITV authorities weren't impressed by the angle at all. If this wasn't the last All-Star Promotions' show screened on ITV then more about it might have been said. It was an interesting thing to attempt to do and the subsequent rematches around the circuit did good business at the box office so it was a success in that respect although some people hated the whole thing. The other match on that week saw British Middleweight Champion Brian Maxine take on Lucky Gordon. The match ended in the fifth round when a dropkick from Maxine which barely touched Gordon saw him fall through the ropes and not beat referee Roger Brown's count of ten.

October 22nd on ITV saw a Joint Promotions' show from Keighley feature two title matches. The first of them saw British Light/Heavyweight Champion Alan Kilby take on Chris Cougar. Cougar had only been seen once on TV losing to Richie Brooks in a Grand Prix Belt heat so it's hard to see how he warranted a title match. A rather dour, uninteresting match saw Kilby take the first fall in the second round. A mule kick left Cougar weakened for the body slam and cross press pinfall. Cougar equalised in the fourth with a hip toss leading to another cross press. The match ended in the sixth round when an awkward landing by Cougar from a high back drop left referee Jeff Kaye no choice but to stop the bout and Kilby retained the belt. The second title match saw Kid McCoy defend his British Lightweight Title against 'Mad Dog' Ian Wilson, like Cougar in the previous match Wilson was yet another random challenger with no back story to create any interest in the match. McCoy got the winning fall in the fifth round when he pinned Wilson after a nice reversal.

All that was wrong with Joint Promotions' TV shows was on offer on October 29th with two matches of which neither promised anything special to make you want to tune in. The first saw Johnny Saint against 'Rocker' Pete LaPaque. Saint's tricks were far too much for LaPaque with a Saint submission on the veteran Leicester man ending it in the fifth round. The other match was at heavyweight between Gil Singh and Rory Campbell. This replaced a billed tag match between the 'Wrecking Crew' & the 'Tyneside Tearaways' of which I hadn't heard of either team. Instead we got a slow paced, typical British heavyweight match with plenty of botches in it. Singh got the first fall in the second round following a hip toss and cross press. Singh recorded a two straight falls win with a kick that didn't connect which led to a suplex for the winning fall in the fourth round.

Wrestling was missing on November 5th as ITV showed a recording of the Thomas Hearns v James Kinchen fight which had already been shown live in the early hours of that morning.

Big Daddy made his last appearance on ITV on November 12th as the first part of the last ever Joint Promotions' ITV show recorded at Rickmansworth. This would be a six man tag match with Daddy partnering Tom Thumb and Kashmir Singh against the 'Task Force III' team of Sid Cooper, Bulldog Brown and John Wilkie accompanied by 'Ayatollah' Tony Francis. Strangely enough it was Gordon Pryor doing the MC duties and not Brian Crabtree for this final show. It was what it was, a typical Daddy match with the crowd loving it and the purists hating it. There was just over eight minutes of Daddy's 'greatest hits' routine before the ending came when all the members of 'Task Force III' left the ring and were counted out by referee Roy Harding. The programme's first match was yet another horribly dull, dated heavyweight match in which John Elijah wrestled a one fall each draw over six rounds with Prince Mann Singh. There was also a quick glimpse of Johnny Kidd pinning Eddie Riley in the third round of a bonus bout.

Wrestling was again missing on ITV on November 19th. For no apparent reason why the film 'Guys and Dolls' was shown in the usual TV time slot instead of wrestling.

November 26th saw the last All-Star Promotions' show shown on ITV which was the second half of the one recorded at Bedworth back in August. The first match saw the ITV debut of the young Canadian Steve Adonis against Sandy Scott. Kent Walton was immediately gushing in his praise of Adonis 'His name is Adonis and he looks like one', Walton also introduced Adonis' manager the lady wrestler Donna Marie and she was shown during the interval between round's one and two. A flying clothesline from Adonis knocked out Scott in the fourth round. Adonis went onto to wrestle in this country for the next few years before returning home and giving up wrestling. As for Adonis' manager Donna Marie she continued wrestling in Britain until she emigrated to Australia in the early 2000's and is now serving a life sentence there for murdering her husband. The main event for that week's programme was a tag match which should have seen Fit Finlay and Skull Murphy take on Marty Jones and Danny Collins but it was altered to Murphy partnering Johnny South and Jones tagging with Steve Taylor. Despite the changes it was still a solid, hard hitting match. Jones got the first fall in seven minutes with a folding press on Murphy. Murphy equalised with the gator hold on Taylor in the eleventh minute before a confusing ending. South pinned Jones following a suplex with assistance from Murphy outside of the ring after which referee Roger Brown disqualified South to give Marty Jones and Steve Taylor a popular win.

The following week on December 3rd it was time for the last WWF show in that ITV slot with Hulk Hogan defeating Ted Dibiase and King Haku beating S.D. Jones as the featured matches.

December 10th was the day no wrestling fan in Britain wanted to come. After thirty three years of coverage there would no longer be traditional British wrestling on ITV. Unfortunately rather than go out with a bang the final show went out with a whimper. The final Joint Promotions' show was the second half of the Rickmansworth bill with three low key matches on offer for the last time. First up was Greg Valentine who took on Jimmy Ocean. With only one fall needed to win Valentine naturally got the win in the second round when he pinned Ocean following a backdrop. The second match saw the ITV debut of Robbie Hagen against Mel Stuart, both wrestlers well known to each other from years on the holiday camp circuit. Hagen got the win in the seventh minute with the one fall needed in the match following a backdrop and a cross press. So the final match to be seen on ITV was between Pat Roach and Caswell Martin. Maybe it was fitting that the last contest on ITV was another old style British heavyweight match. Pat Roach got the winning fall in the final round of six. Kent Walton spent the final round telling people to go to their local hall for their fix of live wrestling before a body slam and cross press brought proceedings to an end.

A 'best of' highlights show was broadcast on December 17th to mark the occasion introduced by Kent Walton. A wander through the archives saw footage of Mike Marino, Johnny Kwango, Adrian Street, Tibor Szakacs, Big Bruno, Steve Logan, Bert Royal, Mick McManus, Johnny Saint, Billy Two Rivers, Les Kellett, Ricki Starr and Big Daddy amongst others. On the other hand just to emphasise how the sport had never moved on and was still seen to be old fashioned the final words came from Pat Roach. Roach mentioned about watching wrestling in your front parlour which I doubt anyone had done for twenty years or more and then thanking everyone for viewing over the years.

THE TOWN HALL · HOVE
D.M.P.
Dale Martin Promotions Limited
present
WRESTLING
TUESDAY, 19th JANUARY at 7.45p.m.
SENSATIONAL DOUBLE CHAMPIONSHIP BILL
Sponsored by The Evening Argus
FOR THE FIRST TIME IN SUSSEX....
WORLD MID-HEAVYWEIGHT CHAMPIONSHIP 15 rds.
THE HOLDER
MARTY JONES
versus
THE CHALLENGER
INDESTRUCTIBLE
SKULL MURPHY
STAR CELEBRITY
REFEREE
MICK McMANUS
ALAN KILBY
BRITISH LIGHT-HEAVYWEIGHT CHAMPIONSHIP
ALAN KILBY
THE CHAMPION versus
BERNIE WRIGHT
THE CHALLENGER
FULL SUPPORTING PROGRAMME ★ featuring Stars of T.V.
PRICES: £3.50 Adults : £2.50 Children & O.A.P. See Evening Argus for Special Offers
Advance Booking from Evening Argus Offices, North Road, Brighton & Church Road, Hove
KING OF THE ACTION SPORTS ★ THRILLS ★ SPILLS ★ EXCITEMENT

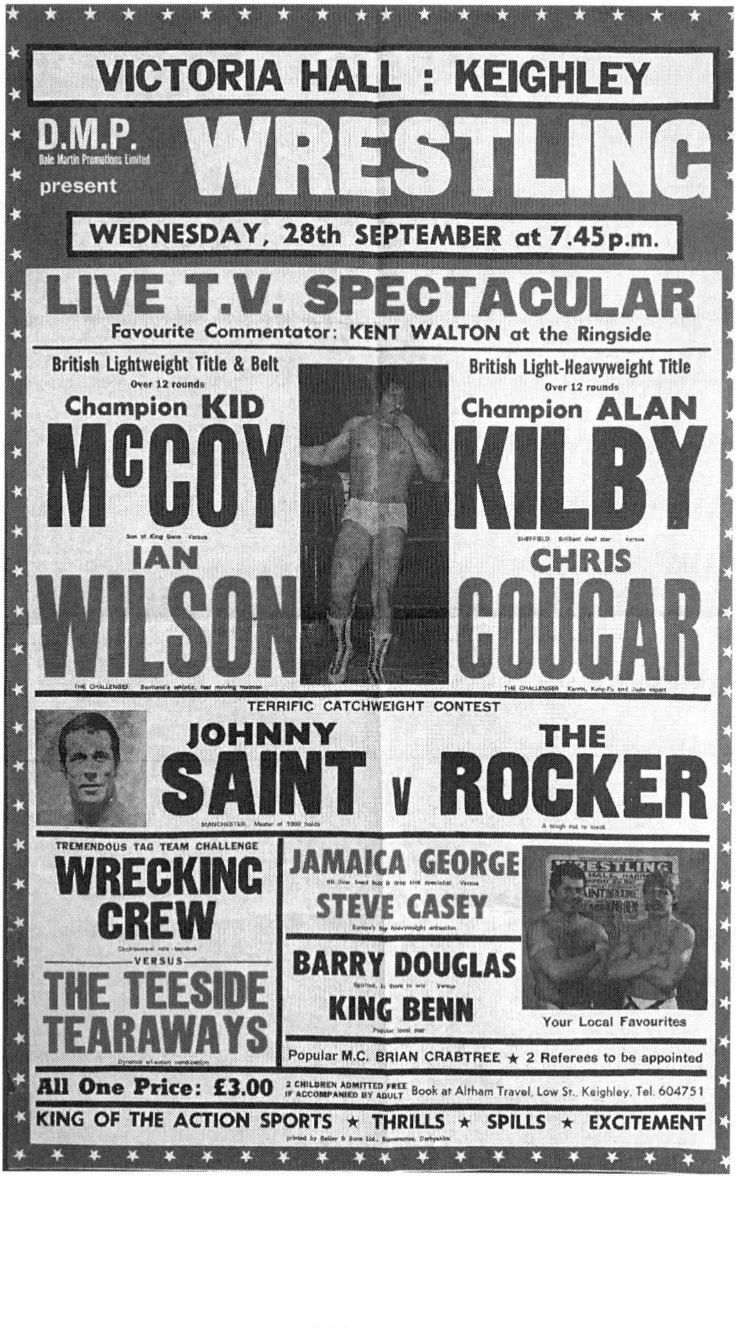
VICTORIA HALL : KEIGHLEY
D.M.P.
Dale Martin Promotions Limited
present
WRESTLING
WEDNESDAY, 28th SEPTEMBER at 7.45 p.m.
LIVE T.V. SPECTACULAR
Favourite Commentator: KENT WALTON at the Ringside
British Lightweight Title & Belt
Over 12 rounds
Champion KID McCOY
Son of King Benn Versus
IAN WILSON
THE CHALLENGER
British Light-Heavyweight Title
Over 12 rounds
Champion ALAN KILBY
SHEFFIELD. Brilliant deaf star Versus
CHRIS COUGAR
THE CHALLENGER Karate, Kung-Fu and Judo expert
TERRIFIC CATCHWEIGHT CONTEST
JOHNNY SAINT v THE ROCKER
MANCHESTER. Master of 1000 holds
A tough nut to crack
TREMENDOUS TAG TEAM CHALLENGE
WRECKING CREW
VERSUS
THE TEESIDE TEARAWAYS
JAMAICA GEORGE
Versus
STEVE CASEY
BARRY DOUGLAS
Versus
KING BENN
Popular local star
WRESTLING
Your Local Favourites
Popular M.C. BRIAN CRABTREE ★ 2 Referees to be appointed
All One Price: £3.00
2 CHILDREN ADMITTED FREE IF ACCOMPANIED BY ADULT
Book at Altham Travel, Low St., Keighley. Tel. 604751
KING OF THE ACTION SPORTS ★ THRILLS ★ SPILLS ★ EXCITEMENT

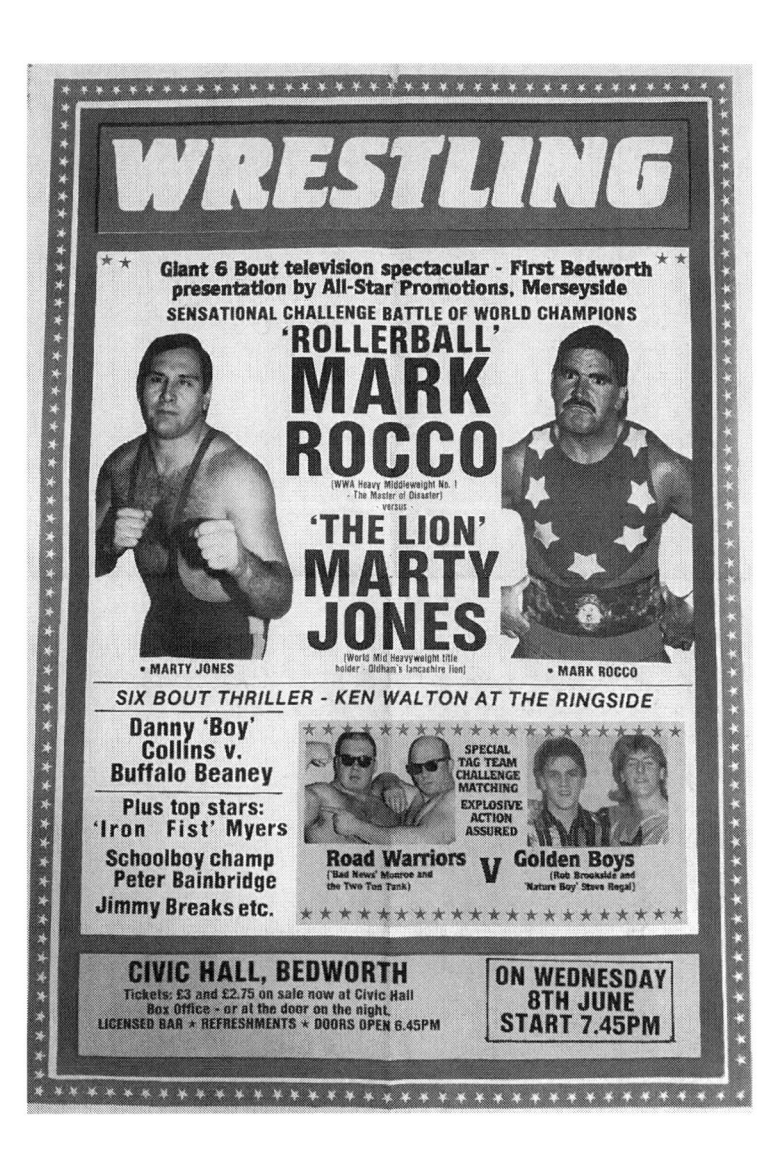

WRESTLING

Giant 6 Bout television spectacular - First Bedworth presentation by All-Star Promotions, Merseyside

SENSATIONAL CHALLENGE BATTLE OF WORLD CHAMPIONS

'ROLLERBALL' MARK ROCCO
(WWA Heavy Middleweight No. 1 - The Master of Disaster)

- versus -

'THE LION' MARTY JONES
(World Mid Heavyweight title holder - Oldham's Lancashire Lion)

• MARTY JONES   • MARK ROCCO

SIX BOUT THRILLER - KEN WALTON AT THE RINGSIDE

Danny 'Boy' Collins v. Buffalo Beaney

Plus top stars:
'Iron Fist' Myers
Schoolboy champ Peter Bainbridge
Jimmy Breaks etc.

SPECIAL TAG TEAM CHALLENGE MATCHING
EXPLOSIVE ACTION ASSURED

Road Warriors ('Bad News' Monroe and the Two Ton Tank) **V Golden Boys** (Rob Brookside and 'Nature Boy' Steve Regal)

CIVIC HALL, BEDWORTH
Tickets: £3 and £2.75 on sale now at Civic Hall Box Office - or at the door on the night.
LICENSED BAR ★ REFRESHMENTS ★ DOORS OPEN 6.45PM

ON WEDNESDAY 8TH JUNE START 7.45PM

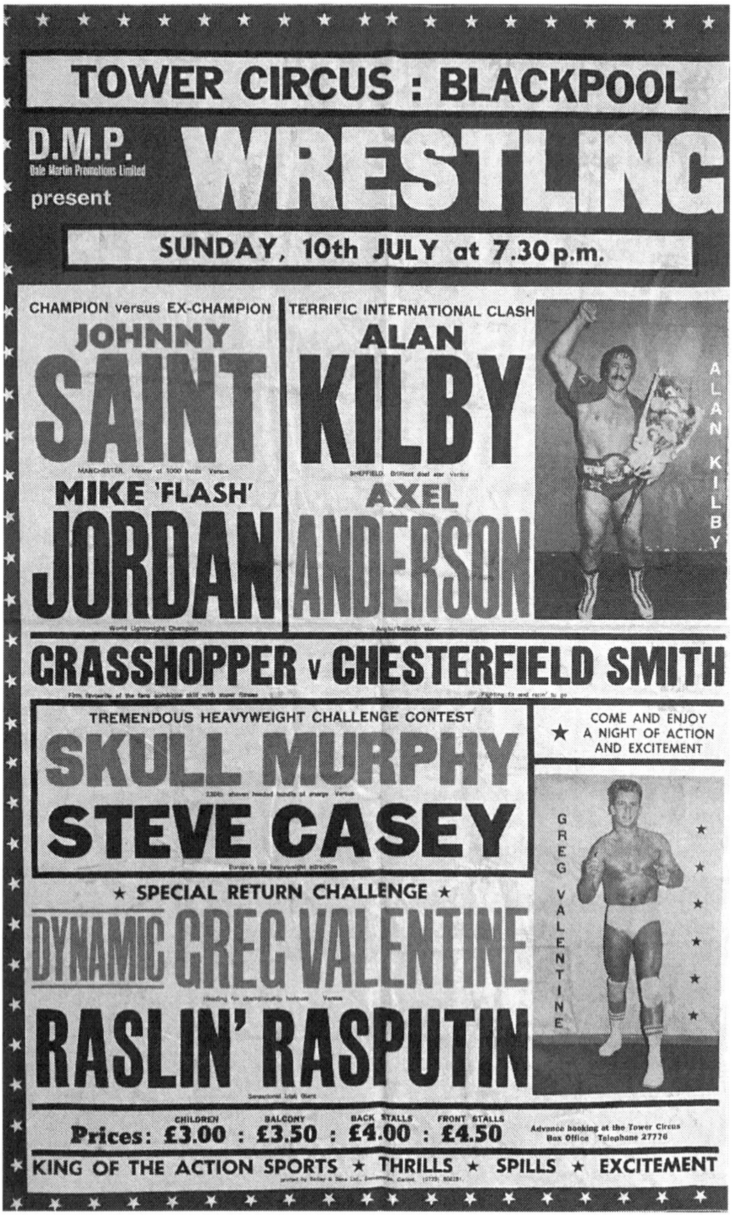
TOWER CIRCUS : BLACKPOOL
D.M.P.
Dale Martin Promotions Limited
present
WRESTLING
SUNDAY, 10th JULY at 7.30 p.m.
CHAMPION versus EX-CHAMPION
JOHNNY
SAINT
MANCHESTER. Master of 1000 holds Versus
MIKE 'FLASH'
JORDAN
World Lightweight Champion
TERRIFIC INTERNATIONAL CLASH
ALAN
KILBY
SHEFFIELD. Brilliant deaf star Versus
AXEL
ANDERSON
Anglo/Swedish star
ALAN KILBY
GRASSHOPPER v CHESTERFIELD SMITH
Fighting fit and racin' to go
TREMENDOUS HEAVYWEIGHT CHALLENGE CONTEST
SKULL MURPHY
STEVE CASEY
Europe's top heavyweight attraction
COME AND ENJOY A NIGHT OF ACTION AND EXCITEMENT
★ SPECIAL RETURN CHALLENGE ★
DYNAMIC GREG VALENTINE
RASLIN' RASPUTIN
Sensational Irish Giant
GREG VALENTINE
CHILDREN BALCONY BACK STALLS FRONT STALLS
Prices: £3.00 : £3.50 : £4.00 : £4.50
Advance booking at the Tower Circus Box Office Telephone 27776
KING OF THE ACTION SPORTS ★ THRILLS ★ SPILLS ★ EXCITEMENT

Chapter 10 - The Aftermath

Without any TV coverage Joint Promotions carried on with the Big Daddy roadshow throughout 1989 and still drew big crowds everywhere. The formula remain unchanged with Daddy's opponents now being carefully booked due to his spells of ill health. Due to the lack of shows being promoted by Max Crabtree personally for Joint Promotions he started booking Big Daddy out to other promoters who paid a booking fee to Max as well as Daddy's wages that night. Max drove Daddy to the show wherever it was that night and then drove him back home afterwards. Daddy insisted on going home every night even if they were at Penzance or other far flung places. This continued into the 1990's with the Joint Promotions organisation a shell of its former self. Apart from Big Daddy, shows promoted under the Dale Martin banner were few and far between. Regular venues like Croydon, Derby and Hanley had shows but of varying quality with often the bill nothing like what had been advertised on the posters around town. Max Crabtree would simply make up names or use names of American wrestlers to put on a bill with on the night none of them to be seen. There was an attempt to get wrestling back onto ITV in 1991 when the Grampian region filmed two shows at Aberdeen featuring Big Daddy, local favourite Andy Robbins and Giant Haystacks as well as seeing Klondyke Kate on ITV for the first time. Despite being shown in a few regions nothing came of it and it wasn't the great return we all wished for. The first of the shows was screened on Saturday January 19th at 345pm with the show introduced by Robin Galloway with Kent Walton commentating, this was broadcast for the next three weeks with another series a while later. Eventually the name of Dale Martin Promotions as a company was dissolved in October 1991 with the Joint Promotions organisation following a year later to bring to an end of over forty years of being the premier name of British wrestling. Max Crabtree started to promote under the name 'Ring Wrestling Stars' with a new poster design but the same promotional tactic of a Big Daddy show or things like a 'rumble' with made up names or local talent as the participants. This carried on for a year until the end of 1993 when Big Daddy had his final ever match at Margate on December 29th. Daddy partnered his by then usual partner Tony Stewart took on the masked Undertakers who were usually the father and son duo of Dave Adams and Johnny Angell. There was no fanfare or any recognition of the occasion. Big Daddy just returned to Yorkshire that night and the end of an era.

Shirley Crabtree died after suffering a stroke in December 1997.

After the retirement of Big Daddy Max Crabtree had the opportunity to bring the 'British Bulldog' Davey 'Boy' Smith back to the UK to wrestle as he was in a period of not being contracted to either the WWF or WCW. The tour began in February 1994 and it did incredible business at the box office with sold out venues every night and even putting on matinee shows to cope with the demand. The quality of the matches with Smith in was to put it kindly not good, Davey 'Boy' doing a version of a Big Daddy tag. His partner on the tour was Tony Stewart who would do all the work before the hot tag brought Smith in and following a running powerslam it would be all over. Smith spent more time selling polaroid photos in the ring than he did wrestling each night. Max Crabtree brought back Smith for a further tour later that summer in 1994 but this time business was not nearly so good. Smith had brought Ross Hart with him for company and he wrestled a few matches on the bills eleven years after he was in the UK with brother Owen. After the end of the tour Crabtree shut up shop and retired to his farm in Yorkshire to where he lives to this day.

The promoters Relwyskow & Green carried on running shows in Yorkshire especially the Bridlington summer season under the control of George Relwyskow's daughter Anne until she dissolved that company in 1992. Anne Relwyskow then started promoting at a few venues in the area under the 'Wrestling Superstars' name before she called it a day in April 1996.

Another promoter who was affiliated with Max Crabtree at the end of the 1980's was John Freemantle who after running his second Brighton 'Evening Argus' Christmas Appeal show in December 1988 decided to promote wrestling under his own company 'Premier Promotions'. The first show he ran under his own name was at Brighton Corn Exchange in January 1989 with Johnny Saint defending his World Lightweight Title against Kid McCoy in the main event. It was then announced that Freemantle would have the exclusive use of Big Daddy on his shows and with that he started to promote outside of Brighton & Hove. He first used Daddy at Worthing in February 1989 before bringing him to Burgess Hill for the first time in over ten years in March of that year. Freemantle and Premier Promotions started to run many venues in the south including some shows at the Brighton Centre which had only seen one Dale Martin Promotions show in its history before in 1981. The Centre is now a regular stop off when the WWE tours the UK. Despite the down turn in business towards the end of the 1990's John Freemantle carried on promoting and to this day is still putting on shows making him Britain's second longest running promoter.

At the start of 1980 I don't think anyone would have predicted that just over ten years later that Brian Dixon and All-Star Promotions would have seen off Joint Promotions as rivals and they would no longer be around. Having spent his two years of coverage on ITV to build-up his wrestlers and their feuds Brian Dixon and All-Star Promotions started 1989 strongly with the return of Fuji Yamada accompanied by Flyin' Funaki to add to the mix. Mark Rocco had plenty of great matches with the likes of Yamada, old rival Marty Jones, Fit Finlay and Danny Collins. Watching Rocco wrestle in his matches every night at 100mph it came as a terrible shock when after a match with Finlay at Worthing in January 1991 he was taken unwell and admitted to hospital. Rocco was diagnosed with a heart condition which forced his immediate retirement from the ring to which he was greatly missed.

Throughout 1989 and into the 90's there were plenty of very good shows put on by All-Star Promotions and they even managed to get ladies wrestling onto BBC TV in 1989 with the 'Raging Belles' documentary starring Klondyke Kate and Nicky Monroe's battle over the British title vacated by the retired Mitzi Mueller. Another welcome renaissance was the return of regular tag teams feuding with the likes of 'Liverpool Lads' Robbie Brookside and Doc Dean, 'The Superflys' Jimmy Ocean and Ricky Knight, father & son duos Alan and Adam Kilby & King Ben and Kid McCoy plus the 'Task Force I' team of Vic Powers and Steve Prince having some great matches up and down the country which deserved more coverage. As well as the British talent on offer Brian Dixon brought in plenty of overseas wrestlers to freshen things up with 'The Mongolian Mauler' being one of the most controversial whilst Owen Hart made a return to compete for Mark Rocco's now vacant World Heavy/Middleweight Title. Unfortunately the good times didn't last and by the mid 1990's crowds had disappeared and All-Star Promotion's shows were few and far between in the town venues as the WWF with their regular UK tours had taken over as far as the fans were concerned. Thankfully business began to pick up again in the new millenium with a new 'Superslam' product featuring the best of the UK and oversea's talent and has continued to this day having good crowds wherever they promote. This year (2020) Brian Dixon entered his fiftieth consecutive year as a wrestling promoter in Britain.

Giant Haystacks continued to be a top of the bill attraction and started to be used increasingly more by All-Star Promotions in 1989 and the years after. Apart from his commitments in Britain with All-Star and Joint Promotions he was still wrestling regularly for Orig Williams in Ireland and in the European tournaments as well. Haystacks had finally got his big break in the USA as 'The Loch Ness Monster' in WCW in 1996 when he was diagnosed with cancer and had to return home.

Giant Haystacks died in November 1998.

Kendo Nagasaki continued his tag team with Blondie Barratt into the 1990's as well as having several bloody matches with Giant Haystacks as they fought for the UK version of the World Heavyweight Title. Nagasaki retired from full time wrestling in 1993. Since then he has written an interesting autobiography and is very active in the spiritual world.

Chapter 11 - Facts & Figures

TV Shows Trivia :-
In the timescale this book records wrestling it was recorded for ITV at 102 different venues across England. The TV cameras never visited either Scotland or Wales during this period.

The Fairfield Halls in Croydon had most visits from Kent Walton and the cameras with ten shows recorded for TV broadcasting. Honourable mentions to the Civic Hall in Bedworth, the St.Georges Hall in Bradford and the Floral Hall in Southport who each had six shows broadcast on ITV.

The bout that was broadcast the most times was Pat Roach v Ray Steele and was seen nine times on TV through the 1980's.

Honourable mentions go to Steele again v Gil Singh which was seen seven times. Skull Murphy v Pete Roberts and Steve Grey v Jim Breaks was on six times each.

Big Daddy Data -
Big Daddy made fifty seven appearances on *World of Sport* or the ITV Wrestling Show with the most being seven in any one year, surprisingly few for the biggest draw in British wrestling during this time. Daddy had forty eight different opponents in this time with twenty six different partners in tag matches. The opponent he met most times on TV was Scrubber Daly with ten appearances as himself and a further three as the Masked Marauder. The wrester he partnered most was Danny Collins with seven occasions that they shared the tag rope. Naturally the fifty seven matches ended with fifty seven victories, a combination of singles matches, tags, lumberjack matches and a win in a Battle Royale. Daddy had not been seen in a televised defeat since September 30th 1978 when he and his partner Gary Wensor lost to Giant Haystacks and Big Bruno who beat them in under seven minutes with Wensor being flattened for the winner. Wensor was a late replacement for Daddy's advertised partner Jack Armstrong. Armstrong was a good looking young heavyweight from Croydon who was getting a big push at the time in 1978 and was being booked in tags partnering Big Daddy on the circuit. Unfortunately

Armstrong had a predilection for committing armed robbery and was locked up in prison hence the call for Wensor to replace him. Away from the TV cameras Big Daddy met defeat on three occasions during the 1980's, at Bath on March 16th 1983 when Giant Haystacks and King Kong Kirk beat Daddy and Mal Sanders. At Derby on November 21st 1983 in a six man tag, Daddy and his partners Johnny Kidd and Pat Patton lost to Giant Haystacks, Masked Marauder and Charlie McGee. Finally at Wolverhampton on April 8th 1986 Daddy and Richie Brooks lost to Fit Finlay and Bully Boy Muir which also was Big Daddy's last recorded loss in any match until he retired.

Longest running rivalry -

Mick McManus first fought Johnny Kwango back in 1957 and were matched against each other right up until McManus retired in 1982.

The Champions -

The Lord Mountevans Belt holders at January 1980 were :-

Heavyweight :- Tony St Clair. St Clair refused to drop the belt to Pat Roach in his last TV appearance for Joint Promotions in August 1980. He then defended the title on the independent circuit until early 1982 when it became the open title thus ending the linear history of the Mountevans title.

Mid/Heavyweight :- Mike Marino. Marino hadn't appeared in the ring for eighteen months before making a comeback in May 1980. He made the odd title defence before his death in August 1981. The title died with Marino and there was no tournament to crown a new champion although Marty Jones did win the vacant world title that had been held by Marino.

Light/Heavyweight :- Marty Jones. Jones held the title until November 1982 when he relinquished it on winning the World Mid/Heavyweight Title. Fit Finlay beat Ringo Rigby in the final of the tournament to decide the new champion. The title swapped between Finlay and Jones until Jones relinquished it on regaining the World Mid/Heavyweight Title in November 1984. Alan Kilby won the vacant title beating Steve Logan in January 1985 and was still champion at the end of 1988.

British Heavy/Middleweight Title :- Mark Rocco. Rocco was the champion until he won the world version in August 1981. Alan Kilby won the tournament to win the vacant title beating King Ben the following month. Kilby proceeded to swap the title with Fit Finlay until he lost it to Chic Cullen at the Royal Albert Hall in March 1984. Cullen then lost it to Finlay in 1987 and who was still champion at the end of 1988. Finlay lost the title to Danny Collins in July 1989 and moved up to the full heavyweight division.

Middleweight :- Brian Maxine. Maxine won the middleweight title on June 1st 1971 and the only time he lost his belt was when it was stolen from the dressing room at Brent Town Hall in September 1980. He was still champion at the end of 1988 and has never officially relinquished the title. Various promotions since have claimed to have middleweight champions but none of them have any legitimacy outside of their company.

Welterweight :- Jim Breaks. At the start of 1980 Breaks was concluding a feud with Young David for the title. David's mentor Alan Dennison then defeated Breaks at the Wembley Arena show in June 1980 to become new champion. Breaks and Dennison swapped the belt several times till Breaks regained the title in December 1983. Danny Collins beat Breaks at the Royal Albert Hall in March 1984 and was still champion at the end of 1988. He had lost the title to Steve Grey and Sid Cooper in the intervening period but regained the belt a short time after on both occasions.

Lightweight :- Steve Grey. Grey was champion through most of this period, he did lose the title to Jim Breaks on three occasions but regained it swiftly afterwards. He finally lost it to Kid McCoy who was still champion at the end of 1988.

Acknowledgements –

I'd like to thank the following Brian Dixon, Bob Bartholomew, Steve Barker and Dave Icke for their assistance, encouragement and help with researching and writing this book.

This book is dedicated to the memories of Mark Rocco and Ray Plunkett who both died during the writing of this book.

Mark was one of the greatest British wrestlers ever. A true legend of the sport whose influence is still very much apparent today.

Ray was an MC and referee who made one appearance on the ITV Wrestling show compering a bill from Bradford in 1986. That wasn't what set him apart though. Ray was a historian of British wrestling and collected the bills , the results and the details of anything to do with the sport. He spent much of his own time giving wrestlers details of their careers which had been long forgotten.

Mark and Ray are both very much missed by everyone.

Printed in Great Britain
by Amazon